·⌣ The Near-Death Experience ⌣·

The Near-Death Experience

·~ A Reader ~·

Lee W. Bailey
and
Jenny Yates

Routledge
New York & London

Published in 1996 by

Routledge
29 West 35th Street
New York, NY 10001

Published in Great Britain by
Routledge
11 New Fetter Lane
London EC4P 4EE

Library of Congress Cataloging-in-Publication Data

Bailey, Lee Worth
The near-death experience: a reader / by Lee W. Bailey and Jenny Yates.
    p.   cm.
Includes bibliographical references.

ISBN 0-415-91430-2 (cl) — ISBN 0-415-91431-0 (pbk)
    1. Near-death experiences. 2. Near-death experiences—Religious aspects.
I. Yates, Jenny L. II. Title.

BF1045.N4B35 1996   95-26366
133.9'01'3 — dc20   CIP

Contents

·⁓ Acknowledgments ⁓·

This book began with our study and teaching of death-related issues for several years. As we spoke to people who had near-death experiences and did further research, we became increasingly convinced of the importance of this topic for interdisciplinary analysis. The project took off at the conference at Cornell University on "Religion, Politics, and Cultural Dynamics" in 1994, where Lee and Jenny discovered a common interest through their presentations on near-death experiences. Thanks to Barry Adams and Parviz Morewedge for that beginning. Thanks to the editors and staff at Routledge.

Thanks also to the Institute of Noetic Sciences for their conference "The Sacred Source: Life, Death, and the Survival of Consciousness" in Chicago in 1994, for bringing together several of our authors with the editors.

Thanks to the International Association for Near-Death Studies, for their annual conferences and support for research.

Thanks to our many colleagues who helped us develop and refine the book: especially Kenneth Ring, Richard Creel, Alice McDowell, Brian Karafin, Aurelio Torres, Hana Rab, and Jill Swenson. Thanks to Ithaca College and Wells College for research support. Thanks to the Ithaca College Academic Computing Services for computer scanning support. Thanks to Anne Brinton and Barbara Baroshian for word-processing assistance. Thanks to Paul Barton of Paul Barton Studios in New York for the cover photo. Thanks to all the authors in the book whose thinking and writing is moving the study of NDEs forward.

Thanks most of all to all the survivors of near-death experiences who have struggled to heal and adjust, both those we know personally and those whose writings we have learned from. They have inspired and opened so many doors for more people than they know. To them this book is dedicated.

·⁓ A Note on the Text ⁓·

·⌣ Introduction ⌣·

And they that dwell in the land of the
   shadow of Death
Upon them hath the Light shined.
                           — Isaiah 9:2

A young woman was riding 70 MPH on a motorcyle around a curve on a country road, suddenly skidded on gravel, and BAM! slammed into the guard rail. She fell off, while the cycle flipped over the rail and tumbled downhill. Her body lay there in a mangled, bleeding pile. The next thing she knew, she was floating up above her crumpled body, between two treetops, looking at the leaves' vibrant colors. She sensed a tunnel of light above her and heard pleasant music. Her sister, who had just died two months before, seemed to be present, coaxing her toward the tunnel. She looked down at her physical body lying along the road, and felt a strong desire to live. Then suddenly a "swooshing" sound pulled her back into her body, and she awoke, looking up at faces. Since the experience she has become a successful businesswoman and says that her personal relationships are more meaningful. She has no fear of death, is more upbeat, calm, philosophical, and has a clearer sense of her life's purpose.

Another woman abused drugs for twenty-three years, her life scraping the bottom of the barrel over and over again, until she had a near-death experience (NDE). Because she was familiar with so many drugs, she was also familiar with hallucinations. She says that her NDE was different, "a very real voyage" (Ring, 1991, 24; use the Bibliography at the back of the book). In 1987 she overdosed on two bags of heroin mixed with cocaine and died. She rose out of her body while watching it turn purple, blue, then gray. She watched the paramedics, unable to get a pulse for almost three minutes, working on her body, injecting Narcan and using a defibrillator. She then floated away into a dimension of total peace and serenity, better than any drug-induced feeling. She went toward a Light, "more brilliant than a diamond" (26), into a beautiful city, and saw her life flash before her. Then she felt the Light's total love, acceptance, and peace. But she was jolted back into her body, annoyed at having to be back on earth. But now she knew she was forgiven and had things to do. She was transformed:

> I am a recovering addict that unless you knew me before, you would never
> know that I had such a life of despair. I am now a happy, good-hearted,
> honest, wholesome person. I have this inner peace about me that is incred-
> ible. I attribute the way I am now to my NDE. (Ring, 1991, 23–27)

These are not unusual examples of near-death experiences, a phenomenon that we are now discovering is much more widespread than researchers expected. With the increased efficiency of medical resuscitation technology, more people are coming back from the edge of death, and a good percentage of them are reporting visionary experiences. The surprise is that, for the most part, they are not reporting that death is a terrifyingly painful and horrible ordeal. Instead, they are reporting beautiful, peaceful feelings, out-of-body experiences floating and moving anywhere at will. They may move through a dark tunnel and encounter an astonishing Light with personal qualities of total love and acceptance. For many this is the presence of the creator of the universe: God. Returning to their bodies, these survivors report boldly changed lives, usually with no fear of death and new values and spirituality.

At this point the skeptic bell rings for many people and the questions begin: Are these experiences real or just hallucinations? Do we have any scientific documentation? How common are near-death experiences? Do these people really die? Are all NDEs pleasant or are some distressing? Could this affect our religious beliefs? These are questions that are currently being asked and answered. This book is intended to provide you with the most current research and analysis. There are so many aspects to the near-death experience that a wide spectrum of disciplines must be represented, from neurological to mystical. Research on NDEs must be an interdisciplinary task. But the "Big Secret"... ah, the "Big Secret". One NDE survivor said:

> I think once you've penetrated the big secret just a bit like I did, it's enough to convince you. [God] wanted me to get a peek into this big secret and shove me right back again. (Sabom, 186)

What is the Big Secret? What experience lies waiting behind the curtain when we die? Does consciousness disappear—poof!—into an empty void because it is a by-product of the physical body that no longer functions? Does a deeper consciousness appear when the veil is lifted? Or does the soul lift gracefully above the physical world into a majestic, incredibly beautiful realm full of love and joy, our true home before and after this brief incarnation? The answer to *that* is the Big Secret, and no one is exempt from its implications. Are our research techniques and philosophical angles sufficient to explain the unbelievable clues we are hearing from NDE survivors? That is the challenge.

We have gathered in this book two types of readings: cases and interpretations. First, we have a number of *cases* of near-death experiences, some from well-known individuals, such as Carl G. Jung, and others less known, such as Mellen-Thomas Benedict; some from best-selling contemporary books, such as Betty Eadie's, some from ancient texts, such as Plato's; some from contemporary lives: Dannion Brinkley, Peter Sellers, Eddie Rickenbacker, and George Ritchie.

Second, the *interpretations* of NDEs strive to answer many questions, such as: What is death? What are the types of near-death experiences? Are certain people more likely to have NDEs? How widespread are NDEs? Do children have NDEs? Do some people have distressing NDEs? What after-effects do NDEs have? What have we learned from grief counseling that may help heal survivors of NDEs?

No study concerning death would be complete without acknowledging the pioneering role of Elisabeth Kübler-Ross. A psychiatrist who removed the repressions blocking the honest discussion of death, she defined the classic types of grieving in her 1969 book, *On Death and Dying:* denial, anger, bargaining, depression, and acceptance. As she sat with her dying patients, Kübler-Ross heard numerous accounts of near-death experiences. Before working with terminally ill patients, she was not particularly religious and did not believe in an afterlife. First she noticed that on their deathbeds

patients often spoke to people who had preceded them in death, and after
the moment of clinical death, most of their faces became incredibly peaceful
(Nietzke, 21). Then Kübler-Ross collected hundreds of accounts of out-of-
body travel and other elements of NDEs (Neitzke, 21). She also had her own
mystical experiences. One was a vision of a dead patient, Mrs. Schwartz, who
encouraged her not to give up her work (Kübler-Ross, 1991, 33–36). Another
was a painful identification with her dying patients that turned into a blissful
rebirth experience (Kübler-Ross, 1991, 62–69). "It is impossible to die alone,"
she concludes, because of the many near-death experiences reported by her
patients (Kübler-Ross, 1991, 50). These mystical experiences have made her
a very spiritual psychiatrist who can say, "We have all been endowed by a
facet of divinity" (Kübler-Ross, 1991, 52).

WHAT IS DEATH?

One of the first objections to validating the NDE phenomenon is the critique
that these people did not really die. Survivors of NDEs cannot report on any
reality beyond death, the argument goes, because they did not really die. As
Karl Jansen and others argue, death is by definition that state from which a
person does not return to life. Therefore anyone who returns *by definition* did
not really die, no matter how long their heart, brain, and lungs may have been
nonfunctional. Philosophically, as Jenny Yates points out, this is a *deductive*
argument by definition, because death is being defined as a one-way trip.
What shall we call that state with no life signs but not really dead? Well, this
is why we use the term "near-death" experience.

By contrast, the *inductive* definition accepts the absence of life signs as the
definition of death, rather than the one-way trip. So if a person suffers from a
lack of heart, brain, and lung functioning for a certain period of time, the
physician can sign the death certificate, and that is death. But if on the way to
the morgue the dead patient comes back to life and regains health, it is a bit
awkward for the staff, who have been trained to expect major brain damage
after about five minutes without oxygen flow to the brain. The alternative is
simply to accept the possibility of near-death experiences, mysterious as they
are. Furthermore, our innovative technological environment keeps the
inductive definition open to change. The borderline has shifted recently from
heart death to brain death, as new machines carry on the functions. What is
death? The answer is not so clear, in light of near-death experiences. We must,
as Ian Stevenson points out, whenever possible investigate the medical
records to see whether people reporting NDEs were ever inductively
declared dead. Then we can reflect on our definitions of death.

WHAT ARE THE TYPES OF NEAR-DEATH EXPERIENCES?

Numerous phenomena have been called near-death experiences, ranging from peaceful out-of-body travel to spectacular visions of God. Because of this researchers have offered a number of typologies, or lists of typical elements of NDEs. Raymond Moody was the first researcher to bring NDEs to public attention in 1975, with his book *Life After Life*. A physician and a philosopher in Virginia, Moody studied 150 cases of NDEs for that book and found the following phenomena to be typical recurring elements of a near-death experience:

1. *Ineffability:* Survivors of NDEs often say that ordinary language is too restrictive to express the power and mystery of the experience.
2. *Hearing the News:* Often NDErs hear someone pronounce them dead.
3. *Feelings of Peace and Quiet:* Instead of intolerable pain, NDErs report surprising feelings of calm, relief, relaxed peace, and quiet.
4. *The Noise:* They often hear noises such as buzzing, roaring, banging, whistling, or beautiful music.
5. *The Dark Tunnel:* Frequently survivors are pulled rapidly through a dark space like a tunnel, a well, a funnel, a sewer, a valley, or a cylinder.
6. *Out of Body Experiences (OBEs):* Many NDErs find themselves rising up above their dead bodies and able to see below, hear conversation, and move elsewhere at will.
7. *Meeting Others:* Survivors become aware of a presence or see other beings who died before them, who may aid in their transition to death or send them back to life.
8. *The Being of Light:* The most important phenomenon reported is the appearance of a brilliant Light, described by survivors of NDEs to be loving, accepting, caring, non-judgmental, and often an angel, Christ, or God.
9. *The Life Review:* A rapid review of one's life, stressing love and knowledge.
10. *The Border or Limit:* A door, fence, line, river, or barrier of some kind is recognized as the line that, if crossed, allows no return to life.
11. *Coming Back:* The beauty of the other side convinces many that they do not want to come back, so waking up back here, they take a while to adjust.
12. *Telling Others:* Returnees have absolutely no doubt—the experience was real, but rejection and scorn upon telling others often cause pain, conflict, and withdrawal.
13. *Effects on Lives:* NDErs find not instantaneous salvation or moral purity, but a more philosophical view of life's meaning.
14. *New Views of Death:* Loss of the fear of death is common.

15. *Corroboration:* Survivors can often report events while they were dead and out of their bodies, such as details of medical procedures or words said by grieving family members in another room.

Surprising many people, Moody's book became a best-seller worldwide. With his book, the near-death experience entered global consciousness. Our selection from Moody's writings comes from his later book, *The Light Beyond* (1988), where he goes beyond his initial research and explores new questions, such as the way science would be altered if NDEs were proven, and why NDEs are not mental illness. In the essay here he reports on the Gallup poll on NDEs and explains his NDE typology in a new way.

Soon after Moody's initial research surfaced, Kenneth Ring, a psychologist in Connecticut, began rigorous scientific research into NDEs. Using carefully crafted statistical analyses, he concluded that Moody's initial findings were generally correct. In his first book, *Life at Death* (1980), Ring developed the Weighted Core Experience Index to measure the most frequently recurring or core elements in 102 cases, and found that the core NDE tends to fall into five stages: 1. *peace*, 2. *body separation*, 3. *entering the darkness*, 4. *seeing the Light*, and 5. *entering the Light*. Most common was the first sense of peace, calm, and joy, occuring in 60 percent of his subjects. Next most common was the body separation, a floating sensation, sometimes including out-of-body travel and seeing one's own body below (37 percent). Third was entering a darkness, floating in a dimensionless realm, or moving through a tunnel-like space (23 percent). Fourth came seeing the Light, feeling drawn to its comforting, beautiful brightness, perhaps being surrounded by the Light (16 percent). Finally, according to Ring, least common in the core experience was entering the Light, seeing its incredibly beautiful realm of heavenly scenes, meeting deceased family, hearing music, and sensing the presence of psychic beings such as angels (10 percent) (Ring, 1980).

Bruce Greyson, a psychiatrist then at the University of Connecticut, proposed a fourfold typology of NDEs: 1. *cognitive*, involving thought process alterations, such as time shifts, life review, and sudden understanding. 2. *affective*, involving peace, joy, painlessness, cosmic unity, and apparent encounters with a loving being of Light, 3. *paranormal*, involving apparent out-of-body travel, precognitive visions, extrasensory perception, and hyperacute physical senses, and 4. *transcendental*, involving apparent travel to an unearthly realm, encounters with a mystical being, visible spirits of deceased or religious figures, and a final point of no return. He emphasized that sudden, unexpected brushes with death produce more cognitive features than do anticipated crises (1993).

HOW WIDESPREAD ARE NEAR-DEATH EXPERIENCES?

Reports of NDEs can be found in the ancient past and around the world. Plato reports an ancient NDE in his legend of Er, in the *Republic.* The ancient *Tibetan Book of the Dead* suggests familiarity with NDEs. Carol Zaleski, in her book *Otherworld Journeys,* reports on records of many archaic and medieval NDEs and parallels. The Native American Lakota Sioux, Black Elk, had two NDEs in the nineteenth century. Recent public figures such as Eddie Rickenbacker and Peter Sellers had NDEs, as Lee W. Bailey explains in his first essay in this book.

As twentieth-century scientific studies enter the picture, these few reports seem to be the tip of an iceberg. George Gallup studied the phenomenon statistically, and reported in 1982 that about "15 percent of all adult Americans, or about 23 million people, said they had a close brush with death" involving an unusual experience (Gallup, 76), and "of that number about eight million have experienced some sort of mystical encounter along with the death event" (Gallup, 6). This means that roughly one in twenty Americans have survived an NDE. Gallup's unpublished 1990 survey of 1018 adults found that 12 percent reported being on the verge of death or having a close call which involved an unusual experience.

The list of international literature on contemporary NDEs is small but growing. For example, British parapsychological literature (Crookall), Swiss studies of falling mountain climbers (Heim), and studies of death-bed visions in India (Osis and Haraldsson) give remarkable early parallels to NDEs. Contemporary studies in England (Grey), Italy (Giovetti), Zambia (Morse,1992, 129–33), China, Japan (Becker), the South Pacific (Kellehear), and Australia (Sutherland) are confirming many patterns found worldwide. How widespread are NDEs? They are as ancient as Plato, as contemporary as a television talk show, and as worldwide as researchers on each continent are beginning to report.

ARE CERTAIN PEOPLE MORE LIKELY TO HAVE NEAR-DEATH EXPERIENCES?

Many factors have been explored to find what factors might affect NDEs. Kenneth Ring looked at the differences between NDE survivors of illness, accidents, and suicide. He found that the suicide survivors tended to have more experiences of the peaceful first stage, but none of the later—seeing and entering the Light. Illness victims were less likely to feel the initial peace, but more likely to enter the Light (Ring, 1980). Although they related and highlighted different experiences during the actual NDE, Ring found they still were just as likely to have a core NDE.

Ring also studied whether any demographic factors make one more likely to have a core NDE. He found that age, social class, race, and marital status have little influence on whether a person had a core NDE or not. Explicit and implicit religiousness also had little influence on the likelihood of having a core NDE. Prior knowledge of NDEs did not increase the likelihood of having a core NDE; indeed it may have decreased it (Ring, 1980).

Bruce Greyson reports other findings. He found that, while age and gender did not influence NDEs, the type of death may have more of an impact. He found that the cognitive features of NDEs do seem to be related to the suddenness of death. Anticipated deaths produce fewer experiences of time distortion, thought acceleration, and life review; but sudden deaths, such as in a car accident, stimulate more cognitive experiences, such as a rapid life review. He found that surrender to the process of dying seemed to permit deeper affective and transcendental aspects. And cardiac arrest also appeared to be highly connected to the NDE (Greyson, 1993).

In more recent research, Kenneth Ring has found that one factor may make a person more likely to have a near-death or another extraordinary experience: a childhood history of abuse or trauma. These people, he suggests, may be more likely to dissociate from a painful reality and tune into other realities to feel safe (1992,144).

DO CHILDREN HAVE NEAR-DEATH EXPERIENCES?

Melvin Morse, a pediatrician in Seattle, opened the path of research into children's near-death experiences in his book *Closer to the Light: Learning From the Near-Death Experiences of Children* (1990). He studied a control group of 121 hospitalized children who were seriously ill, but not near death—none of whom had experienced anything like a NDE, even though they were treated with various tranquilizers and anesthetics. He first interviewed twelve children who had NDEs, then interviewed and studied cases of many more children and adults who had survived childhood NDEs. In a second study Morse interviewed 100 adults who had survived NDEs as children. He reported this in his second book, *Transformed by the Light: The Powerful Effect of Near-Death Experiences on People's Lives* (1992). Many of the children had out-of-body experiences, reported the events of their resuscitation from above, went through a tunnel into the Light and a heavenly realm, and met deceased family and religious figures.

DO SOME PEOPLE HAVE DISTRESSING NEAR-DEATH EXPERIENCES?

The early reports of near-death experiences described incredibly beautiful, healing, and loving transcendent experiences. All of Raymond Moody's early cases were positive and uplifting. The 1982 Gallup poll found that 32 percent of NDE survivors experienced feelings of peace and painlessness. Betty Eadie's report, in this book, is one of the most elaborate, detailed, heavenly experiences of love and light. But, by contrast, subsequent reports of negative, miserable, distressing NDEs have emerged. This shadowy issue is increasingly discussed, because some researchers present negative cases and insist on asking: What percentage of NDEs are distressing? What are tormenting NDEs like? Do frightening NDEs reflect religious beliefs about Hell?

Gallup found that only about 1 percent of his respondents reported NDEs with "a sense of hell or torment" (Gallup, 76). Early research on death-bed visions in hospitals in India and the United States by Osis and Haraldsson found that between 9% and 14% of those studied experienced death visions as threatening or frightening (Osis, 235-236). Another report came from Maurice Rawlings, a cardiologist and a conservative Christian in Tennessee. He welcomes the heavenly visions of NDE survivors, but believes that patients who survive a NDE soon repress the distressing aspects of their experiences. Dr. Rawlings hypothesized this when one patient being resuscitated cried out to him: "Don't let me go back to hell!" but later denied any painful experience (1978, 19).

P. M. H. Atwater also speaks firmly about the importance of recognizing painful NDEs. Her three experiences blended painful and beautiful elements. Her research has convinced her that dark, distressing experiences are a basic type of NDE. Atwater has heard survivors describe a horrendous blackness, grinning skulls, and screaming deceased spirits (1994).

Atwater includes unpleasant experiences in her typology of NDEs: 1. *initial "seed" experience:* a loving nothingness, friendly voice or living darkness, 2. *unpleasant or Hell-like experience:* a threatening void, hellish purgatory, or "hauntings", 3. *pleasant or Heaven-like experience:* heavenly scenes, spirits of the recently deceased, loving family reunions, affirmation, validation, inspiration, and 4. *transcendent experience:* expansive revelations, alternate realities, and otherworldly scenes. As she explains in her article in this book, she believes that each type of NDE comes to the kinds of people who are ready for it and need it. She is a leading voice speaking against suppressing or ignoring unpleasant, distressing experiences (1994).

Nancy Evans Bush and Bruce Greyson report on distressing NDEs in their essay in this book, and identify three types: 1. prototypical NDEs with a tunnel and a bright Light, but experienced as terrifying, 2. a sense of nonexistence, eternal void or absurdity, and 3. classical hellish imagery of tormenting demons and agonizing pain (Greyson/Bush, 1992). Their differentiation between the *experience* of the phenomena, which may be fearful and hellish, and the phenomena itself, is crucial to understanding distressing accounts.

Dannion Brinkley says that during his journey to the Light he encountered a distressing life review. He was made to feel all the pain that he had caused in his many angry childhood fistfights. Then he relived the pain and grief of the people he killed during the war in Vietnam. Of one victim he said: "I felt his confusion at having his head blown off and sadness as he left his body"

(Brinkley, 1994, 17). Hitler, Brinkley believes, will feel and become the pain that he created, over and over again, until he learns. Brinkley says that seeing his personal shadow and accepting responsiblity for the way that he had harmed other people led him to be transformed by the Light:

> I looked at the Being of Light and felt a deep sense of sorrow and shame. I expected a rebuke, some kind of cosmic shaking of my soul....As I gazed at the Being of Light...I felt a love and joy that could only be compared to the nonjudgmental compassion that a grandfather has for a grandchild. (Brinkley, 1994, 20)

Brinkley's experience of courageously facing the dark side and acknowledging it transformed him so much that now he is committed to visiting terminally ill patients in hospice centers.

WHAT AFTER-EFFECTS DO NEAR-DEATH EXPERIENCES HAVE?

Kenneth Ring's research into the after-effects of a NDE show that the NDE is most often a spiritual awakening. It is the beginning of a challenging soul journey demanding serious self-reflection and change. He found that the NDE itself does not automatically provide easy answers to one's life problems. It simply jump-starts a spiritual quest. The return to ordinary life filled with a new Light can be difficult. One woman from an alcoholic family had a NDE during surgery. She saw her deceased father and entered the Light with its incredible wisdom and love. She came back unable to continue drinking, but also unable to convince her husband of the reality and importance of her NDE. She and her husband divorced as a result. But she is now an active sponsor in Alcoholics Anoymous and a better parent (Cox-Chapman, 165–69).

Ring's research describes the NDE's typical after-effects: a heightened appreciation of life, a sense of personal renewal and search for purpose, increased confidence, compassion, empathy, tolerance, and understanding. Do survivors change their spiritual beliefs? A NDE may not lead to an increase in traditional religious activity, such as church attendance, but it does tend to increase a survivor's personal belief in life after death and some understanding of God, although often in unconventional form. NDEs tend to stimulate a life of inward prayer, religious tolerance, and universal faith. NDE survivors become more *spiritual*, Ring says, not more "religious." Fear of death diminishes and is replaced by a sense of the beauty and peace of the afterlife (Ring, 1980). Even though death is no longer feared, suicide is not an option, even for those whose NDE resulted from a suicide attempt. They typically feel that life is too precious a gift (Moody, 1977).

Barbara Harris, whose NDEs caused major changes in her life, including divorce and a new career in medicine, speaks for many survivors when she says:

> Near-death experiencers can tell us what the world needs to be peaceful, but they can't determine how to keep their own lives peaceful after they have been turned inside out by the experience. Not everyone has that problem, but for the ones who do, talking about it in a safe environment like a Friends of IANDS [International Association for Near-Death Studies] support group usually helps. (Harris and Bascom, 164)

HOW CAN I HELP A NEAR-DEATH EXPERIENCE SURVIVOR?

Dr. Bruce Greyson offers several helpful suggestions for professional and caring people who want to support people who have had a NDE:

1. Professional medical staff should assume that unconscious, dying patients may be able to hear what is being said around the bed. Be careful what you say.
2. Respectful touching, outlining the patient's body, helps reorient them back to their bodies.
3. Listen for clues of NDEs in conversations with resuscitated people, but do not expect them to divulge their experiences until they trust you.
4. Do not press your own beliefs about NDEs onto patients, but respectfully listen to them.
5. Help the survivor of a NDE clarify his or her own interpretation of it.
6. Respect the NDE as an extremely powerful agent of transformation.
7. Attempting to label a NDE as a symptom of pathology is neither accurate nor helpful.
8. Honesty and confidentiality are critical and essential to establishing trust.
9. Most helpful is listening carefully to whatever the NDEr is saying.
10. Encourage NDErs to express whatever emotions have been evoked by the experience, no matter how intense.
11. Provide accurate information about NDEs. Knowing the common occurrence of the experience is very reassuring to survivors.
12. If a person is upset by a NDE, help him or her identify exactly what part of it caused the problem.
13. Put NDE survivors in contact with others who have had the same experience. Ask locally and contact the International Association for Near-Death Studies, P. O. Box 502, East Windsor Hill, CT 06028.
14. If you work with a NDE survivor after intial contacts, be prepared for the NDE to raise serious issues about the purpose of life.

15. Avoid glorifying or idealizing the NDE. Help the survivor be grounded in practical life, integrating his or her new understandings into daily living. (Greyson, 1990)

INTERPRETIVE METHODOLOGIES

How are we to interpret these unbelievable experiences? What role does brain chemistry play? What philosophical assumptions are involved in different types of research? Do NDEs have valid religious implications? If we take these stories and the NDE research data seriously, then it seems that the universe is much more complicated and mysterious than ordinary consciousness conceives. So it is important to examine a wide range of interpretations. The various explanations can be grouped roughly into four categories: the biological, the psychological, the philosophical, and the religious, although many interpretations include more than one perspective.

What Are the Biological Interpretations of NDEs?

Some, though not all, medical and psychological researchers argue that NDEs can be explained entirely within the realm of measurable, empirical analysis. Several theories have been proposed. Neurologist Ernst Rodin offers cerebral anoxia, or lack of oxygen supply to the brain, as a possible cause of the dying brain's near-death experience (Rodin). Such anoxia produces a confusing dream-like state of delusions and hallucinations. But the cardiologist Michael Sabom responds that the NDE involves a clear awareness and a more mystical content, and NDEs have also occured in people without anoxia (Sabom). Yet it is possible that anoxia could be one of several physical components of NDEs.

The brain's naturally produced narcotics, such as the endorphins, have been offered by endocrinologist Daniel Carr and psychiatrist Karl Jansen to explain why, at the very moment when the body's death would be expected to bring incredible pain and terror, the NDE surprises us with pleasure, calm, and peace (Carr, Jansen). But Dr. Melvin Morse responds that patients receiving prescribed narcotics similar to the endorphins experienced no NDEs. He argues that the opioid peptides in the brain explain less than the serotonin in the brain. Alteration of this chemical could activate certain temporal lobe areas that accompany mystical visions, out-of-body sensations, panoramic memories, and vivid hallucinations (Morse, 1989).

Some neurologists, such as Michael Persinger, argue that instability and activity in the brain's right temporal lobe, above the right ear, is responsible for religious experiences of deep meaningfulness, early memories, and out-of-body experiences (Persinger). The psychologist Susan Blackmore builds on his argument that instability in the temporal lobe, which may show epileptic signs, is responsible for paranormal, mystical, and possibly many other NDE elements (Blackmore). Melvin Morse agrees that the right temporal lobe shows NDE-like activity, but he sees it as the mediating bridge for a spiritual experience, not reductionistically as nothing but a physical cause.

Blackmore also interprets the dark tunnel with light at the end as an optical illusion created by the effects of anoxia and drugs, creating cortical disinhibition, with the effect of random light spots radiating from the center of a dark internal visual field. She also interprets the out-of-body experience as a drug-induced illusion, based on her own experimentation with ketamine. Blackmore sums up the materialist, reductionist position:

> It is my contention that this "real thing"—NDEs, mystical experience and indeed everything encountered on the spiritual path—are products of a brain and the universe of which it is a part. For there is nothing else. It is our longing for something more that leads us astray. It is an illusion that we can find "true spirituality" by looking outside of ourselves. (1993, 111)

Michael Sabom, initially a very skeptical physician, tested and rejected the brain-only argument. While brain neurology is obviously a part of NDEs, he says, it is not a sufficient explanation. NDEs convince Sabom that the soul does leave the body at death, although they do not convince him that there is an afterlife (Sabom).

What Are the Psychological Interpretations of NDEs?

The psychological interpretations of NDEs offer a range of methods for probing their mysteries. Psychiatric categories, statistical analyses, and cognitive, Freudian, and Jungian themes have all been explored. Kenneth Ring and Bruce Greyson, discussed above in the section on types of NDEs, have done much of the groundbreaking statistical analysis establishing the basic empirical facts of the NDE phenomena: the stages and types, the core experience, the after-effects, the heavenly and distressing characteristics.

An early psychiatric analysis of NDEs was the theory of depersonalization. This is a defense of the nervous system, Noyes and Kletti argue, that stalls off mental disorganization during the death crisis by presenting an altered passage of time, vivid and accelerated thoughts, a sense of detachment, unreality, automatic movements, and revival of memories. They interpret mystical elements as extreme extensions of this (Noyes and Kletti). But Michael Sabom argues that depersonalization fails to account for all the elements of NDEs (Sabom).

The psychiatrist Ronald Siegel interprets NDEs and similar imaginative visions of the afterlife as hallucinations, similar to the effects of psychedelic drugs or anesthesia. Both offer vivid, ineffable states, he says, where one may hear sounds or voices, see lights and tunnels or a life review, and even possibly have a mystical illumination (Siegel). The psychologist John Gibbs replies that, compared to NDEs, the various drugs produce a more dissociated, chaotic, idiosyncratic, and varied experience than the more orderly, logical, definable, and predictable NDE, whose memory is uniquely clear and memorable, and distinct from those of people not clinically dead (Gibbs).

The NDE is seen by some Freudians as a denial of death, a hallucinatory wish fulfillment defending the ego from its impending annihilation (Ehrenwald, Menz, Greyson 1983c). A more dramatic Freudian theme was borrowed from Otto Rank, who proposed that the birth trauma is behind all neuroses, for all anxiety-producing experiences of separation reactivate the separation from the mother at birth (Brown, 52–53). This theory has been modified to explain the NDE as a regression to infantile object relations, to preverbal memories of maternal security and bliss, with the dark tunnel as the mother's birth canal, and the bright light as the mother's radiant face (Lowental, Gabbard and Twemlow).

The cosmologist Carl Sagan was drawn to Rank's image. The NDE, he proposed, in its tunnel and light are a reliving of the infant's descent down the birth canal (Sagan, 353–68). But critics have responded that this cannot be literally so. Carl Becker showed that the infant descending the birth canal has its eyes closed and its brain too undeveloped to allow memories of birth (Becker, 1982) . Similarly Susan Blackmore showed that people born by caesarian section have the tunnel experience and OBEs in equal proportion to those born naturally (Blackmore, 1983).

The idea that NDEs relive the birth experience was redirected by the psychologists Grof and Halifax into a symbolic, archetypal image. They saw the birth experience, a sense of cosmic unity, a death-rebirth struggle, and transcendence to be rooted in what Carl Jung called the archetypal patterns of the collective unconscious (Grof/Halifax). Jung describes in this book his own archetypal near-death vision of floating above India and seeing a meditating yogi seated before a temple whose brightly lighted entrance would be his passage out of this world. Marie-Louise von Franz, a Jungian analyst, illustrates Jung's archetypal theory with examples from ancient spiritual texts that illustrate the correspondence of images such as birth, death, and tunnels with NDEs.

Susan Blackwell developed an original view of NDEs based on cognitive psychology's theory of mental models. The mind, she proposes, creates various mental models of reality, based on its experiences, and the most stable one wins out as the favored version. The NDE comes along when the mind in crisis makes up models of reality such as an OBE, imagining the mind to be floating above the body, like a virtual reality computer program. In Blackmore's machine analogy:

This created "you" is no more than information being processed in a computer. In the same way the "you" of our ordinary life is information being processed by our brains. (1993, 175)

What Are the Philosophical Interpretations of NDEs?

What do you think would happen if a seasoned, skeptical philosopher had a NDE? Well, it happened. A. J. Ayer, the founder of early twentieth-century positivist philosophy, had a NDE in old age. He saw a red light, but returned only slightly changed: "My recent experiences," he mused, "have slightly weakened my conviction that my genuine death...will be the end of me, though I continue to hope that it will be. They have not weakened my conviction that there is no god" (Ayer, 1988 a,b). Clearly the NDE does not have a spiritually transforming effect in every case. Positivism assumes that anything not verifiable by the senses is nonsense. Since the NDE marks the end of the senses, strict positivists like Ayer reject anything beyond sense data observation, such as immortal soul or God. Ayer's philosophy is explicit, rooted in John Locke's formula: "Nothing is in the mind that was not first in the senses." Built into any interpretation of NDEs will be some explicit or implicit philosophical position.

One's way of knowing, methodology, epistemology, or hermeneutic, strongly conditions how one seeks to interpret the near-death phenomena. It is important from a larger perspective to see the role of the method in understanding the phenomena. If one's way of knowing is through the senses or empirical, one may follow the method of seeking to explain what is observed during a NDE through sensory means or hidden memories of sensory experiences. If this truth test fails, the empiricist usually moves to skeptical conclusions, striving to reduce NDEs to "nothing but" fantasy, hallucination, or nonsense.

An empirical approach studies observable causes. The psychiatrist Karl Jansen looks for externally verifiable experimental data in brain neurology to explain NDEs in his essay in this book. Susan Blackmore agrees: "Feelings of bliss, love and peace are engendered by specific chemicals acting in specific parts of the brain" (1993, 95). Dr. Melvin Morse sees the brain's right temporal lobe as a necessary mediating factor in NDEs, but he does not believe that NDEs can be reduced to "nothing but" brain activity (Morse, 1992).

Ronald Siegel, a specialist in hallucinations, approaches NDEs through an empirical methodology. For him if NDEs cannot be communicated like sensory perceptions and shared by several observers, and cannot be subjected to objective, consensual validation as events in the external world, then they must be purely subjective events, like hallucinations (Siegel, 1975, 1980).

One aspect of the NDE offering challenging empirical data is the verified or veridical out-of-body experiences. NDE survivors report rising out of their bodies and passing through hospital walls to hear what others are saying in other rooms during their death (Moody 1975, 99), or describe items such as an old sneaker resting way out of sight on a far ledge outside a hospital window (Sharp, 7–16). A Russian scientist, Dr. George Rodonaia, died and observed an infant crying in a nearby room. No one could figure out why the baby was crying so persistently, but he could see, in his OBE, that the child had a broken bone. When he returned to his body and woke up, he told the doctors to look for a broken bone. The X-ray revealed exactly the fracture that he indicated (Schokey).

The study of people blind from birth who report visual information after their NDEs raises the question of the limits of empiricism. A woman named Vicky, recounted by Charles Tart in his essay in this book, was blinded soon after her premature birth, and reported two NDEs. She saw her own body, people in the tunnel and in a life review, then flowers, grass, birds, light, a park shelter, pillars, a gate, and Jesus radiating light. She did not know if she saw color, but she reported seeing "different shades of light." Kenneth Ring is currently researching this and other cases of blind persons' NDEs (Ring, 1995).

Susan Blackmore, while open to new data, tends to be very skeptical of reports of veridical OBEs and blind NDEs, and demands rigorous empirical verification for herself, which is difficult to arrange (1993). Charles Tart responds to this challenge, reporting in his essay on a scientific study of out-of-body travel in his controlled laboratory experiment.

An alternative to empiricism is the philosophical premise that the mind contains inherent *a priori* ideas or psychic patterns that organize experience. Immanuel Kant proposed such *a priori* noumena behind all phenomena. One cannot know the noumena or unconscious directly but only as it manifests through phenomena, such as the tunnel or Light. Thus the study of the correspondences between such phenomena becomes another truth test. The fact that NDE reports are remarkably consistent about the nature of the phenomena given to consciousness is evidence for this truth test. Repeated phenomena reported in NDEs, such as the dark tunnel and the Being of Light, meet this criterion.

According to Michael Grosso, Carl Jung's theory of archetypes is a psychological version of Kant's philosophy. Similar phenomena, such as the Being of Light, can be found that repeat from person to person, culture to culture, and religion to religion. The pattern of such repeating phenomena reveals an unconscious, collective archetype. Jung's archetypes are rooted in Kant's noumena, or underlying structures of the mind, similar to Augustine's storehouse of eternal ideas and Plato's Forms. Jung's archetypal perspective enables one to see one's own visionary and religious symbols in light of similar meaning patterns in other world religions.

Grosso proposes a specific archetype of Death and Enlightenment to unify all the corresponding ideas and images surrounding death. In his essay in this book he proposes: "NDEs activate an archetype of the collective unconscious, a constellation of motifs that guides an enlightenment process, a passage toward greater consciousness of our Self." For Grosso, this theory explains many of the powerful universal spiritual themes of the NDE, such as the overwhelming peace, unconditional love, transformed lives, and psychic energy emerging from the collective unconscious.

Phenomenology is the twentieth-century philosophy that studies phenomena as they are given to consciousness. The phenomenology of archetypal images shows the correspondence of ideas and images across time and cultures. Jenny Yates amplifies the phenomenology of the archetypal Being of Light in world myths and religions to show the archetypal parallels of the Light in the near-death experience. In her article in this book, Yates shows how the phenomenon of the Being of Light of the NDE is parallel to the Light of God's presence reflected in the shining face of Moses on the mountain, the Light of the Shekinah in mystical Judaism, and the Transfiguration of Christ. The Light in the NDE also corresponds to the Light of Sophia in Gnosticism, the union of the individual and the universal soul called Atman-Brahman in Hinduism, and the clear Light of enlightenment in Tibetan Buddhism. She suggests also that the epistemology of the surface is inadequate for the deep, opening a paradigm for exploring the link between word roots and dream images.

The philosopher Carl Becker examines four ways in which NDEs may be considered "objective": 1. paranormal knowledge later verified, 2. the similarity of deathbed events in different cultures, 3. differences between religious expectations and visionary experiences, and 4. third-party observation of visionary figures, indicating that they were not merely subjective hallucinations (Becker, 1984).

Robert Kastenbaum explores empirical and phenomenological methods, emphasizing a number of communication issues, in his essay in this book. The bulk of NDE texts, he observes, are self-reports lacking empirical verification, and possibly allowing elaboration. Conclusions about NDEs must not neglect this. In his view, we should accept NDE literature as descriptions of phenomena as they are given to consciousness, but not assume that they are empirically verifiable by sense data replication.

New developments in physics, some philosophers argue, make positivist assumptions outmoded. Quantum physics teaches that we cannot know phenomena apart from the observer. Arlice Davenport challenges the hallucination view of NDEs as outmoded, because the field theories of physics now suggest new paradigm options available to explain NDEs (Davenport). Mark Woodhouse argues that the traditional materialism/

dualism battle over NDEs may be solved by Einstein. Since matter is now seen as a form of energy, an energy body alternative to the material body could explain the NDE (Woodhouse).

Postmodern philosophical themes have emerged in several discussions of near-death experiences. For example, the Austrialian sociologist Allan Kellehear views NDEs through the prism of life crisis events in his 1996 book *Experiences Near Death: Beyond Medicine and Religion.* Here he points out the rhetorical opinions in some analyses of NDEs that are presented as if they were scientific:

> I will argue that, despite the claim of value neutrality, more than a few current neuroscience explanations are partisan ones. This can be demon-strated through a close inspecton of their choice of language, rhetoric, and metaphors. (Kellehear, 1996, 120)

All language carries implicit social evaluations and exhortations, Kellehear notes, and is highly dependent on imagery. Scientific theories are thus often presented as the most logical, factual, objective, credible, and progressive possiblities, as opposed to the allegedly subjective, superstitious, abnormal, or dysfunctional views of mystics.

Often scientific speculation mistakenly treats as cause what is at best analogy, Kellehear points out (122–23). For example, major speculative theoretical models for the mind, such as the computer, are presumed to solve more problems than they do by appealing to the the prior assumptions of like-minded readers. Such skeptical critiques of NDEs are losing their credibility in the postmodern atmosphere where faith in the authority of a neutral, scientific rationalism has faded in the face of critiques of economic and gender bias, for example. Appeal to the popular stereotype of the dispassionate scientist has been hurt by hidden bias and shrill rhetorical embellishment. Neuroscience needs better arguments than reduction to "nothing but" materialist "mechanisms" to answer the NDE's appeal to personal and religious needs.

What Are the Religious Interpretations of NDEs?

George Ritchie, a physician who introduced Raymond Moody to NDEs, had a NDE in 1943, when he was in the Army. He traveled first to a nightmarish realm, then to a place of learning, and then to a city of Light. He saw the Being of Light as Christ, and returned with a renewed Christian commitment and a gift for both spiritual and physical healing.

There are several examples of elements of the NDE in the Bible, including the mystical powers of God's Light. Moses' call came from the burning bush (Ex. 3:2); the pillar of fire led the Hebrews toward the promised land

(Ex.14:21); Isaiah showed the people walking in darkness "a great Light." (Isa. 9:2). There are several resurrections, aside from Christ's. Elijah raised a widow's son from death (I Kings 17:17–24). Jesus raised Lazarus (John 11), Peter raised Tabitha from death (Acts 9:40), and two prophets were raised after being dead for 3 ½ days (Rev.11:9). Another dramatic occurrence of the phenomenon of the Light was the mystical conversion of Paul. Thrown down by the Light on his way to persecute believers in Damascus, Paul heard the divine voice in the Light. Stunned and blinded by the Light for three days, Paul's life was totally transformed (Acts 9, 22, 26). The Transfiguration of Christ, as Jenny Yates points out, is another remarkable parallel to the NDE. He appeared to the Disciples full of Light: "he was transfigured before them, and his face shone like the sun and his garments as became white as light" (Matt.17, Mk. 9, Lk. 9:28).

The Roman Catholic theologian Hans Küng argues deductively that people having NDEs do not actually die, so the NDE is not proof of eternal life. He is also very skeptical of parapsychological reports and reminds us of the pain of many distressing deaths. Nevertheless, he keeps open the possibility of a blissful transcendence at death (Küng, 8–21).

A major review article in the Protestant journal *Christianity Today* in 1988 gave NDEs the cold shoulder. They do not fall within the range of orthodox Christian tradition, the author argued. They are culturally conditioned, and they likely have natural explanations. For him, NDEs at best offer distorted glimpses of an afterlife, serve little theological purpose other than to remind us of transcendence, and often trivialize problems of evil and suffering (Clapp).

Maurice Rawlings, a cardiologist and conservative Christian, reports that 20 percent of the patients whom he has resuscitated have had NDEs. But he believes half of their experiences to be hellish. For him this confirms the biblical portrayal of judgment and hell, and moves easily from medical description to Christian evangelizing (Rawlings). Other conservative Christians object to NDEs not only as contrary to biblical testimony on final judgment and resurrection, but also because it seems to them to be possibly Satanic in origin (Swihart, 1978; Brooke, 1979; Groothius, 1995).

What do American clergy think about NDEs? David Royse found that half of the 170 clergy he surveyed had read books on NDEs, 71 percent had NDEs confided to them, 66 percent believed NDEs increased religiosity, 13 percent reported personal NDEs, 87 percent found no conflict between NDEs and religious teachings, and 64 percent viewed NDEs as possible evidence for survival after death (Royce).

Some Christians consider near-death experiences to be very much like biblical resurrections (Wilkerson). A 1981 study by a group of Christian educators concludes that the NDE is an authentic experience of transcendence, that it promotes religious life and does not contradict doctrines of heaven and hell, so it can enrich the Christian tradition (Hill). Douglas Hobson argues that there is room for the NDE in Christian varieties of death, resurrection, and the other world, but it does not prove or disprove Christian eschatology (Hobson). A Christian psychotherapist, John McDonagh, believes that the NDE supports abandoning secular psychology and constructing new therapies built on religious premises (McDonagh).

Carol Zaleski's historical research in *Otherworld Journeys* uncovers the medieval parallels to contemporary NDEs. Her research indicates that these medieval pilgrims to other worlds during NDEs, for example, almost always went to hell first, but hell, at least before Dante, was usually pictured as "up there." Her interpretive method is pragmatic, avoiding both extremes of fundamentalist literalism and extreme skepticism. She stresses, in her essay in this book, that the imaginative component of NDEs must be acknowledged and their value must be restricted to the realm of personal conviction:

> At this stage I see no justification for treating contemporary near-death testimony as the foundation for a new eschatology or religious movement. Near-death literature is at its best when it is modest and anecdotal; pressed into service as philosophy or prophesy, it sounds insipid. (1987, 204)

Some Christian theologians object to NDEs because they have spiritualist or universalist implications (Adams, Kuhn). Other Christians are drawn to NDEs for precisely that reason. Charles Flynn taught a universalist and undogmatic Christian view that he believed to be implied by NDEs (Flynn).

Jewish scholars have discovered contemporary NDEs in Israel and found parallels in the Talmud, Zoharic traditions, and later Rabbinic literature and folklore. The theme of judgment before a heavenly court is particularly prominent in the Jewish NDE tradition (Neumann). The Mormon faith is very open to NDEs because it already has a well-developed picture of the next world. Mormons who have reported NDEs are well-received in the Church of Jesus Christ of the Latter Day Saints (Lundahl, Gibson).

The response of traditional religious believers to the NDE's radical implications is mixed, ranging from hostile through lukewarm to enthusiastic. Few mainstream traditions are accustomed to such experiences. But the NDE does appeal to others who see it as a type of universal spiritual or mystical experience related to death.

The Hindu "subtle body" that leaves the body at death, Arvind Sharma shows, is analagous to the spiritual body described in the NDE (Sharma). The flash of light experienced by the youthful guru Yogananda is an archetypal parallel to the NDE light: "An oceanic joy broke upon calm endless shores of my soul. The Spirit of God, I realized, is exhaustless Bliss; his body is countless tissues of light" (Yogananda, 167). Carl Becker reports that Japanese Pure Land Buddhism is grounded upon the reality and accessibility of NDEs for all (1984 b,c). Becker also explores the strong parallels with the *Tibetan Book of the Dead* (1985). The Tibetan Buddhist leader Sogyal Rinpoche explores the parallels between NDEs and the classic *Tibetan Book of the Dead* in his article in this book. But he cautiously limits the NDE to pre-death experiences, since NDE survivors do not cross the point of no return. NDEs have also been compared to mystical shamanic journeys (MacDonald) and to Kundalini yoga's mystical states (Dippong; Ring, 1984).

The eighteenth-century mystic Emanuel Swedenborg's accounts of visionary experiences reveal phenomena corresponding to NDEs. He describes ineffability, peace, joy, the Light, meeting those already dead, cities of Light, frustrated spirits, and the OBE (Schnarr, Rhodes). John Pennachio defines a near-death experience as a mystical state, since NDEs show congruence with Walter Pahnke's nine categories of a mystical experience: intuitive unity, transcendence of space and time, a deeply felt positive mood, a sense of sacredness, a sense of reality, paradoxicality, ineffability, and transiency yet persisting positive changes in attitude and behavior (Pennachio).

But it is not just the confessed mystics who are making this argument. One scientifically trained physician is supplementing scientific inquiry with a mystical interpretation. Dr. Melvin Morse, who says that he himself is not even religious, offers scientific theories to explain the physical aspects of NDEs and also honors the spiritual mystery that they imply. Discussing the electromagnetic field that fills the human body, now made more visible by the new magnetic resonance imaging machines that are replacing x-rays, he proposes that the radiant cosmic Light seen in the NDE realigns the charges in this field so that somehow the brain's "wiring" is renewed. He reports on patients who recovered from pneumonia, cardiac arrest, and cancer after a NDE (1992, 153–54).

Not only can NDEs bring miraculous cures, but they can also give survivors psychic powers. Bruce Greyson's and other surveys of NDErs show significant increases in psychic experiences (Greyson,1983b; Kohr). Virtually every one of the hundreds of NDE survivors studied by Melvin Morse report psychic experiences as a result of their NDEs. "People who have had near-death experiences are four times more likely to have psychic experiences than those who have not had them," he concludes (1992, 89–91). These psychic experiences range from precognitive awareness of incoming telephone calls to verified middle-of-the-night apparitions of faraway loved ones who have just died. One girl, who attempted suicide at age twelve and had a NDE, now regularly has precognitive dreams: "On a regular basis," she says,

> I dream what will happen the next day. I'll often witness conversations
> in my dreams that actually take place the next day...I didn't used to
> believe these were real until I dreamed my uncle's death. He was in per-
> fect health but on this night I dreamed that he was going to die suddenly.
> The next day he died of a heart attack. (Morse,1992, 97)

Morse the physician recognizes both the physical and the mystical sides of
NDEs.

Michael Grosso sets his theory of the archetype of Death and
Enlightenment in the larger tradition of the mystical and parapsychological
vision of "Mind at Large" (Grosso). Struck by the cases of healed survivors
of suicide attempts or drug abuse death, Kenneth Ring speaks of NDEs using
the religious phrase "Amazing Grace" (1991). Ring interprets NDEs
psychologically as archetypal initiatory journeys, involving a death of one's
old ego and a rebirth of a new Self. In addition, he thinks that an adequate
interpretation must incorporate the spiritual realm of Kundalini experiences,
the imaginal realm, and the Mind at Large. As Ring envisions in his essay in
this book, this shift in thinking will deconstruct our traditional Western
worldview. It will bring a dramatic next step in the evolution of a more
ecological and more compassionate consciousness.

David Lorimer interpets NDEs and the psychic experiences of NDE
survivors as their participation in the immanent, divine presence described
in the mystical literature of the Perennial Wisdom, from Plato's Being to
Emerson's Oversoul (Lorimer).

Judith Cressy shows a number of specific parallels between NDEs and
mystics in the classical tradition, such as St.Theresa and John of the Cross.
In her essay in this book, she encourages NDE survivors to seek supportive
spiritual communities that can support their journey of integrating the Light
into daily life.

Lee W. Bailey discerns plenty of ineffable no-thing-ness in NDEs, especially
in the journey behind the Light to the void of the Tao, born before heaven
and earth. No-thing shines through language, meaning, ego-consciousness,
finitude, and God. But to perceive the silent no-thing present in NDEs, the
conventional industrial ego must first welcome the release of experience, the
joy of paradox, and the transparent glass-ness of story. Bailey welcomes more
no-thing-ness in our conceptual formuations about NDEs. Return no-thing to
language, he suggests. Keep it closer to poetry, image, and paradox, in order to
hear the fullness of near-death experiences.

Near-death experiences have a strange effect on thinking. This dramatic
event itself surrounds death, the end. Yet reflections on this end-event push
toward beginnings. NDE survivors begin newly transformed lives. Interpretive
discussions turn on basic questions such as: What is death? which turns back

into: What is life? We ask: what constitutes consciousness? Does it include meaningful unconscious elements? What is truth? the certainty of empirical fact? worldwide patterns of phenomena? What is the significance of transforming spiritual experiences? Does death laugh as it passes, leaving only undecipherable traces? Or does death gently compel a turn to unanticipated truth? Each passing life turns the soul back to such beginnings. As T. S. Eliot put it in *Four Quartets*, "We are born with the dead" (Little Gidding, 230). What is born with near-death experiences? Perhaps a new, but very old, consciousness. William James seemed to know about this type of mystery when he said,

> Our normal waking consciousness is but one special type of consciousness, whilst all about it, parted by the filmiest of screens, there lie potential forms of consciousness entirely different. We may go through life without suspecting their existence. But apply the requisite stimulus and at a touch they are there in all their completeness, definite types of mentality which probably somewhere have their field of application and adaptation. No account of the universe in its totality can be final which leaves these other forms of consciousness quite disregarded. (James, 305)

· 1 ·

The Light Beyond
The Experience of
Almost Dying

Raymond Moody

I am convinced the NDEers do get a
glimpse of the beyond.

Raymond A. Moody, Ph.D., M.D., is the grandfather of the
twentieth-century study of near-death experiences. He was bold
enough to undertake the scholarly study of this phenomenon
despite widespread scepticism. As he explained in his first book,
now a classic, *Life After Life* (1975), Moody initially collected 150
cases of people who had died and come back, and identified the
typical elements of a near-death experience: 1. the ineffability of
the experience, 2. hearing the news of your own death, 3. feelings
of great peace and quiet, 4. some type of noise or music, 5. a dark
tunnel, 6. rising up out-of-body, 7. meeting others who have

already died, 8. the incredible Being of Light, 9. a rapid review of one's life, 10. reaching a border or limit beyond which one cannot return to life, 11. coming back to life, 12. finding it difficult to tell others who often refuse to believe, 13. the transforming effect on one's spirituality and values, and 14. loss of the fear of death. This book has been translated into 26 languages and is being read from South America and Europe to Asia.

Subsequently Moody wrote several other books, including *The Light Beyond* (1988), which we excerpt here. He continues to explore the many factual and interpretive questions that have emerged in the expanding discussion of NDEs. Does he believe that NDEs *prove* life after death? At first Moody was cautious and neutral on this question. But by 1988 he had become more definite. No, NDEs do not scientifically *prove* life after death, he now says. But, following what Pascal called the "reason of the heart," Moody believes that these experiences do open a passageway to another reality. Always pressing forward the frontiers of thought, he is currently exploring visionary reunions with the dead, without undergoing death, in his remarkable "Theatre of the Mind." This is described in his book *Reunions: Visionary Encounters with Departed Loved Ones.*

Raymond A. Moody, Jr., M.D., Ph.D., is a psychiatrist and philosopher who studied at the University of Virginia and now does research, writes, speaks, and trains other professionals. He is the author of *Life After Life* (1975), *Reflections on Life After Life* (1977), *The Light Beyond* (1988), and *Reunions* (1993).

·⁓ The Light Beyond ⁓·
The Experience of Almost Dying

What happens when people die? That is probably mankind's most often asked and perplexing question. Do we simply cease to live, with nothing but our mortal remains to mark our time on earth? Are we resurrected later by a Supreme Being only if we have good marks in the Book of Life? Do we come back as animals, as the Hindus believe, or perhaps as different people generations later?

We are no closer to answering the basic question of the afterlife now than we were thousands of years ago when it was first pondered by ancient man. But there are many ordinary people who have been to the brink of death and reported miraculous glimpses of a world beyond, a world that glows with love and understanding that can be reached only by an exciting trip through a tunnel or passageway.

This world is attended by deceased relatives bathed in glorious light and ruled by a Supreme Being who guides the new arrival through a review of his life before sending him back to live longer on earth.

Upon return, the persons who "died" are never the same. They embrace life to its fullest and express the belief that love and knowledge are the most important of all things because they are the only things you can take with you.

For want of a better phrase to describe these incidents, we can say these people have had near-death experiences (NDEs).

I coined this phrase several years ago in my first book, *Life After Life*. Other people have called it other things, including "other world journeys, "flight of the alone to the Alone," "breaking of the plane," "near-death visions." But the traits of these episodes—no matter what they are called—all point to a similar experience. NDEers experience some or all of the following events: a sense of being dead, peace and painlessness even during a "painful" experience, bodily separation, entering a dark region or tunnel, rising rapidly into the heavens, meeting deceased friends and relatives who are bathed in light, encountering a Supreme Being, reviewing one's life, and feeling reluctance to return to the world of the living.

I isolated these traits over two decades ago in personal research that started by coincidence when I was a twenty-year-old philosophy student at the University of Virginia.

I was sitting with a dozen or so students in a seminar room listening to Professor John Marshall discuss the philosophical issues related to death. Marshall mentioned that he knew a psychiatrist in town—Dr. George Ritchie—who had been pronounced dead of double pneumonia and then successfully resuscitated. While he was "dead," Ritchie had the remarkable experience of passing through a tunnel and seeing beings of light.

This experience, my professor remarked, had profoundly affected this physician, who was convinced that he had been allowed to peek into the afterlife.

Frankly, at that point in my life, the prospect that we might survive spiritually after physical death had never occurred to me. I had always assumed that death was an obliteration of one's physical body as well as one's consciousness. Naturally I was intrigued that a respected physician would be confident enough to publicly admit having a glimpse of the afterlife.

A few months later I heard the psychiatrist himself describe his experience to a group of students. He told us of viewing from a distance his own apparently dead body as it lay on a hospital bed, of entering into a brilliant light that emanated love, and of seeing every event of his life reviewed in a three-dimensional panorama.

I filed Ritchie's story away in my memory and went on with my studies, finishing my Ph.D in philosophy in 1969. It was when I began teaching at the university that I ran into another near-death experience.

One of my students had almost died the year before, and I asked him what the experience was like. I was overwhelmed to find that he'd had an episode almost exactly like the one I had heard from Ritchie over four years before.

I began to find other students who knew of other NDEs. By the time I entered medical school in 1972, I had no fewer than eight NDE case studies from reliable, sincere people.

In medical school I found more cases and soon had enough case studies to compile *Life After Life*, which became an international best-seller. There was clearly a thirst for knowledge about what happens to us in the hereafter.

The book posed many questions it couldn't answer and raised the ire of skeptics who found the case studies of a few hundred people to be worthless in the realm of "real" scientific study. Many doctors claimed that they had never heard of near-death experiences despite having resuscitated hundreds of people. Others claimed it was simply a form of mental illness, like schizophrenia. Some said these NDEs only happened to extremely religious people, while others felt it was a form of demon possession. These experiences never happen to children, some doctors said, because they haven't been "culturally polluted" like adults. Too few people have NDEs for them to be significant, others said.

Some people were interested in researching the subject of NDEs further, myself included. The work we have done over the last decade has shed a tremendous amount of light on this subject. We have been able to address most of the questions put forth by those who feel that the near-death experience is little more than a mental illness or the brain playing tricks on itself.

Frankly, it has been good to have the skeptics around, because it has made us look at this phenomenon much harder than we probably would have otherwise. Much of what we researchers have found is included in this book.

WHO, HOW MANY, AND WHY

One thing I would like to discuss in this chapter is the great number of NDEs that actually happen. When I started looking into this phenomenon, I thought there were very few people who actually experienced it. I had no figures and there were certainly none referred to in medical literature, but if I had to guess I would say that one in eight people who were resuscitated or had a similar brush with mortality had at least one of the traits of an NDE.

When I began lecturing and asking large groups of people if they had ever had an NDE themselves or knew anyone who had, my perception of the frequency of this phenomenon changed dramatically. At lectures I would ask the audience, "How many of you have had a near-death experience or know of someone who has?" About one person in thirty raised his hand in reply.

Pollster George Gallup, Jr., found that eight million adults in the United States have had an NDE. That equals one person in twenty.

He was further able to analyze the content of these NDEs by polling for their elements. Here is what he found:

ELEMENT	PERCENT
Out of Body	26
Accurate Visual Perception	23
Audible sounds or voices	17
Feelings of peace, painlessness	32
Light phenomena	14
Life review	32
Being in another world	32
Encountering other beings	23
Tunnel experience	9
Precognition	6

Such a poll clearly showed the NDEs are much more common in society than any of the NDE researchers ever thought.

THE NDE TRAITS

As I mentioned earlier, I was able to derive a set of nine traits that define the near-death experience. I did this by questioning hundreds of people and examining their unique episodes for those common elements.

In *Life After Life* I said that I had never met anyone who had experienced all of these traits while undergoing an NDE. But since writing that book, I have interviewed more than a thousand NDEers and have found several who had "full-blown" episodes that exhibited all nine NDE traits.

Still, it's important to note that not all people who undergo a near-death experience have all of the following symptoms. Some might have one or two, others five or six. It is the presence of one or more of these traits that defines the NDE.

A Sense of Being Dead

Many people don't realize that the near-death experience they are having has anything to do with death. They will find themselves floating above their body, looking at it from a distance, and suddenly feel fear and/or confusion. They will wonder, "How is it that I can be up here, looking at myself down there?" It doesn't make any sense to them and they become very confused.

At this point, they may not actually recognize the physical body they are looking at as being their own.

One person told me that while he was out of his body, he passed through an army hospital ward and was amazed at how many young men there were who were about his age and shape who looked like him. He was actually looking at these different bodies, wondering which one was his.

Another person who was in a horrible accident in which he lost two of his limbs remembered lingering over his body on the operating table and feeling sorry for the maimed person on it. Then he realized it was him!

NDEers often feel fear at this point, which then gives way to perfect understanding of what is going on. They can understand what the doctors and nurses are trying to convey to each other (even though they frequently have no formal medical training), but when they try to talk to them or other people present, no one is able to see or hear them.

At this point, they may try to attract the attention of the people present by touching them. But when they do, their hands go right through the person's arm as though nothing was there.

This was described to me by a woman I personally resuscitated. I saw her have a cardiac arrest and immediately started chest massage. She told me later that while I was working on restarting her heart, she was going up above her body and looking down. She was standing behind me, trying to tell me to stop, that she was fine where she was. When I didn't hear her, she tried to grab my arm to keep me from inserting a needle in her arm for injecting intravenous fluid. Her hand passed right through my arm. But when she did that, she later claimed that she felt something that was the consistency of "very rarified gelatin" that seemed to have an electric current running through it.

I have heard similar descriptions from other patients.

After trying to communicate with others, NDEers frequently have an increased sense of self-identity. One NDEer described this stage as being "a time when you are not the wife of your husband, you are not the parent of your children, you are not the child of your parents. You are totally and completely you." Another woman said she felt like she was going through "a cutting of ribbons," like the freedom given to a balloon when its strings are cut.

It is at this point that fear turns to bliss, as well as understanding.

Peace and Painlessness

While the patient is in his or her body, there can frequently be intense pain. But when the "ribbons are cut," there is a very real sense of peace and painlessness.

I have talked to cardiac arrest patients who say that the intense pain of their heart attack turns from agony to an almost intense pleasure. Some researchers have theorized that the brain, when it experiences such intense pain, releases a self-made chemical that stops the pain. I discuss this theory [elsewhere] but I will say here that no one has ever done experiments to prove or disprove it. But even if it is true, it doesn't explain the other symptoms of this phenomenon.

Out-of-Body Experience

Frequently about the time that the doctor says, "We've lost him (or her)," the patient undergoes a complete change of perspective. He feels himself rising up and viewing his own body below.

Most people say they are not just some spot of consciousness when this happens. They still seem to be in some kind of body even though they are out of their physical bodies. They say the spiritual body has shape and form unlike our physical bodies. It has arms and a shape although most are at a loss to describe what it looks like. Some people describe it as a cloud of colors, or an energy field.

One NDEer I spoke to several years ago said he studied his hands while he was in this state and saw them to be composed of light with tiny structures in them. He could see the delicate whorls of his fingerprints and tubes of light up his arms.

The Tunnel Experience

The tunnel experience generally happens after bodily separation. I didn't notice until I wrote *Life After Life* that it isn't until people undergo the "cutting of the ribbons" and the out-of-body experience that they truly realize that their experience has something to do with death.

At this point, a portal or tunnel opens to them and they are propelled into darkness. They start going through this dark space and at the end they come into the brilliant light that we'll deal with next.

Some people go up stairways instead of through a tunnel. One woman said she was with her son as he was dying of lung cancer. One of the last things he said was that he saw a beautiful spiral staircase going upward. He put his mother's mind at peace when he told her that he thought he was going up those stairs.

Some people have described going through beautiful, ornate doors, which seems very symbolic of a passage into another realm.

Some people hear a *whoosh* as they go into the tunnel. Or they hear an electric vibrating sensation or a humming.

The tunnel experience is not something I discovered. There is a fifteenth-century painting by Hieronymus Bosch called "The Ascent into the Empyrean" that virtually describes this experience. In the foreground are people who are dying. Surrounding them are spiritual beings who are trying to direct their attention upward. They pass through a dark tunnel and come out into a light. As they go into this light, they kneel reverently.

In one of the most amazing tunnel experiences I've ever heard the tunnel was described as being almost infinite in length and width and filled with light.

The descriptions are many, but the sense of what is happening remains the same: the person is going through a passageway toward an intense light.

People of Light

Once through the tunnel, the person usually meets beings of light. These beings aren't composed of ordinary light. They glow with a beautiful and intense luminescence that seems to permeate everything and fill the person with love. In fact, one person who went through this experience said, "I could describe this as 'light' or 'love' and it would mean the same thing." Some say it's almost like being drenched by a rainstorm of light.

They also describe this light as being much brighter than anything we experience on earth. But still, despite its brilliant intensity, it doesn't hurt the eyes. Instead, it's warm, vibrant, and alive.

In this situation, NDEers frequently meet up with friends and relatives who have died. Often, they speak of these people as being in the same indescribable bodies as theirs.

Besides bright light and luminescent friends and relatives, some people have described beautiful pastoral scenes. One woman I know spoke of a meadow that was surrounded by plants, each with its own inner light.

Occasionally, people see beautiful cities of light that defy description in their grandeur.

In this state, communication doesn't take place in words as we know them, but in telepathic, nonverbal ways that result in immediate understanding.

The Being of Light

After meeting several beings in light, the NDEer usually meets a supreme Being of Light. People with a Christian background often describe Him as God or Jesus. Those with other religious backgrounds may call him Buddha or Allah. But some have said that it's neither God nor Jesus, but someone very holy nonetheless.

Whoever he is, the Being radiates total love and understanding. So much so, that most people want to be with it forever.

But they can't. At this point they are told, usually by the Being of Light, that they have to return to their earthly body. But first it's his job to take them on a life review.

The Life Review

When the life review occurs, there are no more physical surroundings. In their place is a full color, three-dimensional, panoramic review of every single thing the NDEers have done in their lives.

This usually takes place in a third-person perspective and doesn't occur in time as we know it. The closest description I've heard of it is that the person's whole life is there at once.

In this situation, you not only see every action that you have ever done, but you also perceive immediately the effects of every single one of your actions upon the people in your life.

So for instance, if I see myself doing an unloving act, then immediately I am in the consciousness of the person I did that act to, so that I feel their sadness, hurt, and regret.

On the other hand, if I do a loving act to someone, then I am immediately in their place and I can feel the kind and happy feelings.

Through all of this, the Being is with those people, asking them what good they have done with their lives. He helps them through this review and helps them put all the events of their life in perspective.

All of the people who go through this come away believing that the most important thing in their life is love.

For most of them, the second most important thing in life is knowledge. As they see life scenes in which they are learning things, the Being points out that one of the things they can take with them at death is knowledge. The other is love.

When people come back they have a thirst for knowledge. Frequently, NDEers become avid readers, even if they weren't very fond of books before, or they enroll in school to study a different field than the one they are in.

Rising Rapidly into the Heavens

I should point out that not all NDEers have a tunnel experience. Some report a "floating experience," in which they rise rapidly into the heavens, seeing the universe from a perspective reserved for satellites and astronauts.

The psychotherapist C.G. Jung had an experience like this in 1944 when he had a heart attack. He said that he felt himself rise rapidly to a point far above the earth.

One child I talked to said that he felt himself rise far above the earth, passing through the stars and finding himself up with the angels. Another NDEer described himself as zooming up and seeing the planets all around him and the earth below, like a blue marble.

Reluctance to Return

For many people, the NDE is such a pleasant event that they don't want to return. As a result, they are frequently very angry at their doctors for bringing them back.

Two physician friends of mine first discovered NDEs for themselves when patients they saved became hostile.

One of them was resuscitating another physician who had just had a cardiac arrest. When the stricken man revived, he said angrily: "Carl, don't you ever do that to me again."

Carl was bewildered as to why this anger should arise. But later the revived physician took him aside and apologized for his behavior and explained his experience. "I was mad because you brought me back to death instead of life."

Another physician friend of mine discovered the NDE phenomenon when he resuscitated a man who then yelled at him for taking him out of "that beautiful and bright place."

NDEers frequently act this way. But it is a short-lived feeling. If you talk to them a week or so later, they are happy to have returned. Although they miss the blissful state, they are glad to have the chance to go on living.

Interestingly, many NDEers feel they are given a choice to return or stay. It may be the Being of Light who offers this choice to them, or a relative who has died.

All of the persons I have talked to would stay if they had only themselves to think of. But they usually say they want to go back because they have children left to raise or because their spouses or parents might miss them.

One woman in Los Angeles has faced this question from the Being of Light twice in her life. Once in the late fifties when she was in a coma following an automobile accident, the Being told her it was time to die and go to heaven.

She argued with him, complaining that she was too young to die. But the Being wouldn't budge until she said, "But I'm young, I haven't danced enough yet."

At that point the Being gave out a hearty laugh and allowed her to live.

About thirty years later, she had a cardiac arrest while undergoing minor surgery. Again she passed through the tunnel and found herself with the Being, and again he told her it was her time to die.

This time she argued that she had children to raise and couldn't leave them at this point in their lives.

"Okay," said the Being. "But this is the last time. The next time you have to stay."

Different Time and Space

In addition to these nine traits, people who have undergone NDEs say that time is greatly compressed and nothing like the time we keep with our watches. NDEers have described it as "being in eternity." One woman, when asked how long her experience lasted, told me, "You could say it lasted one second or that it lasted ten thousand years and it wouldn't make any difference how you put it."

The boundaries imposed by space in our everyday lives are often broken in NDEs. During the experience, if NDEers want to go somewhere, they can often just think themselves there. People say that while they were out of their body but watching the doctors work on them in the operating room, they could simply wish their way into the waiting room to see their relatives.

Such experiences are perhaps the best answer to people who think NDEs are the brain playing tricks on itself. After all, on the surface it is entirely possible that the brain, while in great distress, could try to calm itself by creating tunnel experiences and Beings of Light to put the person to rest. But NDEers who can tell you what was going on in other rooms while having their episodes are truly having out-of-body experiences.

I have several examples of people who had out-of-body experiences during their resuscitations and were able to leave the operating room to observe relatives in other parts of the hospital.

One woman who left her body went into the waiting room and saw that her daughter was wearing mismatched plaids.

What had happened was that the maid had brought the child to the hospital and in her haste had just grabbed the first two things off the laundry pile.

Later, when she told her family about her experience and the fact that she had seen the girl in these mismatched clothes, they knew that she must have been in that waiting room with them.

Another woman had an out-of-body experience and left the room where her body was being resuscitated. From across the hospital lobby, she watched her brother-in-law as some business associate approached him and asked what he was doing in the hospital.

"Well, I was going out of town on a business trip," said the brother-in-law. "But it looks like June is going to kick the bucket, so I better stay around and be a pallbearer."

A few days later when she was recovering, the brother-in-law came to visit. She told him that she was in the room as he spoke to his friend, and erased any doubt by saying, "Next time I die, you go off on your business trip because I'll be just fine." He turned so pale that she thought he was about to have a near-death experience himself.

Another of these experiences happened to an elderly woman I was resuscitating. I was giving her closed heart massage on an emergency room examining table and the nurse assisting me ran into another room to get a vial of medication that we needed.

It was a glass-necked vial that you're supposed to hold in a paper towel while breaking off the top so you don't cut yourself. When the nurse returned, the neck was broken so I could use the medicine right away.

When the old woman came to, she looked very sweetly at the nurse and said, "Honey, I saw what you did in that room, and you're going to cut yourself doing that." The nurse was shocked. She admitted that in her haste to open the medicine, she had broken the glass neck with her bare fingers.

The woman told us that while we were resuscitating her, she had followed the nurse back to the room to watch what she was doing.

*****

In the absence of firm scientific proof, people frequently ask me what I believe: Are NDEs evidence of life after life? My answer is "Yes."

There are several things about NDEs that make me feel so strongly. One of these is the verifiable out-of-body experiences that I mentioned [above]. What greater proof is needed that persons survive the death of their physical bodies than many examples of individuals leaving their bodies and witnessing attempts to save it?

Although these out-of-body experiences might be the most solid scientific reason to believe in life hereafter, the most impressive thing about NDEs to me is the enormous changes in personality that they bring about in people. That NDEs totally transform the people to whom they happen shows their reality and power.

After twenty-two years of looking at the near-death experience, I think there isn't enough scientific proof to show conclusively that there is life after death. But that means scientific proof.

Matters of the heart are different. They are open to judgments that don't require a strictly scientific view of the world. But with researchers like myself, they do call for educated analysis.

Based on such examination, I am convinced that NDEers do get a glimpse of the beyond, a brief passage into a whole other reality.

The psychotherapist C. G. Jung summed up my feeling on life after life in a letter he wrote in 1944. This letter is especially significant since Jung himself had an NDE during a heart attack just a few months before he wrote it:

> What happens after death is so unspeakably glorious that our imaginations and our feelings do not suffice to form even an approximate conception of it....
>
> Sooner or later, the dead all become what we also are. But in this reality, we know little or nothing about that mode of being. And what shall we still know of this earth after death? The dissolution of our timebound form in eternity brings no loss of meaning. Rather, does the little finger know itself a member of the hand.

Through the Light and Beyond

Mellen-Thomas Benedict

This body, that you are in, has been alive *forever*. It comes from an unending stream of life, going back to the Big Bang and beyond.

Mellen-Thomas Benedict is an artist who survived a near-death experience in 1982. He died extremely discouraged about the nuclear and ecology crises on our planet. He was dead over an hour and a half, during which he felt that he rose up out of his body and went to the Light. Curious about the universe, he says, he was taken far into the remote depths of existence, and even beyond, into the energetic Void of Nothingness behind the Big Bang. He brought back deep and fascinating insights into scientific and spiritual questions. Now full of faith and healed of his illness, he lives in California, helping heal others and working with university scientists to explore theoretical frontiers. "His story is one of the most remarkable I have encountered in my extensive research on near-death experiences." says Professor Kenneth Ring, at the University of Connecticut.

Dr. Janice Holden, in the Department of Counselor Education at the University of North Texas, confirms that Mellen-Thomas, under hypnosis, was able to give accurate information about and draw the genetic makeup of a rare neuromuscular disease. She was astounded by this, saying "It's not the kind of thing where one could cheat" (Blaser).

Dr. Beverly Rubik, a bio-physicist and founding Chair of the Center for Frontier Sciences at Temple University, has also tested Mellen-Thomas' insight. She let him try his technique for healing with light on her. She had some raspberry bramble scratches on her arm and let him shine his light treatment on half the scratches for ten minutes. The treated scratches healed twice as fast as the untreated. "I am very much impressed with the ideas that he gets for future medical technology," she says, "especially since he's not a trained bio-physicist or engineer" (Blaser).

Mellen-Thomas Benedict lives in California, speaking, leading workshops, and researching new healing techniques from the Light.

·⁓ Through the Light and Beyond ⁓·

In 1982 I died from terminal cancer. The condition I had was inoperable, and any kind of chemotherapy they could give me would just have made me more of a vegetable. I was given six to eight months to live. I had been an information freak in the 1970's, and I had become increasingly despondent over the nuclear crisis, the ecology crisis, and so forth. So, since I did not have a spiritual basis, I began to believe that nature had made a mistake, and that we were probably a cancerous organism on the planet. I saw no way that we could get out from all the problems we had created for ourselves and the planet. I perceived all humans as cancer, and that is what I got. That is what killed me. Be careful what your world view is. It can feed back on you, especially if it is a negative world view. I had a seriously negative one. That is what led me into my death. I tried all sorts of alternative healing methods, but nothing helped.

So I determined that this was really just between me and God. I had never really faced God before, or even dealt with God. I was not into any kind of spirituality at the time, but I began a journey into learning about spirituality and alternative healing. I set out to do all the reading I could and bone up on the subject, because I did not want to be surprised on the other side. So I started reading on various religions and philosophies. They were all very interesting, and gave hope that there was something on the other side. On the other hand, as a self-employed stained-glass artist at the time, I had no medical insurance whatsoever. So my life savings went overnight in testing. Then I was facing the medical profession without any kind of insurance. I did not want to have my family dragged down financially, so I determined to handle this myself. There was not constant pain, but there were blackouts. I got so that I would not dare to drive, and eventually I ended up in hospice care. I had my own personal hospice caretaker. I was very blessed by this angel who went through the last part of this with me. I lasted about eighteen months. I did not want to take a lot of drugs, since I wanted to be as conscious as possible. Then I experienced such pain that I had nothing but pain in my consciousness, luckily only for a few days at a time.

I remember waking up one morning at home about 4:30 AM, and I just knew that this was it. This was the day I was going to die. So I called a few friends and said goodbye. I woke up my hospice caretaker and told her. I had a private agreement with her that she would leave my dead body alone for six hours, since I had read that all kinds of interesting things happen when you die. I went back to sleep. The next thing I remember is the beginning of a typical near-death experience. Suddenly I was fully aware and I was standing up, but my body was in the bed. There was this darkness around me. Being out of my body was even more vivid than ordinary experience. It was so vivid that I could see every room in the house, I could see the top of the house, I could see around the house, I could see under the house.

There was this Light shining. I turned toward the Light. The Light was very similar to what many other people have described in their near-death experiences. It was so magnificent. It is tangible; you can feel it. It is alluring; you want to go to it like you would want to go to your ideal mother's or father's arms. As I began to move toward the Light, I knew intuitively that if I went to the Light, I would be dead. So as I was moving toward the Light I said, "Please wait a minute, just hold on a second here. I want to think about this; I would like to talk to you before I go." To my surprise, the entire experience halted at that point. You are indeed in control of your near-death experience. You are not on a roller coaster ride. So my request was honored and I had some conversations with the Light. The Light kept changing into different figures, like Jesus, Buddha, Krishna, mandalas, archetypal images and signs. I asked the Light, "What is going on here? Please, Light, clarify yourself for me. I really want to know the reality of the situation." I can not really say the exact words, because it was sort of telepathy. The Light responded. The information transferred to me was that your beliefs shape the kind of feedback you are getting before the Light. If you were a Buddhist or Catholic or Fundamentalist, you get a feedback loop of your own stuff. You have a chance to look at it and examine it, but most people do not. As the Light revealed itself to me, I became aware that what I was really seeing was our higher Self matrix. We all have a higher Self, or an oversoul part of our being. It revealed itself to me in its truest energy form. The only way I can really describe it is that the being of the higher Self is more like a conduit. It did not look like that, but it is a direct connection to the Source that each and every one of us has. We are directly connected to the Source. So the Light was showing me the higher Self matrix. I was not committed to one particular religion. So that is what was was being fed back to me.

As I asked the Light to keep clearing for me, to keep explaining, I understood what the higher Self matrix is. We have a grid around the planet where all the higher Selves are connected. This is like a great company, a next subtle level of energy around us, the spirit level, you might say. Then, after a couple of minutes, I asked for more clarification. I really wanted to know what the universe is about, and I was ready to go at that time. I said "I am ready, take me." Then the Light turned into the most beautiful thing that I have ever seen: a mandala of human souls on this planet. Now I came to this with my negative view of what has happening on the planet. So as I asked the light to keep clarifying for me, I saw in this magnificent mandala how beautiful we all are in our essence, our core. We are the most beautiful creations. The human soul, the human matrix that we all make together is absolutely fantastic, elegant, exotic, everything. I just cannot say enough about how it changed my opinion of human beings in that instant. I said, "Oh, God, I did not know how beautiful we are." At any level, high or low, in whatever shape you are in, you are the most beautiful creation, you are.

The revelations coming from the Light seemed to go on and on, then I asked the Light, "Does this mean that Mankind will be saved?" Then, like a trumpet blast with a shower of spiraling lights, the Great Light spoke, saying, "Remember this and never forget; you save, redeem and heal youself. You always have. You always will. You were created with the power to do so from before the beginning of the world."

In that instant I realized even more. I realized that WE HAVE ALREADY BEEN SAVED, and we saved ourselves because we were designed to self-correct like the rest of God's universe. This is what the second coming is about. I thanked the Light of God with all my heart. The best thing I could come up with was these simple words of total appreciation: "Oh dear God, Dear Universe, dear Great Self, I Love My Life." The Light seemed to breathe me in even more deeply. It was as if the Light was completely absorbing me. The Love Light is, to this day, indescribable. I entered into another realm, more profound than the last, and became aware of something more, much more. It was an enormous stream of Light, vast and full, deep in the Heart of Life. I asked what this was.

The Light responded, "This is the RIVER OF LIFE. Drink of this manna water to your heart's content." So I did. I took one big drink and then another. To drink of Life Itself! I was in ecstasy.

Then the Light said, "You have a desire." The Light knew all about me, everything past, present and future.

"Yes!" I whispered.

I asked to see the rest of the Universe; beyond our solar system, beyond all human illusion. The Light then told me that I could go with the Stream. I did, and was carried Through the Light at the End of the Tunnel. I felt and heard a series of very soft sonic booms. What a rush!

Suddenly I seemed to be rocketing away from the planet on this stream of Life. I saw the earth fly away. The solar system, in all its splendor, whizzed by and disappeared. At faster than light speed, I flew through the center of the galaxy, absorbing more knowledge as I went. I learned that this galaxy, and all of the Universe, is bursting with many different varieties of LIFE. I saw many worlds. The good news is that we are not alone in this Universe! As I rode this stream of consciousness through the center of the galaxy, the stream was expanding in awesome fractal waves of energy. The super clusters of galaxies with all their ancient wisdom flew by. At first I thought I was going somewhere; actually travelling. But then I realized that, as the stream was expanding, my own consciousness was also expanding to take in everything in the Universe! All creation passed by me. It was an unimaginable wonder! I truly was a Wonder Child; a babe in Wonderland!

It seemed as if all the creations in the Universe soared by me and vanished in a speck of Light. Almost immediately, a second Light appeared. It came from all sides, and was so different; a Light made up of more than every frequency in the Universe. I felt and heard several velvety sonic booms again. My consciousness, or being, was expanding to interface with the entire Holographic Universe and More. As I passed into the second Light, the awareness came to me that I had just Transcended the Truth. Those are the best words I have for it, but I will try to explain. As I passed into the second Light, I expanded beyond the First Light. I found myself in a profound stillness, beyond all silence. I could see or perceive FOREVER, beyond Infinity.

I was in the Void.

I was in pre-creation, before the Big Bang. I had crossed over the beginning of time/the First Word/the First vibration. I was in the Eye of Creation. I felt as if I was touching the Face of God. It was not a religious feeling. Simply I was at one with Absolute Life and Consciousness.

When I say that I could see or perceive forever, I mean that I could experience all of creation generating itself. It was without beginning and without end. That's a mind-expanding thought, isn't it? Scientists perceive the Big Bang as a single event which created the Universe. I saw that the Big Bang is only one of an infinite number of Big Bangs creating Universes endlessly and simultaneously. The only images that even come close in human terms would be those created by super computers using fractal geometry equations.

The ancients knew of this. They said Godhead periodically created new Universes by breathing out, and de-created other Universes by breathing in. These epochs were called Yugas. Modern science called this the Big Bang. I was in absolute, pure consciousness. I could see or perceive all the Big Bangs or Yugas creating and de-creating themselves. Instantly I entered into them all simultaneously. I saw that each and every little piece of creation has the power to create. It is very difficult to try to explain this. I am still speechless about this.

It took me years after I returned to assimilate any words at all for the Void experience. I can tell you this now: the Void is less than nothing, yet more than everything that is! The Void is absolute zero; chaos forming all possibilities. It is Absolute Consciousness; much more than even Universal Intelligence.

Where is the Void? I know.

The Void is inside and outside everything. You, right now even while you live, are always inside and outside the Void simultaneously. You don't have to go anywhere or die to get there. The Void is the vacuum or nothingness between all physical manifestations. The SPACE between atoms and their components. Modern science has begun to study this space between everything. They call it Zero-point. Whenever they try to measure it, their instruments go off the scale, or to infinity, so to speak. They have no way, as of yet, to measure infinity accurately. There is more of the 0 space in your own body and the Universe than anything else!

What mystics call the Void is not a void. It is so full of energy, a different kind of energy that has created everything that we are. Everything since the Big Bang is vibration, from the first Word, which is the first vibration. The biblical "I am" really has a question mark after it. "I am—What am I?" So creation is God exploring God's Self through every way imaginable, in an on-going, infinite exploration through every one of us. Through every piece of hair on your head, through every leaf on every tree, through every atom, God is exploring God's Self, the great "I am." I began to see that everything that is, is the Self, literally, your Self, my Self. Everything is the great Self. That is why God knows even when a leaf falls. That is possible because wherever you are is the center of the universe. Wherever any atom is, that is the center of the universe. There is God in that, and God in the Void.

As I was exploring the Void and all the Yugas or creations, I was completely out of time and space as we know it. In this expanded state, I discovered that creation is about Absolute Pure Consciousness, or God, coming into the Experience of Life as we know it. The Void itself is devoid of experience. It is pre-life, before the first vibration. Godhead is about more than Life and Death. Therefore there is even more than Life and Death to experience in the Universe!

When I realized this, I was finished with the Void, and wanted to return to this creation, or Yuga. It just seemed like the natural thing to do. Then I suddenly came back through the second Light, or the Big Bang, hearing several more velvet booms. I rode the stream of consciousness back through all of creation, and what a ride it was! The super clusters of galaxies came through me with even more insights. I passed through the center of our galaxy, which is a black hole. Black holes are the great processors or recyclers of the Universe. Do you know what is on the other side of a Black Hole? We are; our galaxy, which has been reprocessed from another Universe. In its total energy configuration, the galaxy looked like a fantastic city of lights. All energy this side of the Big Bang is light. Every sub-atom, atom, star, planet, even consciousness itself is made of light and has a frequency and/or particle. Light is living stuff. Everything is made of light, even stones. So everything is alive. Everything is made from the Light of God; everything is very intelligent.

As I rode the stream on and on, I could eventually see a huge Light coming. I knew it was the First Light; the higher Self Light Matrix of our solar system. Then the entire solar system appeared in the Light, accompanied by one of those velvet booms.

I could see all the energy that this solar system generates, and it is an incredible light show! I could hear the Music of the Spheres. Our solar system, as do all celestial bodies, generates a unique matrix of light, sound and vibratory energies. Advanced civilizations from other star systems can spot life as we know it in the universe by the vibratory or energy matrix imprint. It is child's play. The earth's Wonder child (human beings) make an abundance of sound right now, like children playing in the backyard of the universe.

I rode the stream directly into the center of the Light. I felt embraced by the Light as it took me in with its breath again, followed by another soft sonic boom. I was in this great Light of Love with the stream of life flowing through me. I have to say again, it is the most loving, non-judgmental Light. It is the ideal parent for this Wonder Child.

"What now?" I wondered.

The Light explained to me that there is no death; we are immortal beings. We have already been alive forever! I realized that we are part of a natural living system that recycles itself endlessly. I was never told that I had to come back. I just knew that I would. It was only natural, from what I had seen.

I don't know how long I was with the Light, in human time. But there came a moment when I realized that all my questions had been answered and my return was near. When I say that all my questions were answered on the other side, I mean to say just that. All my questions have been answered. Every human has a different life and set of questions to explore. Some of our questions are Universal, but each of us is exploring this thing we call Life in our own unique way. So is every other form of life, from mountains to every leaf on every tree.

And that is very important to the rest of us in this Universe. Because it all contributes to the Big Picture, the fullness of Life. We are literally God exploring God's self in an infinite Dance of Life. Your uniqueness enhances all of Life.

As I began my return to the life cycle, it never crossed my mind, nor was I told, that I would return to the same body. It just did not matter. I had complete trust in the Light and the Life process. As the stream merged with the great Light, I asked never to forget the revelations and the feelings of what I had learned on the other side.

There was a "Yes." It felt like a kiss to my soul.

Then I was taken back through the Light into the vibratory realm again. The whole process reversed, with even more information being given to me. I came back home, and I was given lessons on the mechanics of reincarnation. I was given answers to all those little questions I had: "How does this work? How does that work?" I knew that I would be reincarnated. The earth is a great processor of energy, and individual consciousness evolves out of that into each one of us. I thought of myself as a human for the first time, and I was happy to be that. From what I have seen, I would be happy to be an atom in this universe. An atom. So to be the human part of God…this is the most fantastic blessing. It is a blessing beyond our wildest estimation of what blessing can be. For each and every one of us to be the human part of this experience is awesome, and magnificent. Each and every one of us, no matter where we are, screwed up or not, is a blessing to the planet, right where we are.

So I went through the reincarnation process expecting to be a baby somewhere. But I was given a lesson on how individual identity and consciousness evolve. So I reincarnated back into this body. I was so surprised when I opened my eyes. I do not know why, because I understood it, but it was still such as surprise to be back in this body, back in my room with someone looking over me crying her eyes out. It was my hospice caretaker. She had given up an hour and a half after finding me dead. She was sure I was dead; all the signs of death were there—I was getting stiff. We do not know how long I was dead, but we do know that it was an hour and a half since I was found. She honored my wish to have my newly dead body left alone for a few hours as much as she could. We had an amplified stethoscope and many ways of checking out the vital functions of the body to see what was happening. She can verify that I really was dead. It was not a near-death experience. I experienced death itself for at least an hour and a half. She found me dead and checked the stethoscope, blood pressure and heart rate monitor for an hour and a half. My body was stiff and inflexible. She went into the other room. Then I awakened and saw the light outside. I tried to get up to go to it, but I fell out of the bed. She heard a loud "clunk", ran in and found me on the floor.

When I recovered, I was very surprised and yet very awed about what had happened to me. At first all the memory of the trip that I have now was not there. I kept slipping out of this world and kept asking, "Am I alive?" This world seemed more like a dream than that one. Within three days I was feeling normal again, clearer, yet different than I had ever felt in my life. My memory of the journey came back later. I could see nothing wrong with any human being I had ever seen. Before that I was really judgmental. I thought a lot of people were really screwed up, in fact I thought that everybody was screwed up but me. But I got clear on all that.

About three months later a friend said I should get tested, so I went and got the scans and so forth. I really felt good, so I was afraid of getting bad news. I remember the doctor at the clinic looking at the before and after scans, saying, "Well, there is nothing here now." I said, "Really, it must be a miracle!" He said "No, these things happen; they are called spontaneous remission." He acted very unimpressed. But here was a miracle, and I was impressed, even if no one else was.

The mystery of life has very little to do with intelligence. The universe is not an intellectual process at all. The intellectual is helpful; it is brilliant, but right now that is all we process with, instead of our hearts and the wiser part of ourselves.

The center of the earth is this great transmuter of energy, just as you see in pictures of our earth's magnetic field. That's our cycle, pulling reincarnated souls back in and through it again. A sign that you are reaching human level is that you are beginning to evolve an individual consciousness. The animals have a group soul, and they reincarnate in group souls. A deer is pretty much going to be a deer forever. But just being born a human, whether deformed or a genius, shows that you are on the path to developing an individual consciousness. That is in itself part of the group consciousness called humanity. I saw that races are personality clusters. Nations like France, Germany and China each have their own personality. Cities have personalities, their local group souls that attract certain people. Families have group souls. Individual identity is evolving like branches of a fractal; the group soul explores in our individuality. The different questions that each of us has are very, very important. This is how Godhead is exploring God's Self— through you. So ask your questions, do your searching. You will find your Self and you will find God in that Self, because it is only the Self.

More than that, I began to see that each one of us humans are soul mates. We are part of the same soul fractaling out in many creative directions, but still the same. Now I look at every human being that I ever see, and I see a soul mate, my soul mate, the one I have always been looking for. Beyond that, the greatest soul mate that you will ever have is yourself. We are each both male and female. We experience this in the womb and we experience this in reincarnation states. If you are looking for that ultimate soul mate outside of yourself, you may never find it; it is not there. Just as God is not "there." God is *here*. Don't look "out there" for God. Look *here* for God. Look through your Self. Start having the greatest love affair you ever had…with your Self. You will love everything out of that.

I had a descent into what you might call Hell, and it was very surprising. I did not see Satan or evil. My descent into Hell was a descent into each person's customized human misery, ignorance, and darkness of not-knowing. It seemed like a miserable eternity. But each of the millions of souls around me had a little star of light always available. But no one seemed to pay attention to it. They were so consumed with their own grief, trauma and misery. But, after what seemed an eternity, I started calling out to that Light, like a child calling to a parent for help. Then the Light opened up and formed a tunnel that came right to me and insulated me from all that fear and pain. That is what Hell really is. So what we are doing is learning to hold hands, to come together. The doors of Hell are open now. We are going to link up, hold hands, and walk out of Hell together. The Light came to me and turned into a huge golden angel. I said, "Are you the angel of death?" It expressed to me that it was my oversoul, my higher Self matrix, a super-ancient part of ourselves. Then I was taken to the Light.

Soon our science will quantify spirit. Isn't that going to be wonderful? We are coming up with devices now that are sensitive to subtle energy or spirit energy. Physicists use these atomic colliders to smash atoms to see what they are made of. They have got it down to quarks and charm, and all that. Well, one day they are going to come down to the little thing that holds it all together, and they are going to have to call that…God. With atomic colliders they are not only seeing what is in here, but they are creating particles. Thank God most of them are short-lived milliseconds and nanoseconds. We are just beginning to understand that we are creating too, as we go along. As I saw forever, I came to a realm in which there is a point where we pass all knowledge and begin creating the next fractal, the next level. We have that power to create as we explore. And that is God expanding itself through us.

Since my return I have experienced the Light spontaneously, and I have learned how to get to that space almost any time in my meditation. Each one of you can do this. You do not have to die to do this. It is within your equipment; you are wired for it already. The body is the most magnificent Light being there is. The body is a universe of incredible Light. Spirit is not pushing us to dissolve this body. That is not what is happening. Stop trying to become God; God is becoming you. Here.

The mind is like a child running around the universe, demanding this and thinking it created the world. But I ask the mind: "What did your mother have to do with this?" That is the next level of spiritual awareness. Oh! my mother! All of a sudden you give up the ego, because you are not the only soul in the universe.

One of my questions to the Light was "What is Heaven?" I was given a tour of all the heavens that have been created: the Nirvanas, the Happy Hunting Grounds, all of them. I went through them. These are thought form creations that we have created. We don't really go to heaven; we are reprocessed. But whatever we created, we leave a part of ourself there. It is real, but it is not all of the soul. I saw the Christian Heaven. We expect it to be beautiful place, and you stand in front of the throne, worshipping forever. I tried it. It is boring! This is all we are going to do? It is childlike. I do not mean to offend anyone. Some heavens are very interesting, and some are very boring. I found the ancient ones to be more interesting, like the Native American ones, the Happy Hunting Grounds. The Egyptians have fantastic ones. It goes on and on. There are so many of them. In each of them there is a fractal that is your particular interpretation, unless you are part of the group soul that believes in only the God of a particular religion. Then you are very close, in the same ball park together. But even then, each is a little bit different. That is a part of yourself that you leave there. Death is about life, not about Heaven.

I asked God: "What is the best religion on the planet? Which one is right?" And Godhead said, with great love: "I don't care." That was incredible grace. What that meant was that we are the caring beings here. The Ultimate Godhead of all the stars tells us: "It does not matter what religion you are." They come and they go, they change. Buddhism has not been here forever, Catholicism has not been here forever, and they are all about to become more enlightened. More light is coming into all systems now. There is going to be a reformation in spirituality that is going to be just as dramatic as the Protestant Reformation. There will be lots of people fighting about it, one religion against the next, believing that only they are right. Everyone thinks they own God, the religions and philosophies, especially the religions, because they form big organizations around the philosophy. When Godhead said, "I don't care," I immediately understood that it is for *us* to care about. It is important, because we are the caring beings. It matters to us and that is where it is important. What you have is the energy equation in spirituality. Ultimate Godhead does not care if you are Protestant, Buddhist, or whatever. It is all a blooming facet of the whole. I wish that all religions would realize it and let each other be. It is not the end of each religion, but we are talking about the same God. Live and let live. Each has a different view. And it all adds up to the big picture; it is all important.

I went over to the other side with a lot of fears about toxic waste, nuclear missiles, the population explosion, the rainforest. I came back loving every single problem. I love nuclear waste. I love the mushroom cloud; this is the holiest mandala that we have manifested to date, as an archetype. It, more than any religion or philosophy on earth, brought us together all of a sudden, to a new level of consciousness. Knowing that maybe we can blow up the planet fifty times, or 500 times, we finally realize that maybe we are all here together now. For a period they had to keep setting off more bombs to get it in to us. Then we started saying, "we do not need this any more." Now we are actually in a safer world than we have ever been in, and it is going to get safer. So I came back loving toxic waste, because it brought us together. These things are so big. As Peter Russell might say, these problems are now "soul size." Do we have soul size answers? YES!

The clearing of the rain forest will slow down, and in fifty years there will be more trees on the planet than in a long time. If you are into ecology, go for it; you are that part of the system that is becoming aware. Go for it with all your might, but do not be depressed. It is part of a larger thing. Earth is in the process of domesticating itself. It is never again going to be as wild a place as it once was. There will be great wild places, reserves where nature thrives. Gardening and reserves will be the thing in the future. Population increase is getting very close to the optimal range of energy to cause a shift in consciousness. That shift in consciousness will change politics, money, energy.

What happens when we dream? We are multi-dimensional beings. We can access that through lucid dreaming. In fact, this universe is God's dream. One of the things that I saw is that we humans are a speck on a planet that is a speck in a galaxy that is a speck. Those are giant systems out there, and we are in sort of an average system. But human beings are already legendary throughout the cosmos of consciousness. The little bitty human being of Earth/Gaia is legendary. One of the things that we are legendary for is dreaming. We are legendary dreamers. In fact, the whole cosmos has been looking for the meaning of life, the meaning of it all. And it was the little dreamer who came up with the best answer ever. We dreamed it up. So dreams are important.

After dying and coming back, I really respect life and death. In our DNA experiments we may have opened the door to a great secret. Soon we will be able to live as long as we want to live in this body. After living 150 years or so, there will be an intuitive soul sense that you will want to change channels. Living forever in one body is not as creative as reincarnation, as transferring energy in this fantastic vortex of energy that we are in. We are actually going to see the wisdom of life and death, and enjoy it. As it is now, we have already been alive forever. This body, that you are in, has been alive *forever*. It comes from an unending stream of life, going back to the Big Bang and beyond. This body gives life to the next life, in dense and subtle energy. This body has been alive forever already.

REFERENCES

Blaser, Janet. "Gifts from the 'other side:' Mellen-Thomas died, saw the light, and brought it back with him." *Santa Cruz County Sentinel.* Santa Cruz, CA. Sat. July 29, 1995. pp. C1–2.

Mellen-Thomas Benedict is writing a book and currently has available a series of audiotapes, beginning with "Journey Through the Light and Back!" Golden Tree Productions, PO Box 1898, Soquel, CA 95073.

⌣ 3 ⌣

Embraced by the Light

Betty Eadie

I saw that we all volunteered for our positions and stations in the world, and that each of us is receiving more help than we know.

Recovering from surgery in 1973, Betty Eadie, a mother of seven children, died and rose above her hospital bed. She floated up through a dark, tornado-like tunnel toward the brilliant Light, where she felt the incredible power of life itself and love itself. The Light was Jesus Christ, and Betty did not want to return to earth. She had so many questions! Why are there different religions? Why did I fear God as a child? How do spirit and body interact in illness? Why is there sin and despair? Guided through a bookless library of understanding, she received her answers in full. Walking through a glowing garden, she became a rose, feeling

God's love pouring into plants, into humans, into all of existence, because we are all one.

Betty saw how each incarnation is a chosen learning experience. Each spirit volunteers to live a certain life in order to call up needed spiritual strengths. Each weakness is given as a challenge to our spirit. We are all on earth for one great purpose—to learn to love each other. Reluctantly Betty returned home to Washington state, where her physician confirmed that she had indeed died from a hemmorhage. Nineteen years later, Betty finally was persuaded to write her story in *Embraced by the Light* (1992) with Curtis Taylor. The book soon soared to the top of *The New York Times* best-seller list.

Betty Eadie lives in Seattle and speaks widely. Her book has been translated and published by over twenty international presses, from Sweden to Taiwan.

·⁓ Embraced by the Light ⁓·

I saw a pinpoint of light in the distance. The black mass around me began to take on more of the shape of a tunnel, and I felt myself traveling through it at an even greater speed, rushing toward the light. I was instinctively attracted to it, although again, I felt that others might not be. As I approached it, I noticed the figure of a man standing in it, with the light radiating all around him. As I got closer the light became brilliant—brilliant beyond any description, far more brilliant than the sun—and I knew that no earthly eyes in their natural state could look upon this light without being destroyed. Only spiritual eyes could endure it—and appreciate it. As I drew closer I began to stand upright.

I saw that the light immediately around him was golden, as if his whole body had a golden halo around it, and I could see that the golden halo burst out from around him and spread into a brilliant, magnificent whiteness that extended out for some distance. I felt his light blending into mine, literally, and I felt my light being drawn to his. It was as if there were two lamps in a room, both shining, their light merging together. It's hard to tell where one light ends and the other begins; they just become one light. Although his light was much brighter than my own, I was aware that my light, too, illuminated us. And as our lights merged, I felt as if I had stepped into his countenance, and I felt an utter explosion of love.

It was the most unconditional love I have ever felt, and as I saw his arms open to receive me I went to him and received his complete embrace and said over and over, "I'm home. I'm home. I'm finally home." I felt his enormous spirit and knew that I had always been a part of him, that in reality I had never been away from him. And I knew that I was worthy to be with him, to embrace him. I knew that he was aware of all my sins and faults, but that they didn't matter right now. He just wanted to hold me and share his love with me, and I wanted to share mine with him.

There was no questioning who he was. I knew that he was my Savior, and friend, and God. He was Jesus Christ, who had always loved me, even when I thought he hated me. He was life itself, love itself, and his love gave me a fullness of joy, even to overflowing. I knew that I had known him from the beginning, from long before my earth life, because my spirit *remembered* him.

All my life I had feared him, and I now saw—I *knew*—that he was my choicest friend. Gently, he opened his arms and let me stand back far enough to look into his eyes, and he said, "Your death was premature, it is not yet your time." No words ever spoken have penetrated me more than these. Until then, I had felt no purpose in life; I had simply ambled along looking for love and goodness but never really knowing if my actions were right. Now, within his words, I felt a mission, a purpose; I didn't know what it was, but I knew that my life on earth had not been meaningless.

It was not yet my time.

My time would come when my mission, my purpose, my *meaning* in this life was accomplished. I had a reason for existing on earth. But even though I understood this, my spirit rebelled. Did this mean I would have to go back? I said to him, "No, I can never leave you now."

He understood what I meant, and his love and acceptance for me never wavered. My thoughts raced on: "Is this Jesus, God, the being I feared all my life? He is nothing like what I had thought. He is filled with love."

Then questions began coming to my mind. I wanted to know why I had died as I had not prematurely, but how my spirit had come to him before the resurrection. I was still laboring under the teachings and beliefs of my childhood. His light now began to fill my mind, and my questions were answered even before I fully asked them. His light was knowledge. It had power to fill me with all truth. As I gained confidence and let the light flow into me, my questions came faster than I thought possible, and they were just as quickly answered. And the answers were absolute and complete. In my fears, I had misinterpreted death, had expected something that was not so. The grave was never intended for the spirit—only for the body. I felt no judgment for having been mistaken. There was just a feeling that a simple, living truth had replaced my error. I understood that he was the Son of God, though he himself was also a God, and that he had chosen from before the creation of the world to be our Savior. I understood, or rather, I *remembered*, his role as creator of the earth. His mission was to come into the world to teach love. This knowledge was more like remembering. Things were coming back to me from long before my life on earth, things that had been purposely blocked from me by a "veil" of forgetfulness at my birth.

As more questions bubbled out of me, I became aware of his sense of humor. Almost laughing, he suggested that I slow down, that I could know all I desired. But I wanted to know *everything*, from beginning to end. My curiosity had always been a torment to my parents and husband—and sometimes to me—but now it was a blessing, and I was thrilled with the freedom of learning. I was being taught by the master teacher! My comprehension was such that I could understand volumes in an instant. It was as if I could look at a book and comprehend it at a glance—as though I could just sit back while the book revealed itself to me in every detail, forward and backward, inside and out, every nuance and possible suggestion. All in an instant. As I comprehended one thing, more questions and answers would come to me, all building on each other, and interacting as if all truth were intrinsically connected. The word "omniscient" had never been more meaningful to me. Knowledge permeated me. In a sense it became me, and I was amazed at my ability to comprehend the mysteries of the universe simply by reflecting on them.

I wanted to know why there were so many churches in the world. Why didn't God give us only one church, one pure religion? The answer came to me with the purest of understanding. Each of us, I was told, is at a different level of spiritual development and understanding. Each person is therefore prepared for a different level of spiritual knowledge. All religions upon the earth are necessary because there are people who need what they teach. People in one religion may not have a complete understanding of the Lord's gospel and never will have while in that religion. But that religion is used as a stepping stone to further knowledge. Each church fulfills spiritual needs that perhaps others cannot fill. No one church can fulfill everybody's needs at every level. As an individual raises his level of understanding about God and his own eternal progress, he might feel discontented with the teachings of his present church and seek a different philosophy or religion to fill that void. When this occurs he has reached another level of understanding and will long for further truth and knowledge, and for another opportunity to grow. And at every step of the way, these new opportunities to learn will be given.

Having received this knowledge, I knew that we have no right to criticize any church or religion in any way. They are all precious and important in his sight. Very special people with important missions have been placed in all countries, in all religions, in every station of life, that they might touch others. There is a fullness of the gospel, but most people will not attain it here. In order to grasp this truth, we need to listen to the Spirit and let go of our egos.

I wanted to learn the purpose of life on the earth. Why are we here? As I basked in the love of Jesus Christ, I couldn't imagine why any spirit would voluntarily leave this wonderful paradise and all it offered—worlds to explore and ideas to create and knowledge to gain. Why would anyone want to come here? In answer, I *remembered* the creation of the earth. I actually experienced it as if it were being reenacted before my eyes. This was important. Jesus wanted me to internalize this knowledge. He wanted me to know how I felt when the creation occurred. And the only way to do that was for me to view it again and feel what I had felt before.

All people as spirits in the pre-mortal world took part in the creation of the earth. We were thrilled to be part of it. We were with God, and we knew that he created us, that we were his very own children. He was pleased with our development and was filled with absolute love for each one of us. Also, Jesus Christ was there. I understood, to my surprise, that Jesus was a separate being from God, with his own divine purpose, and I knew that God was our mutual Father. My Protestant upbringing had taught me that God the Father and Jesus Christ were one being. As we all assembled, the Father explained that coming to earth for a time would further our spiritual growth. Each spirit who was to come to earth assisted in planning the conditions on earth, including the laws of mortality which would govern us. These included the laws of physics as we know them, the limitations of our bodies, and spiritual powers that we would be able to access. We assisted God in the development of plants and animal life that would be here. Everything was created of spirit matter before it was created physically—solar systems, suns, moons, stars, planets, life upon the planets, mountains, rivers, seas, etc. I saw this process, and then, to further understand it, I was told by the Savior that the spirit creation could be compared to one of our photographic prints; the spirit creation would be like a sharp, brilliant print, and the earth would be like its dark negative. This earth is only a shadow of the beauty and glory of its spirit creation, but it is what we needed for our growth. It was important that I understand that we all assisted in creating our conditions here.

Many times the creative thoughts we have in this life are the result of unseen inspiration. Many of our important inventions and even technological developments were first created in the spirit by spirit prodigies. Then individuals on earth received the inspiration to create these inventions here. I understood that there is a vital, dynamic link between the spirit world and mortality, and that we need the spirits on the other side for our progression. I also saw that they are *very* happy to assist us in any way they can.

I saw that in the pre-mortal world we knew about and even chose our missions in life. I understood that our stations in life are based upon the objectives of those missions. Through divine knowledge we knew what many of our tests and experiences would be, and we prepared accordingly. We bonded with others—family members and friends—to help us complete our missions. We needed their help. We came as volunteers, each eager to learn and experience all that God had created for us. I knew that each of us who made the decision to come here was a valiant spirit. Even the least developed among us here was strong and valiant there.

We were given agency to act for ourselves here. Our own actions determine the course of our lives, and we can alter or redirect our lives at any time. I understood that this was crucial; God made the promise that he wouldn't intervene in our lives *unless we asked him*. And then through his omniscient knowledge he would help us attain our righteous desires. We were grateful for this ability to express our free will and to exercise its power. This would allow each of us to obtain great joy or to choose that which will bring us sadness. The choice would be ours through our decisions.

I was actually relieved to find that the earth is not our natural home, that we did not originate here. I was gratified to see that the earth is only a temporary place for our schooling and that sin is not our true nature. Spiritually, we are at various degrees of light—which is knowledge—and because of our divine, spiritual nature we are filled with the desire to do good. Our earthly selves, however, are constantly in opposition to our spirits. I saw how weak the flesh is. But it is persistent. Although our spirit bodies are full of light, truth, and love, they must battle constantly to overcome the flesh, and this strengthens them. Those who are truly developed will find a perfect harmony between their flesh and spirits, a harmony that will bless them with peace and give them the ability to help others.

As we learn to abide by the laws of this creation, we learn how to use those laws to our own good. We learn how to live in harmony with the creative powers around us. God has given us individual talents, some more and some less according to our needs. As we use these talents, we learn how to work with, and eventually understand, the laws and overcome the limitations of this life. By understanding these laws we are better able to serve those around us. Whatever we become here in mortality is meaningless unless it is done for the benefit of others. Our gifts and talents are given to us to help us serve. And in serving others we grow spiritually.

Above all, I was shown that love is supreme. I saw that truly without love we are nothing. We are here to help each other, to care for each other, to understand, forgive, and serve one another. We are here to have love for every person born on earth. Their earthly form might be black, yellow, brown, handsome, ugly, thin, fat, wealthy, poor, intelligent, or ignorant, but we are not to judge by these appearances. Each spirit has the capacity to be filled with love and eternal energy. At the beginning, each possesses some degree of light and truth that can be more fully developed. We cannot measure these things. Only God knows the heart of man, and only God can judge perfectly. He knows our spirits; we see only temporary strengths and weaknesses. Because of our own limitations, we can seldom look into the heart of man.

I knew that anything we do to show love is worthwhile: a smile, a word of encouragement, a small act of sacrifice. We grow by these actions. Not all people are lovable, but when we find someone difficult for us to love, it is often because they remind us of something within ourselves that we don't like. I learned that we must love our enemies—let go of anger, hate, envy, bitterness, and the refusal to forgive. These things destroy the spirit. We will have to account for how we treat others.

Upon receiving the plan of creation, we sang in rejoicing and were filled with God's love. We were filled with joy as we saw the growth we would have here on earth and the joyous bonds we would create with each other.

Then we watched as the earth was created. We watched as our spirit brothers and sisters entered physical bodies for their turns upon the earth, each experiencing the pains and joys that would help them progress. I distinctly remember watching the American pioneers crossing the continent and rejoicing as they endured their difficult tasks and completed their missions. I knew that only those who needed that experience were placed there. I saw the angels rejoicing for those who endured their trials and succeeded and grieving for those who failed. I saw that some failed because of their own weaknesses, and some failed because of the weaknesses of others. I sensed that many of us who were not there would not have been up to the tasks, that we would have made lousy pioneers, and we would have been the cause of more suffering for others. Likewise, some of the pioneers and people from other eras could not have endured the trials of today. We are where we need to be.

As all of these things came to me, I understood the perfection of the plan. I saw that we all volunteered for our positions and stations in the world, and that each of us is receiving more help than we know. I saw the unconditional love of God, beyond any earthly love, radiating from him to all his children. I saw the angels standing near us, waiting to assist us, rejoicing in our accomplishments and joys. But above all, I saw Christ, the Creator and Savior of the earth, my friend, and the closest friend any of us can have. I seemed to melt with joy as I was held in his arms and comforted—home at last. I would give all in my power, all that I ever was, to be filled with that love again—to be embraced in the arms of his eternal light.

⁓ **4** ⁓

Saved by the Light

Dannion Brinkley

Now, in the life review, I was forced
to see the death and destruction that
had taken place in the world as a
result of my actions.

Conversing on the phone at home in South Carolina in 1975,
Dannion Brinkley was struck by an enormous bolt of lightning.
After being thrown up to the ceiling, his dead body crashed down
to the floor. Before he woke up on a hospital gurney headed for
the morgue, he took the tunnel to eternity. Dannion had been an
angry and violent youth. Then, beginning in Vietnam, he got
involved in clandestine government operations, specializing in
sniping and demolition around the world. So in his near-death
experience, he says, he was made to relive all the pain and grief
that his victims and their families suffered.

He felt ashamed, but the Being of Light did not convey judgment. Instead, it communicated an intense grandfatherly love that relieved his guilt. By this gift of forgiveness, Dannion was transformed, now filled with the joyous desire to spread the cosmic love he had just received. He was also shown several remarkable prophetic visions of earthly events. On returning to life, Dannion overcame severe paralysis and heart damage, then discovered that he had psychic insights. He could easily win card games, because he knew everybody else's hand. He eventually stopped playing with cards and began the more serious task of talking to gamblers about spiritually fulfilling goals. Today Dannion volunteers in hospice programs and gives passionate public speeches. "Go die with somebody!" he says, "You are a co-creator with God."

Dannion Brinkley is from South Carolina. He wrote his book *Saved by the Light* (1994) with Paul Perry, which soon appeared on the *New York Times* best-seller list. His second book was entitled *At Peace in the Light* (1995).

· Saved by the Light ·

THE TUNNEL TO ETERNITY

I actually didn't move at all; the tunnel came to me.

There was the sound of chimes as the tunnel spiraled toward and then around me. Soon there was nothing to be seen—no crying Sandy, no ambulance attendants trying to jump-start my dead body, no desperate chatter with the hospital over the radio—only a tunnel that engulfed me completely and the intensely beautiful sound of seven chimes ringing in rhythmic succession.

I looked ahead into the darkness. There was a light up there, and I began to move toward it as quickly as possible. I was moving without legs at a high rate of speed. Ahead the light became brighter and brighter until it overtook the darkness and left me standing in a paradise of brilliant light. This was the brightest light I had ever seen, but in spite of that, it didn't hurt my eyes in the least. Unlike the pain one might feel when walking into sunlight from a dark room, this light was soothing to my eyes.

I looked to my right and could see a silver form appearing like a silhouette through mist. As it approached I began to feel a deep sense of love that encompassed all of the meanings of the word. It was as though I were seeing a lover, mother, and best friend, multiplied a thousandfold. As the Being of Light came closer, these feelings of love intensified until they became almost too pleasurable to withstand. I had the sense of becoming less dense, as though I had lost twenty or thirty pounds. The burden of my body had been left behind, and now I was an unencumbered spirit.

I looked at my hand. It was translucent and shimmering and moved with fluidity, like the water in the ocean. I looked down at my chest. It, too, had the translucence and flow of fine silk in a light breeze.

The Being of Light stood directly in front of me. As I gazed into its essence I could see prisms of color, as though it were composed of thousands of tiny diamonds, each emitting the colors of the rainbow.

I began to look around. Below us were other Beings who looked like me. They appeared to be lost and shimmered at a rate that was far slower than the rate at which I shimmered. As I watched them I noticed that I slowed down as well. There was a discomfort in this reduced vibration that made me look away.

I looked above me. There were more Beings, these brighter and more radiant than I. I felt discomfort when looking at them as well because I began to vibrate faster. It was as though I had drunk too much coffee and was now speeding up and moving too fast. I looked away from them and straight ahead at the Being of Light, who now stood before me. I felt comfortable in his presence, a familiarity that made me believe he had felt every feeling I had ever had, from the time I took my first breath to the instant I was sizzled by lightning. Looking at this Being I had the feeling that no one could love me better, no one could have more empathy, sympathy, encouragement, and nonjudgmental compassion for me than this Being.

Although I refer to the Being of Light as a "he," I never saw this Being as either male or female. I have gone over this initial meeting many times in my head and can honestly say that none of the Beings I met had gender, just great power.

The Being of Light engulfed me, and as it did I began to experience my whole life, feeling and seeing everything that had ever happened to me. It was as though a dam had burst and every memory stored in my brain flowed out.

This life-review was not pleasant. From the moment it began until it ended, I was faced with the sickening reality that I had been an unpleasant person, someone who was self-centered and mean.

The first thing I saw was my angry childhood. I saw myself torturing other children, stealing their bicycles or making them miserable at school. One of the most vivid scenes was of the time I picked on a child at grade school because he had a goiter that protruded from his neck. The other kids in the class picked on him too, but I was the worst. At the time I thought I was funny. But now, as I relived this incident, I found myself in his body, living with the pain that I was causing.

This perspective continued through every negative incident in my childhood, a substantial number to be sure. From fifth to twelfth grade, I estimate that I had at least six thousand fist fights. Now, as I reviewed my life in the bosom of the Being, I relived each one of those altercations, but with one major difference: I was the receiver.

I wasn't the receiver in the sense that I felt the punches I had thrown. Rather, I felt the anguish and the humiliation my opponent felt. Many of the people I fought had it coming, but others were innocent victims of my anger. Now I was forced to feel their pain.

I also felt the grief I had caused my parents. I had been uncontrollable and proud of it. Although they had grounded me and yelled at me, I had let them know by my actions that none of their discipline really mattered. Many times they had pleaded with me and many times they had met frustration. I had often bragged to my friends about how I had hurt my parents. Now, in my life-review, I felt their psychological pain at having such a bad child.

My grade school in South Carolina had a demerit system. Students who received 15 demerits had their parents called in for a conference, while those who had 30 demerits on their record were suspended. In seventh grade, I had received 154 demerits by the third day of school. I was that kind of student. Now they call students like that "hyperactive" and do something about it. Back then we were just called "bad kids" and were thought to be lost causes.

When I was in the fourth grade, a redheaded boy named Curt would wait for me every day before school and threaten to beat me up if I didn't give him my lunch money. I was afraid, and gave him the money.

Finally, I got tired of going all day without eating and told my father what was happening. He showed me how to make a blackjack out of a pair of my mother's nylon stockings by pouring sand into them and tying the ends. "When he bothers you again, hit him with the blackjack," he told me.

My father didn't mean any harm—he was just showing me how to protect myself from the older kids. The problem was that after I bludgeoned Curt and took his money, I developed a taste for fighting. From that point on, all I wanted to do was inflict pain and be tough.

When I was in the fifth grade I polled all my friends to find out who they thought was the toughest kid in the neighborhood. They all agreed that it was a stocky kid named Butch. I walked up to his house and knocked on the door. "Is Butch here?" I asked his mother. When he came out the door I beat him until he fell off the porch, and then I ran away.

I didn't care who I fought, or how big or old they were. All I wanted to do was draw blood.

Once, in sixth grade, a teacher asked me to stop disrupting class. When I refused, she grabbed my arm and began marching me toward the principal's office. As we walked out of the classroom I pulled loose and hit her with an uppercut that knocked her to the ground. As she held her bleeding nose, I walked myself to the principal's office. As I explained to my parents, I didn't mind going to the office, I just didn't want to be pulled there by a teacher.

We lived next door to the junior high school I attended, and I could sit on the porch and watch the kids in the playground on the days that I was suspended from school. One day I was sitting there when a group of girls came to the fence and started making fun of me. I wasn't going to take that.

I went into the house, got my brother's shotgun, and loaded it with rock salt. Then I came back out and shot the girls in the back as they fled, screaming.

By the time I was seventeen, I was known as one of the best fighters in my high school. I fought almost daily to maintain my reputation. When I couldn't find kids from my own school to beat up, I relied on the bad kids from other schools for competition.

At least once a week we had staged fights in a parking lot near school. Students would come from as far as thirty miles away to participate in these fights. On the days that I fought, many of the kids wouldn't get out of their cars, because after I beat up my opponent, I would take on a few spectators just for fun.

These were the days of segregated high schools, and we would have great wars between blacks and whites.

The black champion was a giant named Lundy. No one wanted to fight him after he beat the white champion in a savage two-minute battle. Even I tried to avoid him, knowing there was no way that I could win.

One day we ran into each other at a hamburger stand. I tried to leave quickly but he stepped in my way.

"Meet me tomorrow morning at the parking lot," he said.

"I'll be there," I promised. Then, as he turned to walk away, I hit him with such force on the right side of the face that he couldn't open his eyes for at least ten minutes. As he lay struggling on the ground, I walked around him and kicked him in the chest a couple of times as hard as I could.

"I won't be able to make it tomorrow," I said. "So I thought I would take care of it today."

I knew I couldn't beat him in a fair fight, so I jumped him when his back was turned.

That was the world I lived in through high school.

Twenty years later, at my high school reunion, a classmate cornered my date to tell her what kind of student I had been.

"Let me tell you what he was famous for," he said. "He would beat your ass, steal your girlfriend, or do both."

In retrospect, I couldn't have agreed with him more. By the time I was finished with high school, that is exactly who I was. And by the time I had reached that point in my review, I was ashamed of myself. Now I knew the pain I had caused everyone in my life. As my body lay dead on that stretcher, I was reliving every moment of my life, including my emotions, attitudes, and motivations.

The depth of emotion I experienced during this life-review was astonishing. Not only could I feel the way both I and the other person had felt when an incident took place, I could also feel the feelings of the next person they reacted to. I was in a chain reaction of emotion, one that showed how deeply we affect one another. Luckily, not all of it was bad.

One time, for instance, my great-uncle and I were driving down the road when we saw a man beating a goat that had somehow gotten its head stuck in a fence. The man had a branch, and he was hitting the goat across the back as hard as he could while the goat bleated in fear and agony. I stopped the car and jumped across a ditch. Before the man could turn around, I was pounding him as hard as I could in the back of the head. I only stopped when my great-uncle pulled me off, I freed the goat and we left in a cloud of burnt rubber.

Now, as I relived that incident, I felt satisfaction at the humiliation that farmer had felt and joy in the relief the goat had felt. I knew that in the animal's own way, he had said "thank you."

But I wasn't always kind to animals. I saw myself whipping a dog with a belt. I had caught this dog chewing on our living room carpet and lost my temper. I had pulled my belt off and let him have it without trying a lesser form of discipline. Reliving this incident, I felt the dog's love for me and could tell that he didn't mean to do what he was doing. I felt his sorrow and pain.

Later, as I thought about these experiences, I realized that people who beat animals or are cruel to them are going to know how those animals felt when they have a life review.

I also discovered that it is not so much what you do that counts, but why you do it. For example, having a fistfight with someone for no real reason hurt me far more in the life-review than having one with someone who had picked a fight with me. To relive hurting someone just for fun is the greatest pain of all. To relive hurting someone for a cause you believe in is not as painful.

This became obvious to me when my review took me back through my years in military and intelligence work.

In the span of what must have been a few seconds, I went through basic training, where I learned to channel my anger into my new role as a combat soldier. On through special training I went, watching and feeling my character being molded for the purpose of killing. This was the era of the Vietnam War, and I found myself back in the muggy jungles of Southeast Asia doing what I liked to do most—fight.

I spent very little time in Vietnam. I was attached to an intelligence unit that operated mainly in Laos and Cambodia. I did a bit of "observation work," which amounted to little more than watching enemy troop movements through binoculars. My main job was to "plan and execute the removal of enemy politicians and military personnel." In short, I was an assassin.

I didn't operate alone. Two other Marines worked with me as we scoured the jungles looking for specific targets. Their jobs were to spot the target with a high-powered telescope and verify that the desired person had been eliminated. My job was to pull the trigger.

Once, for example, we were sent to "terminate" a North Vietnamese colonel who was with his troops in the jungles of Cambodia. Aerial photographs showed us where this colonel was holed up. It was our job to tramp through the jungle and find him. Although this kind of attack was especially time consuming, it was considered crucial, for it broke the morale of the enemy troops to have their leader killed in their midst.

We found the colonel right where the maps said we would. We sat quietly about seven hundred yards from their camp, waiting for the perfect moment to "drop" him.

That moment came early the next morning, when the troops lined up for their daily review. I got into position, bringing the crosshairs of my high-powered sniper rifle on the head of the colonel, who was standing before the unsuspecting soldiers.

"Is that him?" I asked the spotter, whose job it was to identify the targets with the photographs intelligence had given us.

"That's him," he said. "The man standing right before the troops is him."

I squeezed off the round and felt the rifle kick. A moment later I saw his head explode and his body crumple before the shocked troops.

That is what I saw when the incident happened.

During my life-review, I experienced this incident from the perspective of the North Vietnamese colonel. I didn't feel the pain that he must have felt. Instead, I felt his confusion at having his head blown off and sadness as he left his body and realized that he would never go home again. Then I felt the rest of the chain reaction—the sad feelings of his family when they realized they would be without their provider.

I relived all of my kills in just this fashion. I saw myself make the kill and then I felt its horrible results.

While in Southeast Asia I had seen women and children murdered, entire villages destroyed, for no reason or for the wrong reasons. I had not been involved in these killings, but now I had to experience them again, from the point of view not of the executor, but the executed.

On one occasion, for example, I was sent to a country bordering Vietnam to assassinate a government official who did not share the "American point of view." I went in with a team. Our goal was to eliminate this man at a small rural hotel where he was staying. This would make the unspoken statement that no one was out of reach of the United States government.

We sat in the jungle for four days, waiting for a clear shot at this official, but he was always surrounded by an entourage of bodyguards and secretaries. Finally, we gave up and decided on another tack: Late at night, when everyone was asleep, we would simply plant explosives and blow up the hotel.

That is exactly what we did. We surrounded the hotel with plastic explosives and leveled it at sunrise, killing the official along with about fifty people who were staying there. At the time I laughed about it and told my control officer that all the people deserved to die because they were guilty by association.

I saw this incident again during my near-death experience, but this time, I was hit by a rush of emotions and information. I felt the stark horror that all of those people felt as they realized their lives were being snuffed out. I experienced the pain their families felt when they discovered that they had lost loved ones in such a tragic way. In many cases I even felt the loss their absence would make to future generations.

All in all I contributed to the deaths of dozens of people in Southeast Asia, and reliving them was hard to take. The one saving grace was that at the time, I thought what I was doing was right. I was killing in the name of patriotism, which took the edge off the horrors I had committed.

When I returned to the United States after my military duty, I continued to work for the government, performing clandestine operations. This largely involved the transport of weapons to people and countries friendly to the United States. Sometimes I was even called upon to train these people in the fine art of sniping or demolition.

Now, in the life-review, I was forced to see the death and destruction that had taken place in the world as a result of my actions. "We are all a link in the great chain of humanity," said the Being. "What you do has an effect on the other links in that chain."

Many examples of this came to mind, but one in particular stands out. I saw myself unloading weapons in a Central American country. They were to be used to fight a war that was supported by our country against the Soviet Union.

My task was simply to transfer these weapons from an airplane to our military interests in the area. When this transfer was completed, I got back on the airplane and left.

But leaving wasn't so easy in my life-review. I stayed with the weapons and watched as they were distributed at a military staging area. Then I went with the guns as they were used in the job of killing, some of them murdering innocent people and some the not so innocent. All in all it was horrible to witness the results of my role in this war.

This weapons transfer in Central America was the last job I was involved in before being struck by lightning. I remember watching children cry because they had been told that their fathers were dead, and I knew these deaths were caused by the guns I had delivered.

Then that was it, the review was over.

When I finished the review, I arrived at a point of reflection in which I was able to look back on what I had just witnessed and come to a conclusion. I was ashamed. I realized I had led a very selfish life, rarely reaching out to help anyone. Almost never had I smiled as an act of brotherly love or just handed somebody a dollar because he was down and needed a boost. No, my life had been for me and me alone. I hadn't given a damn about my fellow humans.

I looked at the Being of Light and felt a deep sense of sorrow and shame. I expected a rebuke, some kind of cosmic shaking of my soul. I had reviewed my life and what I had seen was a truly worthless person. What did I deserve if not a rebuke?

As I gazed at the Being of Light I felt as though he was touching me. From that contact I felt a love and joy that could only be compared to the nonjudgmental compassion that a grandfather has for a grandchild. "Who you are is the difference that God makes," said the Being. "And that difference is love." There were no actual words spoken, but this thought was communicated to me through some form of telepathy. To this day, I am not sure of the exact meaning of this cryptic phrase. That is what was said, however.

Again I was allowed a period of reflection. How much love had I given people? How much love had I taken from them? From the review I had just had, I could see that for every good event in my life, there were twenty bad ones to weigh against it. If guilt were fat, I would have weighed five hundred pounds.

As the Being of Light moved away, I felt the burden of this guilt being removed. I had felt the pain and anguish of reflection, but from that I had gained the knowledge that I could use to correct my life. I could hear the Being's message in my head, again as if through telepathy: "Humans are powerful spiritual beings meant to create good on the earth. This good isn't usually accomplished in bold actions, but in singular acts of kindness between people. It's the little things that count, because they are more spontaneous and show who you truly are."

I was elated. I now knew the simple secret to improving mankind. The amount of love and good feelings you have at the end of your life is equal to the love and good feelings you put out during your life. It was just that simple.

"My life will be better now that I have the secret," I said to the Being of Light.

It was then that I realized that I wouldn't be going back. I had no more life to live. I had been struck by lightning. I was dead.

[Editors' note: Dannion continued his remarkable near-death journey into a crystal city, was shown twelve "boxes of knowledge," and then woke up, paralyzed. But he slowly recovered and rebuilt his life.]

Unknown Well-Known Near-Death Experiences

Peter Sellers, Eddie Rickenbacker, Plato, and Black Elk

Lee W. Bailey

The purpose of philosophy for Plato
is to unforget that primal vision of
pure, powerful Light.

Lee W. Bailey, Ph.D., is a religious studies scholar who discusses the near-death experiences, unknown and well-known, in a handful of ancient and contemporary public figures. Imagine Peter Sellers, who you may have enjoyed in some hilarious movies, or Eddie Rickenbacker, the Ace of Aces pilot in World War I. How do you think they might have been changed by a near-death experience? The answers suggest the range of experiences and the range of after-effects.

The brilliant comic actor Peter Sellers died of a heart attack in 1964, rose out of his body, and reached for a hand in a bright, loving light. He came back saying he lost his fear of death, became more introspective, and found tranquility in yoga. But he still felt lost.

Eddie Rickenbacker was a heroic American pilot in World War I. Known as a reckless race car driver and pilot, he came close to death following surgery, felt serene, had a life review, and saw sensuous forms which he spoke of as hallucinations. Again, in a plane crash, he was brushed by the Grim Reaper's shadow and felt he was being tested. Afterward, he spoke more openly about his religious faith and had psychic insights.

Plato reports one of the oldest NDE records, the legend of Er, an ancient warrior in the *Republic* who woke up at his cremation. He came back telling of the afterlife judgment and a bright, pure light that was the cosmic axis. Plato integrated this image of cosmic light into his philosophy in the cave myth in the *Republic* and the myth of the soul's journey to the heavenly realm of pure Being in the *Phaedrus*.

Black Elk, a Lakota Sioux Native American, came close to death twice. First at age nine he nearly died and journeyed into a transcendent realm where he saw a great vision. This later became the experiential basis for his role as a wise, healing shaman who spoke reverently of "seeing in a sacred manner."

Lee W. Bailey, Ph.D., teaches Religion and Culture at Ithaca College in upstate New York. His publications include *Rudely Stamp'd: Imaginal Disability and Prejudice* and articles on mythology, projection in psychology and religion, and the philosophy of technology. He is listed in *Who's Who in the East*.

ᴗ Unknown Well-Known
Near-Death Experiences ᴗ
Peter Sellers, Eddie Rickenbacker,
Plato, and Black Elk

ᴗ PETER SELLERS: REACHING FOR THE HAND OF LIGHT

I felt myself leave my body. I just floated out of my
physical form and I saw them cart my body away to the
hospital. I went with it.... I wasn't frightened.

Peter Sellers was the comic genius of a generation of actors.
He brought brilliant characterization to numerous films,
including *The Mouse That Roared* (1959), *Dr. Strangelove*
(1964), *The Pink Panther* (1964), and *Being There* (1979). He
was known for his enthusiastic way of totally absorbing
himself in his characters, even carrying roles offstage. He also
suffered from sad moods between films. While he knew his
characters thoroughly, he said that he really did not know
who he was. Then Peter Sellers, the brilliant, confused actor,
had a near-death experience.

Seated in a Hollywood mockup of a limousine's back seat
while shooting his last great film, *Being There*, he told Shirley
MacLaine about his near-death experience, astonished that
she did not consider him "bonkers." In 1964, during the first
of a rapid series of eight heart attacks, when his heart stopped
and he was clinically dead, he had an out-of-body experience
and saw the bright, loving light:

> Well, I felt myself leave my body. I just floated out of my
> physical form and I saw them cart my body away to the
> hospital. I went with it.... I wasn't frightened or anything
> like that because *I* was fine; and it was my body that was
> in trouble. (MacLaine, 172)

The doctor saw that he was dead and massaged his heart
vigorously. Meanwhile,

> I looked around myself and I saw an incredibly beautiful bright loving
> white light above me. I wanted to go to that white light more than any-
> thing. I've never wanted anything more. I know there was love, real love,
> on the other side of the light which was attracting me so much. It was
> kind and loving and I remember thinking 'That's God'. (MacLaine, 172)

Peter's out-of-body soul tried to elevate itself toward the light, but he fell
short: "Then I saw a hand reach throught the light. I tried to touch it, to grab
onto it, to clasp it so it could sweep me up and pull me through it"
(MacLaine, 172). But just then his heart began beating again, and at that
instant the hand's voice said: "It's not time. Go back and finish. It's not time."
As the hand receded he felt himself floating back down to his body, waking
up bitterly disappointed (MacLaine, 173).

What effect did his NDE have on Sellers? His biographer says that "The
repeated act of 'dying' became for Peter Sellers the most important
experience of his life" (Walker 158). Sellers said of death: "I'll never fear it
again." Family and friends found him more spiritual and reflective than
before:

> The experience of resurrection intensified Sellers's spiritual concern and
> friends discerned the start of a new introspectiveness, a sense of his not
> 'being there' in spirit, though present in body. (Walker, 158)

His wife Britt Ekland found it unnerving that her previously restless
husband had now become so quiet. He was now "sitting still over lengthy
periods, saying nothing, but staring at her with his thoughts turned inward"
(Walker, 158). He returned to England for an extended convalescence, but
soon reverted to old habits and bought his 84th car, an expensive Ferrari.

A couple of years before the NDE, Peter had played an earnest priest in
Heavens Above, and developed a serious interest in Christianity (although he
was born Jewish). During this time, following his father's death in 1962,
Sellers was drawn to long, serious discussions about life's meaning with a
neighboring vicar in London, the Rev. John Hester, "to try to reconcile the
world of plenty he inhabited with the emptiness of soul that oppressed him"
(Walker, 143). After his NDE he deepened his quest for spiritual truth,
continuing his discussions with Rev. Hester, coming close to joining the
church. In later years he practiced yoga, saying once that "Yoga has given me
a tranquility I wouldn't have thought possible" (Walker, 217). The NDE
strengthened Sellers' conviction that he was a reincarnated soul whose power
of mimicry sprang from memories of past lives. But in this incarnation, at
least, he felt lost. He did not know who he was and why he was on this earth.

He explained to Shirley MacLaine:

> I know I have lived many times before…that experience confirmed it to me, because in *this* lifetime I felt what it was for my soul to actually be *out* of my body. But ever since I came back, I don't know why I don't know what it is I'm supposed to do, or what I came back for.(MacLaine, 174)

Spirituality gave Sellers some peace, but did not still his restless drift. In 1977 he complained that his yoga practice did not stop his heart disease:

> After all, what did it do for me? I obeyed all the instructions. I said my prayers regularly. I did all the exercises for peace, tranquility, and happiness. And all that happened was that I got steadily worse. (Walker, 227)

Peter Sellers' NDE awakened him to a deepened spirituality, but it did not usher in a major, lasting change in his soul's makeup. This brilliant actor still felt lost.

REFERENCES

Evans, Peter. (1968). *Peter Sellers: The Mask Behind the Mask.* Englewood Cliffs, NJ: Prentice-Hall.

MacLaine, Shirley. (1983). *Out on a Limb.* New York: Bantam Books.

Walker, Alexander. (1981). *Peter Sellers: The Authorized Biography.* New York: Macmillan.

·- EDDIE RICKENBACKER: SAVED TO SERVE

You may have heard the dying is unpleasant, but don't you believe it. Dying is the sweetest, tenderest, most sensuous sensation I have ever experienced.

Eddie Rickenbacker was World War I's Ace of Aces; he shot down 26 enemy planes, more than any other American pilot. Before the Great War he was known as a clever automobile inventor and a daring race car driver. He survived an airplane crash in the South Pacific in 1942, floating for 24 days in a rubber raft. This swashbuckling American pioneer boldly risked his life repeatedly for adventure, technological development and patriotism. Eddie ran close to the shadow of the Grim Reaper. So it is no surprise that he had more than one near-death experience. In 1917, just before becoming a pilot over the European battlefield, he had this tonsils removed. But his surgeon accidentally nicked an artery in his throat and the bleeding would not stop. Ironically, this reckless man had his first near-death experience neither in a flaming auto crash nor in an airplane plunging to certain death, but safely tucked in a hospital bed. Spitting up blood, he felt his life slipping away:

> Even though I was vaguely aware that I was in a critical stage, I felt no sense of discomfort, no panic. Rather, everything seemed serene and lovely. Still I continued to bleed, and still I remained in a quiet, almost pleasurable state accepting death. Hallucinations began to enter my blood-drained brain. I lived again the happy scenes of my childhood. I saw strange shapes and beautiful colors. It was truly a sensuous experience. How easy it was to lie there and, with a heavenly sensation of contentment, die. (Rickenbacker, 84)

But Rickenbacker fought back, as he fought against so many other odds. He was determined to fight, to live, to survive. He prayed for God's help. The doctor arrived, clamped the artery, and Eddie was soon on his way to the War.

At death this hard-bitten fighter felt not anger, not terror, but the peace and contented acceptance of the early elements of a NDE. He went through a life review, reliving childhood's happy scenes. He saw colorful visual patterns and sensuous images that he called "hallucinations."

Again in 1941 Rickenbacker, now in charge of Eastern Air Lines, was a passenger in a plane crash in Atlanta. Later, in the hospital, he felt the same sensation of dying that he felt in 1917:

> You may have heard that dying is unpleasant, but don't you believe it. Dying is the sweetest, tenderest, most sensuous sensation I have ever experienced. Death comes disguised as a sympathetic friend. All was serene; all was calm. How wonderful it would be simply to float out of this world. It is easy to die. You have to fight to live. (Rickenbacker, 243)

Rickenbacker struggled for many days, barely surviving on blood transfusions, repeatedly slipping out of this world and back:

> Time and time again I felt myself slipping into that sensuous and beautiful state. How sweet it would have been simply to let go and slip off into that lovely land where there is no pain. (Rickenbacker, 243)

But Eddie kept fighting his way back from the edge, determined to live. Encased in a body cast and dosed with morphine for pain, he thought he was hallucinating:

In some of my hallucinations I thought the doctors and nurses were abusing me.... I would complain bitterly.... Later I would snap out of it and have to explain to [my doctor] that I had dreamed the whole thing. (Rickenbacker, 245)

Here the peace and beautiful contentment of the early elements of a NDE reoccur, with what seemed to be hallucinations, possibly aided by morphine.

What effects did Rickenbacker's NDE have on him? While many NDErs overcome their fear of death, we cannot say this happened to Eddie, because he was already fearless, happy to roar around a race track or zoom around in a rickety new-fangled airplane! But he did express an increased sense of his life's purpose: The crash, he reflected, had a beneficial result:

It brought home to me once again the conviction that surely I was being permitted to continue living for some good purpose. I was being tested for some great opportunity to serve.... (Rickenbacker, 249)

After another crash in 1942, bobbing helplessly in a rubber raft in the South Pacific with six other young airmen, Rickenbacker realized that his earlier brushes with death had prepared him for this demanding challenge:

More than anyone else on those three rafts, more than all of them combined, I had faced death and had learned from those encounters the meaning of life, the meaning of God, the meaning of the Golden Rule.

It was clear to me that God had had a purpose in keeping me alive. It was to help the others, to bring them through. I had been saved to serve. It was an awesome responsibility, but I accepted it gladly and proudly. (Rickenbacker, 323–24)

Eddie struggled against thirst, hunger, sharks, fatigue, blistering sunburn and the death of one of the men, to maintain morale for 24 days. After their rescue he became more openly religious. He had always been quietly religious, but now, he said, he *knew* God and spoke openly about his strengthened faith. A newspaper columnist wrote: "Rickenbacker has become an evangelist without knowing it. There is an unworldly gleam in his eyes and a quaver in his voice these days" (Rickenbacker, 344). Many who have had a brush with death without a vision have felt this increased sense of life's purpose and spirituality, so this element of Rickenbacker's reaction may have not been stimulated only by his NDE.

One more effect that Rickenbacker felt subsequent to his brushes with death was his psychic experiences. In France in 1918, leading his new squadron of pilots, Eddie had just figured out how to overcome jammed machine guns in the planes, but was grounded by mastoiditis, a swelling behind the ear. Dreaming during a painful semicoma, he saw two of his men's planes collide: "It seemed to happen in a cloud, yet I saw it clearly. Their wings touched and fell off, and I saw both planes pummeting to earth." Awakening, he reported the pilots' deaths before being told. It happened exactly as he dreamed (Rickenbacker, 119–20).

Again in 1965, Rickenbacker dreamed that his brother Bill phoned him, explaining that he was close to death: "I am not going to stay here very long. I wish you'd come out and see me—the sooner the better, I'd like to have a last word with you…" Later that day Eddie received a phone call telling him that Bill had died suddenly. Like many a survivor of NDEs, Rickenbacker concluded that ESP was real and encouraged research in parapsychology (Rickenbacker, 435).

Eddie Rickenbacker's two near-death experiences showed him the peace and calm, the life review, the dramatic visual patterns, the increased sense of life's purpose for him, and strengthened spirituality that are typical of NDE survivors. He also described his experiences as hallucinations, perhaps at times stimulated by medications such as morphine. His story presents an interesting case for interpretation: were his NDEs actually "hallucinations," or were they authentic transcendental visits from beyond?

REFERENCE

Edward V. Rickenbacker. (1967). *Rickenbacker.* Englewood Cliffs, NJ: Prentice-Hall.

·– PLATO: FLIGHT OF THE SOUL

> *He once upon a time was slain in battle…at the moment of his funeral, on the twelfth day as he lay on the pyre, revived, and after coming to life related what, he said, he had seen in the world beyond.*

One of the oldest surviving explicit reports of a near-death experience in Western literature is Plato's legend of Er, a soldier who awoke on his funeral pyre. But this story is not just a random anecdote for Plato. He integrated at least three elements of the near-death experience into his philosophy: the departure of the soul from the cave of shadows to see the light of truth, the flight of the soul to a vision of pure celestial being and its subsequent recollection of the vision of light, which is the very purpose of philosophy.

In the Tenth Book of the *Republic*, Plato concludes his discussion of immortal soul and ultimate justice with the legend of Er. Traditional Greek culture had no strong faith in ultimate justice, as monotheistic faiths do. Ancestral spirits lingered in a dark, miserable underworld Hades, regardless of their behavior in this life, with no reward or punishment, as Odysseus learned in his *Odyssey*. But Plato, perhaps importing some Orphic, Egyptian or Zoroastrian themes, drew on the idea of an otherworldly reward or punishment to motivate virtuous behavior in this life. The first point of Er's story is to report on this cosmic justice; it is:

> the tale of a warrior bold, Er, the son of Armenius, by race a Pamphylian. He once upon a time was slain in battle, and when the corpses were taken up on the tenth day already decayed, was found intact, and having been brought home, at the moment of his funeral, on the twelfth day as he lay upon the pyre, revived, and after coming to life related what, he said, he had seen in the world beyond. He said that when his soul went forth from his body he journeyed with a great company and that they came to a mysterious region where there were two openings side by side in the earth, and above and over against them in the heaven two others, and that judges were sitting between these, and that after every judgment they bade the righteous journey to the right and upward through the heaven with tokens attached to them in front of the judgment passed upon them, and the unjust to take the road to the left and downward, they too wearing behind signs of all that had befallen them, and that when he himself drew near they told him that he must be the messenger to mankind to tell them of that other world, and they charged him to give ear and to observe everything in the place. (*Rep.* X, 614 b,c,d)

From the other tunnels came souls preparing for reincarnation on earth. From above came souls happily reporting "delights and visions of a beauty beyond words." From below came souls lamenting and wailing over a thousand years of dreadful sufferings, where people were repaid manifold for any earthly suffering they had caused. Journeying on, the newcomers saw:

> extended from above throughout the heaven and the earth, a straight light like a pillar, most nearly resembling the rainbow, but brighter and purer...and they saw there at the middle of the light the extremities of its fastenings stretched from heaven, for this light was the girdle of the heavens like the undergirders of triremes, holding together in like manner the entire revolving vault. (*Rep.* X, 616 b,c)

The cosmic axis is a rainbow light holding together the eight spheres revolving around the earth, each guided by its Fate, a daughter of Necessity.

One of these Fates casts before the crowd to be reincarnated a number of earthly destinies from which they may choose to be, for example, a tyrant, an animal, an artist, or, as Odysseus carefully chose, an ordinary citizen who minds his own business. Then, just before returning to earth as a shooting star, each soul is required to drink from the River of Forgetfulness, so that all these cosmic events will fade from memory. Only Er was not allowed to drink and forget.

Thus Plato's cosmology is framed in the story of a near-death experience, although it obviously has been elaborated beyond an individual account into a collective cosmology. This amazing vision of the universal light, immortal soul, reward and punishment, reincarnation and even tunnels, is echoed 2500 years later in our contemporary near-death experiences.

Plato's allegory of the cave in the *Republic* similarly reflects the centrality of the cosmic light of wisdom. Chained inside a cave, looking at a wall dancing with shadowy figures, residents take these figments to be reality: "such prisoners would deem reality to be nothing else than the shadows of the artificial objects." But then one prisoner is freed and, climbing out of the cave with dazzled eyes, discovers the blazing sun and the true world that it floods with light.

> When one was freed from his fetters and compelled to stand up suddenly and turn his head around and walk and to lift up his eyes to the light, and in doing all this felt pain and, because of the dazzle and glitter of the light, was unable to discern the objects whose shadows he formerly saw, what do you suppose would be his answer if someone told him that what he had seen before was all a cheat and an illusion, but that now, being nearer to reality and turned toward more real things, he saw more truly? (*Rep.* VII, 515 c,d)

Plato uses the image to convey the soul's philosophical awakening to the realm of archetypal forms. Several parallels with NDEs stand out. The shock of the discovery through the light, reversing all previous convictions, echoes loudly the near-death experiencer's radical shift in consciousness. When the wanderer returns to the cave and attempts to awaken his mates to the true light, he provokes laughter and even death threats: "And if it were possible to lay hands on and to kill the man who tried to release them and lead them up, would they not kill him?" (*Rep.* VII, 517a). This reference to Socrates' death reflects the pain of misunderstanding and rejection felt by survivors of NDEs, and the consequent difficulty adjusting to the ordinary world of shadows. The returning bearer of visionary discoveries is despised for upsetting the cave's established order.

The flight of the immortal soul toward an incredible vision of pure celestial

Being Plato describes in the *Phaedrus*. Drawn out by love and beauty, the soul is carried as on a chariot pulled by two eager steeds, upward to join a magnificent circular parade of souls (the Milky Way), each following the Greek god it most favors (Ares for warriors, Zeus for wise leaders, Hera for royalty, etc.). All parade around the cosmic cycle, straining for a view of pure Being in the center. Those who see more of it are reincarnated with more memory of the universal forms of pure truth, justice, beauty, temperance and love:

> every human soul has, by reason of her nature, had contemplation of true being; else would she never have entered into this human creature.... Some, when they had the vision, had it but for a moment.... Few indeed are left that can still remember much. (*Phaedrus*, 249e–250a)

Like an initiation into a mystery religion, our eternal souls are enlightened by "the spectacles on which we gaze in the moment of final revelation; pure was the light that shone around us, and pure were we" (*Phadrus*, 250c). The purpose of philosophy for Plato is to unforget that primal vision of pure, powerful Light. The very purpose of life is to remember that journey between lives, that pilgrimage between death and birth, to uncover that transcendent vision of Light revealed in the near-death experience.

REFERENCE
Hamilton, Edith, and H. Cairns, eds. (1978). *The Collected Dialogues of Plato*. Princeton, NJ: Princeton University Press.

·~ BLACK ELK: SEEING IN A SACRED MANNER
I saw more than I can tell and I understood more than I saw; for I was seeing in a sacred manner the shapes of all things in the spirit.

The near-death experiences of the Native American medicine man Black Elk, of the Lakota Sioux nation, echo with the enchanting poetic language of an ancient society. His story reveals a traditional natural world culture, yet also many of the familiar phenomena of near-death experiences that leap across eras. Living between 1863 and 1950, Black Elk survived the collision of two eras, when the ancient primal world of his people was shattered by the violent invasion of the new industrial culture. This remarkable medicine man did not even speak English when he told his visionary experience to the author John Neihardt, who told it in *Black Elk Speaks* in 1932. In this classic of Native American literature, Black Elk's near-death experiences glow through his perceptions of a sacred natural world.

The world of the Lakota Sioux is filled not with souless material objects "out there" but with the manifestations of the presence of being that lies behind all creation: *Wakan Tanka*, the Great Mystery. This spiritual power is not personified as a remote God, but is both transcendent and present in all the world: in thunder, water, blood, birds, buffalo. Since the worldview of industrial society demands the expulsion of these perceptions, they seem like dim archaic memories. But Black Elk's near-death experience was a living, vital way of seeing in a sacred manner.

When Black Elk was a boy of nine, he collapsed with a severe, painful swelling of his legs, arms and face. He lost consciousness and lay in his tipi dying (*Sixth Grandfather*, 111, 142). He was called by two men coming from the clouds, saying "Hurry up, your grandfather is calling you." He was raised up out of his tipi into the clouds, feeling sorry to leave his parents. He was shown an elaborate vision oriented around a classic Native American mandala: the circular hoop, the four directions, and the center of the world on an axis stretching from sky to earth. Numerous neighing, dancing horses, surrounded by lightning and thunder, filled the sky at each direction. He was told to behold this, then to follow a bay horse, which led him to a rainbow door. Inside, sitting on clouds, were six grandfathers, "older than men can ever be—old like hills, old like stars." The oldest grandfather welcomed the boy and said:

> "Your Grandfathers all over the world are having a council, and they have called you here to teach you." His voice was very kind, but I shook all over with fear now, for I knew that these were not old men, but the Powers of the World. (*Black Elk Speaks*, 25)

Each Grandfather gave Black Elk a power. The Grandfather of where the sun goes down began:

> Behold, them yonder where the sun goes down, the thunder beings! You shall see, and have from them my power; and they shall take you to the high and lonely center of the earth that you may see; even to the place where the sun continually shines, they shall take you there to understand. (*BES*, 25–26)

Then the first Grandfather gave Black Elk a cup of water with the power to heal and make live, and a bow with the warrior's power to destroy. From the sunset comes death and life.

The second Grandfather of the North then gave the boy the cleansing power of the white goose and a healing herb of power that immediately healed a sick horse. From the place of snowy winter comes the power of cleansing.

Then the third Power of the World, from the direction of sunrise, "he of where the sun shines continually," said: "Take courage, younger brother…for across the earth they shall take you!" Then he pointed to two men flying beneath the daybreak star: "From them you shall have power," he said, "from them who have awakened all the beings of the earth with roots and legs and wings" (*BES*, 27). Then he gave the boy a peace pipe with a fluttering eagle on it. From the place where the sun shines continually comes the power of awakening and its peace.

From the Grandfather of the South, whence comes the power of growth, the boy was shown the power of the holy flowering tree in the middle of the hoop of the people. Crossing at the center he saw two roads, one of troubles, one of good. From the southern warmth comes flowering renewal.

The fifth Grandfather, the Spirit of the Sky, now showed Black Elk the soaring strength of flight:

> "My boy," he said, "I have sent for you and you have come. My power you shall see!" He stretched his arms and turned into a spotted eagle hovering. "Behold," he said, "all the wings of the air shall come to you, and they and the winds and the stars shall be like relatives. You shall go across the earth with my power." (*BES*, 29–30)

From the sky comes the power of transcendent vision.

Now the sixth Grandfather spoke, the Spirit of the Earth. From a very old man he incredibly grew backwards into youth, until he became the boy Black Elk. Growing older again he said, "My boy, have courage, for my power shall be yours, and you shall need it, for your nation on the earth will have great troubles" (*BES*, 30). From the earth spirit comes embodiment in space/time.

Then the boy, now named Eagle Wing Stretches, was taken out through the rainbow door and rode with the thunderous storm clouds to attack a blue man with lightning and plant the revitalizing flowering stick in the midst of his people. Then the gentle winds sang and the peace pipe flew from the east, spreading its deep peace. And as the daybreak star rose, sparkling from the horizion,

> a Voice said, "It shall be a relative to them; and who shall see it, shall see much more, for thence comes wisdom; and those who do not see it shall be dark." And all the people raised their faces to the east, and the star's light fell upon them, and all the dogs barked loudly and the horses whinnied.

> Then when the many little voices ceased, the great Voice said: "Behold
> the circle of the nation's hoop, for it is holy, being endless, and thus all pow-
> ers shall be one power in the people without end...." (*BES*, 35)

Then Black Elk led his people through the powers and the struggles that
would be theirs to come. Standing on the highest mountain, surveying the
grand vista of the hoop of the world, Black Elk said:

> I saw more than I can tell and I understood more than I saw; for I was see-
> ing in a sacred manner the shapes of all things in the spirit, and the shape
> of all shapes as they must live together like one being. (*BES*, 43)

After returning to the six grandfathers once again to receive his powers, the
boy was sent back to his dying body. When he awoke, his overjoyed parents
told him that he "had been sick twelve days, lying like dead all the while" (*BES*,
48) His friend Standing Bear, then age thirteen, testified that Black Elk was
unconscious twelve days, "dying and just breathing barely" (*Sixth GF*, 143).

Black Elk was afraid to tell his experience, and moped around as a shy,
withdrawn boy for eight years. Finally he told a medicine man who helped
him reenact the vision as a ritual. At that moment he became a powerful
medicine man or shaman, healing, he said, many people of illnesses from
tuberculosis to despair. He kept his vision alive with daily practices, such as
meditation on the daybreak star. But the great sadness of his life was his
inablity to stop the destructive onslaught of industrial culture, in search of
gold and land, that almost destroyed his people.

Black Elk had a second NDE, this time in Europe, when he was 26. He
had joined the Buffalo Bill's travelling show to learn about white culture.
They went to New York, then to London to perform for Queen Victoria, then
on to Paris and the Continent. In 1889 Black Elk was accidentally separated
from the troupe and left behind. He fell ill in Paris and was cared for by
friends. For over 24 hours he was dead:

> I had actually dropped over and died. They had announced me dead and
> had a coffin ready to put me in.... Once in a while my heart would beat a
> little bit. Several doctors came and they all thought that there wasn't
> enough life in me to bring me to. (*Sixth GF*, 253)

Meanwhile Black Elk was out of body, taking a Spirit Journey home. He
journeyed on clouds back to the Black Hills and Pine Ridge reservation in
South Dakota. He saw his mother, her tipi and some of the people he knew.
Then he was carried on the clouds back to Europe, heard bells ringing and
woke up to face his coffin. He rejoined Buffalo Bill, who sent him home to

Pine Ridge, where he saw his mother and friends exactly where they were camped in his vision. "During the the time of my vision, my mother had dreamed during her sleep that I had come back on a cloud" (*Sixth GF*, 252–55).

Among Black Elk's after-effects were a lessened fear of death, psychic foresight, and healing powers. During a battle he said, "I did not care whether I got killed or not, that probably I would be better off in the other world anyway" (*Sixth GF*, 230). Some degree of such bravery was cultivated among warriors, who would typically say just before a battle: "It is a good day to die! Remember those back in camp." But his fearlessness was firmly rooted in his NDE. He also developed psychic, prophetic powers, he said, sensing unknowns, such as approaching buffalo to hunt or enemies to avoid. Once, during a winter famine, they were out hunting in the snow, and "we heard a coyote howling and then I heard a voice say: 'Two-legged man, on this ridge west of you over there are buffalo. Beforehand you shall see two two-legged people.'" Heading west, they found two men and some buffalo (*Sixth GF*, 205, 208). Black Elk also gained healing powers after his vision and practiced traditional shamanic healing rituals until the reservation missionary priests stopped him.

Similar to many a twentieth-century near-death survivor, Black Elk almost died and took an out-of-body journey. He was directed to the high and holy center of the world so that he might see, and to the place where the sun continually shines. From a council of Powers of the World he was given powers not unlike Platonic forms or Jungian archetypes: life, death, healing, awakening, peace, renewal, transcendent vision.

Of course Black Elk's collective worldview shaped his vision. Unlike most twentieth-century near-death survivors, Black Elk was helped along the path of developing his awakening experience into a spiritual practice by a medicine man who understood his experience. He was led to ritualize his vision, keep it alive in consciousness, and serve his people with the powers he gained. As a Christian might see Christ or a Hindu see Vishnu, Black Elk saw six Grandfathers, old like hills, old like stars, representing the traditional six directions of the Sioux world picture. Black Elk saw not European cities of light, but familiar horses, migrating geese, spotted eagles and the peace pipe. Near-death experiences integrate local cultural symbols such as these with worldwide images such as light, mandalas, and rainbows. This is the collective langue of seeing in a sacred manner.

Why would Black Elk tell a white man such sacred secrets? This question has been raised by Steve Straight, who observes that not only were his experiences sacred, but it was against the law for Indians to discuss the old ways (Straight). In addition, Black Elk was a devoted member of the missionary church at Pine Ridge and did not want to antagonize the priests.

Black Elk had refused to speak to other white people about his history, so why would he tell John Neihardt? Even to the surprise of Neihardt's guide Afraid of Hawk, Black Elk seemed ready for Neihardt when he arrived, and did not hesitate to share his remarkable story. The two men quickly developed a strong rapport, and Black Elk said, after a long silence, "As I sit here, I can feel in this man beside me a strong desire to know the things of the Other World. He has been sent to learn what I know, and I will teach him" (*BES*, xvii).

Later Neihardt told Black Elk that he, too, had experienced a boyhood vision. When he was eleven years old he had a powerful dream that in some ways reflected Black Elk's. Neihardt had also fallen suddenly ill, and saw himself flying through a vast emptiness, arms before him, at a frightening speed. There was a powerful voice urging him on. The dream was repeated three times during the night. In the morning his fever was gone and he regained his health. He interpreted the dream as a calling to his literary work (Neihardt,1972,47; DeMallie, 42). Straight believes that Black Elk, with his superior intuition, may have recognized a fellow visionary in Neihardt, and thus trusted him with his story. Black Elk said to Neihardt:

> this vision of mine ought to go out, I feel, but somehow I couldn't get anyone to do it. I would think about it and get sad. I wanted the world to know about it. It seems that your ghostly brother has sent you here to do this for me.... I hope that we can make the tree bloom for your children and mine. (DeMallie, 43–44)

REFERENCES
Black Elk, as told through John G. Neihardt. *Black Elk Speaks.* (1932). Lincoln: University of Nebraska Press; paperback (1972). New York: Washington Square Press.
DeMallie, Raymond J., ed. (1984). *The Sixth Grandfather: Black Elk's Teachings Given to John G. Neihardt.* Lincoln: University of Nebraska Press. This is the original English transcript of the stenographic notes, with commentary, of Black Elk's verbal account to Neihardt.
Neihardt, John. (1972). *All Is But a Beginning.* New York: Harcourt, Brace, Jovanovich.
Neihardt, John. (1978). *Patterns and Coincidences.* Columbia: University of Missouri Press.
Straight, Steve. (1995). "The NDEs of Black Elk & John Neihardt." Paper presented at IANDS Fifth Annual North American Conference, August 1995. Audiotape. Boulder, CO: Perpetual Motion Unlimited.

My Life After Dying

George Ritchie

I was suddenly propelled up and off the bed. Out of the brilliant light at the head of the bed stepped the most magnificent Being I have ever known.

George Ritchie, M.D., had a near-death experience in 1943, during his World War II Army service. It was a milestone NDE, because it was the first NDE account heard by Raymond Moody. Ritchie's story opened the door to contemporary near-death studies. Moody dared to begin research on NDEs in part because Dr. Ritchie, who affirmed the reality of the near-death experience, had such a solid reputation as a psychiatrist at the University of Virginia Medical Center. Dr. Ian Stevenson, at the same Medical Center, expresses the same respect for Ritchie's reputation in his foreword to Ritchie's book, *My Life After Dying,* from which we have excerpted part of the original experience. Dr. Ritchie first published the account in his book, *Return from Tomorrow,* which sold over 200,000 copies. The more recent book tells how the near-death experience has affected his life. Dr. Richie now has a gift for healing that involves faith as well as medicine.

George Ritchie, M.D., is now retired from his practice at the University of Virginia Medical Center.

·- My Life After Dying ·-

September, 1943

What 20-year-old would believe that he would be pronounced dead before the end of the year? Sure, this sort of thing could happen to others, but the human mind's ability to use massive denial is so powerful that I believed when I took out my G.I. insurance I was guaranteed my three score and ten years.

Some very shocking circumstances changed my mind.

In September 1941, I entered the University of Richmond just outside of Richmond, Virginia, to study pre-medicine. I expected to graduate in 1945, enter the Medical College of Virginia, and receive my degree as a Doctor of Medicine in 1949. After my hospital training, I would go into practice either in my own home town of Richmond, Virginia, or possibly with my uncle-in-law, Dr. John A. Coleman, who was a family physician in Plant City, Florida. I loved and admired Dr. Coleman. In fact, the interest he had shown in me as a child and teen-ager was one reason I had decided to study medicine. The other reason was my desire to help the disabled, for I had grown up with a wonderful, spirited grandfather who, ever since I had known him, had been crippled with severe rheumatoid arthritis.

Robert Burns, the great Scottish poet, wrote: "Man proposes but oft-times God disposes," and this certainly turned out to be my case, though I doubt God's will had anything to do with it. Rather, it was Mr. Hitler and the Japanese attack on Pearl Harbor that were to radically change my schedule.

My first hint of the change came when my father, who was too old to be drafted, accepted a commission as a major in the Army. He was in charge of fuel for the U.S. Army camps and would help plan for the storage of fuel for the D-Day invasion of Normandy.

Dad, who was one of the two top experts in the United States on coal utilization, worked for the Chesapeake & Ohio Railroad. The railroad sent him, their top fuel service engineer, as a consultant to any other railroad or large company that was having trouble with the utilization of coal.

After Pearl Harbor, most pre-med students began to go to summer school, in addition to the regular classes, in order to complete as much education as possible before being called into service. By 1943, I had completed most of my courses for a bachelor of science degree. Because I could no longer feel comfortable sitting in college studying when I knew it was a matter of months before my Dad would be sent overseas, I volunteered from inactive army reserve for active duty. I was soon called to active duty and told to report to Camp Lee, Virginia.

After a stay there of two weeks, I was loaded on a train and sent to Camp Barkeley, Texas. It is situated in the Texas panhandle and is the only place I have ever been where I could march in mud up to my ankles and still have dust blowing in my face.

I had almost completed basic training when I was told to report to the top sergeant at regimental headquarters. No one told me why, and I began to wonder if I was facing some sort of court martial. These fears didn't abate when I went into headquarters and saw three other soldiers waiting. The top sergeant told me to take a seat and wait until I was called into the room behind the closed doors that he nodded toward. In fact, my fears mounted even higher when a major stuck his head out of the door and called my name. As soon as I went through the door I automatically snapped to attention because I had never seen that much high army brass in one room. They ranked all the way from the major to a major general. Now I was sure I was in deep trouble. Certainly I had bitched and griped like the rest of the G.I.s going through basic training, but I hadn't gone A.W.O.L. or cussed out any noncoms or officers, and I couldn't think of anything I had done that would deserve a general court martial, which this must be, to have all this brass here.

Then the questions began. The officers asked me about things I had accomplished as a teenager, what I had done in college and in college sports. They were even interested in what fraternity I belonged to. They were most interested in why I had volunteered for active duty. Then they told me that I was dismissed but that I was to report back to them the next morning at 1000.

During the rest of the day my buddies gave me a hard time. They wanted to know where I had been. When I told them I had been called before regimental headquarters, the rumors really began to fly as they can only in the army.

The next morning, when I was called into the room again, I was immediately given the order, "Stand at Ease." The major general walked up to me, stuck out his hand and said, "Congratulations, soldier, you have been picked under the Army Specialized Training Program to continue your studies of medicine. As soon as your basic training is complete, you will be sent back to your own home town to the Medical College of Virginia to continue the study of medicine."

I thanked them abundantly, snapped to attention, and gave him the best salute I knew. He returned the salute and I was dismissed. As I left, the top Sergeant congratulated me and promised I would receive my orders so that I would have them in adequate time to reach the medical college a good time before the actual classes began.

During the next two weeks my spirits soared, as did my dreams. I was going to be one of the youngest men ever to graduate from the Medical College of Virginia. I wanted to help people, but I dreamed, too, of having a cottage at the beach and owning a Cadillac before I was 35.

My Dad had already been sent overseas, but I would be home in time for Christmas and would get to see my stepmother, sisters, brother and all of my aunts and uncles. This too was very important to me because, during the three months I had been gone, I had missed them greatly.

Ten days before basic was completed, the unexpected happened. A young shave-tail second lieutenant who was giving us a lecture on the firing range made the entire company sit at attention for five minutes because two soldiers were talking. The temperature was five degrees above zero. As a result of this, at least five percent of our company ended up in the station hospital with an upper respiratory infection.

I was one of that five percent. One week later I was still in the hospital and the regimental sergeant, true to his word, had sent me my orders two days before. They read as follows: "You have your rail tickets enclosed for the train leaving Abilene at 0400 December 20, 1943. A jeep will pick you up at the front door of your ward at 0320 and carry you to the Abilene Station. You should arrive in Richmond in adequate time to report to the Commandant at the Medical College by 1430 on the afternoon of December 22, 1943. You shall be billeted in your own home."

I had shown these orders to the nurses and doctors on the ward. They were a great bunch and all of them were pulling for me. The medical officer in charge of the ward said that if my temperature was down to normal by December 19, there would be no doubt about my catching that train.

On the morning of the 19th my temperature was normal and I was transferred to the recuperation ward. The next morning at 0320, I was to be discharged when the jeep driver came to get me. The night nurse was so nice she even lent me her personal alarm clock.

I continued a hacking cough throughout the day. At supper the guy sitting on the next bed asked me if I would be interested in taking in a movie at the hospital theater with him. I had agreed if we could catch the 7:00 p.m. show so that I could be back and into bed by 9:30 p.m. I was going to have to be up by 3:00 a.m. to be dressed and ready when the jeep driver came to take me into Abilene.

When I returned from the show, I felt a little warm and thought I might be running a fever but I wasn't about to tell anyone on the staff for fear they would put me back into the ward I had just left. This would knock me out of my chances to go to medical school.

I had learned enough in basic training as a medical and surgical technician to know that aspirin and APC tablets would reduce fever, so I told the ward boy that I had a slight headache and asked him to give me six aspirin and three APC tablets so that I would be able to control the headache during my train ride. He gave them to me and I took two aspirin and an APC tablet.

While I was there, I also picked up my G.I. boots, my army overcoat, and my duffel bag that had been sent over from my company when the orders had been delivered. I placed all of these at the foot of my bed so that I would know where they were and not make a lot of noise and awake the rest of the soldiers when I got up in the middle of the night. I set the alarm clock for 3:00 a.m., climbed into bed and went right to sleep.

I awoke later because of coughing, and turned on the bedside light. It was 1:00 a.m., and I was even more feverish than when I had gone to bed, so I took two more aspirin and my second APC tablet. At 2:00 a.m. I awoke again feeling like I was on fire. I took my last three tablets.

Because I was coughing up so much material and spitting it into a sputum cup on the bedside table, I couldn't go back to sleep. Finally after what seemed like an eternity because I felt so bad, I turned on the bedside light to see if it wasn't time for the alarm to go off. It was 2:50 a.m. But what really caught my attention was the sputum cup being full of blood.

Thoroughly frightened, I jumped out of bed, went into the ward boy's office and asked him for a thermometer to take my temperature. A minute later, when I took the thermometer out of my mouth and showed it to him, it registered 106 degrees. He bolted out of the ward and in two minutes was back with the nurse. She took my temperature, read it, then said to the ward boy, "Get the captain in charge of the three wards."

When he came in, he looked at me, put his stethoscope on my chest and told me to breathe through my mouth. A moment later he shouted to the ward boy, "Call for an ambulance to take this soldier to the x-ray section."

While waiting for the ambulance, the doctor called the captain of the x-ray department and told him that he was sending me over and wanted pictures of my chest and the reading on them stat.

"What about me catching my train?" I shouted.

"Forget your train. You are not going anywhere tonight but inside this hospital compound. It will be a long time before you take a train anywhere."

The ambulance men put me on the stretcher, covered me with blankets and carried me out. During the ambulance ride I did all I could to fight back tears. A grown man wasn't supposed to cry—much less a soldier. The chance to be with my family for Christmas had vanished. Was the opportunity to enter medical school also evaporating? I felt so sick, so depressed, that I could hardly keep my senses.

The next thing I realized was that an army captain was standing over me and my stretcher, that had been placed on this x-ray table in front of the x-ray machine.

"Do you think you can stand long enough, soldier, for us to get a picture of your chest?"

"Certainly, Sir."

I got up and walked to the machine.

"Raise your arms over your head and lean forward against that panel. Take a deep breath and hold it."

I heard the machine make a funny whirling sound and the click that followed. Then everything began to go dark.

Faintly I heard the Captain shout to the nurse and the ambulance driver.

"Grab him."

PREAMBLE

Since I collapsed in front of the x-ray machine at approximately 3:10 a.m. on December 20, 1943, and remained unconscious until the morning of December 24, 1943, what is recorded here has been related to me by other people.

The doctor in charge of the medical ward to which I was carried was Donald G. Francy, M.D. The nurse assigned to my case was First Lieutenant Retta Irvine. Statements by both of these attendants were sent to Mrs. Catherine Marshall when she was writing her book, *To Live Again*. Mrs. Marshall and I tried to locate the other attendants on the case but because 13 years had elapsed and I couldn't remember their names, we were unable to locate the ward attendant or the medical officer who pronounced me dead. Nevertheless, she included my story in the chapter, "Is There Life after Death?"

That morning my condition continued to deteriorate. When the ward enlisted man made his rounds, he could find no vital signs. He quickly summoned the officer of the day, but this medical officer could detect no evidence of respiration, blood pressure or cardiac impulse. He pronounced me dead, and ordered the attendant to prepare my body for the morgue.

The ward boy had to finish his medication rounds before he could carry out the doctor's orders. Then he came back to the little isolation room to which I had been brought. Because I was the same age as he, and because he was having trouble accepting the pronouncement of death on someone as young, the ward boy went back to the officer of the day and told him he thought he had seen my chest move. He asked the medical officer if he wouldn't make up a hypo of adrenalin to have ready to give to me. The medical officer did this and followed the attendant back into my room.

The doctor again checked me for vital signs and found none. When the officer was about to tell the attendant to go ahead and prep me for the morgue this young attendant asked the doctor to please give me the hypo to be sure. Though the doctor was sure of his diagnosis of death, he could see that this young man was having a hard time dealing with my death. For the ward boy's benefit, he plunged the hypo directly into my heart. To his surprise my heart started beating. It was four more days and nights before I regained consciousness.

The doctor knew for a certainty that it had been 8 to 9 minutes between the two times I had been pronounced dead. I'm sure, as an M.D. myself, the doctor must have become very worried, since no one was sure of how long my vital signs had ceased before the ward boy made his rounds. For then, as now, doctors knew the chance of brain damage after five minutes without oxygen to the brain was profound. This is why Dr. Francy made this statement in his notarized statement, *"I, speaking for myself, feel sure that his virtual call from death and return to vigorous health has to be explained in terms of other than natural means."*

Lieutenant Retta Irvine, in her notarized note, says, *"Although fourteen years have elapsed and some of the details are not quite clear, I remember that this patient was pronounced dead at two different times by the Medical Officer who was on duty, yet after he was given an injection into the heart muscle the patient revived and in due time regained his health. During his convalescence Private Ritchie asked me how near dead he had been. When I told him what had happened he said that he thought that he had been dead. Although he did not go into detail he told me that he had an experience that would probably change his life. Even though this experience was most unusual, I did not doubt this man's sincerity either then or now."*

There is one other bit of evidence which is extremely important. In the next chapter, I relate that I left my human body and traveled to a city beside a large river before I realized no one could see me. I came down in front of a white, rectangular all-night cafe. There was a front door, flanked by large windows. In one window was a Pabst Blue Ribbon Beer neon sign.

Ten months later, while driving through Vicksburg, Mississippi, on the way from Cincinnati, Ohio to New Orleans, Louisiana, I recognized this same building. The color of the building and the neon sign were the same. The topographical location on the land as it related to the Mississippi River was the same. This removed any possibility of my experience being a delusion or a dream as so many of the skeptics wanted to believe.

Before my turn for the worse began, on the morning of December the 19th, as soon as I had been sent to the recuperation ward, I telegraphed my stepmother so she would be able to meet me in Richmond, Virginia.

On the 21st, when my stepmother found I was not on the train on which I was due to arrive, she became very worried. When she still had not heard anything from me by the morning of the 22nd, she called the Barkeley Station Hospital. After a great deal of trouble the hospital operator located the new ward where I had been placed and got the head nurse on the telephone. When Mother asked why I was still there in the hospital, she was told that I had relapsed into pneumonia, was in critical condition and not expected to live.

The nurse asked Mother if it was possible for her to come to the hospital since my condition was possibly terminal. All of this was an extreme shock to her. Mother told the nurse my father, Major Ritchie, was in England and she could not come because she had two small children, my half-brother Henry, who was nine, and my half-sister, Bruce, who was only six and a half, and was in bed with virus pneumonia. (My older sister, Mary Jane, had already married and was not living in Richmond.) After suggesting my mother notify the Commandant at the Medical College of Virginia what had happened, she took Mother's phone number in case they had to reach her.

Seven weeks later when I finally arrived in Richmond and she met me at the station, she was somewhat prepared for how I looked as a result of her phone call to Texas but not totally. When I entered the hospital with the upper respiratory infection, I was finishing my basic training and was in excellent physical condition. I was 6 feet 2 inches tall and weighed 175 pounds. The first time the nurse weighed me a week after my return to consciousness, I weighed 107 pounds.

The doctor who was in charge of my case stated emphatically there was no way that he would sign my discharge until my weight reached 135 pounds. When they were sure there was no brain damage, one of the medical staff called the Medical College of Virginia and found they were saving my place. During the next five weeks, the nurses and ward men fed me more milk shakes, fruit juices, snacks and extra helpings at meals than I had ever had. They were a terrific group and did everything they could to help me gain weight.

EXPERIENCING THE EPIPHANY

The night was getting stranger and stranger, I thought. Here I was sitting on the side of the bed; I felt like I just woke up but I did not remember sitting up. What was going on? The last thing I could remember was my standing in front of the x-ray machine. What was I doing in this little room?

Had I missed my train? What time was it? Where was the watch I usually wore on my left arm? I knew it must be night because it was still dark.

The only light in the room was the little bulb in the stalk of the lamp and it was not putting out much light. In fact, it put out so little, I could not see my uniform anywhere in the room.

I knew I had to get out of this place and go to Richmond or I would be A.W.O.L., and if I was, that would be a heck of a way to start to medical school. I had to leave immediately. I didn't have any more time to waste.

With that thought, I walked to the ward hall. The room that I had left was a middle room, for there were rooms on each side. There were three rooms across the hall, the first the doctor's office, next the nurse's office with a wall of filing cabinets. Next to the nurse's office, before you entered the double doors into the big ward, was a ward attendant's office and storage room. I could see out through the glass windows of the double doors. Facing into the connecting corridor was a door, opposite the ward doors, going outside.

As I passed through the ward door a ward man, carrying a covered tray, came toward me.

"Watch where you are going," I said. He acted as through he could neither see nor hear me.

He walked right through me!

This surprised and confused me but I did not have time to stop and mull over it. I had to get to Richmond.

I passed through the outside door and as soon as I did, to my amazement, I found myself approximately five hundred feet above the ground, traveling at a terrific speed. It was a clear night. I was sure, from the position of the North Star, that I was headed in an easterly direction. I could also see the little hills covered with mesquite trees. As I continued to speed eastward they gave way to more pine trees and trees like we had in Virginia. The ground did not seem so desert-like as it had in the western part of Texas.

From the appearance of the crystal-clear sky and from seeing some ice on the smaller rivers I was crossing, I realized that I should be cold but for some strange reason I did not feel cold. My flying through the night well above the earth without knowing how I was accomplishing this was even more startling but I decided I would take the Scarlett O'Hara approach. I would think about that tomorrow, after I reached Richmond.

Quite a bit of distance later, I saw a large river with a big bridge crossing over it. There was a city located on the eastern banks. I thought I had better slow down, land there, and find if I was going in the right direction to reach Richmond.

I came down closer to the ground when I noticed bright blue color coming from a Pabst Blue Ribbon Beer neon sign in front of a white cafe. I was on the corner of the street ahead of me. I saw a tall, thin man, bundled in a dark overcoat coming up the sidewalk, heading toward the door of this car.

I lit down about twelve feet in front of him to ask directions. I had no idea where I was or how far I had traveled.

"What is the name of this city? Do you know where Richmond, Virginia, is and in what direction I should go to get there?"

For the second time that night, here was another man who acted as though he could neither see nor hear me.

In fact he also walked right through me.

This was too much.

I went over to lean against the guy wire, the cable coming from the telephone pole, and my hand went through it.

I suddenly thought, "What has happened to me? No one can see or hear me. Is this a coincidence that I have bumped into two men with this trouble? If the wardman and this man can not hear or see me, will Mother be able to see or hear me? Will the commandant or any of the professors or students be able to know I am there? What is the use of going on if they can not?

"I have never had to face any problem like this. If I don't continue going where I'm going, wherever that may be, then do I go back? If I do, why and to what? The hospital wardman couldn't see me either.

What was that covered mound I left in the bed after I stood up back in the room in Texas? Could that have been a body? I don't like this line of thought: A human isn't separated from their body unless…*they are dead!*

"If I am, then what is this thing that I am in now? It can go through doors without opening them. It can fly. It does not feel cold. As remarkable as these qualities are, they are no good to me if I cannot be seen. I have to go back to that hospital in Camp Barkeley and get my other body!

"I am too young to die. I'm only 20 years old. I have too many things to do with my life. I *have to get back to that hospital.*"

I had no sooner thought about returning to the hospital when I found myself up in the air and traveling, this time rapidly, in a westerly direction. Before I could adequately take in what was happening to me, I found myself standing in front of the Barkeley Station Hospital.

I had made two other discoveries about this strange out-of-body realm. First, one goes wherever his/her soul's sincere desire leads him/her. Secondly, time in this realm, if it exists at all, is much shorter than our normal human realm, or the capacity to cover great distances in a regular period of time is vastly increased, for the distance I knew I had traveled could not be covered in our fastest airplanes.

I was in trouble now, for when I left the hospital, I was in such a great rush that I had not taken the trouble to look and see which ward I had left. What had happened with the human beings before was still true. These people, the doctors and nurses now, also could not see or hear me and there was no way I could ask them for information about where my room was located. This was a much larger hospital than I had realized since I had been in only two wards and the movie theater. Now I found myself wandering from ward to ward, room to room, trying to find that little room that I had been in before I left.

I could see the nurses, doctors, and ward attendants, but as I have said, they could not see me. I could see the soldiers lying in the beds because I was trying to find my body. I saw several who looked like me but the ones that had their left hand out from under the cover did not have my Phi Gamma Delta fraternity ring on their ring finger. I was becoming increasingly discouraged and frightened and feeling alone and separated from the rest of the human race.

I continued to search from ward to ward and room to room.

I had begun to believe I was going to be condemned to spending an eternity doing this when I came into a poorly lit room. It had only a night light on in the stalk of the lamp.

Lying in the bed with a sheet pulled up over the head was this body. When they pulled up the sheet to cover the body, they left the left arm and hand uncovered. *There on the left ring finger was my Phi Gamma Delta and University of Richmond ring with 19 on one side and 45 on the other side of the oval black onyx with the silver owl on front of it.* The onyx even had the chip on the side that had happened when I knocked my hand against something going through the obstacle course.

I did not like the color of the hand because it had the same appearance my grandfather's hand had had three years before when I saw it right after he died. Now my massive denial was breaking down and I was going to have to accept the fact that I was dead.

I could not believe this had happened to me. I was supposed to become the outstanding young doctor. I was going to have a wonderful Christmas with my family after being away so long. I was the one whom my good friends back in college were going to be so glad to see and I was going to be so excited to see them.

Now I would not be able to see any of them again. No, not even my family, whom I now missed so deeply. I could not even communicate with the staff and soldiers I could see in the ward. I have never felt so alone, discouraged and frightened.

"Oh God, where are you when I am so lost and discouraged?"

I could walk through the bed and walls. I could not pick up the sheet when I wanted to pull back the covers to look at the face to make sure it was my body. I could, by a manner of thinking, manage to sit on the bed beside the body.

I had discovered it was impossible to get the spiritual or soul body into or through any of the small openings in the human body. I was fini, caput, at my end, and giving up.

I had been raised a Southern Baptist. At eleven years of age I had gone to the country to visit some friends of a family who lived fifteen miles outside of Mineral, Virginia. Their Presbyterian church, The Kirk of the Cliff, was holding a fire-and-brimstone revival. I believe it must have been the last one the Presbyterians held in the state of Virginia.

When I did not join the church the first night, I became so frightened, I joined it the second night. Fortunately, when I returned to Richmond, I was transferred to Ginter Park Presbyterian Church which was only five blocks from where we lived. There I came under the care of one of the finest and most wonderful ministers I have ever known, Dr. John MacLean. I was a member of this church when I joined the service.

I still carried the concept that when one died, he/she slept until judgment day when he/she would be judged and then sent to heaven or hell. The experience I was having now had never been mentioned.

Suddenly an amazing thing began. The light at the end of the bed began to grow brighter and brighter. I first thought it was the little night light until I realized it was coming from beside the white bedside table at the head of the bed. It continued to increase in intensity until it seemed to be equal to a million welders' lights. I knew if I had been seeing through my human eyes instead of those of my spiritual body I would have been blinded.

Then three things happened instantaneously. *Something deep inside of my spiritual being said, "STAND UP. YOU ARE IN THE PRESENCE OF THE SON OF GOD."*

I was suddenly propelled up and off the bed. Out of the brilliant light at the head of the bed stepped the most magnificent Being I have ever known.

The hospital walls disappeared and in the place of them was a living panorama of my entire life where I saw in detail everything I had ever experienced, from my own caesarean birth through my present death.

I was in the presence of the One who said, "I am the Alpha and the Omega who is and who was and who is to come, the sovereign Lord of all."

Visions/Life After Death

Carl G. Jung

The visions and experiences were
utterly real; there was nothing
subjective about them.

In a hospital in Switzerland in 1944, the world-renowned
psychiatrist Carl G. Jung, M.D., had a heart attack, then a near-
death experience. On that day, in an out-of-body experience, Jung
envisioned the earth from over a thousand miles out in space.
High above India, he could see the Arabian deserts and the snow-
capped Himalayas. Then he spotted a huge meteorite floating
toward him; it was carved out like an ancient Hindu temple. The
doorway was surrounded by a wreath of bright lights from
numerous flaming lamps. Just to the right a Hindu man wearing a
white gown sat meditating in lotus posture on a stone bench.

Inside the temple, Jung felt, were the answers to all his life's most important questions. But before he could enter, the strange appearance of a spirit who was to die in his place called him back to earth. Reluctantly Jung returned to earth's "box system."

This vivid encounter with the sacred presence, the Light, plus the intensely meaningful insights led Jung to conclude that his experience came from something real and eternal. Subsequently, as he reflected on life after death, Jung recalled the meditating Hindu from his near-death vision and read it as a parable of the archetypal higher Self, the God-image within.

Carl G. Jung, M.D., founded analytical psychology, centered on the archetypes of the collective unconscious. His *Collected Works* are published by Princeton University Press, and have been the best-selling books published by a university press in the United States. This selection is from Jung's autobiography, *Memories, Dreams, Reflections* (1961).

⸱⤳ Visions / Life After Death ⤳⸱

At the beginning of 1944 I broke my foot, and this misadventure was followed by a heart attack. In a state of unconsciousness I experienced deliriums and visions which must have begun when I hung on the edge of death and was being given oxygen and camphor injections. The images were so tremendous that I myself concluded that I was close to death. My nurse afterward told me, "It was as if you were surrounded by a bright glow." That was a phenomenon she had sometimes observed in the dying, she added. I had reached the outermost limit, and do not know whether I was in a dream or an ecstasy. At any rate, extremely strange things began to happen to me.

It seemed to me that I was high up in space. Far below I saw the globe of the earth, bathed in a gloriously blue light. I saw the deep blue sea and the continents. Far below my feet lay Ceylon, and in the distance ahead of me the subcontinent of India. My field of vision did not include the whole earth, but its global shape was plainly distinguishable and its outlines shone with a silvery gleam through that wonderful blue light. In many places the globe seemed colored, or spotted dark green like oxidized silver. Far away to the left lay a broad expanse—the reddish-yellow desert of Arabia; it was as though the silver of the earth had there assumed a reddish-gold hue. Then came the Red Sea, and far, far back—as if in the upper left of a map—I could just make out a bit of the Mediterranean. My gaze was directed chiefly toward that. Everything else appeared indistinct. I could also see the snow-covered Himalayas, but in that direction it was foggy or cloudy. I did not look to the right at all. I knew that I was on the point of departing from the earth.

Later I discovered how high in space one would have to be to have so extensive a view—approximately a thousand miles! The sight of the earth from this height was the most glorious thing I had ever seen.

After contemplating it for a while, I turned around. I had been standing with my back to the Indian Ocean, as it were, and my face to the north. Then it seemed to me that I made a turn to the south. Something new entered my field of vision. A short distance away I saw in space a tremendous dark block of stone, like a meteorite. It was about the size of my house, or even bigger. It was floating in space, and I myself was floating in space.

I had seen similar stones on the coast of the Gulf of Bengal. They were blocks of tawny granite, and some of them had been hollowed out into temples. My stone was one such gigantic dark block. An entrance led into a small antechamber. To the right of the entrance, a black Hindu sat silently in lotus posture upon a stone bench. He wore a white gown, and I knew that he expected me. Two steps led up to this antechamber, and inside, on the left, was the gate to the temple. Innumerable tiny niches, each with a saucer-like concavity filled with coconut oil and small burning wicks, surrounded the door with a wreath of bright flames. I had once actually seen this when I visited the Temple of the Holy Tooth at Kandy in Ceylon; the gate had been framed by several rows of burning oil lamps of this sort.

As I approached the steps leading up to the entrance into the rock, a strange thing happened: I had the feeling that everything was being sloughed away; everything I aimed at or wished for or thought, the whole phantasmagoria of earthly existence, fell away or was stripped from me—an extremely painful process. Nevertheless something remained; it was as if I now carried along with me everything I had ever experienced or done, everything that had happened around me. I might also say: it was with me, and I was it. I consisted of all that, so to speak. I consisted of my own history and I felt with great certainty: this is what I am. "I am this bundle of what has been and what has been accomplished."

This experience gave me a feeling of extreme poverty, but at the same time of great fullness. There was no longer anything I wanted or desired. I existed in an objective form; I was what I had been and lived. At first the sense of annihilation predominated, of having been stripped or pillaged; but suddenly that became of no consequence. Everything seemed to be past; what remained was a *fait accompli*, without any reference back to what had been. There was no longer any regret that something had dropped away or been taken away. On the contrary: I had everything that I was, and that was everything.

Something else engaged my attention: as I approached the temple I had the certainty that I was about to enter an illuminated room and would meet there all those people to whom I belong in reality. There I would at last understand—this too was a certainty—what historical nexus I or my life fitted into. I would know what had been before me, why I had come into being, and where my life was flowing. My life as I lived it had often seemed to me like a story that has no beginning and end. I had the feeling that I was a historical fragment, an excerpt for which the preceding and succeeding text was missing. My life seemed to have been snipped out of a long chain of events, and many questions had remained unanswered. Why had it taken this course? Why had I brought these particular assumptions with me? What had I made of them? What will follow? I felt sure that I would receive an answer to all the questions as soon as I entered the rock temple. There I would learn why everything had been thus and not otherwise. There I would meet the people who knew the answer to my question about what had been before and what would come after.

While I was thinking over these matters, something happened that caught my attention. From below, from the direction of Europe, an image floated up. It was my doctor, Dr. H.—or, rather, his likeness—framed by a golden chain or a golden laurel wreath. I knew at once: "Aha, this is my doctor, of course, the one who has been treating me. But now he is coming in his primal form, as a *basileus* of Kos.[1] In life he was an avatar of this *basileus*, the temporal embodiment of the primal form, which has existed from the beginning. Now he is appearing in that primal form."

Presumably I too was in my primal form, though this was something I did not observe but simply took for granted. As he stood before me, a mute exchange of thought took place between us. Dr. H. had been delegated by the earth to deliver a message to me, to tell me that there was a protest against my going away. I had no right to leave the earth and must return. The moment I heard that, the vision ceased.

I was profoundly disappointed, for now it all seemed to have been for nothing. The painful process of defoliation had been in vain, and I was not to be allowed to enter the temple, to join the people in whose company I belonged.

In reality, a good three weeks were still to pass before I could truly make up my mind to live again. I could not eat because all food repelled me. The view of city and mountains from my sickbed seemed to me like a painted curtain with black holes in it, or a tattered sheet of newspaper full of photographs that meant nothing. Disappointed, I thought, "Now I must return to the 'box system' again." For it seemed to me as if behind the horizon of the cosmos a three-dimensional world had been artificially built up, in which each person sat by himself in a little box. And now I should have to convince myself all over again that this was important! Life and the whole world struck me as a prison, and it bothered me beyond measure that I should again be finding all that quite in order. I had been so glad to shed it all, and now it had come about that I—along with everyone else—would again be hung up in a box by a thread. While I floated in space, I had been weightless, and there had been nothing tugging at me. And now all that was to be a thing of the past!

I felt violent resistance to my doctor because he had brought me back to life. At the same time, I was worried about him. "His life is in danger, for heaven's sake! He has appeared to me in his primal form! When anybody attains this form it means he is going to die, for already he belongs to the 'greater company.'" Suddenly the terrifying thought came to me that Dr. H. would have to die in my stead. I tried my best to talk to him about it, but he did not understand me. Then I became angry with him. "Why does he always pretend he doesn't know he is a *basileus* of Kos? And that he has already assumed his primal form? He wants to make me believe that he doesn't know." That irritated me. My wife reproved me for being so unfriendly to him. She was right; but at the time I was angry with him for stubbornly refusing to speak of all that had passed between us in my vision. "Damn it all, he ought to watch his step. He has no right to be so reckless! I want to tell him to take care of himself." I was firmly convinced that his life was in jeopardy.

In actual fact I was his last patient. On April 4, 1944—I still remember the exact date I was allowed to sit up on the edge of my bed for the first time since the beginning of my illness, and on this same day Dr. H. took to his bed and did not leave it again. I heard that he was having intermittent attacks of fever. Soon afterward he died of septicemia. He was a good doctor; there was something of the genius about him. Otherwise he would not have appeared to me as a prince of Kos.

During those weeks I lived in a strange rhythm. By day I was usually depressed. I felt weak and wretched, and scarcely dared to stir. Gloomily, I thought, "Now I must go back to this drab world." Toward evening I would fall asleep, and my sleep would last until about midnight. Then I would come to myself and lie awake for about an hour, but in an utterly transformed state. It was as if I were in an ecstasy. I felt as though I were floating in space, as though I were safe in the womb of the universe—in a tremendous void, but filled with the highest possible feeling of happiness. "This is eternal bliss," I thought. "This cannot be described; it is far too wonderful!"

Everything around me seemed enchanted. At this hour of the night the nurse brought me some food she had warmed—for only then was I able to take any, and I ate with appetite. For a time it seemed to me that she was an old Jewish woman, much older than she actually was, and that she was preparing ritual kosher dishes for me. When I looked at her, she seemed to have a blue halo around her head. I myself was, so it seemed, in the Pardes Rimmonim, the garden of pomegranates,[2] and the wedding of Tifereth with Malchuth was taking place. Or else I was Rabbi Simon ben Jochai, whose wedding in the afterlife was being celebrated. It was the mystic marriage as it appears in the Cabbalistic tradition. I cannot tell you how wonderful it was. I could only think continually, "Now this is the garden of pomegranates! Now this is the marriage of Malchuth with Tifereth!" I do not know exactly what part I played in it. At bottom it was I myself: I was the marriage. And my beatitude was that of a blissful wedding.

Gradually the garden of pomegranates faded away and changed. There followed the Marriage of the Lamb, in a Jerusalem festively bedecked. I cannot describe what it was like in detail. These were ineffable states of joy. Angels were present, and light. I myself was the "Marriage of the Lamb."

That, too, vanished, and there came a new image, the last vision. I walked up a wide valley to the end, where a gentle chain of hills began. The valley ended in a classical amphitheater. It was magnificently situated in the green landscape. And there, in this theater, the *hierosgamos* was being celebrated. Men and women dancers came onstage, and upon a flower-decked couch All-father Zeus and Hera consummated the mystic marriage, as it is described in the *Iliad*.

All these experiences were glorious. Night after night I floated in a state of purest bliss, "thronged round with images of all creation."[3] Gradually, the motifs mingled and paled. Usually the visions lasted for about an hour; then I would fall asleep again. By the time morning drew near, I would feel: Now gray morning is coming again; now comes the gray world with its boxes! What idiocy, what hideous nonsense! Those inner states were so fantastically beautiful that by comparison this world appeared downright ridiculous. As I approached closer to life again, they grew fainter, and scarcely three weeks after the first vision they ceased altogether.

It is impossible to convey the beauty and intensity of emotion during those visions. They were the most tremendous things I have ever experienced. And what a contrast the day was: I was tormented and on edge; everything irritated me; everything was too material, too crude and clumsy, terribly limited both spatially and spiritually. It was all an imprisonment, for reasons impossible to divine, and yet it had a kind of hypnotic power, a cogency, as if it were reality itself, for all that I had clearly perceived its emptiness. Although my belief in the world returned to me, I have never since entirely freed myself of the impression that this life is a segment of existence which is enacted in a three-dimensional boxlike universe especially set up for it.

There is something else I quite distinctly remember. At the beginning, when I was having the vision of the garden of pomegranates, I asked the nurse to forgive me if she were harmed. There was such sanctity in the room, I said, that it might be harmful to her. Of course she did not understand me. For me the presence of sanctity had a magical atmosphere; I feared it might be unendurable to others. I understood then why one speaks of the odor of sanctity, of the "sweet smell" of the Holy Ghost. This was it. There was a *pneuma* of inexpressible sanctity in the room, whose manifestation was the *mysterium coniunctionis*.

I would never have imagined that any such experience was possible. It was not a product of imagination. The visions and experiences were utterly real; there was nothing subjective about them; they all had a quality of absolute objectivity.

We shy away from the word "eternal," but I can describe the experience only as the ecstasy of a non-temporal state in which present, past, and future are one. Everything that happens in time had been brought together into a concrete whole. Nothing was distributed over time, nothing could be measured by temporal concepts. The experience might best be defined as a state of feeling, but one which cannot be produced by imagination. How can I imagine that I exist simultaneously the day before yesterday, today, and the day after tomorrow? There would be things which would not yet have begun, other things which would be indubitably present, and others again which would already be finished—and yet all this would be one. The only thing that feeling could grasp would be a sum, an iridescent whole, containing all at once expectation of a beginning, surprise at what is now happening, and satisfaction or disappointment with the result of what has happened. One is interwoven into an indescribable whole and yet observes it with complete objectivity.

I experienced this objectivity once again later on. That was after the death of my wife. I saw her in a dream which was like a vision. She stood at some distance from me, looking at me squarely. She was in her prime, perhaps about thirty, and wearing the dress which had been made for her many years before by my cousin the medium. It was perhaps the most beautiful thing she had ever worn. Her expression was neither joyful nor sad, but, rather, objectively wise and understanding, without the slightest emotional reaction, as though she were beyond the mist of affects. I knew that it was not she, but a portrait she had made or commissioned for me. It contained the beginning of our relationship, the events of fifty-three years of marriage, and the end of her life also. Face to face with such wholeness one remains speechless, for it can scarcely be comprehended.

The objectivity which I experienced in this dream and in the visions is part of a completed individuation. It signifies detachment from valuations and from what we call emotional ties. In general, emotional ties are very important to human beings. But they still contain projections, and it is essential to withdraw these projections in order to attain to oneself and to objectivity. Emotional relationships are relationships of desire, tainted by coercion and constraint; something is expected from the other person, and that makes him and ourselves unfree. Objective cognition lies hidden behind the attraction of the emotional relationship; it seems to be the central secret. Only through objective cognition is the real *coniunctio* possible.

After the illness a fruitful period of work began for me. A good many of my principal works were written only then. The insight I had had, or the vision of the end of all things, gave me the courage to undertake new formulations. I no longer attempted to put across my own opinion, but surrendered myself to the current of my thoughts. Thus one problem after the other revealed itself to me and took shape.

Something else, too, came to me from my illness. I might formulate it as an affirmation of things as they are: an unconditional "yes" to that which is, without subjective protests— acceptance of the conditions of existence as I see them and understand them, acceptance of my own nature, as I happen to be. At the beginning of the illness I had the feeling that there was something wrong with my attitude, and that I was to some extent responsible for the mishap. But when one follows the path of individuation, when one lives one's own life, one must take mistakes into the bargain; life would not be complete without them. There is no guarantee—not for a single moment — that we will not fall into error or stumble into deadly peril. We may think there is a sure road. But that would be the road of death. Then nothing happens any longer—at any rate, not the right things. Anyone who takes the sure road is as good as dead.

It was only after the illness that I understood how important it is to affirm one's own destiny. In this way we forge an ego that does not break down when incomprehensible things happen; an ego that endures, that endures the truth, and that is capable of coping with the world and with fate. Then, to experience defeat is also to experience victory. Nothing is disturbed— neither inwardly nor outwardly, for one's own continuity has withstood the current of life and of time. But that can come to pass only when one does not meddle inquisitively with the workings of fate.

I have also realized that one must accept the thoughts that go on within oneself of their own accord as part of one's reality. The categories of true and false are, of course, always present; but because they are not binding they take second place. The presence of thoughts is more important than our subjective judgment of them. But neither must these judgments be suppressed, for they also are existent thoughts which are part of our wholeness.

*****

I had dreamed once before of the problem of the self and the ego. In that earlier dream I was on a hiking trip. I was walking along a little road through a hilly landscape; the sun was shining and I had a wide view in all directions. Then I came to a small wayside chapel. The door was ajar, and I went in. To my surprise there was no image of the Virgin on the altar, and no crucifix either, but only a wonderful flower arrangement. But then I saw that on the floor in front of the altar, facing me, sat a yogi—in lotus posture, in deep meditation. When I looked at him more closely, I realized that he had my face. I started in profound fright, and awoke with the thought: "Aha, so he is the one who is meditating me. He has a dream, and I am it." I knew that when he awakened, I would no longer be.

I had this dream after my illness in 1944. It is a parable: My self retires into meditation and meditates my earthly form. To put it another way: it assumes human shape in order to enter three dimensional existence, as if someone were putting on a diver's suit in order to dive into the sea. When it renounces existence in the hereafter, the self assumes a religious posture, as the chapel in the dream shows. In earthly form it can pass through the experiences of the three dimensional world, and by greater awareness take a further step toward realization.

The figure of the yogi, then, would more or less represent my unconscious prenatal wholeness, and the Far East, as is often the case in dreams, a psychic state alien and opposed to our own. Like the magic lantern, the yogi's meditation "projects" my empirical reality. As a rule, we see this causal relationship in reverse: in the products of the unconscious we discover mandala symbols, that is, circular and quaternary figures which express wholeness, and whenever we wish to express wholeness, we employ just such figures. Our basis is ego-consciousness, our world the field of light centered upon the focal point of the ego. From that point we look out upon an enigmatic world of obscurity, never knowing to what extent the shadowy forms we see are caused by our consciousness, or possess a reality of their own. The superficial observer is content with the first assumption. But closer study shows that as a rule the images of the unconscious are not produced by consciousness, but have a reality and spontaneity of their own. Nevertheless, we regard them as mere marginal phenomena.

The aim of both these dreams is to effect a reversal of the relationship between ego consciousness and the unconscious, and to represent the unconscious as the generator of the empirical personality. This reversal suggests that in the opinion of the "other side," our unconscious existence is the real one and our conscious world a kind of illusion, an apparent reality constructed for a specific purpose, like a dream which seems a reality as long as we are in it. It is clear that this state of affairs resembles very closely the Oriental conception of Maya.

Unconscious wholeness therefore seems to me the true *spiritus rector* of all biological and psychic events. Here is a principle which strives for total realization—which in man's case signifies the attainment of total consciousness. Attainment of consciousness is culture in the broadest sense, and self-knowledge is therefore the heart and essence of this process. The Oriental attributes unquestionably divine significance to the self, and according to the ancient Christian view self-knowledge is the road to knowledge of God.

The decisive question for man is: Is he related to something infinite or not?

That is the telling question of his life. Only if we know that the thing which truly matters is the infinite can we avoid fixing our interest upon futilities, and upon all kinds of goals which are not of real importance. Thus we demand that the world grant us recognition for qualities which we regard as personal possessions: our talent or our beauty. The more a man lays stress on false possessions, and the less sensitivity he has for what is essential, the less satisfying is his life. He feels limited because he has limited aims, and the result is envy and jealousy. If we understand and feel that here in this life we already have a link with the infinite, desires and attitudes change. In the final analysis, we count for something only because of the essential we embody, and if we do not embody that, life is wasted. In our relationships to other men, too, the crucial question is whether an element of boundlessness is expressed in the relationship.

The feeling for the infinite, however, can be attained only if we are bounded to the utmost. The greatest limitation for man is the "self"; it is manifested in the experience: "I am *only* that!" Only consciousness of our narrow confinement in the self forms the link to the limitlessness of the unconscious. In such awareness we experience ourselves concurrently as limited and eternal, as both the one and the other. In knowing ourselves to be unique in our personal combination—that is, ultimately limited—we possess also the capacity for becoming conscious of the infinite. But only then!

In an era which has concentrated exclusively upon extension of living space and increase of rational knowledge at all costs, it is a supreme challenge to ask man to become conscious of his uniqueness and his limitation. Uniqueness and limitation are synonymous. Without them, no perception of the unlimited is possible—and, consequently, no coming to consciousness either—merely a delusory identity with it which takes the form of intoxication with large numbers and an avidity for political power.

Our age has shifted all emphasis to the here and now, and thus brought about a daemonization of man and his world. The phenomenon of dictators and all the misery they have wrought springs from the fact that man has been robbed of transcendence by the shortsightedness of the superintellectuals. Like them, he has fallen a victim to unconsciousness. But man's task is the exact opposite: to become conscious of the contents that press upward from the unconscious. Neither should he persist in his unconsciousness, nor remain identical with the unconscious elements of his being, thus evading his destiny, which is to create more and more consciousness. As far as we can discern, the sole purpose of human existence is to kindle a light in the darkness of mere being. It may even be assumed that just as the unconscious affects us, so the increase in our consciousness affects the unconscious.

NOTES

1. *Basileus* = king. Kos was famous in antiquity as the site of the temple of Asklepios, and was the birthplace of Hippocrates.

2. *Pardes Rimmonim* is the title of an old Cabbalistic tract by Moses Cordovero (sixteenth century). In Cabbalistic doctrine Malchuth and Tifereth are two of the ten spheres of divine manifestation in which God emerges from his hidden state. They represent the female and male principles within the Godhead.

3. *Faust*, Part Two.

· ⌣ 8 ⌣ ·

On Dreams and Death

Marie-Louise von Franz

In the Mithraic cult, this light-glory...envelops the entire soul of the dying man, like a "shining illumination by a spiritual fire which inflames the soul to ardor."

Marie-Louise von Franz, Ph.D., is one of the founding members of the C. G. Jung Institute in Küsnacht, Switzerland, where she is a supervising analyst. She collaborated with Jung and has written numerous influential books, including *Projections and Recollection; The Aurora Consurgens; Number and Time; Jung: His Myth in Our Time,* and several volumes on the archetypal motifs in fairy tales.

During her training as a Jungian analyst, Jenny Yates heard Dr. von Franz lecture on death and dreams at the University of Zurich. She vividly recalls von Franz telling the story of a dying woman's dream of a candle going out on one side of a window, then lighting up on the other side. What an apt metaphor for the near-death experience.

The following selection is an excerpt from von Franz' comments on near-death experiences in her 1984 book, *On Dreams and Death*. She illustrates the classic Jungian method of seeking to understand the correspondence of phenomena through amplification or illustration from parallel symbols in the world's storehouses of the archetypes of the collective unconscious: dreams, myths, fairy tales, and religious literature, such as *The Egyptian Book of the Dead*. She begins with a discussion of the archetypal image of the birth/death passage in the Komairos text, which is a highly symbolic ancient alchemical text (Berthelot).

⁓ On Dreams and Death ⁓

THE DARK BIRTH PASSAGE AND THE SPIRIT OF DISCOURAGEMENT

The image of a dark, narrow birth passage also belongs among those archetypal motifs which anticipate the course of death. In the Komarios text, the production of gold, or the "stone of the wise," was represented as taking place through a pregnancy and the birth of a child. This is a leitmotif that runs through many centuries of the alchemical tradition.

Similar to the birth image is another motif in the Komarios text: the suggestion that adepts should treat their material like a bird which "hatches its eggs…in mild warmth." This idea also occurs over and over again in the alchemical texts. From the beginning of time, antique man wondered with fascination how an egg, which when opened contains only half-liquid "dead" substances, could still produce a living being, only by being warmed and without the help of any external agent. The alchemists compared the production of their stone to this "miracle."

The *I Ching*, the Chinese oracle book, provides a parallel to this, which seems to me worth mentioning. It concerns the description of a time condition called Chung Fu, "Inner Truth." Richard Wilhelm comments: "The character *fu* ('truth') is actually the picture of a bird's foot over a fledgling. It suggests the idea of brooding. An egg is hollow. The light-giving power must work to quicken it from the outside, but there must be a germ of life within, if life is to be awakened" (Vol.I, 250). In a similar manner, and in this case certainly without any cultural transfer, the alchemist Gerhard Dorn (sixteenth century) called the innermost soul, the Self of man, an "inner truth," and he looked upon alchemical work as a "hatching out" of this truth from physical matter.

Birth symbolism is especially and intensively elaborated in the Egyptian death liturgy. Thus in Rubric 170 of the Book of the Dead we read: "Shake off the earth which is in your flesh;

you are Horus in his egg" (Hornung, 1979, 348). Or, Rubric 85: "I am the
Heightened, the Lord of the Ta-Tebu; my name is the Boy in the Place, the
Child in the Field" (Hornung, 1979, 174). Or: "I am yesterday. My name is
He Who Has Seen Millions of Years…. I am the Lord of Eternity…. I am the
one in the Udjat Eye, and I am the one in the egg…with it life is given to me."
(Hornung, 1979, 115) Or: "I enter the world from which I emerged, after
having counted (renewed) my first birth" (Hornung, 1972, 325). It is true
that this last rubric concerns the sun god, but every dead person repeats the
fate of the god and, like the sun, is reborn as child and hatched out as a bird.

To date I have heard only once of such a birth motif in the dream of a
dying person. This was the case of a seventy-four-year-old woman who died
from carcinoma metastases. She had the dream just two weeks before her
death. She had been very ill the day before, yet she made much seemingly
futile effort to bring some order into her outer affairs. As a result, she
developed painful stomach cramps, after which she dreamed:

> She was lying across the opening of a cement pipe about one meter wide,
> whose upper edge pressed painfully against her stomach. The pipe itself
> was stuck into the earth. She knew that she had to emerge from it head-
> first and intact into another land.

Upon awakening, her association for the "other land" was a "land of dwarfs
and spirits" of which she had previously dreamed.

The later dream seems to me to express the following: The pipe appears as
a birth passage into another existence. The dreamer was supposed to go
through it head first, like an infant when it is being born. For the moment,
however, she lies across it, because she is still engaged with the concerns of
this world and resists the dark passage. The land into which she is supposed to
be born is the "land of dwarfs and spirits"—psychological language for the
collective unconscious, which indeed has always been and still is "under" our
world of consciousness, even when we do not notice it.

The physicians Raymond Moody (1976, 1978) and Michael Sabom (1982)
and the theologian Johann Christoph Hampe (1975) report similar "passage"
motifs in their respective works (Lindley, 1981). They deal with cases of heart
failure, after which the patients were "brought back to life" artificially. Most
of these patients describe their experience as one of being in a very happy
state, but quite often some of them had first to go through something
resembling a short blackout (Hampe, 1975, 52–57) or through a dark valley
or tunnel before they could arrive at a new state of existence. A clinically
dead woman who was reanimated by means of an adrenalin injection
described her experience in the following terms:

I was floating in a long tunnel, which at first seemed quite narrow, then became wider and wider. It was dark red over me and blue-black in front of me. However, the higher I looked the brighter it became. The feeling of weightlessness was wonderful. (Hampe, 1975, 83)

Another case:

I found myself again inside a dark spiral-shaped tunnel. At the far end of the tunnel, which was very narrow, I saw a bright light. (Hampe, 89)

When obliged to return to life by medical treatment, some of these patients reported that they had to come back through the same tunnel by which they departed.

THE PASSAGE THROUGH FIRE AND WATER

In the Isis procession described at end of the *Metamorphoses*, Apuleius tells us that the most holy object carried in the procession was a vessel full of Nile water. This is the previously mentioned Osiris Hydreios, a new symbol which appeared in Graeco-Roman Egypt (first century A.D.). It represented a kind of matrix out of which the dead would be reborn and presumably, at the same time, an image of the goddess Isis, who begets the dead once again. The vessel contains water from the Nile, from that primal water, Nun, out of which, according to the Egyptian view, all the gods emerged at the creation of the universe. As Nun, the primal waters from which all creation emerged, this water, which is also fire, is, in addition, a symbol of the collective unconscious. It would then figure as a matrix of images and symbolic insights, whereas fire would be more representative of its emotional quality (Lauf, 1974, 95).

Both of these aspects of the unconscious appear in death experiences reported by Moody and Hampe. In describing their experiences, the patients were often overcome by profound emotions of bliss or of suffering. They emphasized time after time that they were unable to find words to describe their feelings adequately. They experienced an inexpressible emotion (fire).

On the other hand, these experiences often depict a kind of *flowing* of light, colors, images, souls, which are not clearly discernible in detail. They have a greater resemblance to the water aspect of the unconscious:

A woman goes first through a tunnel: "I had to search for my escort somewhere in there, where the dark blue grew toward me from the opening of this tunnel. The hum became brighter and more beautiful. The colors, too, became clearer and then to fall apart again like the colors in a bouquet. Every color had a sound. And all those colors and sounds together produced a wonderful music which filled me and drew me forward." (Hampe, 83)

Or:

More and more I became enveloped in a magnificent blue sky with pink clouds and soft violet sounds. I floated along in this ideal atmosphere, smoothly and painlessly. (Hampe, 85)

Or:

In an unconscious state I saw in front of me pictures of myself in which all of the colors of the rainbow ran into one another. (Hampe, 91)

This streaming element is apparently met with very frequently in near-death experiences. It corresponds to the water aspect of the unconscious. Hindu burials, in which the ashes of the dead are scattered in the Ganges, or the Balinese custom of taking the ashes out to sea in a boat and scattering them there, express symbolically the idea of a redeeming dissolution, of a return to the primal ocean. At the same time, the symbolism represents the water aspect of the unconscious, something in which "the images of creation" float, somehow more beautiful and intense than in a dream, but even less comprehensible.

THE SHIFTING EGO-IDENTITY, MULTIPLE SOULS, AND THEIR FIXATION IN THE FRUIT

When one compares the near-death and dying experiences published by Moody, Osis, Hampe, and Sabom, one notices that the factors of ego and ego consciousness are often strangely shifting. In many accounts the survivor relates his entire experience from the ego point of view, that of an ego which seems to be equivalent to the normal ego of everyday life. This everyday ego is then confronted with a "voice" or with an "inner friend," who in Jungian psychology would be interpreted as a personification of the Self.

In some instances the everyday ego seems also to merge partially somehow with this Self being. Moody cites the case of a man who first met the "being of light" in a deep coma (caused by bronchial asthma): "It was just a ball of light, almost like a globe, and it was not very large, I would say no more than twelve to fifteen inches in diameter" (Moody, 1975, 102). A hand, reaching out to him, invited him to come along so that he himself floated aloft and then moved with the light being here and there in the hospital room. "Now, immediately, when I had joined him…and had become a spirit myself, in a way we had been fused into one. We were two separate ones, too, of course.

Yet, he had full control of everything that was going on as far as I was concerned" (Moody, 1976, 104). An intimate association between ego and Self is described here *but not a complete merging of the two.*

In another report the everyday ego is so greatly altered that it closely resembles the Self:

> My new ego was no longer the old familiar ego, but rather a sublimate of it, as it were, even if it did seem to me somehow familiar, like something I had always known but which had been deeply buried under a super-structure of fears, hopes, wishes and desires. This ego had nothing to do with the ego of this world. It was a spirit, absolute, unchangeable, indivis-ible, indestructible. Although absolutely unique, as individual as a finger-print, it was at the same time part of an infinite, well ordered whole. (Hampe, 92 f.)

The two aspects, ego and Self, are almost completely united here, but the ego feeling remains *part* of a larger whole; it is not the whole itself. In his visions on the brink of death, Jung describes a similar change in his everyday ego:

> I had the feeling that everything was being sloughed away; everything I aimed at or wished for or thought, the whole phantasmagoria of earthly existence, fell away or was stripped from me—an extremely painful process. Nevertheless something remained; it was as if I now carried along with me everything I had ever experienced or done, everything that had happened around me. I might also say: it was with me, and I was it. I con-sisted of all that, so to speak. I consisted of my own history, and I felt with great certainty: this is what I am. "I am this bundle of what has been, and what has been accomplished."
>
> This experience gave me a feeling of extreme poverty, but at the same time of great fullness. There was no longer anything I wanted or desired. I existed in an objective form; I was what I had been and lived. At first the sense of annihilation predominated, of having been shipped or pil-laged; but suddenly that became of no consequence. Everything seemed to be past, what remained was a *fait accompli*, without reference back to what had been. There was no longer any regret that something had dropped away or been taken away. On the contrary: I had everything that I was, and that was everything. (Jung, 1961, 290 f.)

Jung's altered, "objective" ego, which had "everything that (it) was," reminds one of Simon Magus' idea of that "fruit" of the life-tree which survives the destruction of the tree. This new ego seems to be a kind of lived quintessence, which at the same time is also a termination of life. Buddhism also teaches that our experiences and actions are transformed into "grain" which represents the "fruit of our deeds." This grain survives in an after-death dimension (Gaskell, 157). In the previously cited passage from Simon Magus, the fruit of the world-tree which survives death is God's image in the human soul—the Self, in Jungian language. The immortal *doppelgänger* in man is also referred to in the Persian religion as a fruit of man's lived faith. And finally the motif of the fruit also appears in modern dreams. The psychotherapist Liliane Frey relates a dream which illustrates this motif. It is the case of a dying eighty-year-old man who entertained doubts in consciousness about survival after death.

Then shortly before he died he dreamed:

> A sick old plum tree unexpectedly bears a lot of fruit on one of its branch-
> es. At the edge of one bough there are even two golden plums. Full of joy,
> I show this miracle to my daughter and to my son. (Frey-Rohn, 1980, 34)

In alchemy the lapis is often described as the fruit of the sun tree and the moon tree, a final transfiguration of the life that has been lived and which is represented by the tree itself. This fruit or end result even seems capable of continuing to have effects in the collective unconscious. Thus a man who had suffered a great deal in his professional life dreamed a short time before his death:

> A voice speaking in an oriental language says to me: "Your work and your
> life, which you have endured consciously, have redeemed hundreds in
> your generation and will have an illuminating influence upon hundreds
> of generation to come." (Frey-Rhon, 34)

This dream seems to answer a question which is often of concern to any reflective person: Why must highly valuable "important" people often go unnoticed and unappreciated by the public at large and suffer thereby throughout their lives, whereas heartless, empty-headed individuals are praised by almost everyone? According to this dream, there exists an invisible compensation. Suffering and pain which are *consciously* lived often seem to have their own rewards—their fruit—but often only in the Beyond, as is indeed emphasized in Christian teaching. The difference, however, is that in the dream the image is not that of reward or punishment but of something more objective. Consciously lived suffering has a redeeming effect on the past and on the future of mankind, an effect which is exerted invisibly from the Beyond (from the collective unconscious). To understand this, however, is surely the highest reward which an individual may expect from life. In this connection, Edinger reports an impressive dream of a person fated soon to die:

> I have been set a task nearly too difficult for me. A log of hard and heavy wood lies covered in the forest. I must uncover it, saw or hew from it a circular piece, and then carve through the piece a design. The result is to be preserved at all cost, as representing something no longer recurring and in danger of being lost. At the same time, a tape recording is to be made describing in detail what it is, what it represents, its whole meaning. At the end, the thing itself and the tape are to be given to the public library. Someone says that only the library will know how to prevent the tape from deteriorating within five years. (Edinger, 1972, 218)

As Edinger interprets it, this object is a unique quintessence—the goal and completion of physical existence. This quintessence is to be deposited as a permanent increment to a collective or transpersonal library as a kind of "spirit treasury." In an astonishing way this resembles Simon Magus' idea of a "heavenly barn" into which the "fruit" is brought.

This fruit in the Beyond is often described as the philosopher's stone, as gold fruit, diamond body, etc., that is, as something static, completed, whereas ego consciousness, which is still living in time, experiences itself more as a "flow" of representations. In Jung's report, what seems to drop away from the everyday ego is the hoping, wishing, desiring, fearing, etc., that is, the affective emotional relation to the future; what remains is only that which was and is. This wishing, fearing, desiring, etc. seems to have its source in Geddee's B-consciousness, which appears to be closely related to the somatic realm.

Another of Moody's cases describes the relation of the "purified ego" to the Self (the being of light) in the following way: "When my heart stopped beating...I felt like I was a round ball and almost maybe like I might have been a little sphere—like a B-B—on the inside of this round ball. I just can't describe. it to you" (Moody, 1976, 49). This is an especially striking image, for it seems to describe the "correct" relation of the ego to the Self, that is, the ego is a part of the whole and is at the same time one with the whole. It is just this relation between ego and Self which Jungian depth psychology attempts to establish in every analysand during his or her lifetime (Jung, 1963, par. 129). For if the ego identifies with the Self, then it suffers an inflation. If it goes too far away from the Self, then it sinks into "wishing, hoping, fearing and desiring" and loses itself in the world. The above examples illustrate the strange and paradoxical relation between the purified ego and the Self. Sometimes the ego is described as identical with the Self, at other times as separate or as a smaller ball united with a larger one. As long as the everyday ego is not purified, it experiences itself as distinctly separate from the Self, whereas when it is completed it becomes to a large extent identical with the Self; however, the ego awareness which is necessary for the perception of the Self seems thereby not to cease. The ego, says Jung,

> is an essential part of the self, and can be used *pars pro toto* when the significance of consciousness is borne in mind. But when we want to lay emphasis on the psychic totality it is better to use the term "self." There is no question of a contradictory definition, but merely of a difference of standpoint. (Jung, 1963, par.133)

The image of the relation between ego and Self as a smaller ball within a larger one is beautifully represented in the above pre-death vision.

FINAL RESURRECTION AS A REUNION OF THE PSYCHE WITH THE BODY

In Egypt…the mummy was called an "image." The earth god Aker guards the "great image," but at the same time the mummy is a "mystery," because it is precisely on or in it that the transformation process begins anew. The *ka*—with the qualities the Romans attributed to the *genius*—remains close to the mummy or to a statue of the deceased, whereas the *ba* is also able to accompany the sun god in the upper world on his journey across the sky or joins the "never setting" circumpolar stars. In the Komarios text, which is undoubtedly based on Egyptian ideas, pneuma, psyche and soma are once again united. Pneuma most probably refers to the *ba* and psyche to the *ka*. Admittedly, one should not take such "translations" too literally, for even with the Greeks and Egyptians themselves these terms were applied to vague and flexible concepts. The third element in the Komarios text is the purified body, clothed in glory *(doxa)*, which is the mummy after its reanimation through pneuma and psyche. This whole, newly animated corpse is also what the Egyptian texts often called the *ach*, the transfigured one.

Transfiguration is also described as the acquisition of a garment of light. In the Egyptian Book of Am-Tuat, Re says to the mummy gods in the eighth hour: "You are ornamented with your clothing, you are protected by your garments." And in the Book of Gates, the reanimated mummies are addressed: "Hail to you, Achu (transfigured, blessed dead)…hail to you, underworld ones…. May you shine through your (white!) garments, may you be bright in the brilliance of Re." In the Book of Caves, it is said that mummies are "dressed in the form of Osiris," (Hornung, 1972, 204, 263, 330–33) in the same way that the Komarios text speaks of the body of the dead as being decorated "with divine glory" *(doxa)*.

This motif of the *doxa* seems to me to point not only to Egyptian tradition but even more to the influence of Persian ideas, possibly through the mediation of Gnostic sources. The *doxa* reminds one of the Persian *xvarnah* which comes to meet the newly deceased and which is variously called "light of glory," a "victory," a "victorious fire." In the Mithraic cult this light-glory also meant the fulfillment of individual fate. It illuminates the dead, along with his *daena*—his other-worldly anima (cf. Corbin, 37f). This *imago gloriae* "envelops" the entire soul of the dying man, like a "shining illumination by a spiritual fire which inflames the soul to ardor"; it is at the same time the light of healing knowledge. This same image is to be found in the Gnostic Acts of Thomas.

After the reunion, continues the Komarios text, the house was sealed and "the statue was erected, filled with light and divinity." This probably refers to the end of the Egyptian burial ceremony, when the grave chamber is sealed and the so-called *djed* pillar is erected, along with the statue of the dead, in the *serdab*. The statue *(andrias)* is also called *eikon*, "image." It consists of the four elements that have been united as one and it is also a medicine (elixir) which penetrates everything and is, at the same time, something solid.

The homunculus-priest who, in the visions of Zosimos, first tears himself to pieces is transformed eventually into a "man of gold." The text continues:

> In short, my friend, build a temple from a single stone, like to white lead, to alabaster, to Proconnesian marble[1] with neither end nor beginning in its construction. Let it have within it a spring of the purest water, sparkling like the sun.... A dragon lies at the entrance, guarding the temple. Lay hold upon him; immolate him first; strip him of his skin and, taking his flesh with the bones, separate the limbs; then, laying (the flesh of the limbs) together with the bones at the entrance of the temple, make a step of them, mount thereon, and enter, and you will find what you seek. The priest, that brazen man, whom you see seated in the spring and composing the substance, (look on) him not as the brazen man, for he has changed the colour of his nature and has become the silver man; and if you will, you will soon have him (as) the golden man. (Jung, 1953, par. 87)

In the same text it is also said of the homunculus-priest that "he makes the eyes clairvoyant, and raises the dead" (Jung, 1953, par. 86). The dismembering (and, in variants, the cooking) of the initial substance is also explicitly described as *taricheia* (mummification) (Jung, 1953, pars. 91ff.). The sacrifice of the dragon is in some variants also a sacrifice of the priest himself. In the alchemical view, he represents the microcosmos or the *monas*, the initial matter, which also contains the goal of the work. His dismemberment signifies a new conscious ordering of his initial chaotic nature (cf. Jung, 1953, par. 118).

Important for us here is the monolithic temple, the temple built of a single stone, in which there springs a fountain of life, and "this is a hint that the production of the round wholeness, the stone, is a guarantee of vitality.

Similarly, the light that shines within it can be understood as the illumination which wholeness brings. Enlightenment is an increase of consciousness" (Jung, 1953, par. 112). The golden man sitting on the stone represents the inner man who has gradually become the highest value. (Jung, 1953, pars. 118–19).

*****

What the stone might mean to the postmortal condition can also be seen in a vision which Jung reports in his memoirs. In a near-death experience he seemed to be floating over the earth from a height of "approximately a thousand miles!" As he gazed around him he saw "a tremendous dark block of stone, like a meteorite…floating in space." Near an entrance in the stone sat a black Hindu who seemed to expect him. "Tiny niches" with "small burning wicks surrounded the door" (Jung, 1961, 290). Jung felt certain that he "was about to enter an illuminated room and would meet there all those people to whom (he belonged) in reality." There he would also understand what "historical nexus" his life fitted into. "I would know what had been before me, why I had come into being, and where my life was flowing" (Jung, 1961, 291). At that moment he was called back to earth by the emerging image of his doctor.

The same stone, although in somewhat different form, appeared to Jung a second time a few days before his actual death. It was the last dream he was able to communicate:

> He saw a great round stone in a high place, a barren square, and on it were engraved the words: "And this shall be a sign unto you of Wholeness and Oneness." Then he saw many vessels to the right in an open square and a quadrangle of trees whose roots reached around the earth and enveloped him and among the roots golden threads were glittering. (von Franz, 1975, 287)

JUNG'S NEW HYPOTHESIS

The image of light appears more often than any other image in our quoted material. Jung has expressed the assumption that psychic reality might lie on a supraluminous level of frequency, that is, it could exceed the speed of light. "Light," in this case, would appropriately enough be the last transitional phenomenon of the process of becoming unobservable, before the psyche fully "irrealizes" the body, as Jung puts it, and its first appearance after it incarnates itself in the space-time continuum by shifting its energy to a lower gear. In addition to Moody's witnesses cited earlier, one also finds with him, and especially in the familiar parapsychological literature, numerous reports of such light phenomena accompanying death or connected with ghosts. A dream reported by John Sanford illustrates Jung's hypothesis most graphically. It is the dream of a Protestant clergyman, dreamed a few days before his death:

> ...he sees the clock on the mantlepiece; the hands have been moving, but now as they stop, a window opens behind the mantlepiece clock and a bright light shines through. The opening widens into a door and the light becomes a brilliant path. He walks out on the path of light and disappears. (Sanford, 1968, 60)

NOTE

1. "The island of Prokonessos was the site of the famous Greek marble quarry, now called Marmara (Turkey)" (Jung, *Alchemical Studies*, par. 87, fn.14).

REFERENCES

Berthelot, Marcillin. "Instructions of Cleopatra by the Archpriest Komairos." *Collection des anciens alchimistes grecs.* Paris. 3 Vols. pp. 187–88. See C. G. Jung. *Collected Works.* Vols. 12, 13 & 14.)

Corbin, Henri. (1977). *Spiritual Body and Celestial Earth: From Mazdean Iran to Shi'ite Iran.* (Nancy Pearson, trans.). (Bollingen Series XCI:2). Princeton: Princeton University Press.

Edinger, Edward. (1972). *Ego and Archetype: Individuation and the Religious Function of the Psyche.* New York: Putnam's Sons, for the C. G. Jung Foundation.

Franz, Marie-Louise von. (1975). *C. G. Jung: His Myth in Our Time* (Willam Kennedy, trans.). New York: Putnam's Sons, for the C. G. Jung Foundation.

Franz, Marie-Louise von, Liliane Frey-Rohn, and Aniela Jaffé. (1980). *Im Unkreis des Todes.* Zurich: Daimon.

Frey-Rohn, Liliane. (1980). Sterbeerfahrungen psychologisch beluchtet. In Marie-Louise von Franz, et.al., eds. *Im Umkreis des Todes.* Zurich: Daimon. pp. 29–95.

Gaskell, G. A. (1960). *A Dictionary of All Scriptures and Myths.* New York: Julian Press.

Hampe, Johann Christoph. (1975). *Sterben is doch ganz anders: Erfahrungen mit dem eigenen Tod.* Berlin: Kreuz Verlag.

Hornung, Erik, ed. (1972). *Aegyptische Unterweltsbücher.* Zurich/Munich: Artemis.

Hornung, Erik, ed. (1979). *Das Totenbuch der Aegypter.* Zurich/Munich: Artemis.

I Ching, or the Book of Changes. (1950). The German translation by Richard Wilhelm rendered into English by Cary Baynes. 2 vols. (Bollingen Series XIX). New York: Pantheon Books.

Jung. C. G. (1953). *Psychology and Alchemy. Collected Works.* Vol. 12. Princeton: Princeton University Press.

Jung.C. G. (1961). *Memories, Dreams, Reflections.* Recorded and edited by Aniela Jaffé. (Trans. R. and C. Winston). New York: Pantheon Books.

Jung, C. G. (1963). *Letters.* Vol. 1: 1906–1950. Princeton: Princeton University Press.

Jung, C. G. (1963). *Mysterium Coniunctionis. Collected Works,* Vol. 14. Princeton: Princeton University Press.

Jung. C. G. (1967). *Alchemical Studies. Collected Works,* Vol. 13. Princeton: Princeton University Press.

Lauf, Detlef Ingo. (1974). *Leben nach dem sterben.* (A. Rosenberg, ed.). Munich: Kosel Verlag.
Linley, J. (1981, December). Near-Death Experiences. *Anabiosis, The Journal for Near-Death Studies, 1.*
Moody, Raymond. (1975). *Life After Life.* New York: Mockingbird/Bantam Books.
Moody, Raymond. (1978). *Reflections on Life After Life.* New York: Bantam Books.
Sabom, Michael B. (1982). *Recollections of Death: A Medical Investigation.* New York: Harper and Row.
Sanford, John A. (1968). *Dreams: God's Forgotten Language.* Philadelphia/New York: Lippincott.
Von Franz, Marie-Louise. (1975). C. G. *Jung: His Myth in Our Time.* New York: Pantheon.

·⁓ **9** ⁓·

The Archetype of Death and Enlightenment

Michael Grosso

What we call death is archetypally portrayed as the road to a greater and more fulfilling reality than what we know in life.

Michael Grosso, Ph.D., is a philosopher who presents the case that Carl Jung's theory of archetypes is especially helpful in understanding near-death experiences. Grosso sets archetypal theory in a philosophical context that preserves the meaningfulness of NDEs, in contrast with interpretations that reduce them to hallucinations. Archetypal theory, he says, helps one cope with death out of the deep resources of the archetypal Self, which parallels the God-image within. Grosso proposes a specific archetype of transformation at death, which he calls the archetype of Death and Enlightenment. This underlying dynamic, he says, has the advantage of being consistent with several important aspects of the NDE: the neurological, the psychodynamic, the paranormal, and the religious.

Jung's theory of archetypes includes unconscious, collective primordial images that are the psychic end on a continuum with biological instincts at the other end. Archetypal theory sees the world's religious imagery and mystical experiences through universal archetypal images such as God, the Light, the mandala, the wise woman/man, and the treasure. When such images appear in near-death experiences, they echo archetypal themes from around the world.

Michael Grosso, Ph.D., teaches Philosophy and the Humanities at Jersey City State College. His books include *Final Choice* (1985), *Frontiers of the Soul* (1992), *Soulmaker* (1992), and *Millenium Myth: Love and Death at the End of Time.* (1995).

The Archetype of Death and Enlightenment

*A man should be able to say he has done his best to form
a conception of life after death, or to create some image of
it—even if he must confess his failure. Not to have done so
is a vital loss.*

— C. G. Jung

What difference does the near-death experience (NDE) make
to our life here and now? What I attempt to show here is that
near-death experiences point to a deep inner resource for
coping with death. Carl Jung's theory of archetypes seems
especially helpful in trying to articulate the nature of this
resource. I feel, in fact, that near-death data suggest the
existence of a specific archetype associated with death and
dying. I call this the *archetype of death and enlightenment*.

Let us begin by reminding ourselves that NDEs are
primarily mental images experienced on the threshold of
death. What kind of mental images are they? What is their
function? What do they mean? What are their aftereffects?
What, if anything, do they tell us about the objective world
and our relationship to death? Are they of any special use in
bringing a healing vision of death into focus?

What follows is an attempt to answer these questions in
the light of Carl Jung's theory of archetypes. It develops a
transpersonal paradigm of NDEs that I believe is useful for
the following reasons:

(1) To begin with, NDEs are themselves evidence for the
    theory of archetypes, the universal patterns of imagery,
    affect and behavior, the unconscious, collective, psychic
    instincts central to Jungian theory.
(2) The theory respects the intrinsic value of the near-death
    experience, especially the sense of tremendous mean-
    ingfulness, of having encountered a supremely important

reality. It is true that not all NDEs are tremendously meaningful; more-over, the NDE may be a complex phenomenon with multicausal ori-gins. Nevertheless, the impact on those who have the core near-death experience is usually quite powerful. By contrast, reductionistic theo-ries tend to devalue and derealize the intrinsic NDE by categorizing it as hallucinatory, illusory, or epiphenomenal.

(3) The archetype theory is compatible with what psychiatrist Bruce Greyson has called a "normal neurophysiological adaptive response." For instance, evidence for temporal-limbic activity or endorphin release would be compatible with the idea that NDEs activate archetypal psychic contents. In general, the notion of archetypes, as developed by Jung, is in tune with the biological perspective; although he never fully developed his thinking here, Jung saw the archetypal layer of the human unconscious as organically adaptive.

(4) The present view complies with another point made by Greyson: the need for a psychodynamic interpretation of near-death phenomena. However, there is a crucial addition: Jungian psychodynamics posits a transpersonal level of psychic reality, the level of the "collective" unconscious.

(5) The theory, unlike many psychodynamic theories, is compatible with the paranormal elements often reported in near-death research. The fifth point is linked to the fourth. The transpersonal level of psychic reality works relatively free from the constraints of time and space, which is another way of talking about the paranormal.

(6) The archetype theory is consistent with the idea that human consciousness survives bodily death.

The theory of archetypes enables us to view NDEs as evidence for a general psychic function associated with the dying process. This function I call the archetype of death and enlightenment (ADE). As Jung knew from clinical experience, "modern man"—solitary, anxious, driven, traditionless and spiritually uprooted—has lost touch with the healing symbols and energies for coping with death. The NDE is a clue to rediscovering the healing force within, the living answer in our own psyches to the riddle of death.

THE ARCHETYPAL NATURE OF NEAR-DEATH EXPERIENCES

The nature and origin of "archetypes" is obscure and controversial. Jung was not a philosopher, a fact he often stressed with relish, and so he was never systematic. Like Freud and Plato, his thought was always in process; there is a seminal ambiguity in his writings. Let us then just try for a good working definition of the archetype; we will illustrate its nuances by means of the NDE itself.

Archetype, primordial image, psychic dominant—Jung used these terms to refer to a dynamic, organizing psychic content, a center of psychic energy, that forms part of the ground plan of the human mind. There are similarities to the Platonic Form and to the Kantian categories. Jung sometimes thought of the archetype as a psychic equivalent to the biological concept of instinct. The similarity lies in the *a priori* and nonpersonal derivation of these concepts, their regulative and ordering function on human experience. Jung repudiates the Lockean notion of the mind as a *tabula rasa*, a blank slate upon which historical and cultural contingencies can write their own arbitrary dictates. People, in short, have an inner destiny; a principle of self-development presides over human fate. The archetypes, viewed as an organic psychic system, guide the development of the human soul.

Archetypes comprise the collective unconscious. Jung distinguishes between the "archetype as such" and its particular psychic manifestation in images, as in dream or myth. Let us now look in detail at the archetypal aspects of the near-death experience.

ARCHETYPES AND TYPICAL SITUATIONS

"There are as many archetypes as there are typical situations in life… [They represent] merely the possibility of a certain type of perception and action," wrote Jung (1971). Dying is one of the typical situations of life; it would therefore be surprising if there were no archetype related to dying. The archetypes express the great forms and residues of the human condition, the permanent impulses, conditions and tendencies that belong to humanity at large: womanhood, childhood, heroism, wisdom, the dark side of the human soul, birth, death, rebirth, and so on. We can hardly suppose a more permanent and fateful condition that imposes itself on human life than death. Now, just as more primitive organisms are fitted with means to assist in birth, growth and adaptation, so, I believe, evolution has fitted the human organism with means for adapting to the stage of development called death.

The archetype is a psychic dynamism that cannot be traced to the subject's personal history. Neither can the prototypical NDE be traced to the subject's personal history. Researchers are generally impressed by the common patterns of the experience; typical features occur independently of personal variables such as age, sex, education, religion and culture. Apparently, a pattern of images and feelings occurs to people on the verge of death with striking regularity. It is hard to avoid the conclusion that the NDE pattern is, so to speak, "built in" to the deep psyche.

This seems especially so when subjects are children. In one account, particularly intriguing from a Jungian viewpoint, a seven-year-old girl, deathly ill, heard a chorus of heavenly voices, experienced peace, went out of her body, met beings who sparkled like stars in her room, and sailed through a dark tunnel at the end of which she saw a robed Christlike figure. Children, even much younger than this seven-year-old, envisioned similar archetypal near-death scenarios. It seems unlikely that these images were based on personal history, on the personal unconscious or on anything learned. They seem more like crystallizations of a "preformed faculty" of their minds.

FLUIDITY AND INEFFABILITY OF THE ARCHETYPE

The archetypes, according to Jung, "appear under an almost infinite variety of aspects." "A kind of fluid interpretation belongs to the very nature of the archetype," he said, and further, "no archetype can be reduced to a formula...but they change their shape continually." This is somewhat overstated since, if there were no continuity of form at all, there would be no way to talk of the Shadow, the Wise Old Man, the Anima, and so on. Still, there is a point in stressing that fixed labels are pale reminders of the richness of the archetypal experience. The often reported ineffability of the NDE comes, therefore, as no surprise.

Archetypes mark a point of meeting between the personal and the collective experience of humankind. They are charged with a surplus of meanings and associations; they reverberate with human memories, nostalgias and aspirations. Truly to evoke these images, resonant with the passions of the human race, would take the poetic genius of a Dante or a Blake. No wonder the ordinary person returns from the NDE stammering hyperboles.

AN ARCHETYPE OF TRANSFORMATION

Jung spoke of a category of archetype that, in addition to personified imagery (the Trickster, the Child, the Hero, etc.), consists of "typical situations, places, ways and means...." These he called archetypes of transformation. If the NDE is anything, it is surely an archetype of transformation; for death, symbolically and in fact, is certainly a dramatic case of transformation.

The term *archetype* does not here denote a single thing or a simple, static formula; it is shorthand for a constellation of recurrent, though fluid, motifs. We find not one thing but a family of psychic processes. In the near-death experience we find personifications, guides, light-beings, deceased relatives, religious and mythical figures, voices and presences. We also observe situations, ways and places, such as coming to a border, beholding heavenly (and sometimes infernal) landscapes and cities, hearing the music of the spheres, passing through tunnels, cones, whorls, caves, soaring through darkness into the light, having prophetic visions of global catastrophe and a new age. The common thread of the various elements of the near-death archetype is the theme of transformation.

The archetypes of the collective unconscious express themselves through spontaneous sources: dreams, "active imagination," trance states, fantasy, psychotic delusions, dreams of early childhood and so forth. A weakening of ordi-nary waking consciousness is a condition for their appearance; clearly, being near-death drastically weakens ordinary consciousness and so is likely to give rise to archetypal motifs. The millions of near-death experiences, the sponta-neous uniformity and universality of the imagery, the profound similarity in the aftereffects, provide a mass of primary evidence for the reality of the archetype of death and enlightenment in the collective unconscious.

THE AUTONOMY OF THE ARCHETYPES

Archetypes behave autonomously; they have a life of their own and "come upon us like fate." This tallies with the near-death experience in which the figures, the messengers from beyond, have a life of their own. They come like fate, apart from religious beliefs and expectations, although, once the visions intrude, their interpretation is conditioned by prior religious beliefs.

The autonomy of near-death archetypes is illustrated in the "no-consent" cases (otherworldly messengers who impose their wills on dying subjects) and the "hellish" visitants reported in NDEs. Osis and Haraldsson cite the case of an avowed atheist who had a deathbed vision of Christ. According to the theory of archetypes, dominants of the collective unconscious are activated to compensate for the one-sided attitudes of the conscious mind. So atheism would be an extreme state of one-sidedness and alienation from the powers of the unconscious. A vision of Christ might well occur to such an atheist.

On the other hand, most NDErs in America who have a vision of Christ are Christians. Yet even here, there is support for the autonomy of the near-death imagery. The literature is full of accounts of dying people whose visions conflicted with their conventional expectations. For instance, they expected to see angels with wings, but instead saw transfigured beings in human form. Further, we have little information about the depth of religious belief in most NDErs. Weak, merely nominal Christians would need to compensate for their spiritual needs as much perhaps as atheists. In either case, atheist or faithful Christian, dying is an extreme situation, and one is liable to fall back upon the resources of the collective treasure trove. Archetypes, like NDEs, just happen, in spite of, and even because of, the limitations of the personal ego. The archetypes of the near-death experience are harbingers of the Self that is greater than the personal ego.

According to Jung (1959), Christ is the chief symbol of the archetype of the Self in the Western world. The Self is the totality of the psyche, realized, symbolically, in the death and crucifixion of Christ. In the near-death experiences of modern Westerners, there are frequent reports of visions of Christ. Often, however, what is actually "seen" is a pure light, a content without form; the Christ-form is usually projected onto this pure light.

The psychological significance of the eruption of the Self-archetype is that wholeness, symbolized by Christ, is won through "crucifixion," through death. Wholeness means welding together opposing forces, somehow taking in pain, evil, darkness and helplessness, all that we consciously dread and wish to avoid. The epiphany of the Christ-image in the midst of being near-death is a living message from the death of our Selves; it boldly declares that there is hope of renewed being in the menace of nonbeing. The near-death experience, against the dictates of everyday reasonableness, hints of a much fuller potential for coping with death. It encourages us to trust in the power of life to transcend death.

The phenomenology of near-death experiences displays different symbols for the archetype of the Self. Among Christians, Christ is the chief symbol; even atheists (in a Christian culture) or persons who only experience the light without form, project the Christ image or interpretation. In the cross-cultural studies of Osis and Haraldsson, Hindu religious figures were "seen" during NDEs. In Carl Becker's study of NDEs and Pure Land Buddhism, deathbed visions of the Buddha were reported. The basic function of the near-death archetype appears to be constant, although the contents vary, depending on culture and other personal variables.

"Otherworldly messengers" seem to count as "messengers" from the "other world" of the collective unconscious. Such messengers, or archetypes, proceeding from the "wholly other" regions of the collective mind, bearing their own messages with their own purposes, profoundly affect experiencers. The majesty, the fascination, the power of these emissaries from Mind at Large might indeed be so great as to rob the visionary of his or her most deeply ingrained habit: the habit, the instinct, to live. Nothing provides better testimony of the power of the near-death archetype than this.

THE NUMINOUS AND THE WILL TO LIVE

It often happens that, on the threshold of death, people catch glimpses of something that lures them away from life itself. Like wandering sailors who hear the song of the Sirens and drift toward disaster, those near death hear a strange melody that weakens their grip on life and makes them want to go all the way into the abyss. What could it be that reverses the instinct of self-preservation? So much anxiety is spent in the course of life struggling to fend off death, yet at the verge of death, the struggle sometimes mysteriously subsides, anxiety vanishes and life in the body becomes a reason for regret. That to which we clung so grimly all our lives, now we are ready to discard.

Whatever the true explanation, we might at least be glad that nature has a few secrets up her sleeve and that she knows how to make even the dark god Thanatos so enchantingly irresistible. Perhaps this is done by means of endogenous opiates produced by the brain under the stress of dying. Somewhere in the secret codes of our genes there may be instructions for making dying easy, especially after the struggle for survival ceases. If that code is part of a ground plan that understands, as Hindu scripture does, that everything is food for everything, then there might be provisions for easing individual death, for the benefit of the food chain as a whole. In the ecosystems of life, every death is a sacrifice to the whole; individual death is nutrition for the biosphere.

This is not a view of the NDE that experiencers are likely to fancy. Research shows that "encounters with ostensible messengers from the other world seemed to be so gratifying that the value of this life was easily outweighed" (Osis, Haraldsson, 1977). As bearers of meaning, seeming centers of awareness, the messengers cast a spell on the experiencer. This outweighing of life's value is a prominent feature of NDEs and deathbed visions. Reports are frequent of patients irked, angry or disappointed over being revived. They do not like being torn from a world more vivid and marvelous than ordinary reality. The experience is a blunting of a painful and frightening reality, but a sharpened sense of an alternate reality.

Jung himself had a remarkable near-death experience when he had a heart attack after breaking his foot. "I felt violent reistance to my doctor because he had brought me back to life," he wrote in his autobiography (Jung, 1961). Jung said it took him more than three weeks to make up his mind to live again. He regretted having to return to this "gray world with its boxes." The other world he glimpsed was fuller, not broken up into bits of time and pieces of space. "Although my belief in the world returned to me, I have never since entirely freed myself from the impression that this life is a segment of existence which is enacted in a three-dimensional boxlike universe especially set up for it." It is hard to see this shattering of one's basic sense of reality as caused by a dousing the brain with endorphins. Judging from Jung's and related accounts, the reluctance to return to life is based on the appeal of something positive in itself. The archetypes, as reservoirs of the deepest feelings of the human race, are saturated with numinous power, and might indeed induce a sense of the unimportance of finite life. Jung had a vision of Zeus and Hera in a mystical marriage ceremony during his NDE; his feelings of awe may well have temporarily weakened his will to live (Jung, 1961, "Visions").

THE FEELING OF IMMORTALITY

Closely related to this weakening of the will to live are feelings of immortality. Studies of Ring, Sabom and others show that NDErs undergo a dramatic reduction of the fear of death. The fear of death would decline with feeling immortal. For Jung, this feeling was associated with the non-temporal and non-spatial aspect of the collective unconscious. "The feeling of immortality," Jung wrote, "has its origins in a peculiar feeling of extension in time and space."

NDEs may induce this feeling of extension in space and time, along with the reduction of the fear of death, in at least two ways: first, by activating the archetypes. Archetypes represent points of entry into the world of the collective unconscious. Vivid archetypal experience would enhance the feeling of being extended in time and space.

Jung understood ancient deification rites as group techniques for project-ing archetypal imagery: Dionysos, Persephone, Isis and so on. Using hypnotic suggestion, right-hemisphere languages, sensory overload, psychoactive drugs, trance-dancing and the like, celebrants were led into altered states and exalt-ed visionary encounters. They experienced temporary union with the gods or archetypes, causing the extended sense of immortality.

A second way NDEs might induce feelings of being extended in space and time is by means of the out-of-body experience (OBE). The experience of being extended in space is dramatic and often causes feelings of immortality and reduced death anxiety. The after-effects of such OBEs are often profound and long-lasting. A twenty-eight-year-old woman who nearly died during an emergency caesarean section wrote the following:

> I was in excruciating pain, physically exhausted, and in labor for fifteen hours. Dr. R. said, "I'm sorry, M., I'm going to have to put you to sleep." The next thing I remember was being above the room. I looked down and could see everything and everyone including my body with Dr. R. and two nurses standing over it. I felt terrified and panic-stricken at first, but then the feeling passed. I realized I was very big, I was taking up the whole room. I also felt very, very good. Better than I've ever felt before or since. The feeling was extreme, extreme exhilaration. I felt brilliantly, totally alive—like all my senses were tuned to maximum awareness. I was very interested in what was going on. Dr. R. yelled: "Her pressure is still drop-ping!" The anesthesiologist started squeezing a black rubber ball that was connected to an apparatus over my face. Dr. R. said some numbers I can't remember, and then, "OK, she's stable." My husband was sitting in the corner. He looked scared and had a sad look on his face and tears in his eyes. A nurse was wheeling in a bassinet that squeaked a little. . . .The next thing I can remember was being awakened by the nurses washing me. They said, "You had a girl."

The woman who wrote this account for me adds that people in the room confirmed the accuracy of her out-of-body observations. The result of her experience was to profoundly change her sense of self-identity; she claimed to have discovered she was a spiritual being, an idea previously foreign to her. Her brush with death activated the archetype of death and enlightenment.

THE BIPOLARITY OF ARCHETYPES AND NDES

Collective psychic phenomena also involve extensions in time, which calls to mind another archetypal aspect of NDEs. The Jungian analyst Jolande Jacobi writes of the bipolarity of the archetypes: "Like a Janus head, [the archetype] is turned both 'forwards' and 'backwards,' integrating into a meaningful whole all the possibilities of that which has been and of that which is still to come" (Jacobi, 1974). NDEs furnish ample evidence for this polarity.

First, consider the phenomenon of panoramic memory or flashback. On the threshold of death, subjects often claim to experience their lives passing in review before them. The customary separation of time and space breaks down; past events, beyond the reach of immediate consciousness, are raised from oblivion into an enlarged present. In fact, the idea of a present resonant with the presence of the past gives an empirical model for the idea of eternity.

Poets like Wordsworth, Pound and Eliot, and novelists like Joyce and Proust (following Bergson) made their art a rite for capturing eternity in the forms of time. The image was the vehicle for condensing the fullness and pattern of life into a concentrated presence. It is interesting to see how the medieval philosopher Boethius spoke of eternity in *The Consolation of Philosophy*: it is "one thing," he said, "to live an endless life…and another for the whole of unending life to be embraced all at once as present." The latter, Boethius said, is the mark of the divine mind or, we might say, the collective mind.

The "divine" mind, the divine dimension of our own minds, doesn't survive as a succession of discrete states; it expands its present, penetrates the depth of its own presence. Boethius helps us distinguish between mere survival of bodily death (which by itself says nothing of value or quality) and eternity, which is the plenitude of the present, the psychic fruit of enlightenment. "Eternity," writes Boethius, "is the whole, perfect, and simultaneous possession of endless life." Elsewhere he speaks of the divine being as "in full possession of itself, always present to itself."

These descriptions of eternity figure in Jung's concept of individuation; the individuated being is fully in possession of itself, is present to its past, its conflicts and varied energies subdued and reconciled in a higher harmony. The panoramic disclosure of the total Self in the near-death experience is an empirical model of mystical eternity.

Sartre, by the way, says that the meaning of a life can only be known after it is over; for as long as one is alive, an action may be performed that could change the whole pattern of a life. The near-death experience apparently affords some people a glimpse of "eternity," in other words, the full pattern of their lives, and hence the deepest meanings.

The total pattern, the bipolarity of the archetypes, not only points backward, gathering up moments of the past into the present, but forward, foreshadowing things to come. And in fact there are reports in NDEs of what Ring calls "flashforwards." General future trends are forecasted or there may be specific items of precognition. I might add here that it is a very old belief that people on the threshold of death acquire prophetic powers. Let us call these extensions of time consciousness in the NDE the horozontal axis of the archetype.

There is also a vertical, qualitative axis. Archetypal experiences stretch backwards and forwards in time. They are bipolar in a second way: they have a bright and high side as well as a dark and low one. "Just as all archetypes have a positive, favorable, bright side that points upwards, so also they have one that points downwards, partly negative and unfavorable, partly chthonic…" (Jung, 1967, in Evans-Wentz). The bright, favorable side of the NDE is well known, but there also have been dark, chthonic encounters, perhaps underreported (Rawlings, 1978).

The dark, hellish visions have probably been reported less because they were pushed out of consciousness. Some may have withheld their reports because they don't fit into the widely publicized format. In any case, the Shadow content (devils, lakes of fire and brimstone, etc.) of these frightening visions is patently archetypal. Once we include the negative features, the NDE more clearly resembles the mythical and religious view of the afterlife. See, for instance, Jung's 1967 psychological commentary on the *Tibetan Book of the Dead*. (Evans-Wentz). The stronger this resemblance, the stronger the case for the NDE as archetypal.

METANOIA AND THE NDE

Reduction of the fear of death is only part of a larger pattern of trans-formative NDE after-effects. In cases where this larger pattern is displayed in full, the experience has all the earmarks of a religious conversion. We could describe the full-fledged NDE as an archetypal conversion process. Converts undergo a pervasive change of value and outlook (Flynn, 1983). The Greek word for such a transformation of mind in the New Testament is *metanoia*, and it might be useful to speak of the metanoid component of the NDE. Saint Paul's experience on the road to Damascus, which had some of the classic features of the NDE, is a historically dramatic case in point.

The metanoid component of the NDE is sometimes expressed as unconditional love. In the words of one experiencer: "I would describe this love I encountered in dying as 'unconditional.' It was so powerful, so complete, so forgiving, so all-knowing, so encompassing, it transcended all forms of earthly love." The awakening of this all-encompassing, unearthly love makes the NDE even more paradoxical. Several experiencers have described to me how normal relations were disturbed by their NDE. Customary attachments became an obstacle to further growth. The experience seemed to release a force that disrupted their everyday routines. A new, transpersonal dynamic of love was set in motion. The approach of death doesn't just intensify the need to preserve the old ego; it seems rather to liberate forces that dissolve the ego's ordinary boundaries. The expansive tendency of the near-death process reflects something positive in itself, not merely the ego struggling to defend itself against extinction.

Problems result from releasing this metanoid energy and transforming love. For example, the NDEr returns from an experience that she or he is unable to describe in ordinary language. This puts the experiencer at a disadvantage. Deep NDErs become obsessed with their experiences; they sometimes complain of loneliness and find it hard to adjust to a world that falls short of the perfection glimpsed. They return to ordinary life haunted by a sense of incompleteness, a nostaglia for paradise.

The power of near-death archetypes sometimes touches those who allow themselves to be receptive to experiencers, according to Kenneth Ring, who has spent a good deal of time listening to NDErs. There are analogies for this sort of "direct transmission," "contact high," or "*shaktipat*" in the group dynamics of religious experience. An example of spiritual power (*dynamis*) apparently transmitted by touch is mentioned in Luke:

> And a woman having an issue of blood twelve years, which had spent all her living upon physicians, neither could be healed of any, came behind him, and touched border of his garment; and immediately her issue of blood stanched.... And Jesus said, "Somebody touched me; for I perceive that power (dynamis) is gone out of me." (Luke 8: 43–46)

THE SELF AND THE NEAR-DEATH ARCHETYPE

On the threshold of death, the unprepared ego may for the first time come face to face with its unknown Self. This larger pattern of psychic reality submerged below the threshold of the everyday mind, but making up the fuller potential of our human identity, Jung calls the Self or Objective Psyche. The Self comes upon us from outside, as transcendent; Ring also thinks that the being of light, the voice, the presence experienced during near-death states, is the larger pattern of oneself. "It is not merely a projection of one's personality, however, but one's *total self*, or what in some traditions is called the *higher self*. In this view, the individual personality is but a split-off fragment of the total self with which it is reunited at the point of death" (Ring, 1980).

With regard to his study of alchemy, Jung remarked that "the arche- types have about them a certain effulgence or quasi-consciousness...and numinosity entails luminosity." So powerful are these luminous effects, symbolic and expressive of an extended consciousness, that they seem to stand outside the normal personality. Experiencers therefore tend to believe that the "being of light" is God. "We know that an archetype can break with shattering force into individual life…. It is therefore not surprising that it is called God." Theological speculation aside, the most we might say here is that for the person who has this type of experience, the upper limits of the Self seem to border on the lower limits of the Divine.

In the Western tradition, to claim identity of Self with God is blasphemous. But perhaps in light of what we are learning about the near-death experience, and what Jung believed to be latent in the human psyche, we can understand how some people might be led to identify themselves with God. Jesus was accused of blasphemy because he claimed a special intimacy with the Father (John, 10:33). The Hindu doctrine of the oneness of Atman and Brahman is not shy about asserting this lofty equation. Tibetan Buddhist teachings say that we must recognize that the divine light before which we stand in awe is the Self. The Gnostic and enthusiastic traditions of Christianity, the Sufis and cabbalists of the Islamic and Judaic traditions, drew inspiration, often at great risk, from the well of this Supreme Identity.

The NDE shows that psychological experiences of such power are possible, that claims of the reality of the Divine, even of the Self's identity with the Divine, were bound to occur in history. One can also see how such archetypal experiences would, in some hardy spirits who trusted their own instincts above tradition, form the kernel of a new authority, a new interpretation of reality and a new myth of personal identity.

The encounter with the archetypes has its malevolent side, to be sure. Mix these inner urgencies with ignorance of the universals of spiritual life, spice with envy, intolerance and faction, and it's easy to see how the energies of spiritual transformation often worked their way into the ugly and tragic blunderings of history. Perhaps the study of archetypal psychodynamics might help reduce these misunderstandings by showing that behind the many masks of the gods is the one eternal Self in transformation.

THE ARCHETYPE OF DEATH AND ENLIGHTENMENT

In light of the foregoing, it seems reasonable to suggest that NDEs activate an archetype of the collective unconscious, a constellation of motifs that guides an enlightenment process, a passage toward greater consciousness of our Self. Let us call this constellation the archetype of death and enlightenment (ADE). The NDE is a dramatic expression of the ADE but not the only context in which it appears. Psychological, spiritual, and cultural "near-death" states may bring forth the ADE. Any crisis of transformation, spontaneous or artificial, individual or collective, could stir up these psychic dominants.

Near-death imagery is oriented around the process of becoming a Self. The various images reflect overlapping goals. For example, there is the abstract image of moving from darkness to light, from unconsciousness to consciousness. Light emerging from darkness is a universal symbol. "And the light shines in darkness; and the darkness comprehended it not" (John: 1.5). From the *Bradarankaya Upanishad*: "From non-being lead me to being, from darkness lead me to the light, from death lead me to immortality." In the NDE, the sequence is also from darkness to light. We find a similar sequence in many creation myths: in the *Rig-Veda*, Hesiod's *Theogony*, the Old Testament and the Scandinavian *Eddas*. For Jews, Arabs, Germanic peoples, Celts and many others, day begins with night; darkness precedes the dawning of the light. Light is a primordial image of consciousness; it always rises from the depths of darkness.

Another common near-death image is passage through caves, canals, holes, tunnels and the like, into a clearing. This motif symbolizes birth and rebirth, passage to a new and higher plane of being. The Allegory of the Cave in Plato's *Republic* (Bk. 7) is a landmark in Western philosophy. Enlightenment is portrayed as escape from bondage in a cave into the light of the sun. The cave motif appears again in the Myth of the True Earth in the *Phaedo*. There we find an image of struggle to emerge from the mist and shadow of a false earth, along with the task of learning to endure the light of the true earth. Plato's myths contained some of his deepest insights, the healing truths that modern philosophy has, for the most part, neglected and to which the NDE might hopefully point the way back.

The guides NDErs reportedly meet—deceased persons, otherworldly messengers, light-beings—are personifications of the same theme: of coming to a border, of passage from dark to light, cave to clearing, bondage to release. The guides oversee the transition, the vision of wholeness and knowledge, and the return. They reveal the higher truths, encourage self-assessment, sometimes terrify into humility and prescribe the tasks of the future. The guides deepen the connection between our present and our past and future, between our own lives and those of our ancestors or offspring. Whether the imagery is abstract (dark-light, tunnel-opening) or personal (guide, deceased relative, religious figure), the basic idea is passage from enclosure to disclosure.

The out-of-body motif expresses the same unit of meaning. Going out of the body means exiting the enclosure of embodied existence. The body itself is a cave, hole or tunnel that one escapes from in the near-death experience. Dying, like being born, is a release from enclosure. One thinks of the ancient Orphic formula *soma sema* (the body is a tomb); true life must then be to exit from the body. The symbolism of the NDE throws down a gauntlet before gray common sense and black scientific materialism. Dying, as it appears to the sharp but short-sighted ego, is the ultimate disaster; but before the dream-lit collective psyche, it is the gateway to self-transformation.

The unifying symbol of light is not just symbolic or abstract. The light is an intense, awe-inspiring *experience*. It is brilliant, dazzling, warm, peaceful, elating, vivid and sensuous. It is a pure and formless illumination, and at the same time an aspect of recognizable forms: jewelled cities of light, human figures or "angels" luminously clothed, landscapes bathed in celestial radiance. The light, concrete and abstract, universal and particular, symbolizes the individuated Self, marked by a coincidence of opposites, a fusion of opposing principles and energies. Mircea Eliade, in a study of the experience of the mystic light, wrote: "Experience of the Light signifies primarily a meeting with ultimate reality; that is why one discovers the interior Light when one becomes conscious of the Self (*Atman*) or when one penetrates into the very essence of life and the cosmic elements, or, last of all, at one's death" (Eliade, 1965).

Archetypes are intentional, directed, dynamic. One function of the ADE is to compensate for the ego's onesided view of death. Affectively, this means overcoming the fear of death. Existentially, it means that death promises rebirth, a change in the state of one's being. Cognitively, it signifies an expansion of consciousness. Metaphysically, it points toward a universal, indestructible spiritual reality. The ADE heralds a new mode of being, a new birth. In revealing for the ego a new consciousness of the Self, the ADE rescues death from the curse of meaninglessness. In Jung's words:

> Hence it would seem to be more in accord with the collective psyche of humanity to regard death as the fulfillment of life's meaning and as its goal in the true sense, instead of a mere meaningless cessation. Anyone who cherishes a rationalistic opinion on this score has isolated himself psychologically and stands opposed to his own basic human nature. (Jung, 1978)

In my view, this passage, perhaps more than any other from Jung's writings, is the best possible commentary on the meaning of the near-death experience. But let us not fool ourselves here; the idea that death is somehow the goal of life runs totally counter to the modern outlook. It also runs totally counter to common sense. Nevertheless, this is the symbolic message that emerges from the near-death archetype, echoing the mythic claims of the collective psyche of humanity.

What we call death is archetypally portrayed as the road to a greater and more fulfilling reality than what we know in life. Such a conception implies a Copernican revolution: It places the sun of the objective psyche at the center of spiritual reality, challenging what may be an illusion of the conscious ego—that death is a meaningless cessation.

REFERENCES

Becker, Carl. (1985, Spring). Views from Tibet: NDEs and the Book of the Dead. *Anabiosis 5,1*, 3–20.

Boethius. (1960). *The Consolation of Philosophy.* Indianapolis: Bobbs-Merrill.

Eliade, M. (1965). *The Two and the One.* New York: Harper Torchbooks.

Evans-Wentz, W. Y. Compiler and Translator. (1927/1960). *The Tibetan Book of the Dead.* New York: Oxford University Press.

Flynn, Charles. (1983). Meanings and implications of NDE transformations. *Anabiosis 2.*

Grosso, Michael. (1985). *Final Choice.* Walpole, NH: Stillpoint Publishing.

Grosso, Michael. (1992). *Frontiers of the Soul.* Wheaton, IL: Quest Books.

Grosso, Michael. (1992). *Soulmaker.* Norfolk, VA: Hampton Roads Publishing.

Grosso, Michael. (1995). *Millenium Myth: Love and Death at the End of Time.* Wheaton, IL: Quest Books.

Jacobi, Jolande. (1974). *Complex, Archetype, Symbol in the Psychology of C. G. Jung.* Princeton: Princeton University Press.

Jung, C. G. (1959). *Aion. Collected Works*, Vol. 9ii. Princeton: Princeton University Press.

Jung, C. G. (1961). *Memories, Dreams, Reflections.* New York: Random House.

Jung, C. G. (1971). *The Archetypes of the Collective Unconscious. Collected Works*, Vol. 9i. Princeton: Princeton University Press.

Jung, C. G. (1978) *Structure and Dynamics of the Psyche. Collected Works*, Vol. 8. Princeton: Princeton University Press.

Osis, K., and E. Haraldsson. (1977). *At the Hour of Death.* New York: Avon Books.

Rawlings, M. (1978). *Beyond Death's Door.* New York: Thomas Nelson.

Ring, K. (1980). *Life at Death.* New York: Coward, McCann & Geoghegan.

Sabom, Michael. (1982). *Recollections of Death: A Medical Investigation.* New York: Harper and Row.

Being of Light
Dreaming the Vision Onward

Jenny Yates

> [Jesus] was transfigured before them;
> and his face did shine as the sun, and
> his raiment was white as the light.
> — Matthew 17:2

Dr. Jenny Yates, a Jungian analyst trained in Zurich and a professor of religion, philosophy, and psychology at Wells College, seeks to understand the phenomena of near-death experience through archetypal amplification. She focuses on archetypal parallels to the Being of Light, including resurrection and transfiguration in Christianity, the clear light at death in Tibetan Buddhism, and the female light being Sophia Zoe in Gnosticism. Using dreams as a clue, she amplifies themes such as the mythic task of the legendary Greek female Psyche to take a box to the land of the dead and return, an apt parallel for the near-death journey.

Drawing on her research as a Visiting Associate with Professor Roger Sperry at the California Institute of Technology, Yates suggests the paradigm of parallel processing of image and word roots between the brain hemispheres, noting especially that the etymological root of the "tunnel" through which near-death experiencers pass is "skin." Her research published in *Psyche and the Split Brain* shows that the left hemisphere of our brain sees the actual physical object, whereas the right hemisphere of the brain does not see the thing, but rather reports a phenomenon that shares the same symbolic meaning pattern, which is the basis of Jung's archetypal images.

Jenny Yates, Ph.D., has published *Woman's Transformations: A Psychological Theology* and *Psyche and Split Brain.* She is listed in the *International Who's Who of Women.* Her doctoral dissertation was *Existential Conceptions of Death: Tillich, Heidegger, Rilke.* She chairs the major in Religious Studies, Human Nature, and Values at Wells College in Aurora, New York. She also has a private analytical practice in Ithaca, New York. For 1996–97 she was appointed a Research Fellow at Yale Divinity School.

·⸱ Being of Light ⸱·
Dreaming the Vision Onward

When I was invited to give a presentation at Cornell University on the archetypal phenomena of the near-death experience, I focused on what my unconscious had to say. The night of the invitation I dreamed I was going to the center of a mountain, through the middle of the mountain to the center of the center. As I reached a certain barrier a voice said: "If you go across this barrier, you have to return quickly." As I crossed the barrier in the dream, I came to a cave that had the sense of a tomb. I placed a chair of clear light to the right of the entry. The voice said: "It is easier to do it now than after the funeral." When I awakened, I reflected on how similar the dream was to a near-death experience in which people go across a barrier, encounter a dark tunnel, see a light or Being of Light, and then return. Only hours after the dream, my mother telephoned to tell me that my next door neighbor from childhood died the same evening of my dream. When such an inner experience coincides with an outer event without causal connection, Jung calls it synchronicity. Hence, I decided to give the presentation, which led to my being invited to co-edit this book.

One of the closest states of consciousness to death is sleep. In scripture when people were raised from the dead, it was said they were only sleeping. In 1900 Sigmund Freud turned the century with the publication of *The Interpretation of Dreams*, in which he calls dreams the royal road to the unconscious mind. Carl Jung moved beyond the personal unconscious, where the dreams only belong to the individual, to the collective unconscious, where an individual's dreams join the universal image language of humanity across time, culture, myth, and religions. When the same images repeat they are called archetypal images. I suggest that the current repeating images from near-death experiences, such as the move through a cave or tunnel to a light or Being of Light, can best be understood through the tools for archetypal dream interpretation. The epistemology of the surface is inadequate for the deep. What follows is a summary of my research on how common archetypal themes in literature and my own dreams relate to the phenomenon of the Being of Light in near-death experiences.

The methodology of Jungian dream interpretation includes, in addition to the day's conscious residue which triggers the unconscious, both personal and collective amplifications from parallel phenomena and symbols in the world's religions, mythologies, and literature. When phenomena repeat themselves across times and cultures, as in the near-death experiences, Jung speaks of archetypes of the collective unconscious. I shall amplify my dream clue in seeking to understand the meaning of the phenomena of the Being of Light in near-death experiences. Also I shall cite other archetypal parallels. Dreams are personal at one level, but may open to universal symbols of the human psyche at the deeper level and give us clues for deciphering other unconscious states, such as the near-death experience.

ARCHETYPAL PARALLEL BETWEEN TRANSFIGURATION AND THE BEING OF LIGHT

Now let us return to the dream amplification. A more exact context for seated beings outside a cave tomb is found in the gospel story of Mary Magdalene coming to the empty tomb of Jesus and finding a Being of Light sitting beside the cave. Let us begin with amplification from these gospel accounts of resurrection and transfiguration, which parallel the phenomena of the Being of Light in near-death experiences.

In the three synoptic gospels, Matthew, Mark, and Luke, there are often slight variations on the same account. In Luke's account it is recorded that the woman came to Jesus' tomb to anoint the body and found the stone rolled away from the cave sepulchre. "And it came to pass, as they were much perplexed thereabout, behold, two men stood by them in shining garments," who asked, "Why seek ye the living among the dead?" (Luke 24:4–5, King James version). The Being of Light in near-death experience likewise is described in shining white garment. Mark records that after they saw the stone rolled away "they saw a young man *sitting* on the right side, clothed in a long white garment who says, "Ye seek Jesus of Nazareth, which was crucified: he is risen…" (Mark 16:5–6). Matthew tells us "the angel of the Lord…rolled back the stone from the door, and *sat* upon it. His countenance was like lightning, and his raiment white as snow" (Matthew 28:2–3). Until my dream, I had never noticed that these beings of light were seated outside the cave tomb.

In John, the Fourth Gospel, it is recorded that Mary Magdalene looked into the cave tomb and saw "two angels in white *sitting*, the one at the head, and the other at the feet, where the body of Jesus had lain." "And they say unto her, woman, why weepest thou?.... She turned herself back, and saw Jesus standing, and knew not that it was Jesus. Jesus saith unto her, woman, why weepest thou? whom seekest thou? She supposing him to be the gardener...Jesus saith unto her, touch me not; for I am not yet ascended..." (John 20:11–17). The phenomena of transfiguration are archetypal parallels to the phenomena of the beings of light seen in near-death experiences.

The word used in Mark 16:5 for the "young man" in the white garment at the tomb is the same description used for the transfiguration. Mark records that when Jesus was transfigured on the mountain, his garment became white as snow (Mark 9:12–3). Matthew's record at the tomb was that both the face and the garment were like lightning and snow. In his record of Jesus' transfiguration, 17:2, he says Jesus "was transfigured before them: and his face did shine as the sun, and his raiment was white as the light." Jesus then instructed his disciples to tell no one what they had seen "until the Son of Man may be risen again from the dead."

PARALLEL BETWEEN WORD ROOTS AND DREAM IMAGES

Let me now return to my initial dream image of a chair of light placed outside the cave tomb. I muse often over the parallel processing of image and word in the two hemispheres of our brain, which leads me to a method of tracing the link between the etymological roots of words and dream images. Ernest Klein's *Comprehensive Etymological Dictionary* gives two entries under "chair": (1) The root is *F. 'chaire, pulpit, throne; fr.L. cathedra. (2) 'flesh color,' F. chair 'flesh.' (1966, Vol. I)*. Chair as "flesh color" reminds me that my neighbor who died that night used to sit beside me while I painted portraits. Putting the two roots together, to place a chair is simultaneously to place a pulpit, a throne, or a cathedral outside the tomb and to place "flesh" of light, perhaps the resurrected body as a cathedral of light.

Melvin Morse, M.D., a pediatrician who has worked with children's near-death experiences, in a lecture given at a conference in San Antonio in the summer of 1994, told of a dream of an eight-year-old girl just returned from a near-death experience. She dreamed of a tent in a meadow of golden light. He used the dream to talk about how individual our symbols were. However, they may also be universal. Using my tool of tracing the etymological parallel to images in dreams, I discovered that the origin of "light" is akin to the English "lea," "a pasture land, a meadow open to the sun and drenched with light" (Partridge, 1966). "Tent" comes via Latin "tendre" meaning "to stretch skins." The etymology of "tunnel" links to "skin" (Merriam-Webster, 1976). Hence in the near-death experience, the NDEr would go through a tunnel symbolizing passing through their skin, linking to the out-of-body phenomenon. The little girl's vision in the near-death experience was the flesh bathed in light, the glorified body, as in the transfigured body of Christ.

Also the "Shekinah," or feminine presence of God dwelling with us, means "to pitch one's tent."

ARCHETYPAL MYTHIC PARALLELS

Now let us turn for another archetypal parallel to a mythic story of the Psyche's journey to the land of the dead and a return. At the beginning of my training as an analyst, on a night before I flew to Zurich, my initial dream was of looking in a mirror and seeing behind me the white-faced clown Christ, as he appeared in the film "The Parable," originally shown at the World's Fair in 1965. A voice said: "Retrieve the underground compact of woman." On the sink beneath the mirror was a round white powder box. The lid was an amber dove. A "compact" is also a "covenant." My association to a woman's compact was Psyche's beauty box in the myth of Amour and Psyche, as told by Apuleius in *The Golden Ass* (1960). Beauty is one of Plato's Forms, the source of Jung's archetypes. Psyche's fourth task, which was to take the box to the land of the dead to get a secret from Persephone and then to return, became my personal mythic journey during my analysis in Zurich and now surfaces as a parallel story to the near-death journey.

Psyche's first task was to sort a pile of seeds; the second was to gather the golden fleece of the rams in a "sunlit meadow;" the third was to get a vase of the water of life from the river of death; and the fourth was to take a box and go to the land of the dead for a refill and then return. Note the parallel between the little girl's near-death image of the "meadow of golden light," and Psyche's task to get the "golden" fleece from a "sunlit meadow" before her journey to the land of the dead.

Apuleius in his novel on Metamorphoses or *The Golden Ass* used the word "pyxidem" for the box Psyche took to the land of the dead. Excavations of tombs from the time of his novel have uncovered women's mirror boxes in the shape of the Ankh of Isis which contained "pyxes," supposedly bits of amber for collecting eternal light. Some were shaped like shells, others doves (Goodenough, 1953, 175–77). In the Eastern Orthodox Church a "pyx" holds the "body" of Christ for Holy Communion, not unlike the containers which held the body parts of Osiris and Dionysus in the Isis and the Eleusynian mysteries, in which the story of Eros and Psyche is set. One should also note that at the end of the novel, Lucius is wrapped in the garment of light of Isis and sheds the skin of the beast, symbolizing metamorphosis. The transformation comes when the beast eats roses, a symbol of Eros. The Greek for metamorphosis means transformation, as does the Latin for transfiguration. The garment of light of the Egyptian mysteries marking immortality again is parallel to the near-death visions.

One might also see parallels to the Being of Light in the story in *The Nag Hammadi Library* Gnostic myth "On the Origin of the World" in which the daughters of Wisdom pour their blood on the earth and out of it springs Eros. The scattered light of Sophia, feminine goddess of Wisdom, appears as Eros scattered in all creatures. When Wisdom pours her light on the earth, it is because she is in love with the man of light, the Light-Adam. Psyche loved Eros and poured her blood upon him and upon the earth. From the blood sprang the rose and all the fragrant flowers from the blood of the daughters of Wisdom. Sophia Zoe is the daughter of Wisdom and the enlightened blood of woman. The origin of the Greek word "Zoe" meaning life is linked to the Greek "Zen" meaning to live. Sophia sent her daughter Zoe, who is called Eve of Life, as an instructor to raise up Adam, humankind, so that those who are begotten might become vessels of light. Zoe is called the female light-being. The birth of the instructor, inner instructor, came when Sophia cast a drop of light which floated on the water. That drop first patterned the female body (Robinson, ed., 1977, 161–79). The light-being is parallel to the Being of Light in near-death experience.

ARCHETYPAL PARALLEL BETWEEN THE NDE BEING OF LIGHT AND THE TIBETAN CLEAR LIGHT

Another parallel is the Tibetan Buddhist clear light. In the Buddhist teaching on the clear light, there is a teaching of penetrating the center parts of one's body through meditation on the drops as in the yogas of inner fire; but this cannot carry all the way to the clear light. The next step is the melting of the vessel of the universe into you. It melts like the universe as a candle lit from both ends. Your entire body then melts into a drop of light. One meditates this clear light via the name of one's own God/Goddess. Even the clear light of wisdom being becomes the one indestructible drop. This clear light comes as if one were actually dying. This meaning of clear light came to the Buddha sitting under the tree of enlightenment, the chair of the future Buddha (Gyatso, 1982, 205–206).

Reflecting on the link between Buddhist and Christian symbols, I dreamed that Mary and Joseph were on their way again to Bethlehem. I asked Mary if she were going to have another child after 2,000 years! She said, "No, I am pregnant with the light." A Buddha of golden light laughed, saying, "All the tears in the world are turned to amber in the womb of the Buddha." An emerald green wing connected the light in her womb to the womb of the Buddha. Now let us amplify the dream images.

As we approach the year 2000, the Being of Light in near-death experience is parallel both to the inner light of Christ or the Holy Spirit and the enlightened Buddha mind. The color of the Holy Spirit is green, as is the green Tara who directs others to enlightenment. Michael, who guides souls to the land of the dead, is the archangel with emerald green wings (Davidson, 1967). The emerald green and white Taras were formed from the tears of compassion of Avalokiteshvara, of whom the Dalai Lama is an incarnation. Avalokiteshvara was born out of a ray of light from Amitabha. The dream was linked to my attending the Wheel of Time ritual led by the Dalai Lama in Rikon, Switzerland, where he divined that Amitabha, the Buddha of infinite light, was the Buddha for the West. For the Tibetans, The Buddha was Amoghasiddha, whose color is green. Also during the ritual he administered Bodhisattva vows for those who could enter Nirvana but instead vow to return and teach others the way to enlightenment.

As we approach the year 2000, the avatar appearing for the new millenium is a Being of Light who connects rather than divides the world's religions. Many tears have been shed over the battles between names of the Light, tears that now may crystalize into the golden amber light of consciousness and teach us the link between the love of Christ and the compassion of Buddha, an insight shared by those near-death experiencers who, like the Bodhisattva, could enter the bliss of Nirvana but instead return from the other side to teach the path. My dream was given while attending on alternate days for two weeks the Wheel of Time ritual led by the Dalai Lama in Rikon, Switzerland in 1986 at the Tibetan monastery. On the other days I was in training analysis at the Jung Institute in Zurich. On the days I missed the ritual, I dreamed the details I had never heard. Then I understood how in the depths or core of the Psyche we open to the universal Psyche, called the collective unconscious by Jung, or higher consciousness by the Buddhists. I also understood that the distinction between Hinayana, which is the individual spiritual path, and Mahayana, which is the collective enlightenment, are not two but one. From an existential western philosophical perspective, I understood how the depth of one's own existence is grounded in the universal structure of Being, which is Heidegger's contribution in *Being and Time*, where death reveals who we are at the core of existence. I understood Jung's view of where the personal unconscious opens the collective unconscious at the depths of our Self.

The *Tibetan Book of the Dead*, which parallels the phenomena of the near-death experience, says: "Thine own consciousness, shining, void and inseparable from the Great Body of Radiance, hath no birth, nor death, and is the Immutable light. Buddha Amitabha" (Evans-Wentz, ed., 1960, 96).

The clear light is seen at the moment of death, as reported by near-death experiences and by *The Tibetan Book of the Dead*. The instructions say one should tell the person who is dying and about to see the light, Know Thy Self, as is the task also in depth analysis and individuation.

Carl Jung, in his introduction to the Evans-Wentz edition of *The Tibetan Book of the Dead*, says "The whole book is created out of the archetypal contents of the unconscious," reflecting that "these wise old lamas have caught a glimpse of the fourth dimension and twitched the veil from the greatest of life's secrets" (Evans-Wentz, 1960, 1, li). A secret not unlike Psyche's box, or the secret of transfiguration, emerges when the old red garment, the etymology of Adam (Maass, 1974), is removed and the garment of light is bestowed. This is a secret that Jesus asked his disciples to keep until the "Son of Man" is raised from the dead. The term "Son of Man" was earlier used for Ezekiel when he had a vision of God on a throne: "There I beheld, and lo a likeness as the appearance of fire: from the appearance of the loins downward, fire; and from the loins even upward, as the appearance of brightness, as the color of amber" (Ezekiel 8:2). "Behold the glory of the God of Israel was there, according to the vision that I saw in the plain. Then said God unto me, Son of Man, lift up thine eyes...." (Ezekiel 8:4–5). God's appearance as the amber or golden light reminds me that the dove on the box in my dream before leaving for Zurich was amber. The throne is linked to the ark of the covenant in the Old Testament accounts of the "box" carried by the Hebrew people to symbolize God's presence.

CONCLUSION

Now I am coming full circle to understand why I placed a chair, whose etymology is both "throne" and "flesh," outside the cave tomb in seeking to understand near-death experiences. Flesh of light is the Being of Light at Death. To go through the center of the mountain would be to tunnel. The etymology of tunnel is our skin, the "box" of the Psyche, reminding me that Jung, after his near-death vision, did not wish to re-enter the box once it had been opened. The root of "skin" is "that which one peels off" (Partridge, 1966).

Figure 1 is my own vision of Psyche as a Being of Light collecting the seeds or drops of light in her box at the foot of the tree of light. The center sap, whose root is consciousness (Onians, 1951, 61–63), is being collected first in the crown or "cortex" whose etymology means to strip off bark (Klein, 1966, 357), the same etymology as "leaf." The leaves are returning to the light from which they were photosynthesized, an apt metaphor for our return at death to the Being of Light from which we came.

In a larger sense we see humankind's innate similarities across time. These similarities are what Carl Jung called the archetypes of the collective unconscious. The archetype of a journey to the land of the dead and a return is illustrated in the story of Psyche's box, as told in the novel of Lucius' (a name which means light) metamorphosis and initiation into the Egyptian mystery of putting on the garment of the light of Isis. The garment of light is the phenomena marking metamorphosis or transfiguration in the world's religions and in near-death experience.

The box of the Psyche in the dream vision is linked to the cortex of the brain through the etymological parallel between words and dream images. I suggest that this space between is the source of an epistemology for deciphering the move between death and a return to life. Our task is to collect the seeds of light glimpsed in the between. The poet Hölderlin told us that those cast into the between will tell us who God and humans are. For those with eyes to see and ears to hear, the voice of the light may be seen and heard most clearly where the deepest darkness makes even a spark visible.

Figure 1

REFERENCES

Apuleius. (1960). *The Golden Ass.* (Jack Lindsay, Trans.). Bloomington: Indiana University Press.

Davidson, Gustav. (1967). *A Dictionary of Angels.* New York: The Free Press.

Evans-Wentz, W. Y., ed. (1960). *The Tibetan Book of the Dead: On the After-Death Experiences on the Bardo Plane.* (Lama Kazi Dawa-Samdup, Trans.). Introduction by Carl Jung. London: Oxford University Press.

Goodenough, Erwin. (1953). *Jewish Symbols in the Greco-Roman Period (Vol. I, The Archaeological Evidence from Palestine).* New York: Parthenon Books.

Gyatso, Geshe Kelsang. (1982). *Clear Light of Bliss.* London: Wisdom Publications.

Klein, Ernest. (1966, Vol. I); (1967, Vol. II). *A Comprehensive Etymological Dictionary of the English Language.* Amsterdam: Elsevier Publishing Company.

Maass, Fritz. (1974). "adham." In G. Johannes Botterweck and Helmer Ringgram (Eds.), *Theological Dictionary of the Old Testament* (John T. Willis, Trans.). (Revised Edition, vol. I). Grand Rapids, MI: William B. Eerdmans Publishing Company.

Merriam-Webster's Third New International Dictionary. Philip Babcock, ed. (1976). Springfield, MA: G. and C. Merriam Company

Onians, Richard Broxton. (1951). *The Origins of European Thought About the Body, the Mind, the Soul.* Cambridge, England: Cambridge University Press.

Partridge, Eric. (1966). *Origins: A Short Etymological Dictionary of Modern English.* New York: The Macmillan Company.

Robinson, James, ed. (1977). *The Nag Hammadi Library.* "On the Origin of the World." (II, 5 and XIII, 2). (Hans-Gebhard Bethge and Orval S. Wintermute, Trans.). San Francisco: Harper and Row, Publishers.

⁓ 11 ⁓

The Near-Death Experience
A Staircase to Heaven?

Sogyal Rinpoche

The central message that the near-death experiencers bring back from their encounter with death, or the presence or "being of light," is exactly the same as that of Buddha and of the bardo teachings: that the essential and most important qualities in life are love and knowledge, compassion and wisdom.

Sogyal Rinpoche is a Tibetan Buddhist. His name was given prior to the discernment that he was a reincarnation of Tertön Sogyal, a master of the Thirteenth Dalai Lama. "Rinpoche" is a title given to a master. The present Dalai Lama, in the foreword to Sogyal's *The Tibetan Book of Living and Dying* (from which comes this excerpt), notes that he was instructed by some of the greatest Tibetan Lamas. He also studied at Delhi University and Cambridge University, founded the Rigpa Fellowship, and established meditation centers in several countries.

In this essay Sogyal Rinpoche compares the phenomena of the

near-death experience with the states through which one passes in the journey between death and rebirth, as outlined in the *Bardo Tödrol,* or *Tibetan Book of the Dead.* This ancient book, meant to be read to a dying practitioner, describes what can be expected upon death. It points to three "in-between" states, or *bardos.*

At the moment of death, it says, one comes face-to-face with dazzling Light: the "Ground Luminosity" or "Clear Light." This is the culmination of the *Chikhé Bardo,* where the spiritual challenge is to recognize, from a lifetime of study and meditation practice, that you are the Light, the Buddha. To maintain full awareness and to merge with the clear Light at death is to attain liberation. The *Tibetan Book of the Dead* says:

> O son/daughter of an enlightened family...your pure awareness is inseparable luminosity and emptiness and dwells as a great expanse of light; beyond birth or death, it is, in fact, the Buddha of Unchanging Light. To recognize this is all that is necessary. (Rigpa Fellowship translation)

Those who fail to understand this will move on to the second bardo, the *Chönyi Bardo.* Here an astonishing array of deities appears, representing the spontaneous expression of various aspects of the innermost nature of mind. The first group is peaceful, the second wrathful. The spiritual task here is to know that these are merely the radiance of one's own intrinsic nature. This realization frees the awareness to merge inseparably with the Light of wisdom.

Failing this recognition, the consciousness awakens into the third bardo, the *Sipa Bardo.* Here the path to reincarnation begins and one is advised to choose carefully one's birth womb, for it may be as a spirit being, a human or an animal. One's mental body may experience unlimited travel in the bardos, as this portion of the text shows:

> Hey, noble one! What is "unobstructed" is your mental body; your awareness is free from embodiment and you lack a solid body. So now you can move hither and thither everywhere, through walls, houses, land, rocks, and earth.... You now have the power to think about any place you wish and you will arrive there in that very instant. You can reach anywhere and return just as a normal man stretches out and pulls back his arm. But these various magic powers are not so miraculous; if you don't specially need them, ignore them!.... As you have such a ghostly body, you encounter relatives and familiar places as if in a dream. When you meet these relatives, though you communicate with them, they do not answer.... You tell the mourners "Don't cry! Here I am!" They take no notice. (Thurman, 169–71)

Do not be distracted by these experiences, Tibetan Lamas say. Focus on the Light, call to mind an enlighted being, remember your spiritual practice. It is never too late. Even just before rebirth, one may realize the illusory nature of the entire phantasmagoria and merge with the truth. This is an important aspect of Buddhism; one is always free to alter one's destiny through understanding.

How close is the parallel between NDEs and the *Tibetan Book of the Dead*? Is the NDE more about life than death? Sogyal Rinpoche explores this difficult question from within the increasingly influential tradition of Tibetan Buddhism.

(Rigpa Fellowship: P.O. Box 60, Santa Cruz, CA 95061-0607, and 330 Caledonian Road, London N1 1BB)

⤻ The Near-Death Experience ⤸
A Staircase to Heaven?

We have become very familiar now in the West with the near-death experience, the name given to the range of experiences reported by people who have survived an incident of near or clinical death. The near-death experience has been reported throughout history, in all mystical and shamanic traditions, and by writers and philosophers as varied as Plato, Pope Gregory the Great, some of the great Sufi masters, Tolstoy, and Jung. My favorite example from history is the story told by the great English historian, the monk Bede, in the eighth century.

> About this time, a noteworthy miracle, like those of olden days, occurred in Britain. For, in order to assist the living from spiritual death, a man already dead returned to bodily life and related many notable things that he had seen, some of which I have thought it valuable to mention here in brief. There was a head of a family living in a place in the country of the Northumbrians known as Cunningham, who led a devout life with all his household. He fell ill and grew steadily worse until the crisis came, and in the early hours of one night he died. But at daybreak he returned to life and suddenly sat up to the great consternation of those weeping around the body who ran away; only his wife, who loved him more dearly, remained with him, though trembling and fearful. The man reassured her and said: "Do not be frightened; for I have truly risen from the grasp of death, and I am allowed to live among men again. But henceforth I must not live as I used to, and must adopt a very different way of life" ...Not long afterward, he abandoned all worldly responsibilities and entered the monastery of Melrose....

Bede goes on:

> This was the account he used to give of his experience: 'A handsome man
> in a shining robe was my guide, and we walked in silence in what appeared
> to be a northeasterly direction. As we traveled onward, we came to a very
> broad and deep valley of infinite length…. He soon brought me out of
> darkness into an atmosphere of clear light, and as he led me forward in
> bright light, I saw before us a tremendous wall which seemed to be of
> infinite length and height in all directions. As I could see no gate, window,
> or entrance in it, I began to wonder why we went up to the wall. But when
> we reached it, all at once—I know not by what means—we were on top of
> it. Within lay a very broad and pleasant meadow…. Such was the light
> flooding all this place that it seemed greater than the brightness of daylight
> or of the sun's rays at noon….
>
> "(The guide said) 'You must now return to your body and live among
> men once more; but, if you will weigh your actions with greater care and
> study to keep your words and ways virtuous and simple, then when you
> die, you too will win a home among these happy spirits that you see. For,
> when I left you for a while, I did so in order to discover what your future
> would be.' When he told me this I was most reluctant to return to my
> body; for I was entranced by the pleasantness and beauty of the place I
> could see and the company I saw there. But I did not dare to question my
> guide, and meanwhile, I know not how, I suddenly found myself alive
> among men once more."

Bede ends his account with these words:

> This man of God would not discuss these and other things he had seen
> with any apathetic or careless-living people, but only with those who
> were…willing to take his words to heart and grow in holiness (Bede, 1968,
> 420–21).

The skill of modern medical technology has added a new and exciting
dimension to the extent of the near-death experience; many people have now
been revived from "death," for example, after accidents, heart attack, or
serious illness, or in operations or combat. The near-death experience has
been the subject of a great deal of scientific research and philosophical
speculation. According to an authoritative 1982 Gallup poll, an extraordinary
number of Americans—up to 8 million, or one in twenty in the population—
have had at least one near-death experience (Gallup, 1982).

Although no two people have exactly the same experience, just as no two
people could have identical experiences of the bardos, a common pattern of

different phases in the near-death experience, a "core experience," appears:

1. They experience an altered state of feeling, of peace and well-being, without pain, bodily sensations, or fear.
2. They may be aware of a buzzing or rushing sound, and find themselves separated from their body. This is the so-called "out-of-the-body experience": They can view the body, often from a point somewhere above it; their sense of sight and hearing is heightened; their consciousness is clear and vividly alert, and they can even move through walls.
3. They are aware of another reality, of entering a darkness, floating in a dimensionless space, and then moving rapidly through a tunnel.
4. They see a light, at first a point in the distance, and are magnetically drawn toward it and then enveloped in light and love. This light is described as a blinding light of great beauty, but the eyes are unhurt by it. Some people report meeting "a being of light," a luminous, seemingly omniscient presence that a few call God or Christ, who is compassionate and loving. Sometimes in this presence they may witness a life-review, seeing everything they have done in their life, good and bad. They communicate telepathically with the presence, and find themselves in a timeless and usually blissful dimension in which all ordinary concepts like time and space are meaningless. Even if the experience lasts only one or two minutes in normal time, it can be of a vast elaboration and richness.
5. Some see an inner world of preternatural beauty, paradisal landscapes and buildings, with heavenly music, and they have a feeling of oneness. A very few, it seems, report terrifying visions of hellish realms.
6. They may reach a boundary beyond which they cannot go; some meet dead relatives and friends and talk to them. They decide (often reluctantly) or are told to return to the body and this life, sometimes with a sense of mission and service, sometimes to protect and care for their family, sometimes simply to fulfill the purpose of their life, which has not been accomplished.

The most important aspect of the near-death experience, as reported again and again in the literature about it, is the complete transformation it often makes in the lives, attitudes, careers, and relationships of the people who have this experience. They may not lose their fear of pain and dying, but they lose their fear of death itself; they become more tolerant and loving; and they become interested in spiritual values, the "path of wisdom," and usually in a universal spirituality rather than the dogma of any one religion.

How, then, should the near-death experience be interpreted? Some Western writers, who have read the *Tibetan Book of the Dead*, equate these experiences with the experiences of the bardos taught in the Tibetan tradition. At first glance there do seem to be tantalizing parallels between the two, but how exactly do the details of the near-death experience relate to the teachings on the bardos? I feel that this would require a special study beyond the scope of this book, but there are a number of similarities and differences that we can see.

THE DARKNESS AND THE TUNNEL

The final phase of the dissolution process of the bardo of dying, you will remember, is when the black experience of "full attainment" dawns "like an empty sky shrouded in utter darkness." At this point, the teachings speak of a moment of bliss and joy. One of the main features of the near-death experience is the impression of moving "at a terrific speed" and "feeling weightless" through a black space, "a total, peaceful, wonderful blackness," and down a "long, dark, tunnel."

One woman told Kenneth Ring: "It's just like a void, a nothing and it's such a peaceful—it's so pleasant that you can keep going. It's a complete blackness, there is no sensation at all, there was no feeling...sort of like a dark tunnel. Just a floating. It's like being in mid-air" (Ring, 1982,55).

And another woman told him:

> The first thing I remember was a tremendous rushing sound, a tremen-
> dous.... It's hard to find the right words to describe. The closest thing that
> I could possibly associate it with is, possibly the sound of a tornado—a
> tremendous gushing wind, but almost pulling me. And I was being pulled
> into a narrow point from a wide area. (Ring, 1982, 63)

A woman told Margot Grey:

> I was in what felt like outer space. It was absolutely black out there and I
> felt like I was being drawn towards an opening like at the end of a tun-
> nel. I knew this because I could see a light at the end; that's how I knew it
> was there. I was vertical and I was being drawn towards the opening. I
> know it wasn't a dream, dreams don't happen that way. I never once imag-
> ined it was a dream. (Grey, 1985, 42)

THE LIGHT

At the moment of death, the Ground Luminosity or Clear Light dawns in all its splendor. The *Tibetan Book of the Dead* says: "O son/daughter of an enlightened family...your Rigpa is inseparable luminosity and emptiness and dwells as a great expanse of light; beyond birth or death, it is, in fact, the Buddha of Unchanging Light."

Melvin Morse, who has specialized in the research of near-death experiences in children, remarks: "Nearly every near-death experience of children (and about one fourth of those of adults) has in it an element of light. They all report that the light appears at the final stages of the near-death experience, after they have had an out-of-body experience or have travelled up the tunnel" (Morse, 1990, 115).

One of the best descriptions of the approach to the light was reported by Margot Grey:

> Then gradually you realize that way far off in the distance, an unmeasurable distance, you may be reaching the end of the tunnel, as you can see a white light, but it's so far away I can only compare it to looking up into the sky and in the distance seeing a single star but visually you must remember that you are looking through a tunnel, and this light would fill the end of the tunnel. You concentrate on this speck of light because as you are propelled forward you anticipate reaching this light.
>
> Gradually as you travel towards it at an extreme speed it gets larger and larger. The whole process on reflection only seems to take about one minute. As you gradually draw nearer to this extremely brilliant light there is no sensation of an abrupt end of the tunnel, but rather more of a merging into the light. By now, the tunnel is behind you and before you is this magnificent, beautiful blue-white light. The brilliance is so bright, brighter than a light that would immediately blind you, but absolutely does not hurt your eyes at all. (Grey, 1985, 47)

Many near-death experiences describe the light itself:

> My description of the light was—well, it was not a light, but the absence of darkness, total and complete…. Well, you think of light as a big light shining on things making shadows and so forth. This light was really the absence of darkness. We're not used to that concept because we always get a shadow from the light unless the light is all around us. But this light was so total and complete that you didn't look at the light, you were in the light. (Sabom, 1982, 66)

One person told Kenneth Ring, "It was not bright. It was like a shaded lamp or something. But it wasn't that kind of light that you get from a lamp. You know what it was? Like someone had put a shade over the sun. It made me feel very, very peaceful. I was no longer afraid. Everything was going to be all right" (Ring, 1982, 59).

A woman told Margot Grey: "The light is brighter than anything you could possibly imagine. There are no words to describe it. I was so happy, it's impossible to explain. It was such a feeling of serenity, it was a marvelous feeling. The light is so bright that it would normally blind you, but it doesn't hurt one's eyes a bit."

Others recount how they not only see the light, but enter directly into the light, and they speak of the feelings they have: "I had no sense of separate identity. I was the light and one with it" (Grey, 1985, 46).

A woman who had undergone two major operations in two days told Margot Grey: "Only my essence was felt. Time no longer mattered and space was filled with bliss. I was bathed in radiant light and immersed in the aura of the rainbow. All was fusion. Sounds were of a new order, harmonious, nameless (now I call it music)" (Grey, 1985, 33).

Another man who reached this point of entering the light describes it in this way:

> The following series of events appear to happen simultaneously, but in describing them I will have to take them one at a time. The sensation is of a being of some kind, more a kind of energy, not a character in the sense of another person, but an intelligence with whom it is possible to communicate. Also, in size it just covers the entire vista before you. It totally engulfs everything, you feel enveloped.
>
> The light immediately communicates to you, in an instant telekinesis your thought waves are read, regardless of language. A doubtful statement would be impossible to receive. The first message I received was "Relax, everything is beautiful everything is OK, you have nothing to fear." I was immediately put at absolute ease. In the past if someone like a doctor had said "It's OK, you have nothing to fear, this won't hurt," it usually did—you couldn't trust them.
>
> But this was the most beautiful feeling I have ever known, it's absolute pure love. Every feeling, every emotion is just perfect. You feel warm, but it has nothing to do with temperature. Everything there is absolutely vivid and clear. What the light communicates to you is a feeling of true, pure love. You experience this for the first time ever. You can't compare it to the love of your wife, or the love of your children or sexual love. Even if all those things were combined, you cannot compare it to the feeling you get from this light. (Grey, 1985, 53)

A man who had almost drowned at the age of fourteen recalled:

> As I reached the source of the Light, I could see in. I cannot begin to describe in human terms the feelings I had over what I saw. It was a giant infinite world of calm, and love, and energy and beauty. It was as though human life was unimportant compared to this. And yet it urged the impor-

tance of life at the same time as it solicited death as a means to a different and better life. It was all being, all beauty, all meaning for all existence. It was all the energy of the universe forever in one place. (Morse, 1990, 120)

Melvin Morse has written movingly of the near-death experiences of children, and tells how they describe the light in their simple eloquence: "I have a wonderful secret to tell you. I have been climbing a staircase to heaven." "I just wanted to get to that Light. Forget my body, forget everything. I just wanted to get to that Light." "There was a beautiful Light that had everything good in it. For about a week, I could see sparks of that Light in everything." "When I came out of the coma in the hospital, I opened my eyes and saw pieces of the Light everywhere. I could see how everything in the world fits together" (Morse, 1990, 181).

SIMILARITIES WITH THE BARDO OF BECOMING
In the near-death experience, the mind is momentarily released from the body, and goes through a number of experiences akin to those of the mental body in the bardo of becoming.

1. Out-of-Body Experience
The near-death experience very often begins with an out-of-body experience: people can see their own body, as well as the environment around them. This coincides with what has already been said about the *Tibetan Book of the Dead*:

> I remember coming round from the anesthetic and then drifting off and finding myself out of my body, over the bed looking down at my carcass. I was aware only of being a brain and eyes, I do not remember having a body. (Grey, 1985, 35)

A man who had suffered a heart attack told Kenneth Ring:

> It seemed like I was up there in space and just my mind was active. No body feeling, just like my brain was up in space. I had nothing but my mind. Weightless, I had nothing. (Ring, 1982, 45)

2. Helplessly Watching Relatives
I have described how, in the bardo of becoming, the dead are able to see and hear their living relatives, but are unable, sometimes frustratingly, to communicate with them. A woman from Florida told Michael Sabom how she looked down on her mother from a point near the ceiling: "The biggest thing I remember was that I felt so sad that I couldn't somehow let her know

that I was all right. Somehow I knew that I was all right, but I didn't know how to tell her…" (Sabom, 1982, 37).

> I remember seeing them down the hall…. my wife, my oldest son and my oldest daughter and the doctor…. I didn't know why they were crying. (Sabom, 1982, 155)

And a woman told Michael Sabom: "I was sitting way up there looking at myself convulsing and my mother and my maid screaming and yelling because they thought I was dead. I felt so sorry for them…. Just deep, deep sadness. But I felt I was free up there and there was no reason for suffering" (Sabom, 1982, 37).

3. Perfect Form, Mobility, and Clairvoyance

The mental body in the bardo of becoming is described in the *Tibetan Book of the Dead* as being "like a body of the golden age," and as having almost supernatural mobility and clairvoyance. The near-death experiencers also find that the form they have is complete and in the prime of life.

> I was floating and I was a much younger man…. The impression I got was that I was able to see myself some way through a reflection or something where I was twenty years younger than what I actually was. (Sabom, 1982, 40)

They find also that they can travel instantaneously, simply by the power of thought. A Vietnam veteran told Michael Sabom:

> I felt like I could have thought myself anywhere I wanted to be instantly…. I just felt exhilarated with a sense of power. I could do what I wanted to…. It's realer than here, really. (Sabom, 1982, 56)
> I remember all of a sudden going right back to the battlefield where I had been lost…. It was almost like you materialize there and all of a sudden the next instant you were over here. It was just like you blinked your eyes. (Sabom, 1982, 54–55)

Many near-death experiencers also report a clairvoyant sense of total knowledge "from the beginning of time to the end of time" (Ring, 1985, 199). A woman told Raymond Moody: "All of a sudden, all knowledge of all that had started from the very beginning, that would go on without end—for a second I knew all the secrets of the ages, all the meaning of the universe, the stars, the moon—of everything" (Moody, 1978, 10). "There was a moment in this thing—well, there isn't any way to describe it—but it was like I knew all things…. For a moment, there, it was like communication wasn't necessary. I thought whatever I wanted to know could be known" (Moody, 1978, 14). "While I was there I felt at the center of things. I felt enlightened and cleansed. I felt I could see the point of everything. Everything fitted in, it all made sense, even the dark times. It almost seemed, too, as if the pieces of jigsaw all fitted together" (Grey, 1985, 52).

4. Meeting Others

In the Tibetan teachings the mental body in the bardo of becoming is described as meeting other beings in the bardo. Similarly the near-death experiencer is often able to converse with others who have died. Michael Sabom's Vietnam veteran said that as he lay unconscious on the battlefield, viewing his own body,

> The thirteen guys that had been killed the day before that I had put in plastic bags were right there with me. And more than that, during the course of that month of May, my particular company lost forty-two dead. All forty-two of those guys were there. They were not in the form we perceive the human body…. But I knew they were there. I felt their presence. We communicated without talking with our voices. (Sabom, 1982, 71)

A woman whose heart stopped under anesthetic during a dental extraction said:

> Then I found myself I was in a beautiful landscape, the grass is greener than anything seen on earth, it has a special light or glow. The colors are beyond description, the colors here are so drab by comparison…. In this place I saw people that I knew had died. There were no words spoken, but it was as if I knew what they were thinking, and at the same time I knew that they knew what I was thinking. (Grey, 1985, 50)

5. Different Realms

In the bardo of becoming, as well as many other kinds of visions, the mental body will see visions and signs of different realms. A small percentage of those who have survived a near-death experience report visions of inner worlds, of paradises, cities of light, with transcendental music.

One woman told Raymond Moody:

> Off in the distance…I could see a city. There were buildings—separate buildings. They were gleaming, bright. People were happy in there. There

was sparkling water, fountains…a city of light I guess would be the way to say it…. It was wonderful. There was beautiful music. Everything was just glowing, wonderful…. But if I had entered into this, I think I would never have returned…. I was told that if I went there I couldn't go back…that the decision was mine. (Moody, 1978, 17)

Another person told Margot Grey:

I seemed to find myself in what appeared to be some type of structure or building, but there were no walls that I can remember. There was only this all-pervading beautiful golden light…. I noticed about me many people that seemed to be walking or milling about; they didn't even appear to walk, but seemed somehow to glide. I didn't feel apart from them at all; one of the feelings I remember most about them was the feeling of unity, of being totally a part of everything around me and about me. (Grey, 1985, 51)

6. Hellish Visions

Not all descriptions in the near-death experience, however, are positive, as you would expect from what we have spoken of in the Tibetan teachings. Some people report terrifying experiences of fear, panic, loneliness, desolation, and gloom, vividly reminiscent of the descriptions of the bardo of becoming. One person reported by Margot Grey spoke of being sucked into "a vast black vortex like a whirlpool," and those who have negative experiences tend to feel, rather like those about to be reborn in lower realms in the bardo of becoming, that they are traveling downward instead of upward:

I was moving along as part of a river of sound—a constant babble of human noise…. I felt myself sinking into and becoming part of the stream and slowly being submerged by it. A great fear possessed me as if I knew that once overcome by this ever growing mass of noise that I would be lost. (Grey, 1985, 59)

I was looking down into a large pit, which was full of swirling gray mist and there were all these hands and arms reaching up and trying to grab hold of me and drag me in there. There was a temple wailing noise, full of desperation. (Grey, 1985, 65)

Other people have even experienced what can only be called hellish visions, of intense cold or unbearable heat, and heard the sounds of tormented wailing or a noise like that of wild beasts. A woman reported by Margot Grey said:

> I found myself in a place surrounded by mist. I felt I was in hell. There
> was a big pit with vapor coming out and there were arms and hands com-
> ing out trying to grab mine…. I was terrified that these hands were going
> to claw hold of me and pull me into the pit with them…an enormous lion
> bounded towards me from the other side and I let out a scream. I was not
> afraid of the lion, but I felt somehow he would unsettle me and push me
> into that dreadful pit…. It was very hot down there and the vapor or steam
> was very hot. (Grey, 1985, 63)

A man who suffered a cardiac arrest reported: "I was going down, down
deep into the earth. There was anger and I felt this horrible fear. Everything
was gray. The noise was fearsome, with snarling and crashing like maddened
wild animals, gnashing their teeth" (Grey, 1985, 70).

Raymond Moody writes that several people claimed to have seen beings
who seemed trapped by their inability to surrender their attachments to the
physical world: possessions, people, or habits. One woman spoke of these
"bewildered people":

> What you would think of as their head was bent downward; they had sad
> depressed looks; they seemed to shuffle, as someone would on a chain
> gang…they looked washed out, dull, gray. And they seemed to be forever
> shuffling and moving around, not knowing where they were going, not
> knowing who to follow, or what to look for.
>
> As I went by they didn't even raise their heads to see what was hap-
> pening. They seemed to be thinking, "Well, it's all over with. What am I
> doing? What's it all about?" Just this absolute, crushed, hopeless
> demeanor—not knowing what to do or where to go or who they were or
> anything else.
>
> They seemed to be forever moving, rather than just sitting, but in
> no special direction. They would start straight, then veer to the left and
> take a few steps and veer back to the right. And absolutely nothing to
> do. Searching, but for what they were searching I don't know. (Moody,
> 1978, 19)

In the accounts we have of the near-death experience, a border or limit is
occasionally perceived; a point of no return is reached. At this border the
person then chooses (or is instructed) to return to life, sometimes by the
presence of light. Of course in the Tibetan bardo teachings there is no parallel
to this, because they describe what happens to a person who actually dies.
However, in Tibet there was a group of people, called *déloks*, who had
something like a near-death experience, and what they report is fascinatingly
similar.

THE DÉLOK: A TIBETAN NEAR-DEATH EXPERIENCE

A curious phenomenon, little known in the West, but familiar to Tibetans, is the délok. In Tibetan *dé lok* means "returned from death," and traditionally déloks are people who seemingly "die" as a result of an illness, and find themselves traveling in the bardo. They visit the hell realms, where they witness the judgment of the dead and the sufferings of hell, and sometimes they go to paradises and buddha realms. They can be accompanied by a deity, who protects them and explains what is happening. After a week the délok is sent back to the body with a message from the Lord of Death for the living, urging them to spiritual practice and a beneficial way of life. Often the déloks have great difficulty making people believe their story, and they spend the rest of their lives recounting their experiences to others in order to draw them toward the path of wisdom. The biographies of some of the more famous déloks were written down, and are sung all over Tibet by traveling minstrels.

A number of aspects of the délok correspond not only with, as you would expect, the bardo teachings such as the *Tibetan Book of the Dead*, but also with the near-death experience.

Lingza Chökyi was a famous délok who came from my part of Tibet and lived in the sixteenth century. In her biography she tells how she failed to realize she was dead, how she found herself out of her body, and saw a pig's corpse lying on her bed, wearing her clothes. Frantically she tried in vain to communicate with her family, as they set about the business of the practices for her death. She grew furious with them when they took no notice of her and did not give her her plate of food. When her children wept, she felt a "hail of pus and blood" fall, which caused her intense pain. She tells us she felt joy each time the practices were done, and immeasurable happiness when finally she came before the master who was practicing for her and who was resting in the nature of mind, and her mind and his became one.

After a while she heard someone whom she thought was her father calling to her, and she followed him. She arrived in the bardo realm, which appeared to her like a country. From there, she tells us, there was a bridge that led to the hell realms, and to where the Lord of Death was counting the good or evil actions of the dead. In this realm she met various people who recounted their stories, and she saw a great yogin who had come into the hell realms in order to liberate beings.

Finally Lingza Chökyi was sent back to the world, as there had been an error concerning her name and family, and it was not yet her time to die. With the message from the Lord of Death to the living, she returned to her body and recovered, and spent the rest of her life telling of what she had learned.

The phenomenon of the délok was not simply a historical one; it continued up until very recently in Tibet. Sometimes a délok would leave the body for about a week and meet people who had died, sometimes quite unknown to the délok, who would give messages for their living relatives and ask these relatives to do certain kinds of practices on their behalf. The délok would then return to his or her body and deliver their messages. In Tibet this was an accepted occurrence, and elaborate methods were devised for detecting whether déloks were fraudulent or not. Dilgo Khyentse Rinpoche's daughter told Françoise Pommaret, author of a book on the déloks, that in Tibet, while the délok was undergoing his or her experience, the orifices of the body were stopped with butter, and a paste made from barley flour put over the face (Pommaret, 1989). If the butter did not run, and the mask did not crack, the délok was recognized as authentic.

The tradition of déloks continues in the Tibetan Himalayan regions today. These déloks are quite ordinary people, often women, who are very devoted and have great faith. They "die" on special days in the Buddhist calendar, for a number of hours, and their major function is to act as messengers between the living and the dead.

THE MESSAGE OF THE NEAR-DEATH EXPERIENCE

As we have seen, there are significant similarities between the near-death experience and the bardo teachings; there are also significant differences. The greatest difference, of course, is the fact that the near-death experiencers do *not* die, whereas the teachings describe what happens to people as they die, after actual physical death, and as they take rebirth. The fact that the near-death experiencers do not go further on the journey into death—some of them are only "dead" for one minute—must go some way to explaining at least the possibility for disparities between the two accounts.

Some writers have suggested the near-death experience expresses the stages of the dissolution process in the bardo of dying. It is premature, I feel, to try to link the near-death experience too precisely with the bardo descriptions, because the person who has survived the near-death experience has only been—literally—"near death." I explained to my master Dilgo Khyentse Rinpoche the nature of the near-death experience, and he called it a phenomenon that belongs to the natural bardo of *this* life, because the consciousness merely leaves the body of the person who has "died," and wanders temporarily in various realms.

Dilgo Khyentse Rinpoche implied that the near-death experiencers are experiencing their clinical death within the natural bardo of this life. Perhaps they are standing on the threshold of the bardos, but they have not actually entered into them and returned. Whatever they experience, they are still in the natural bardo of this life. Is their experience of the light similar to the dawning of the Ground Luminosity? Could it be that just before its vast sun rises, they catch a strong glimpse of the first rays of dawn?

Whatever the ultimate meaning of the details of the near-death experience, I remain extremely moved by the many accounts I have heard or read, and struck especially by some of the attitudes that flow from these experiences, attitudes that mirror so richly the Buddhist view of life. Two I have already spoken of: the profound transformation and spiritual awakening that takes place in those who have been through this experience; and the implications for our lives of the life-review. The life-review happens again and again in the near-death experience, and demonstrates so clearly the inescapability of karma and the far-reaching and powerful effects of all our actions, words, and thoughts. The central message that the near-death experiencers bring back from their encounter with death, or the presence of "being of light," is exactly the same as that of Buddha and of the bardo teachings: that the essential and most important qualities in life are love and knowledge, compassion and wisdom.

They are surely beginning to see what the bardo teachings tell us: that life and death are in the mind itself. And the confidence that many of them seem to have after this experience reflects this deeper understanding of mind.

There are also certain fascinating similarities between the near-death experience and its results, and mystical states and altered states of consciousness. For example, a number of paranormal phenomena have been reported by the near-death experiencers. Some have precognitive or prophetic planetary visions, or "life previews" that turn out to be uncannily accurate; after the near-death experience, some report experiences of what appears to be the energy of *kundalini*[1]; others find they have real and amazing powers of clairvoyance, or psychic or physical healing.

Many of those who have come near death speak in a personal, undeniably eloquent way of the beauty, love, peace, and bliss and wisdom of what they have experienced. To me this sounds like they have had certain glimpses of the radiance of the nature of mind, and it is hardly surprising that such glimpses should have resulted in true spiritual transformation, again and again. Yet as Margot Grey points out, "We do not need nearly to die in order to experience a higher spiritual reality" (Grey, 1985, 194). That higher spiritual reality is here and now, in life, if only we can discover and enter it.

I would like to make one essential caution: Don't let these accounts of the near-death experience, which are so inspiring, lull you into believing that all you have to do in order to dwell in such states of peace and bliss is to die. It is not, and could not be, that simple.

Sometimes when people are going through suffering and pain, they feel they cannot bear it anymore; and hearing the near-death stories might, it is conceivable, tempt them to put an end to it all by taking their lives. This might seem like a simple solution, but it overlooks the fact that whatever we go through is part of life. It's impossible to run away. If you run away, you will only come to face your suffering in an even deeper way later on.

Besides, while it is true that the majority of near-death experiences that have been collected have been good ones, there is still some speculation as to whether this reflects the actual rarity of negative, terrifying experiences, or merely the difficulty in recollecting them. People may not want or consciously be able to remember the darker or more frightening experiences. Also the near-death experiencers themselves stress that what they have learned is the importance of transforming our lives now while we are still alive, for we have, they say, "a more important mission while we're here" (Ring, 1982, 145).

This transformation of our lives now is the urgent and essential point. Wouldn't it be tragic if this central message of the near-death experience— that life is inherently sacred and must be lived with sacred intensity and purpose—was obscured and lost in a facile romanticizing of death? Wouldn't it be even more tragic if such a facile optimism further deepened that disregard for our actual responsibilities to ourselves and our world that is menacing the survival of the planet?

THE MEANING OF THE NEAR-DEATH EXPERIENCE

Inevitably some have tried to show that the events of the near-death experience constitute something other than a spiritual experience, and reductionist scientists have tried to explain it away in terms of physiological, neurological, chemical, or psychological effects. The near-death experience researchers, however, doctors and scientists themselves, have countered these objections lucidly one by one, and insist that they cannot explain the whole of the near-death experience. As Melvin Morse writes at the end of his magnificent book, *Closer to the Light: Learning from Children's Near-Death Experiences*:

> But near-death experiences appear to be a cluster of events so that one cannot understand the total by looking at its various pieces. One cannot understand music by studying the various frequencies of sound that generate each note, nor does one need to have a deep understanding of acoustical physics to enjoy Mozart. The near-death experience remains a mystery. (Morse, 1990, 193)

Melvin Morse also says:

> I feel that just understanding near-death experiences will be our first step at healing the great division between science and religion that started with Isaac Newton almost three hundred years ago. Educating physicians, nurses, and ourselves about what people experience in those final hours will

shatter our prejudices about the ways we think about medicine and life. (Morse, 1990, 93)

In other words the very advance in medical technology is simultaneously providing the means to revolutionize itself. Melvin Morse, in a lecture for the International Association of Near-Death Studies: *The NDE as Experienced in Children*, says:

> I find it ironic that it is our medical technology that has led to this plethora of near-death experiences.... There have been near-death experiences throughout the centuries, but it has only been in the last twenty years that we have had the technology to resuscitate patients. Now they are telling us about their experiences, so let's listen to them. This to me is a challenge for our society.... Near-death experiences, to my mind, are a natural psychological process associated with dying. I'm going to boldly predict if we can reintegrate this knowledge into our society not only will it help with dying patients, but it will help society as a whole.
>
> I see medicine today as being devoid of spirit.... There is no reason why technology and the spirit cannot exist side by side.

One of the reasons I have written this chapter is to show I believe what Melvin Morse says is possible: Technology and the spirit can and must exist side by side, if our fullest human potential is to be developed. Wouldn't a complete, and completely useful, human science have the courage to embrace and explore the facts of the mystical, the facts of death and dying as revealed in the near-death experience and in this book?

Bruce Greyson, one of the leading figures in near-death research, in an IANDS lecture: *The NDE: Can It Be Explained in Science?* says:

> Science must try to explain the near-death experience because therein lies the key to its own growth.... History tells us that only in trying to explain phenomena which are currently beyond our reach will science develop new methods. I believe the near-death experience is one of the puzzles that just might force scientists to develop a new scientific method, one that will incorporate all sources of knowledge, not only logical deduction of the intellect, and empirical observation of the physical but direct experience of the mystical as well.

Bruce Greyson has also said he believes near-death experiences occur for a reason: "Based on my watching near-death experiences for a number of years, I think that we have these experiences in order to learn how to help others." Kenneth Ring sees yet another extraordinary possibility and meaning to the near-death experiences. He asks why so many people are now having such experiences and going through spiritual transformation at this time. For many years one of the bravest pioneers in the field of near-death research, he has come to see the near-death experiencers as being "messengers of hope," speaking of a higher and more noble spiritual reality, and calling us to change urgently every facet of how we live now; to end all war, all divisions between religions and peoples, and to protect and save the environment:

> I believe…that humanity as a whole is collectively struggling to awaken to a newer and higher mode of consciousness, …and that the near-death experience can be viewed as an evolutionary device to bring about this transformation, over a period of years, in millions of persons. (Ring, 1985, 7)

It may be that whether this is true or not depends on all of us: on whether we really have the courage to face the implications of the near-death experience and the bardo teachings, and by transforming ourselves transform the world around us, and so by stages the whole future of humanity.

NOTE

1. In the Hindu tradition, kundalini refers to the awakening of the subtle energy that can bring about a psycho-physiological transformation and union with the divine.

REFERENCES

Bede. (1968). *A History of the English Church and People.* Translated by Leo Sherley-Price. Harmondsworth, England: Penguin Books.

Evans-Wentz, W. Y., compiler and editor. (1927/1960). *The Tibetan Book of the Dead.* New York: Oxford University Press.

Fremantle, Francesca and Chogyam Trungpa, translators. (1975). *The Tibetan Book of the Dead.* Boston: Shambhala.

Gallup, George, Jr. (1982). With William Proctor. *Adventures in Immortality: A Look Beyond the Threshold of Death.* London: Souvenir.

Grey, Margot. (1985). *Return from Death: An Exploration of the Near-Death Experience.* Boston and London: Arkana.

Moody, Raymond A., Jr. (1978). *Reflections on Life After Life.* London: Corgi.

Morse, Melvin. (1990). *Closer to the Light: Learning from Children's Near-Death Experiences.* New York: Villard.

Pommaret, Françoise. (1989). *Les Revenants de l'Au-Delà dans le Monde Tibétain.* Paris: Editions du CNRS.

Ring, Kenneth. (1982). *Life at Death: A Scientific Investigation of the Near-Death Experience.* New York: Quill.

Ring, Kenneth. (1985). *Heading Towards Omega: In Search of the Meaning of the Near-Death Experience.* New York: Quill.

Thurman, Robert A. F., translator. (1994). *The Tibetan Book of the Dead.* New York: Bantam.

·⌣ **12** ⌣·

Near-Death Experiences
Implications for Human Evolution and Planetary Transformation

Kenneth Ring

The Light comes to show us the way onward. It is up to each of us whether we shall have the courage and the wisdom to follow where it beckons.

Kenneth Ring, Ph.D., stands out among early researchers taking up Raymond Moody's challenge to undertake further scientific research on NDEs. Ring was the psychologist who first established reliable scientific answers to many of the important questions. Does the type of death affect an NDE? Do personal and social backgrounds change NDEs? Do religious people have more NDEs than atheists? Do more people experience certain elements of an NDE, such as the peace and out-of-body travel, while fewer encounter other elements, such as the light? How does an NDE affect one afterward? Are values and religious beliefs changed?

Does one fear death less?

Ring sees the NDE as a hopeful clue to an evolution of planetary consciousness. The Light seems to be sending a powerful message of hope during a violently destructive century, he says. The NDE is a call to transformation, but each person must accept the call with courage and responsibility. Ring's current research is an exploration of the nature of near-death experiences for persons who are blind, either from birth or afterwards. His initial results show that yes, blind people do, in some fashion, indeed see visually during their NDEs.

Kenneth Ring, Ph.D., is Professor of Psychology at the University of Connecticut. Ring's numerous books and articles have been central to NDE research, especially *Life at Death* (1980), *Heading Toward Omega* (1984), and *The Omega Project* (1992). The International Association for Near-Death Studies (IANDS) owes its existence to Ring, who is a past president.

·⤳ Near-Death Experiences ⤳·
Implications for Human Evolution and Planetary Transformation

About a decade ago, the world began to hear about a curious but irresistibly intriguing phenomenon. Called the *near-death experience* (now often abbreviated as NDE) by its chief popularizer, psychiatrist Raymond Moody (1975, 1977), whose books proved to be international best sellers, this moment of transcendental radiance, occurring when individuals reach the apparent threshold of imminent death, somehow fascinated and captured the attention of millions of people around the world. Indeed, one wonders whether, aside from the sexual orgasm, there has ever been an experience whose duration is so brief—many near-death experiences appear to last less than a minute—that has stimulated so much reflection and commentary.

In this connection, and in the wake of this pioneering work,[1] many books and articles examining near-death experiences and their implications have now been published both in the United States and elsewhere. Numerous professional conferences in the United States, Europe, and Asia have likewise dealt with this experience; and an international organization—the International Association for Near-Death Studies (IANDS)[2]—has emerged as a vehicle for disseminating the findings of NDE research around the world. Such attention appears to have triggered a deep and growing absorption with this tiny sliver of life—its apparent last moments—on a very wide scale.

So pervasive is this interest that, at least in the United States, the near-death experience has achieved the status of a *cultural* and not just a clinical phenomenon. Not only have hundreds of radio and television talk shows featured discussions on the subject in addition to countless articles about it in the print media, but also one can scarcely find anyone who has not encountered such an experience in a Hollywood film, a television soap, a short story or novel, or even in a cartoon of a fashionable magazine. If one is sensitized to their existence, they seem to be as ubiquitous as convenience stores and just about as well known. In the United States alone, literally millions of people are now known to have had near-death experiences; this means that many millions of us are directly acquainted with one or more individuals to whom this kind of experience has happened.

Consequently, the near-death experience hardly appears to be a passing fad[3] but is a salient fact of our time and one which continues to exert a very powerful hold on our collective consciousness. In addition to its popular appeal, in recent years it has begun to be appreciated as a phenomenon with the potential for affecting human consciousness and thus life on earth in a very profound way. Some have speculated that it is already beginning to do so (Flynn, 1986; Grey, 1985; Grosso, 1985; Ring, 1984). But before we can meaningfully explore the deeper implications of near-death experiences, specifically those concerned with human evolution and planetary transformation, we must first examine the experience itself more closely, for it is obviously the foundation stone on which our conclusions must rest.

CONTENT AND PATTERNING OF THE NDE

What is it exactly that someone experiences who reports having survived an NDE? Perhaps the best way to grasp this (through the written word) is for you to imagine that this is something that is happening to you. There are, however, two important qualifications. First, though they tend to follow a single common pattern, near-death experiences vary greatly in terms of the number of experiential elements that serve to define the prototypic pattern. In short, some are more complete than others. Second, as one gets deeper into the experience, there are several different "branches" that one may follow after experiencing the basic NDE "stem." For our purposes, you should imagine a fairly full NDE, which will progress along one of the most common branches.

Suppose you are driving in your automobile at a high rate of speed along a crowded highway when suddenly a truck pulls in front of your car, forcing you to jam on the brakes—but too late. In the next instant there is a terrible, sickening collision and then…. If you are typical of the thousands of people researchers have interviewed who have reported NDEs, what would you experience?

Probably the first sensation you'd be aware of would be a feeling of extreme peace and tremendous well-being. You'd feel no pain—nor indeed any bodily sensation of any kind. You might be aware of a kind of crystalline, pure silence unlike anything you'd ever experienced before. You would probably have the direct awareness that whatever this was, you were absolutely safe and secure in this all-pervading atmosphere of peace.

Then you'd begin to have a kind of visual awareness of your environment. The first thing you'd notice is that while you—the real you—appear to be watching everything from above, your *body* is "down there" surrounded by a knot of concerned individuals. You are watching all the frenetic activity below you with a feeling of detached objectivity, perhaps even with a sense of slight amusement. "Why are they making such a fuss about that body?" you might think, *"I'm* perfectly fine." Indeed, you have never felt better in your life—your perception is extremely vivid and clear, your mind seems to be functioning in a hyper-lucid fashion and you are feeling more fully alive than you can ever remember. You watch the scene below you, noting your crumpled car flipped over on its belly by the side of the road, and you observe that off in the distance an ambulance is trying to weave its way through the stalled traffic....

Suddenly your attention is drawn to an inviting, velvety blackness and you find yourself moving through this blackness—without a body but with an unmistakable sense of motion—and, as you do, you are aware that this blackness has the configuration of a tunnel. That is, the black space is bounded (though vast) and cylindrical and you seem to be propelled through it as if you are headed for a definite, but still unknown destination. Although you are travelling through this tunnel with a sense of increasing, indeed extraordinary, speed, you don't feel afraid. You just accept what is happening to you, knowing that everything will be all right.

As you approach what appears to be the end of the tunnel, you become aware of what is at first a pinpoint of light. This light quickly grows bigger and brighter and becomes more effulgent. It is an extremely brilliant light—golden-white—but it absolutely does not hurt your eyes at all. You've never experienced a light like this—it seems to be sourceless and to cover the entire vista before you. As you move closer to the light, you begin to be overwhelmed with the most powerful waves of what can only be described as pure love, which seem to penetrate to the very core of your being. There are no thoughts at all now—only total immersion in this light. All time stops; this is eternity, this is perfection—you are home again in the light.

In the midst of this timeless perfection, however, you become aware that somehow associated with this light there is a definite *presence.* It is not a person, but it is a *being* of some kind, a form you cannot see but to whose consciousness your own mind seems now to be linked. A telepathic dialogue ensues. The presence informs you that you must make a decision whether to remain here or to go back. Even as this thought is communicated to you, you are suddenly seeing, as though in a million simultaneous yet precise and sharp images, everything that has ever happened to you in your life. There is no sense of judgment—you are watching all this like a spectator—but as this patterned fabric of your life unravels before you, you grasp the essential meaning of your life and in the moment of that realization, you see with absolute clarity that you must go back, that your family, especially your children, need you....

That's the last bit of transcendental awareness you have. The next thing you know is that you are in excruciating pain in what is clearly an altogether different and heart-breaking human environment that you eventually recognize to be a hospital room.

It is three days later, you are enmeshed in tubes and IVs in an intensive care unit, unable to talk but able to remember every last detail of what happened to you when your body lay on the roadside and you hung suspended between life and death.

In reflecting on your near-death experience—though you would probably not label it thus—what is clear to you is that this was no dream or hallucination. Nor was it something that you simply imagined. This was compellingly real and absolutely objective: it was more real than life itself. You wish you could talk to somebody about it, but who could understand, even if you found words adequate to describe it? All you know is that this is the most profound thing that has ever happened to you and that your life— and your understanding of life—will never again be the same.

So much for a fairly common *deep* near-death experience and its immediate aftermath. In any event, this is what many people have said "it is like to die." Of course, the bare recital of such an experience only raises a multitude of empirical and interpretative questions; it does not provide any firm answers (except, possibly, to those who have the experience) concerning what occurs at death, much less what, if anything, takes place *after* biological death. However, considerable research has recently been conducted into these experiences and we now know a great deal more about them.

PARAMETERS AND INTERPRETATIONS OF THE NDE[4]

Among the first questions usually asked about this phenomenon is, how often does it actually occur? If one were to take one hundred consecutive cases of patients who clinically died,[5] how many of the survivors would related NDEs?

Early research (Ring, 1980; Sabom, 1982) suggested that the answer might be about 40%, and this estimate has also been supported by the results of a Gallup poll (Gallup, 1982), which was based on a much larger and more representative sample of people who had been close to death.[6] The body of research on near-death experiences is consistent in showing that most people remember nothing as a result of a near-death crisis, but that a very high percentage of those who claim to have some conscious recall report experiences that conform, at least in part, to the prototypic NDE we've already considered. A scattered number will report idiosyncratic experiences that usually seem to be hallucinatory in character; likewise, a tiny fraction of all cases appear to be negative experiences.

If one extrapolates from Gallup's sample base to the population from which it was designed to be representative (160 million adult Americans), it is possible to estimate how many people living in the United States have already had an NDE—about 8 million! This number has astonished many people (including some researchers) and should be carefully noted since it plays a key role in the thesis to be advanced later in this article.

Another question that is often asked is, does the way one nearly dies affect the experience? Investigators have examined a diverse array of conditions associated with the onset of death: combat situations, attempted rape and murder, electrocutions, near-fatal falls, near drownings, vehicular crashes, freezings, hangings, as well as a great range of strictly medical and surgical conditions. Overall, the pattern seems quite clear-cut: by whatever means a person comes close to death, once the NDE begins to unfold, it is essentially invariant and has the form described earlier. In addition, research on suicide-related NDEs (Greyson, 1981; Ring & Franklin, 1981–1982) has shown that these experiences likewise tend to conform to the prototypic pattern. In short, so far as is now known, situations covering a wide gamut of near-death conditions appear to have a negligible effect on the experience itself.

If situational variables do not significantly influence the experience, what about personal characteristics? Are certain people more likely to have such an experience because of social background, personality, prior beliefs, or even prior knowledge of near-death experiences? Once again, the research to date is consistent in finding that individual and social factors appear to play a minimal role. Demographic variables such as gender, race, social class, or education, for example, have been shown not to be connected with NDE incidence and form. Similarly, it is evident that there is no particular kind of person—defined by psychological attributes—who is especially likely to have a near-death experience. It might be thought that people who have a pre-existing or strong religious orientation or who already believe in some form of postmortem existence would be more prone than others. But this is not so. Atheists and agnostics are no less likely to recount prototypic near-death experiences than religious people, though their interpretation of the experience is apt to be different. Finally, prior knowledge does not seem to increase the probability of having one.

Thus, despite persistent inquiry and recently renewed interest into the question, we are obliged to conclude that the near-death experience seems to "select" its recipients in a random manner. At any rate, if there is any type of person who is an especially good candidate, we have not yet succeeded in identifying the characteristics.

When we come to the question—and it is an all-important one—of *universality*, we must admit that this is an area of research that is still lamentably underdeveloped.[7] Nevertheless, we do at least have a fair amount of data from various cultures that afford us some tentative answers concerning the extent to which the NDE is a culture-free phenomenon.

We already have enough information to assert confidently that in England and in continental Europe near-death experiences take the same form as in the United States (Giovetti, 1982; Grey, 1985; Hampe, 1979). This is hardly surprising since these countries share a Judaeo-Christian heritage. In the IANDS archives and in a few scattered articles (Counts, 1983; Green, 1984; Pasricha & Stevenson), there are fragmentary data from a diverse number of cultures whose traditional beliefs are quite different from those of the west. Included here are cases from India, Japan, South America, Melanesia, and Micronesia, among others. In general, these cases show some obvious parallels to the classic pattern, but often involve elements that deviate in specific ways, especially in the deeper stages where more archetypal imagery comes into play. At this point, then, the prudent conclusion must be that, in western cultures, our data are simply too fragmentary to permit any firm judgment concerning the universality of the prototypic NDE model.

Nevertheless, from the body of cross-cultural data that we do have, it seems plausible to infer that despite some degree of cultural variation, there may be certain universal constants such as the out-of-body experience, the passage through a realm of darkness toward a brilliantly illuminated area, and the encounter with "celestial" beings. Only further research, however, can substantiate this hypothesis as well as settle the question of the universality of the prototypic near-death experience as a thanatological phenomenon.

Finally, we must address the issue of the general interpretation of the NDE. As many considerations of this formidable matter have already established (Grey, 1985; Greyson & Flynn, 1984; Grosso, 1981; Moody, 1975; Ring, 1980; Sabom, 1982), there exist a plethora of theories and a minimum of consensus about them. The interested reader is advised to consult the literature in near-death studies for the specifics of the theory, over which debate continues to be heated. These theories tend to fall into three broad classes: biological, psychological, and transcendental, though many interpretations do not confine themselves to a single perspective. The biological theories tend to be reductionistic and anti-survival in tone whereas those with transcendental emphases tend to be empirically untestable but compatible with a survivalistic interpretation. Naturally the psychological theories are intermediate in most respects.

We must emphasize that a decade of research on the near-death experience has utterly failed to produce any kind of generally accepted interpretation, even among those who have spent years carefully examining it. Moreover, I have recently tried to show (Ring, 1984) that the surrounding interpretative issues are even more complex than many theorists have apparently appreciated. At the present time, then, the question of how such an experience can be explained—or, indeed, whether it even can be—remains shrouded in a cloud of obscurity and contentiousness. The irony is that this entire question may well prove to be entirely irrelevant to the issue of its importance to humanity at large.

The larger significance of the near-death experience turns not so much on either the phenomenology or the parameters of the experience but on its *tranformative* effects. For it is precisely these effects that afford us a means of merging it with certain broad evolutionary currents that seem to be propelling humanity toward the next stage of its collective development. To understand the basis of this linkage, we must now explore the ways in which a near-death experience tends to change the lives, conduct, and character of those who survive it.

TRANSFORMATIVE EFFECTS OF NDES

The most recent work in near-death studies (Bauer, 1985; Flynn,1986; Grey, 1985; Ring, 1984) has been increasingly focused on the aftereffects of the NDE, and it is concordant in revealing a very provocative set of findings. First, it appears that just as the near-death experience itself seems to adhere to a common pattern of transcendental elements, so also there seems to be a consistent pattern of transformative aftereffects. Second, this pattern of changes tends to be so highly positive and specific in its effects that it is possible to interpret it as indicative of *a generalized awakening of higher human potential*. To see how this could be so, and to lay the groundwork for its possible evolutionary significance, let us now review the findings of my own study of aftereffects, described in my book *Heading Toward Omega* (Ring, 1984).

This investigation, whose findings rest on the statistical analysis of specially designed questionnaires as well as qualitative data from personal interviews, examined three broad categories of aftereffects: (I) changes in self-concept and personal values; (2) changes in religious or spiritual orientation; and (3) changes in psychic awareness. Wherever possible, the self-reports of respondents were compared to assessments provided by individuals such as close friends or family members who had known the experiencer well both before and after his or her near-death experience. For most statistical analyses, data from appropriate control groups were also available for comparative purposes. What, then, is the psychological portrait that can be drawn from this study?

First, in the realm of personal values, people emerge from this experience with a heightened *appreciation of life*, which often takes the form not only of a greater responsiveness to its natural beauty but also of a pronounced tendency to be focused intently on the present moment. Concern over past grievances and worries about future problems tend to diminish. As a result, these people are able to be more fully present to life now, in the moment, so that an enhanced attentiveness to their environment and a freshness of perception follow naturally. They also possess a greater appreciation of themselves in the sense that they have *greater feelings of self-worth* generally. In most cases, it is not that they show signs of ego inflation, but rather that they are able to come to a kind of acceptance of themselves as they are, which they will sometimes attribute to the tremendous sense of affirmation they received "from the Light."

Perhaps one of the most evident changes that follows a near-death experience is an *increased concern for the welfare of others.* This is a very broad and important domain with many different aspects to it. Here I will only be able to briefly summarize its principal modes of expression—increased tolerance, patience, and compassion for others, and especially an increased ability to express love. Indeed, after a near-death experience, people tend to emphasize the importance of sharing love as the primary value in life. In addition, they seem to feel a stronger desire to help others and claim to have more insight into human problems and more understanding of other human beings. Finally, they seem to demonstrate an unconditional acceptance of others, possibly because they have been able to accept themselves in this way. In a sense, one might characterize all these changes as exemplifying a *greater appreciation of others* and, as such, it may represent still another facet of what appears to be a general appreciation factor that the near-death experience itself serves to intensify.

As there is an overall increase in the aforementioned values, in other values there is a clear and consistent decline. For example, the importance placed on material things, on success for its own sake, and on the need to make a good impression on others, all diminish after individuals undergo a near-death experience. In general, people-oriented values rise while concern over material success plummets.

Finally, one more change in the realm of personal values should be noted. These people tend to seek a deeper understanding of life, especially its spiritual or religious aspects. They tend to become involved in a search for increased self-understanding as well, and appear more inclined to join organizations or engage in reading or other activities that will be conducive to achieving these ends.

Incidentally, with respect to these value changes—as well as to other categories of aftereffects—it appears that these self-reports may well reflect changes in behavior. Though we clearly need more corroborative evidence than is available in *Heading Toward Omega,* statements by close friends and family members tend to provide support for the behavioral changes these people describe in themselves.

Moving to the area of religious and spiritual changes, it will come as no surprise to learn that there are far-reaching aftereffects here, too. In general, however, such changes tend to follow a particular form to which the term *universalistic* might most appropriately be applied. In characterizing this universalistic orientation, it will be helpful to distinguish a number of different components that together make up the model spiritual world-view of those who have experienced a near-death crisis.

First, there is a tendency to describe themselves as more spiritual, not necessarily more religious. By this they appear to signify that they have experienced a deep inward change in their spiritual awareness, but not one that made them more outwardly religious in their behavior. They claim to feel, for example, much closer to God than they had before, but the formal, more external aspects of religious worship often appear to have weakened in importance. They are also more likely to express an unconditional belief in "life after death" for everyone and to endorse the conviction that not only will there be some form of post-mortem existence, but that "the Light" will be there for everyone at death, regardless of one's beliefs (or lack of them) about what happens at death.

Interestingly—and this is a finding also suggested by my earlier research in *Life at Death* (Ring, 1980) as well as Gallup's (1982) survey—a greater openness to the idea of reincarnation is often expressed. It is not that they find themselves ready to subscribe to a formal belief in reincarnation, but rather that it is a doctrine that makes more sense to them than it did prior to their near-death experience. My impression is that this increased receptivity to reincarnational ideas is part of a more general friendliness to and acquaintance with Eastern religions and with some of the more esoteric and mystical variants of Christianity and Judaism.

Finally, the near-death experience draws people to a belief in the idea known to students of comparative religion as "the transcendent unity of religions," the notion that underlying all the world's greatest religious traditions there is a single and shared transcendent vision of the Divine. In espousing this view, people will sometimes aver or imply that they came to this realization directly through their own near-death experiences. Similarly, they are more inclined than others to admit to a desire for a form of universal spirituality that by embracing everyone would exclude no one. This is not a naïve hope or wish that the multitudinous and incredibly diverse religious traditions throughout the world might somehow melt into a single "universal religion," but only that individuals of different and seemingly divisive religious faiths might one day truly realize their unity with one another.

The last domain of aftereffects explored in *Heading Toward Omega* dealt with changes in psychic awareness. Not only my findings but those of others (Greyson, 1983; Kohr, 1983) tend to support the hypothesis that the near-death experience serves to trigger an increase in psychic sensitivity and development—that following their experience they become aware of many more psychic phenomena than had previously been the case. For example, they claim to have had more telepathic and clairvoyant experiences, more precognitive experiences (especially in dreams), greater awareness of synchronicities, more out-of-body experiences, and a generally increased susceptibility to what parapsychologists call "psi-conducive states of consciousness" (that is, psychological states which seem to facilitate the occurrence of psychic phenomena). Although the data on apparent increases in psychic awareness lend themselves to various interpretations, it does seem clear that a heightened sensitivity to psychic phenomena follows a near-death experience (which, of course, may well include subjectively convincing paranormal features in its own right).

Having now reviewed the findings on some of the major aftereffects of near-death experiences, we must seek a coherent framework to place them in so that their implicit patterning may be brought into relief. I believe it is possible and plausible to regard the near-death experience as playing a critical *catalytic* role in personal development. Specifically, it seems to serve as a catalyst to promote the *spiritual awakening and growth* of the individual because of its power to thrust one into a transcendental state of consciousness whose impact is to trigger a release of a universal "inner programming" of higher human potentials. There may be in each of us a latent spiritual core that is set to manifest in a particular form if only it can be activated by a powerful enough stimulus.[8] In the near-death experience it appears that the stimulus is the Light, and the similarity and consistency of the spiritual changes following a near-death experience point to what may be a common "spiritual DNA" of the human species. In these people, the pattern of changes in the consciousness and conduct bears a marked similarity to what Bucke (1969) long ago claimed for his examples of "cosmic consciousness" and to which the modern psychiatrist, Stanley Dean (1975), has more recently called our attention. A near-death experience certainly tends to stimulate a *radical spiritual transformation* in the life of the individual, which affects his self-concept, his relations to others, his view of the world *and* his world-view, as well as his mode of psychological and psychic functioning. But how does any of this—profound as these changes may be—speak to the weighty issues of human evolution and planetary transformation?

IMPLICATIONS OF THE NEAR-DEATH EXPERIENCE FOR HUMAN EVOLUTION AND PLANETARY TRANSFORMATION

I believe only a very partial understanding of the significance of the near-death experience can be attained from a strictly psychological perspective, i.e., one that concentrates on the *individual's* experience and its effects upon him. A more complete appreciation is available, however, if we shift the level of analysis from the individual plane to the sociological, where the meaning of the transformative pattern will be more apparent. We must look at the near-death experience from this broader perspective in order to discern the possible deeper significance for humanity at large.

Recall, first of all, that it has already been projected that perhaps as many as 8 *million* adult Americans have experienced this phenomenon—and we know that American children also report such experiences (Bush, 1983; Gabbard & Twemlow, 1984; Morse, 1983; Morse, Connor, & Tyler, 1985). Although we do not have even a crude estimate of how many people in the whole world may have had this experience, it certainly does not seem unreasonable to assume that additional millions outside the United States must also have had them. But the point is not simply that many millions will know this experience for themselves but also *how the NDE will transform them afterward*. We have already examined how people's lives and consciousness are affected and what values come to guide their behavior. To begin to appreciate the possible planetary impact of these changes, we must imagine these same effects occurring in millions of lives throughout the world, regardless of race, religion, nationality, or culture.

From various studies of transcendental experiences (Bucke, 1969; Dean, 1975; Hardy, 1979; Hay, 1982; Grof, 1985; James, 1958), we know that the radical spiritual transformation which often follows a near-death experience is by no means unique to that experience alone. Rather, as Grof (1985) has recently implied, transcendental experiences, however they may come about, tend to induce similar patterns of spiritual change in individuals who undergo them. In short, the near-death experience is only *one* means to catalyze a spiritual transformation, but many others, which seem to reflect the same underlying spiritual archetype, have unquestionably been triggered by something other than a near-death crisis.

Is there any way to estimate the extent of such transcendental experiences in general? Probably not with any real hope for acceptable accuracy, but we do have at least a basis for a rough sort of guess for English-speaking countries. In national surveys in the United States, England, and Canada, for example, up to *one third* of those polled admit that they have had some kind of powerful spiritual experience (Hay, 1982). Of course, from these data only, it is impossible to claim that such experiences necessarily induce the kind of transformative pattern I have previously delineated. Nevertheless, it does seem warranted to infer that many more people must undergo these transformations by means other than a near-death experience.

Thus, if these other transformations are added to the presumed millions of near-death experiences, we immediately see that we are dealing with a far more pervasive phenomenon than one might have first assumed.

A third consideration in this argument pertains not simply to the number of people in the world who may have experienced a major transformative awakening, however it may have been occasioned, but to the rate of increase in such transformations. In the case of near-death experiences, of course, it is mainly modern resuscitation technology that is responsible for creating such a large pool of survivors. Before the advent of cardiopulmonary resuscitation, for example, most would have died; now many not only are saved but go on to live drastically changed lives because of their close encounter with death. With resuscitation technology likely to improve and to spread in use around the globe, it appears inevitable that many more millions will undergo and survive near-death experiences and thus be transformed according to this archetypal pattern.

Similarly, although there are not, as I have indicated, any systematic studies of the incidence of transcendental experiences in general, various students of higher consciousness (Ferguson, 1980; Grof, 1985; Russell, 1983; White, 1981) have speculated that such experiences are widespread, at least in the western world, and that their number may be growing exponentially.

Such intriguing possibilities fit neatly with the next observation needed to complete the foundation for my argument based on recent theories concerning the spread of behavioral properties throughout a population. I am thinking here particularly of the theory of the young English biologist, Rupert Sheldrake, whose book, A *New Science of Life* (1981), has fanned widespread interest and controversy in scientific circles ever since its publication. In his book, Sheldrake propounds a hypothesis of what he calls "formative causation," which states that the characteristic forms and behavior of physical, chemical, and biological systems are determined by invisible organizing fields—*morphogenetic fields*, in Sheldrake's phrase. Although I cannot review here the author's evidence in support of his hypothesis,[9] Sheldrake's basic idea is that once such fields do become established through some initial behavior, that behavior is then facilitated in others through a process called *morphic resonance*. Thus, for example, once an *evolutionary variant* occurs in a species, it is likely to spread throughout the entire species.

Sheldrake's ideas are similar to (but certainly not identical with) the theme of the popular "hundredth monkey effect," whose empirical authenticity now appears entirely without foundation, but whose appeal as a framework for conceiving social contagion phenomena is almost irresistible. This seemingly apocryphal tale describes how a new behavior, potato washing by monkeys, spread to all monkeys on a certain Japanese island as well as to monkeys on adjacent islands when an imaginary "hundredth monkey" indulged in the new ritual. In principle, once the hundredth monkey engaged in this new behavior, that was all that was needed to create a strong enough field for morphic resonance to occur, thus turning innovation into custom. In this case, the hundredth monkey presumably established the critical mass necessary to transform the eating habits of the entire colony. What is the relevance of all this to the near-death experience and to the issues of the evolution of consciousness and planetary transformation? There is a possible connection stemming from the following observation, which has previously been made by a number of others besides myself. We do not know the limits of Sheldrake's hypothesis. If it is correct—and it is at present the subject of much excited interest and experimental work—it is distinctly possible that it may also apply to states of consciousness as well. This extrapolation has, in fact, been made by science writer Peter Russell (1983) whose commentary will make explicit the connection between our concerns here and Sheldrake's work. According to Russell:

> Applying Sheldrake's theory to the development of higher states of con-
> sciousness, we might predict that the more individuals begin to raise their
> own levels of consciousness, the stronger the morphogenetic field for high-
> er states would become, and the easier it would be for others to move in
> that direction. Society would gather momentum toward enlightenment.
> Since the rate of growth would not be dependent on the achievements
> of those who had gone before, we would enter a phase of super-expo-
> nential growth. Ultimately, this could lead to a chain reaction, in which
> everyone suddenly started making the transition to a higher level of con-
> sciousness. (Russell, 1983, p. 129)

Although Russell's own formulation may seem somewhat hyperbolic and simplistic, it does have the virtue of suggesting both a hopeful and larger vision of the inherent potential of the near-death experience and of other similar transcendental experiences. If we now consider the high base rate of all transcendental experiences generally throughout the world, the likelihood of their increasing incidence, and the possible mechanism by which the effects of such states may spread across a population, we may finally discern the possible global significance of the near-death experience.

May it be that this high rate of transcendental experience *collectively represents an evolutionary thrust toward higher consciousness for humanity at large?* Could it be that the near-death experience is itself an *evolutionary mechanism* that has the effect of jump-stepping individuals into the next stage of human development by unlocking previously dormant spiritual potentials? Indeed, are we seeing in these people, as they mutate from their former personalities into more loving and compassionate individuals, the prototype of a new, more spiritually advanced strain of the human species striving to come into being? Do these people represent the "early maturers" of a new breed of humanity emerging in our time—an evolutionary bridge to the next shore in our progression as a species, a "missing link" in our midst?

These are heady and provocative questions, but they are not entirely speculative ones. Many thinkers before me have dreamed and written of the coming to earth of a higher humanity and have attempted to describe the attributes of such people. Although these visions of a higher humanity are subjective, the transformations I have outlined in this article have happened to real people, and they are among us now. And we can at least ask: How well do these visions of a new humanity match the characteristics of these people?

For one representative portrait of this new humanity,[10] let me draw on the views of the well-known author, John White (1981), who has helped to popularize the term *Homo noeticus* in this connection. In reading his description, bear in mind that it was *not* intended as a characterization of someone who had experienced a near-death crisis, and that it is similar in many ways to accounts provided by other evolutionary thinkers who have addressed the same issue:

> *Homo noeticus* is the name I give to the emerging form of humanity.
> "Noetics" is a term meaning the study of consciousness, and that activity is
> a primary characteristic of members of the new breed. Because of their
> deepened awareness and self-understanding, they do not allow the tradi-
> tionally imposed forms, controls, and institutions of society to be barriers
> to their full development. Their changed psychology is based on expres-
> sion of feeling, not suppression. Their motivation is cooperative and lov-
> ing, not competitive and aggressive. Their logic is multi-level/integrat-
> ed/simultaneous, not linear/sequential/either-or. Their sense of identity is
> embracing-collective, not isolated individual. Their psychic abilities are
> used for benevolent and ethical purposes, not harmful and immoral ones.
> The conventional ways of society don't satisfy them. The search for new
> ways of living and new institutions concerns them. They seek a culture
> founded in higher consciousness, a culture whose institutions are based
> on love and wisdom, a culture that fulfills the perennial philosophy.
> (White, 1981, p. 14)

Although this is an idealized description, the transformative process that the near-death experience tends to set into motion certainly appears to lead to the development of individuals who approximate the ideal type White posits as the prototype of the new humanity.

Even if my own ideas about the seeding of a new humanity through the spread of near-death experiences and other transcendental experiences are found to have some plausibility,[11] their implications for planetary transformation admittedly allow for a variety of short-term scenarios. I am not one who foresees the emergence of a new, cooperative planetary culture as a necessary consequence of the kind of evolutionary shift in consciousness I detect. Rather, I see that shift as a potential of the human species that is beginning to manifest, but whether it takes hold and transforms the earth depends on many factors; not least is the extent to which many of us consciously align with these trends and seek to awaken. Clearly, nothing in the collective human potential emerging from the spawning grounds of transcendental experiences precludes the possibility of our planet's self-destructing. Nothing is assured or inevitable. No one living in the last years of the twentieth century—unarguably the most horrific in history—could deny for a moment that our prospects for surviving intact into the next millennium are shrouded in black uncertainty.

At the same time, human beings live in hope as well as fear and this recent curious phenomenon—the near-death experience—seems to be holding out a powerful message of hope to humanity that even, and perhaps especially, in its darkest moments, the Light comes to show us the way onward. It is up to each of us whether we shall have the courage and the wisdom to follow where it beckons.

NOTES

1. To be sure others had researched the phenomenon long before Moody—and another physician, Elisabeth Kübler-Ross, was already a highly visible international figure who spoke compellingly about the NDE—but it was really Moody's book which, by *labelling* the phenomenon, rooted it in the soil of contemporary western culture.

2. IANDS' address is P.O. Box 502, East Windsor Hill, CT USA 06028.

3. Raymond Moody has said that after his first book, *Life After Life*, came out, he expected that the interest in the NDE that it generated would run its course within just a few months (personal communication, 1981).

4. A more detailed consideration of these issues will be found in my book, *Heading Toward Omega* (1984), especially in Chapter 2.

5. In fact, many individuals who have "only" been close to death but seemingly not "clinically dead" (i.e. without vital signs such as heartbeat and respiration for a short time) have related that they, too, have had NDEs. A broader consideration of the conditions under which individuals may undergo NDEs or similar experiences will be broached later in this article.

6. Actually, Gallup's figure is approximately 35 percent but there are methodological reasons for thinking this may be a slight underestimation of the population parameter.

7. Near-death studies is that branch of thanatology which is especially concerned with the study and understanding of the NDE.

8. In preparing this paper for publication, I discovered that Stanislav Grof, in his book *Beyond the Brain* (1985), had independently arrived at a similar conclusion based on his work of nearly three decades with psychedelic therapy and other forms of deep experiential work. In this connection he writes:

    According to the new data, spirituality is an *intrinsic* property of the psyche that emerges quite spontaneously when the process of self-exploration reaches sufficient depth. Direct experimental confrontation with the [deep] levels of the unconscious *is always* associated with a spontaneous awakening of a spirituality that is quite *independent* of the individual's childhood experiences, religious programming, church affiliation, and even cultural and racial background. The individual who connects with these levels of his or her psyche automatically develops a new world view within which spirituality represents a natural, essential and absolutely vital element of existence. (Grof, 1985, p. 368; my italics)

9. I have discussed some of it briefly elsewhere, however (see Ring, 1984, pp. 261–262).

10. By using this phrase, I of course do *not* mean to imply that NDEers and others who have undergone similar transformations represent a new *biological* species—that would be absurd. Rather, I am suggesting that such persons may be signalling a rapid shift in the overall level of spiritual awareness in homo sapiens, i.e., that humanity at large may be about to move into a higher stage of its inherent evolutionary capacity. The extent to which there may be actual changes in human biological parameters is an open question that will need to be addressed empirically.

11. Interestingly enough, another near-death researcher, Margot Grey (1985), has recently independently arrived at conclusions almost identical to mine on the basis of her own research on NDEs. In addition, Rupert Sheldrake, without having had an opportunity to review my work in detail, has told me (Sheldrake, private communication, 1985) that my extrapolation of his ideas seems legitimate to him.

REFERENCES

Bauer, M. (1985). Near-death experiences and attitude change. *Anabiosis, 5*, 39–47.

Bucke, R. (1969). *Cosmic Consciousness*. New York: E. P. Dutton.

Bush, N. (1983). The near-death experience in children: Shades of the prison house reopening. *Anabiosis, 3*, 177–93.

Counts, D. (1983). Near-death and out-of-body experiences in a Melanesian society. *Anabiosis, 3*, 115–35.

Dean, S. (1975). Metapsychiatry: The confluence of psychiatry and mysticism. In S. Dean (Ed.), *Psychiatry and Mysticism* (pp. 3–18). Chicago: Nelson-Hall.

Ferguson, M. (1980). *The Aquarian Conspiracy*. Los Angeles: J. P.Tarcher.

Flynn, C. (1986). *After the Beyond*. Englewood Cliffs, NJ: Prentice-Hall.

Gabbard, G., and S. Twemiow. (1984). *With the Eyes of the Mind*. New York: Praeger.

Gallup, G., Jr. (1982). *Adventures in Immortality*. New York: McGraw-Hill.

Giovetti, P. (1982). Near-death and deathbed experiences: An Italian survey. *Theta, 10*, 10–13.

Green, J. (1984). Near-death experiences in a Chammorro culture.*Vital Signs, 4*, 6–7.

Grey, M. (1985). *Return from Death*. London: Routledge & Kegan Paul.

Greyson, B. (1981). Near-death experiences and attempted suicide. *Suicide and Life Threatening Behavior, 11*, 1016.

Greyson, B. (1983). Increase in psychic phenomena following near-death experiences. *Theta, 11*, 26–29.

Greyson, B., and C. Flynn, eds. (1984). *The Near-Death Experience*. Springfield, IL: Charles C. Thomas.

Grof, S. (1985). *Beyond the Brain*. Albany: State University of New York Press.

Grosso, M. (1981). Toward an explanation of near-death phenomena. *Journal of the American Society for Psychical Research, 75*, 37–60.

Grosso, M. (1985). *The Final Choice*. Walpole, NH: Stillpoint.

Hampe, J. (1979). *To Die is Gain*. Atlanta, GA: John Knox.

Hardy, A. (1979). *The Spiritual Nature of Man*. New York: Oxford University Press.

Hay, D. (1982). *Exploring Innerspace*. Middlesex, England: Penguin Books.

James, W. (1958). *The Varieties of Religious Experience*. New York: Mentor.

Kohr, R. (1983). Near-death experiences, altered states and psi sensitivity. *Anabiosis, 3*, 157–74.

Moody, R., Jr. (1975). *Life after Life*. New York: Mockingbird/Bantam Books.

Moody, R., Jr. (1977). *Reflections on Life after Life*. New York: Bantam.

Morse, M. (1983). A near-death experience in a 7-year-old child. *American Journal of Diseases in Children, 13 7*, 959–61.

Morse, M., D. Conner, and D. Tyler. (1985). Near-death experiences in a pediatric population. *American Journal of Diseases in Children, 139*, 595–99.

Pasricha, S. and I. Stevenson. (1986). Near-death experiences in India: A preliminary report. *Journal of Nervous and Mental Disease 174,3*, 165–70.

Ring, K. (1980). *Life at Death*. New York: Coward, McCann & Geoghegan.

Ring, K. (1984). *Heading Toward Omega*. New York: William Morrow.

Ring, K. From alpha to omega: Ancient mysteries and the near-death experience. *Anabiosis*.

Ring, K., and S. Franklin. (1981–1982). Do suicide survivors report near-death experiences? *Omega, 12*, 191–208.

Russell, P. (1983). *The Global Brain*. Los Angeles: J. P. Tarcher.

Sabom, M. (1982). *Recollections of Death*. New York: Harper & Row.

Sheldrake, R. (1981). *A New Science of Life*. Los Angeles: J. P. Tarcher.

White, J. (1981, September). Jesus, evolution and the future of humanity. Part 1. *Science of the Mind*, pp. 8–17.

Near-Death Experiences
Relevance to the Question of Survival After Death

Ian Stevenson and *Bruce Greyson*

Some of these universal features may reflect widespread human adaptive responses to stress, but others may be more suggestive of the possibility of another realm of existence into which we pass at death.

Ian Stevenson, M.D., one of the world's foremost researchers in the field of parapsychology, is known best for his scientific investigations of reports of reincarnation. In this early article he collaborates with one of the leaders of near-death research, Bruce Greyson, M.D., editor of the *Journal of Near-Death Studies*. Focusing on the question of whether near-death experiences provide evidence for survival after death, they explore cases of people whose deaths were anticipated but did not occur, and the need to take account of remarkable similarities across cultural accounts of near-death experiences. They question the validity of autobiographical self-reports for understanding the physiological aspects of near-death experiences, however. This is because the independent corroboration from medical examinations is needed to consider possible physical factors inducing "the more impressive subjective experiences."

Ian Stevenson, M.D., is Professor of Psychiatry at the University of Virginia. He is known for his multi-volume, multi-cultural scientific study, *Cases of the Reincarnation Type.* He has also published other studies of near-death experiences.

Bruce Greyson, M.D., is Professor of Psychiatric Medicine at the University of Virginia. He has published numerous studies on NDEs.

·᠆ Near-Death Experiences ᠆·
Relevance to the Question of Survival After Death

During the last two decades, articles and books about death and dying have proliferated, but, with rare exceptions, their authors ignore completely the question of whether man survives after death.

One of us (I.S.) recently has reviewed the evidence that suggests man's survival after death (Stevenson, 1977). The evidence available is far from necessitating a conclusion in favor of such survival, but it is also far from deserving the neglect it has received from most scientists. One type of research that may contribute to this evidence is the investigation of near-death experiences—reports of persons who come close to death but escape. Such experiences include those of persons who are seriously injured or ill and are expected to die or are thought to be dead, but who unexpectedly recover. Also relevant are the experiences of persons who anticipate death during a potentially fatal situation, such as a fall from a great height, but who escape unharmed.

In this article we review published reports of these experiences and discuss some methodological and conceptual aspects of their investigation. In a subsequent report, we will present and analyze some data from cases we have investigated.

PUBLISHED REPORTS OF NEAR-DEATH EXPERIENCES

The Swiss geologist Heim (1972) was the first to collect and report a series of such experiences. In a summary account of more than 30 near-death experiences, mostly of Alpine climbers who (like himself) had fallen while climbing, he noted how frequently his informants, as they thought they were facing death, were free of fear and had an unusual clarity and increased speed of thought, and also panoramic memories, or life-review. Heim offered no interpretation of his reports, but Pfister (1930), on the basis of Heim's experience and one other account of a near-fatal event in trench warfare, ascribed the symptoms of near-death experiences to denial of death and to profound regression under stress.

Druss and Kornfeld (1967) interviewed ten survivors of cardiac arrests, three of whom believed they had entered some unearthly realm or other state of postmortem existence during their periods of unconsciousness before they were resuscitated.

Kalish (1969) published an analysis of 323 accounts of near-death experiences, obtained for him by students. Only 23 percent of the respondents reported fear or panic as they seemed to approach death, and few had unpleasant long range aftereffects.

Dobson et al. (1971) questioned 20 patients who had survived cardiac arrest, only one of whom claimed to remember events of a paranormal or transcendental nature before his resuscitation.

Noyes (1972) and co-workers (Noyes and Kletti, 1976a, 1976b, 1977a, 1977b; Noyes and Hoenk et. al., 1977) reported the accounts of more than 200 persons who came close to death and survived. These authors described sequential phases of (1) resistance to death, (2) life-review, and (3) transcendence of space and time. By factor analysis, they isolated independent symptom clusters of (1) hyperalertness, (2) depersonalization, and (3) mystical consciousness, including panoramic memory. They interpreted the first two of these symptom clusters as adaptive psychological responses to the threat of death, but they concluded that no single or unified interpretation also could account for the reported experiences of mystical consciousness.

Rosen (1975) interviewed seven survivors of suicide attempted by jumps from San Francisco Bay bridges; all seven reported peaceful or tranquil feelings during their jumps, as well as transcendental experiences with spiritual rebirth; none reported life-review. Rosen suggested that the absence of resistance to death and of panoramic memories may be attributed to the volitional and planned aspects of these close brushes with death.

Sabom and Kreutziger (1977a,1977b) questioned "approximately 50" patients who had suffered a near-fatal crisis (mostly cardiac arrest) with unconsciousness. Eleven of their respondents reported either autoscopic or transcendental experiences, or both. The authors found no clear medical or scientific explanation that could adequately account for these experiences.

In the scientific literature, detailed case reports are scanty. We found only fifteen such reports in journals of medicine, psychology, or parapsychology. Memoirs and other works outside the conventional medical literature contain other accounts, mostly autobiographical, which often include vivid details of the authors' recollections of their experiences. But these reports usually lack any independent corroboration and confirmation from medical examinations.

FACTORS ACCOUNTING FOR DIFFERING RESULTS

The different proportions of reported memories of near-death experiences in cardiac arrest survivors obtained in New York, (Druss, 1967), in England (Dobson et. al., 1971), and in Florida (Sabom and Kreutziger, 1977b) may derive from cultural differences among the three groups of patients, from different techniques in eliciting information by the various interviewers, or from a combination of these and other factors. A high incidence of experiences reported in a group of patients, however, does not necessarily imply the investigator's superior skill in obtaining information. In one series, overenthusiastic interviewers may have unwittingly enticed patients to embellish their experiences; in another, skeptical interviewers may have subtly communicated to the patients the wisdom of keeping silent about any puzzling experiences they may remember. Furthermore, interviews or questionnaires administered to groups of patients who are more or less known to each other (as those in intensive care units) may lead to conformities in reporting or suppressing experiences.

Medical documentation of the patient's condition is not necessary to validate the patient's personal report of his near-death experience. It is essential, however, if we are to advance in understanding the physiological conditions that accompany and may induce the more impressive subjective experiences. In a small number of our own cases, we studied reports of a patient's physical condition from hospital or other records. The patient's condition at the time of his experience sometimes was reported to be less grave than he later believed it had been. Such discrepancies may arise from paucity or inadequacy of medical records and even from their distortion, or they may arise from exaggeration on the part of the patient.

Detailed medical reports also may reveal specific conditions determining which survivors will recall events that happen while they are apparently unconscious. For example, if we assume that the principal physiological changes during cardiac arrest are broadly similar in all patients, then some additional feature, such as the duration of the arrest, may determine which patients will have memories of events occurring during the arrest. Also, since patients who have ostensibly similar physical conditions vary widely in what they claim to remember afterward, psychological factors may account for these differences. Detecting these factors, however, will require much more psychological data than those usually included in medical records.

The life-review, or panoramic memory experience, occurs with varying frequency in the published studies. Heim (1972) described it as a consistent feature of near-death experiences due to serious falls with anticipation of death. Noyes and Kletti (1977b) reported life-review in 44% of respondents who believed they were going to die during some life-threatening danger, but in only 12% of those who did not believe they were about to die. As noted previously, Rosen (1975) found that none of the interviewed survivors of suicidal jumps reported panoramic memory. These observations suggest that the suddenness and unexpectedness, which are not necessarily the same, with which a person faces death may importantly influence the occurrence of the life-review experience.

RELEVANCE TO SURVIVAL AFTER DEATH

Comparisons of accounts of near-death experiences obtained in different cultures suggest that the beliefs a person has before he approaches death have an important influence on the kind of experience he will report if he comes close to death and escapes. If these experiences derive solely from the beliefs of the persons having them, then they have no more objective reality than most dreams. In that case, their particularly vivid nature and some of their more impressive features may result only from emotional reactions to the prospect of imminent death. This interpretation is favored by several psychiatrists who have studied these cases, such as Noyes (Noyes and Hoenk et. al., 1977), Ehrenwald (1974), and Lukianowicz (1958). It falls short, however, in several regards.

First, although culture-bound expectations do seem to influence these experiences, reports from different cultures also show remarkable uniformities. Some of these universal features may reflect widespread human adaptive responses to stress, but others may be more suggestive of the possibility of another realm of existence into which we pass at death. For example, subjects frequently report that, while apparently dead, they seemed to view their bodies as if from a different point in space. They usually also claim that their mental processes were remarkably clear when they seemed to be separated from their physical bodies. Most of them become convinced by the experience that they will survive the deaths of their physical bodies when death finally occurs. However, as Ducasse (1961) noted, since persons having near-death experiences escape death, they have not existed independently of their physical bodies. Even though consciousness may seem to become detached from the body, it may actually remain dependent on the life of the body for its continued existence.

Some persons who report such out-of-the-body experiences claim that they became aware of events that they could not have perceived normally. Some remember conversations between the physicians and nurses who were working to revive them. This kind of experience is not necessarily evidence of extrasensory perception; patients who are anesthetized or otherwise ostensibly unconscious sometimes can assimilate, and afterward remember, conversations held in their presence (Cherkin and Harroun, 1971). Other patients, however, make stronger claims of remembering conversations held in adjoining rooms or other events occurring outside the range of their sense organs.

Patients who approach death and recover sometimes report that during the time they seemed to be dying, they met deceased relatives or friends. Visions of this kind, like other aspects of near-death experiences, may represent a defensive attempt to reduce fear of impending death by imagining reunion with familiar persons. There are a small number of cases, however, in which the dying person had a vision of a recently deceased person of whose death he had no normal knowledge (Osis and Haraldsson, 1977).

Cases that include features of extrasensory perception cannot readily be subsumed under the heading of depersonalization. However, veridical extrasensory or autoscopic experiences near-death do not necessarily tell us anything about postmortem conditions. Near-death experiences may be analogous to presently recognized transitional states of consciousness that occur between sleeping and waking—the hypnagogic and hypnopompic states—the particular features of which may not be characteristic of those mental states that lie clearly on either side of the transition.

CONCLUSION

Our purpose in presenting this review is to develop a stance appropriate for the further investigation of near-death experiences. Popular writings on the subject are apt to proclaim rhapsodically that near-death experiences already provide strong evidence of man's survival after death. In contrast, the scientific reports rarely touch on the possibility of postmortem survival or acknowledge that further inquiries into near-death experiences could contribute to the evidence bearing on this question. If we fail even to conjecture about this possibility—of life after death— we shall be unlikely to make appropriate inquiries that could clarify the many questions with which near-death experiences abound.

REFERENCES

Cherkin, A., and P. Harroun. (1971). Anesthesiology and memory processes *Anesthesiology*, *34*, 469–74.

Dobson M., A. E. Tattersfield, and M. W. Adler, et al. (1971). Attitudes and long-term adjustment of patients surviving cardiac arrest. *British Medical Journal*, 3, 207–12.

Druss, R. C., and D. S. Kornfeld. (1967). The survivors of cardiac arrest: A psychiatric study *JAMA*, *201*, 291–296.

Ducasse, C. J. (1961). *A Critical Examination of the Belief in a Life After Death*. Springfield, IL: Charles Thomas Publisher., 164.

Ehrenwald, J. (1974). Out-of-the-body experiences and the denial of death. *Journal of Nervous and Mental Disease, 159*, 227–33.

Heim, A. (1972). Notizen über den Tod durch Absturz. *Jahrbuch des schweizerischen Alpclub, 27*, 327–37, 1892. Translated in *Omega* ,3, 45–52, 1972.

Kalish, R. (1969). Experiences of persons reprieved from death, in Kutscher, A. H., Ed., *Death* and Bereavement. Springfield, IL: Charles C. Thomas Publisher, 84–96.

Lukianowicz, N. (1958). Autoscopic phenomena. AMA Arch Neurol Psychiatry, 80, 199–220.

Noyes, R. (1972). The experience of dying. Psychiatry, 35, 174–84.

Noyes, R., P. R. Hoenk, S. Kuperman, et al. (1977). Depersonalization in accident victims and psychiatric patients. Journal of Nervous and Mental Disease, 164, 401–407

Noyes, R., and R. Kletti. (1976a). Depersonalization in the face of life-threatening danger: A description. Psychiatry, 39, 19–27.

Noyes, R., and R. Kletti. (1976b). Depersonalization in the face of life-threatening danger: An interpretation. Omega 7, 103–14.

Noyes, R., and R. Kletti. (1977a). Depersonalization in response to life-threatening danger Comparative Psychiatry, 18, 375–84.

Noyes, R., and R. Kletti. (1977b). Panoramic memory: A response to the threat of death. Omega, 8, 181–94.

Osis, K., Haraldsson, E. (1977). At the Hour of Death. New York: Avon Books.

Pfister, O. (1930). Schockdenken und Schockphantasien bei höchster Todesgefahr. International Zeitschrift für Psychoanalysis, 16, 430–55.

Rosen D. (1975). Suicide survivors: A follow-up study of persons who survived jumping from the Golden Gate and San Francisco-Oakland Bay Bridges. Western Journal of Medicine, 122, 289–94.

Sabom, M.B., and S. Kreutziger. (1977a). The experience of near death. Death Education, 1, 195–203.

Sabom, M.B., and S. Kreutziger. (1977b). Near-death experiences. Journal of the Florida Medical Association, 64, 648–50.

Stevenson, I. (1977). Research into the evidence of man's survival after death: A historical and critical survey with a summary of recent developments. Journal of Nervous and Mental Disease, 165, 152–70.

· 14 ·

Distressing Near-Death Experiences

Bruce Greyson and *Nancy Evans Bush*

There's a cosmic terror
we have never addressed.

Bruce Greyson and Nancy Evans Bush have both been leaders in
NDE research. Greyson has contributed essential research to help
answer several questions about NDE typologies and relations to
suicide. He has also explored important issues about the role of
scientific methodology in researching NDEs. Bush is a pastoral
counselor who had a frightening near-death experience herself.
Together they give needed clarification to a theme now expanding
in NDE studies: the negative, frightening, or distressing NDE.

After early studies emphasized the beautiful, blissful, and
positive nature of NDEs, reports of negative experiences surfaced,

notably those reported by Maurice Rawlings and P. M. H. Atwater. Greyson and Bush analyze the research on the frequency of these painful events and organize them into three types: 1. possibly peaceful but experienced as unpleasant, 2. a nonexistence or void, and 3. hellish landscapes and entities. While small in percentage, the terrifying NDEs present the shadow side of the soul's journey to other worlds, and call for theories broad enough to incorporate both the bliss and the pain.

Bruce Greyson, M.D., is Professor of Psychiatric Medicine at the University of Virginia, and editor of the *Journal of Near-Death Studies*. He has published numerous studies on NDEs. Nancy Evans Bush, M.A., is a pastoral counselor in Connecticut and President of the International Association for Near-Death Studies (IANDS), which is the growing network providing support for and research about any survivors of near-death experiences.

⋅⌣ Distressing Near-Death Experiences ⌣⋅

Most reported near-death experiences include profound feelings of peace, joy, and cosmic unity. Less familiar are the reports following close brushes with death of experiences that are partially or entirely unpleasant, frightening, or frankly hellish. While little is known about the antecedents or aftereffects of these distressing experiences. there appear to be three distinct types, involving (1) phenomenology similar to peaceful near-death experiences but interpreted as unpleasant, (2) a sense of nonexistence or eternal void, or (3) graphic hellish landscapes and entities. While the first type may eventually convert to a typical peaceful experience, the relationship of all three types to prototypical near-death experiences merits further study. The effect of the distressing experience in the lives of individuals deserves exploration, as the psychological impact may be profound and long-lasting.

The near-death experience is a powerful psychological experience of undetermined origin typically occurring to an individual close to death or in a situation of intense physical or emotional danger. The precipitating event may be obvious, such as a documented cardiac arrest, or it may go unnoted, such as a momentary but quickly corrected hypotensive episode; prototypical near-death experiences have occurred with no recognized antecedent event. Thus, while a life-threatening situation is a reliable trigger for a subsequent report of a near-death experience, such an experience can occur in the absence of any recognized danger.

Most reported near-death experiences have included profound feelings of peace or bliss, joy, and a sense of cosmic unity, as well as a sense of leaving the body, entering a darkness, encountering a light, meeting spiritual beings and/or deceased persons, an uncrossable boundary, a life review, and an altered sense of time.

Further, most experiencers subsequently report profound and long-lasting changes in attitudes, beliefs, and values

(Greyson and Stevenson, 1980; Noyes, 1940; Ring, 1980, 1984; Sabom, 1982; Greyson, 1983a; Grey, 1985; Flynn, 1986; Raft and Andresen, 1986; Atwater, 1988; Roberts and Owen, 1988).

However, sporadic reports have described a smaller number of distressing events that are in some ways similar to the prototypical near-death experience but characterized by feelings of fear or despair and often described as "nightmarish" or "hellish." While the frequency of these distressing events and their relation to the more common peaceful near-death experiences have been questioned, little is known about them, and there is in fact no accepted definition of what constitutes a distressing near-death experience.

PRIOR REPORTS OF DISTRESSING NEAR-DEATH EXPERIENCES

The early phenomenological reports of near-death experiences (Moody, 1975; Noyes and Slymen, 1978–1979; Greyson and Stevenson, 1980; Ring 1980, 1984; Sabom, 1982) contained no distressing experiences, which may have deterred subsequent investigators from seeking or acknowledging them. Moody (1977) reported a vaguely unpleasant affect, primarily in suicide-related experiences and noted that some people described seeing in their peaceful near-death experiences other individuals who appeared bewildered or perplexed; however, he concluded that "in the mass of material I have collected no one has ever described to me a state like the archetypical hell" (p. 169).

Sabom (1982) noted that only 18 percent of near-death experiencers he interviewed reported transitory feelings of fright or bewilderment, which were replaced by tranquility as the experience unfolded. Ring (1984) estimated that unpleasant experiences might account for 1 percent of all reported cases or less, and concluded:

> In my own experience, having talked to or heard the accounts of many hundreds of NDErs [near-death experiencers], I have never personally encountered a fullblown, predominantly negative NDE, though I have certainly found some NDEs to have had moments of uncertainty, confusion, or transitory fears. (p. 44)

Furthermore, the commonly used research instruments for identifying and measuring near-death experiences, based on these early studies, may perpetuate the bias against recognizing distressing experiences. Both the Weighted Core Experience Index (Ring, 1980) and NDE Scale (Greyson, 1983a) include elements such as peace, joy, and a sense of cosmic unity among their diagnostic criteria for near-death experiences.

Frightening deathbed visions were well known in previous centuries. Grosso (1981) noted that Christian and Hindu iconography were replete with examples of postmortem horrors, including dangerous encounters with evil forces; even the Being of Light is described in the *Tibetan Book of the Dead* as terrifying. Zaleski (1987) has documented an abundance of journeys to hell or purgatory and back from the medieval Christian literature, and noted that in contrast to those return-from-death accounts, recent near-death reports suggest that "the modern otherworld is a congenial place…a garden of unearthly delights" (p. 7).

The absence of such distressing experiences from contemporary near-death accounts may be due to their rarity, or the reluctance of individuals to report this type of experience, or to the reluctance of clinicians and researchers to hear them. It is difficult to imagine that an experiencer could be indifferent to the cultural assumption that personal merit determines type of experience; that is, that "heavenly" and "hellish" experiences come to those who have earned them. Distressing near-death experiences have frequently been referred to in the literature as "negative," in contrast to the prototypical "positive" pleasant experiences; this value-laden terminology may lead experiencers to believe they will be similarly characterized. Furthermore, people who have distressing experiences may resist talking about them to avoid reliving a personal horror, or from a sense that others must be spared a knowledge too dreadful to bear. It may seem impossible to be open about a dark and distressing experience, considering how difficult it is for many people to report radiant and peaceful encounters (e.g., Moody, 1975; Ring, 1984; Flynn, 1986; Atwater, 1988).

Clark (in Flynn, 1986) emphasized both the reluctance of individuals who have had distressing experiences to share them with investigators and our resultant underestimation of their frequency. She estimated that patients who had distressing near-death experiences took twice as many sessions to open up about them as did patients with peaceful ones. Elsewhere (Clark, 1984), she emphasized the fear, anxiety, and sense of vulnerability that may follow a distressing experience.

Whether distressing near-death experiences are rare or simply underreported, enough contemporary reports have surfaced to confirm that they do, in fact, exist. Rawlings (1978) speculated that interviewing patients immediately after resuscitation would reveal as many distressing experiences as peaceful ones, on the assumption that terrifying experiences would be quickly repressed. He noted great variety in content among these distressing experiences, in contrast to the consistency among those of a peaceful nature, and recounted twelve examples assembled from a variety of sources; but his anecdotal accounts provided no information about how long after resuscitation these individuals were interviewed. Other researchers have found no evidence that distressing experiences are rapidly repressed, nor of a higher incidence of their report immediately upon resuscitation (Ring, 1980).

Rogo, citing Rawlings's findings that distressing near-death experiences are less consistent in content than peaceful ones and are quickly forgotten, concluded that hellish experiences might be hallucinations produced by the witnesses' minds as a reaction to the violent physical ordeals (such as chest pounding and electrical stimulation) which are part and parcel of normal resuscitation techniques (1989, 136).

Garfield (1979) reported that of 36 individuals he interviewed initially from two hours to three days after the event, eight (22 percent) described demonic or nightmarish visions of great lucidity, and another four (11 percent) reported dream-like images alternating blissful and terrifying features. He further reported that in repeated interviews over a three-week period, there was no change in description of either peaceful or distressing experiences.

Lindley, Bryan, and Conley (1981), in a study of 55 near-death encounters collected through newspaper advertisements, found eleven (20 percent) to be "partially negative or hellish." They defined a "negative" near-death experience as "one that contains extreme fear, panic, or anger. It may also contain visions of demonic creatures that threaten or taunt the subjects (p. 113). They reported that "most negative experiences begin with a rush of fear and panic or with a vision of wrathful or fearful creatures," but that they are "usually transformed, at some point, into a positive experience in which all negativity vanishes and the first stage of death (peacefulness) is achieved" (p. 113).

However, Lindley and his colleagues also found it "common" for the distressing elements to follow a peaceful experience and suggested that the distress may reside in the transition between a peaceful experience and normal consciousness. From their descriptions of and direct quotes from near-death accounts, they seem to have included as "negative" those cases in which the actual experience was completely peaceful but the apparent return to the body and to mundane reality was accompanied by anger or panic.

A nationwide poll conducted in 1980–1981 by the Gallup Organization (Gallup and Proctor, 1982) estimated that 1 percent of near-death experiencers reported having experienced a sense of hell or torment, but these researchers warned that the question of distressing experiences was more complex than their data suggested. Their respondents described such elements as featureless, forbidding faces; beings who were present but not comforting; feelings of discomfort, emotional unrest, and confusion; a sense of being tricked into ultimate destruction; and fear about the finality of death. Nevertheless, the Gallup Poll reported that belief in hell was less pervasive among near-death experiencers (47 percent) than it is among the general population (53 percent).

Grey, in her comparative study of British and American near-death experiencers (1985), noted "indications that pointed to the fact that negative encounters, while infrequent, do however definitely exist" (p. 56). Grey defined a "negative" near-death experience as characterized by feelings of extreme fear or panic, emotional or mental anguish, desperation, intense loneliness, and desolation. She found the environment to be described as either dark and gloomy or barren and hostile; often subjects reported being on the brink of a pit or abyss. She further defined a subcategory of "hell-like" near-death experiences as intense unpleasant events that include a definite sense of some evil force, such as threatening demonic creatures. She found the hellish environment to be described as intensely hot or cold and to often include sounds of torment.

Grey reported that distressing experiences tend to follow a sequence of (1) fear and panic, (2) out-of-body experience, (3) entering a black void, (4) sensing an evil force, and (5) entering a hellish environment. This sequence mimics Ring's (1980) temporal model of the prototypical near-death experience unfolding in stages of (1) peace, (2) out-of body experience, (3) entering the tunnel, (4) seeing the light, and (5) entering the heavenly environment.

Grey noted the belief of physicians she interviewed that distressing experiences were more likely to be reported immediately after a near-death event. On the other hand, she noted that cardiologists such as Sabom (1982), who interviewed patients immediately after cardiac resuscitation, had failed to elicit any hellish experiences, and that the five distressing cases she herself had come across (out of a total of 41 NDEs) were reported long after the event.

Atwater (1988) also noted patterns parallel to prototypical peaceful near-death experiences in her small sample of distressing accounts. She described elements of the latter as lifeless apparitions, barren expanses, threats or silence, danger of violence, a sense of hell, and coldness; these are in contrast to the peaceful experience's friendly beings, beautiful environment, conversations, acceptance and overwhelming love, feeling of heaven, and warmth.

Flynn (1986) reported Clark's clinical impressions indicating a general pattern to distressing experiences, in which evil is experienced as a powerful entity, separate from the positively experienced light.

Aftereffects of peaceful near-death experiences have been documented by Noyes (1980), Sabom (1982), Greyson (1983c), Ring (1984), Grey (1985), Flynn (1986), Atwater (1988), and others. These effects, which are unlike those of any phenomenologically comparable events, are profound and durable. They include long-term pervasive shifts in values and attitudes that may both enrich and disrupt an individual's functioning in relationships, career, and intrapsychic life. The impact of a distressing near-death experience may be of equivalent power and permanence, but that has not been systematically examined.

Now that clinicians and investigators have discovered these distressing experiences, a number of questions arise. Initially, we need to document the incidence and phenomenology of these events. Only then can we begin to address (1) their connection to the prototypical peaceful near-death experience about which we have learned much over the past decade and (2) the more difficult but more meaningful questions about the possible causes or precipitants of distressing experiences and their effect on individuals' subsequent values, beliefs, and attitudes toward life and death.

STUDY SAMPLE

Over the past ten years, some thirty individuals have spontaneously written to the authors to tell of their terrifying near-death experiences. Recently, a notice placed in the newsletter of the International Association for Near-Death Studies requested accounts of distressing experiences. These activities resulted in the collection of 50 accounts, which constituted the study group.

From this self-selected sample, we have identified three distinct types of distressing near-death experiences differing substantially in phenomenology. The first type is similar in features to the prototypical peaceful near-death experience, but is nevertheless interpreted as terrifying.

The second involves a paradoxical experience of nothingness or of existing in an eternal featureless void. The third includes blatant "hellish" images and often begins with a sense of falling down a dark pit.

In this paper we present examples of these three types and some of their discriminating features. Further study of these rare, or rarely reported, cases may elucidate whether these three types also differ in their causes and aftereffects.

PHENOMENOLOGICAL TYPES OF DISTRESSING NEAR-DEATH EXPERIENCES

1. Prototypical Near-Death Experiences Interpreted as Terrifying

The first type of distressing experience often involves the phenomenological features of prototypical peaceful near-death experiences, such as a bright light, a tunnel, a sense of being out of the body, and a life review, but is interpreted by the individual as terrifying rather than comforting. Often the individual identifies loss of ego control as the terrifying aspect of the experience. Following are verbatim accounts of this type.

The first example is the account of a professional author who reported that she had had no religious upbringing and no knowledge of near-death experiences prior to her own, though she has read about them since. She described an experience that occurred during an anaphylactic reaction to multiple black fly bites at age 35:

I was taken to emergency suffering from a severe allergic reaction to black fly bites. Both of my eyes were completely swollen shut, and I was having difficulty breathing. I was placed on a table and immediately given an injection of Benadryl and an IV of adrenalin.

After a few minutes, my body began to shake violently. I then saw a clear picture of myself lying on the table. I saw the doctor and the nurse, whom I had never seen before, and my husband standing by my body. I became frightened and I remember strongly feeling I didn't like what I saw and what was happening. I shouted, "I don't like this!" but I was not heard by those in the room.

I then started to breathe more easily, and after a while one eye opened a little. As I looked around, I saw that the room and the people were exactly as I had seen them during my floating sensation.

The second example was reported by a paramedic instructor who claimed to have heard several patients' accounts of their near-death experiences. She described an event she experienced during a bout of measles at age six, during which, according to her mother, she almost died:

That night I was picked up, unwillingly, by a lady wearing a long, green flowing robe, medieval style. She carried me in her arms down a long, dark, green moldy type dirt-walled tunnel swiftly taking me somewhere I did not want to go. She mind-talked to me, and kept trying to explain that I had to go, and nothing could prevent it, no matter how much I didn't want to leave. I think that was why she was carrying me, for I know I would have run back down the tunnel otherwise.

Suddenly she heard bells bonging from very, very far away. She stopped and turned to listen. She told me there had been a change and I had to go back after all. She had no compassion during all of this, simply a formal, strong approach towards me. Then she carried me back to my bed and placed me on it, still drawn up in a contracted bundle from being carried so long. I called out to her, but she rapidly walked away into the tunnel.

When my mother rushed in and heard my jabbered story—which scared me more than any dream—she became terrified, due to my fragile condition.

The third example was reported by a man to have occurred during a postoperative infection following surgery for an aneurysm at age 64. At the time of his experience, he had never heard of such events, and subsequently, thinking his own experience was unique, he mentioned it to no one but his wife. The day after seeing a television program about near-death experiences, he wrote to one of us (N.E.B.) describing his experience:

As I looked under me…a strong wind was pulling me into what seemed to be a funnel shaped like a cornucopia, only opened at both ends. I was flying, and drawn directly into the vortex or funnel. At the end the lights were blinding, and crystal flashing was unbearable. As I neared the very end, I was reaching for the sides, trying to stop myself from falling off the end into the flashing crystal. I felt that I did not want to go on. If there was some way I could explain to you what happened! I vividly remember screaming, "God, I'm not ready; please help me." As I write this letter I am reliving it. I remember when I screamed an arm shot out of the sky and grabbed my hand and at the last second I was kept from falling off the end of the funnel, the lights flashing; and the heat was really something.

Since this type of distressing experience shares many descriptive features of the peaceful type, it is reasonable to regard it as a variant of the prototypical near-death experience. Supporting that view are the following examples of phenomenologically prototypical but distressing experiences that convert to peaceful ones once the individual stops fighting the experience and accepts it.

The first example was reported by a licensed practical nurse whose family attended a Dutch Reformed Church. She described an experience she had during a documented postoperative fever of 105.6°F, secondary to a pelvic abscess following her hysterectomy at age 36:

After a week or more of continuously increasing temperatures, something happened to me. Tears come to my eyes when I recall it. My body began to shake completely; I knew I was in trouble. A frightened young nurse came and placed a blanket over me and put a thermometer in my mouth and left. I couldn't hold the thermometer and dropped it, but broke it with my teeth. I was alone in my hospital room.

I don't know what happened next or how, but I was no longer in my hospital bed, but I—not as we know me, a solid human form, but myself, my energy, or my mind—was in a place surrounded by a misty gray cloud-like substance. I then began to see lights flashing in a circular shape, advancing towards me at a rapid speed, then retreating after coming inches from my face. This continued for a period of time, and I was terribly frightened. I felt as if I were transfixed. Then I began to talk to myself nonverbally. I said to myself, "You can handle this; you're strong; you'll be okay," and continued to repeat this and pray to God. I felt near death.

Then suddenly I was overcome by a feeling of *complete peace*. My feelings were that I was safe and it was beautiful, weightless. I loved it. I felt at one with all, a great joy and ultimate peace of mind and body. I knew no harm in any way would come to me. All was peaceful and profound love surrounded me. There is no description on earth that can compare with this place and feeling. I felt something was saying, "You're safe now; don't be afraid; this peace will help you."

After this happened, I just came back. I refer to this as leaving and coming back, as that's how I feel. My body was there, but where was I? The beauty of the feeling overwhelms me even now, and sometimes I try to recreate it in my mind. I cannot. The depth of this experience cannot be understood by a person who has not had it happen to themselves. Anyone who has felt this peace would never want to leave or have it leave them.

The second example was reported by a secretary who had been raised as a Congregationalist but had never heard of near-death experiences before her own. She described the following event that occurred at age 27, when, having just delivered her third child, she was given nitrous oxide for the repair of extensive uterine lacerations:

As I breathed in from the anesthesia mask, I felt myself go limp and light-headed. I was happy to give in to the floaty feeling because the bottom half of my body was experiencing intense pain, and a numbing sensation afforded me such wonderful relief! Suddenly I became aware that something really strange was happening. It was as if I had pulled up and away from my body, and I found myself watching my doctor and his nurse working on my body from a corner of the room near the ceiling. I felt so startled at being able to hover above like that. And I wanted to feel in control of my situation but I was unable to do anything except watch helplessly. I made some attempts to get the attention of the other two in the room, but they were totally oblivious to anything I was saying to them.

Then I found myself no longer in the room but traveling through a tunnel, slowly at first, then picking up speed as I went. As I entered the tunnel I began hearing the sound of an engine, the kind that operates heavy machinery. Then, as I was moving slowly I could hear voices on each side of my head, the voices of people whom I've known before because they were vaguely familiar. About this time I became frightened, so I didn't concentrate on trying to recognize any of the voices.

I found myself growing more and more afraid as the speed picked up and I realized that I was headed toward the pinpoint of light at the end of the tunnel. The thought came that this was probably what it was like to die. I decided then and there that I wanted to go no further, and I tried to backpedal, stop, and turn around, but to no avail. I could control nothing, and the pinpoint of light grew larger and larger. Before I knew it, that light exploded around me. I should also report that my attitude at this time was quite terrified; I did not want to be there, and I was determined that

I was *not*, by God, going to stay.

There were beings all around me and they acknowledged my presence. The beings were quite amused at me. They totally accepted me into their midst and didn't seem to mind one bit that I was cranky and demanding to know where I was and who did they think they were anyhow, snatching me away like that! Put me back, damn it, put me back! Slowly my ruffled feathers became smoothed and I felt peaceful and calm. So I began going along with this weird experience and became accepting of them too. We began to have a question and answer time. I would ask the questions and instead of receiving a wordy reply they would *show* me the answer. We moved from place to place with no effort at all and I learned a great deal.

Finally the beings made it clear to me that I could return to the delivery room, and I found myself traveling back through either a tunnel or a hallway of some sort. This went very quickly and I became aware of my doctor and his nurse again. Within a brief instant, I was inside my head and could move my head from side to side. Then I felt the sensation throughout the rest of my body that we would have if we slipped on a glove over our hand.

2. Nonexistence or Eternal Void

The second type of distressing experience involves a paradoxical sensation of ceasing to exist entirely, or of being condemned to a featureless void for eternity. Sometimes this type of experience includes a sense of despair that life as we know it not only no longer exists but in fact never did, that it was all a cruel joke. Unlike the first type of distressing experience, these generally contain fewer features of the prototypical peaceful near-death experience and do not appear to convert to the peaceful kind with time. Following are verbatim accounts of this type.

The first example was reported by an academic administrator, the daughter of Unitarian ministers, who had never heard of such experiences previously and believed she was the only person ever to have had one, unable to tell even her husband about it. Her experience occurred during the delivery of her second child at age 28; the fetus had engaged and labor had begun three weeks early, and she was sent to the hospital where three pitocin drips were started over the next seven hours. She described her mental state as fearful, depressed, and panicky; finally she was given nitrous oxide:

> I remember trying to fight the mask, but they grabbed my wrists and strapped them. First there was only unconsciousness, but at some point farther into delivery my blood pressure suddenly dropped. I was aware, not

of the flurry around me, but of moving rapidly upward into darkness. Although I don't recall turning to look, I knew the hospital and the world were receding below me, very fast; to this day my mind holds a sharp picture of them down there, though I don't know how I could so clearly have seen something I didn't look at. I was rocketing through space like an astronaut without a capsule, with immense speed and great distance.

A small group of circles appeared ahead of me, some tending toward the left. To the right was just a dark space. The circles were black and white, and made a clicking sound as they snapped black to white, white to black. They were jeering and tormenting—not evil, exactly, but more mocking and mechanistic. The message in their clicking was: Your life never existed. The world never existed. Your family never existed. You were allowed to imagine it. You were allowed to make it up. It was never there. There is nothing here. There was never anything there. That's the joke—it was all a joke.

There was much laughter on their parts, malicious. I remember brilliant argumentation on my part, trying to prove that the world—and I—existed. I recall arguing that I knew details of my mother's life before my birth, things about her childhood in another part of the country; how could I have made that up? And my first baby—I *knew* her. I knew I hadn't made her up. And childbirth—why would I ever have made up that? They just kept jeering.

"This is eternity," they kept mocking. This is all there ever was, and all there ever will be, just this despair. It was empty, except for me and them, and dark. Not like night dark somehow, it was thinner—whatever that means. It was very dark and immense all around, but somehow I could see them; the voidness seemed to thin out somewhere off by the horizon, if there had been a horizon, but it wasn't lighter, just thinner. It seemed to go on forever. I was debating and simultaneously grieving for my first baby, and this baby that was never going to get born, and for my mother. That utter emptiness just went on and on, and they kept on clicking. I was trying to summon up some strong memory of my husband and the house, something tangible to argue with, thinking I couldn't bear this for eternity. The grief was just wrenching; this world gone, and grass, and my first baby and all the other babies, and hills. I knew no one could bear that much grief but there didn't seem to be any end of it, and no way out. Everyone I loved was gone.

Time was forever, endless rather than all at once. The remembering of events had no sense of life review, but of trying to prove existence, that existence existed. Yes, it was more than real: absolute reality. There's a cosmic terror we have never addressed. The despair was because of the absolute conviction that I had seen what the other side was—I never thought of it as Hell—and there was no way to tell anyone. It wouldn't matter how I died or when, damnation was out there, just waiting.

Six years later, I was leafing through a book—it may have been Jung's *Man and His Symbols*—and turned a page to discover a picture of one of the circles. The book landed across the room in one shudder. That was terror! It was corroboration: Somebody else knew about the circles. There would be no way I could any longer pretend they were imaginary. It would be several more years before I learned that the circles were the yin/yang of Eastern tradition; their sound had been the black and white sides clicking to the opposite and back again.

The second example was reported by a registered nurse, who had been raised Presbyterian and never heard of near-death experiences. She reported two identical experiences to have occurred during childbirth under anesthesia at ages 24 and 26. With her first delivery, her obstetrician induced labor by a series of three pitocin injections; in her second delivery, she suffered an inverted uterus and began to hemorrhage:

I was given ether in the delivery room. The last thing I saw before going "under" was the monotony of the ceiling tiles in the delivery room, and two nuns, of course, dressed exactly alike. I passed through different stages of "torment." Voices were laughing at me, telling me all of life was a "dream," that there was no Heaven, Hell, or Earth, really, and that all I had experienced in life was actually an hallucination. I remember trying to tell the nuns, who were smiling in happy anticipation of the impending birth, "How can you smile, when you've given your lives for religion, and there is no religion, no Heaven or Hell?"

I passed through the stage of terrible thirst and the voices kept laughing and telling me, "You think this is bad? Wait till the next stage!" I found myself hurling towards the final torment: I was to be suspended in a total vacuum with nothing to see or do for eternity. I was naked and I was sad about that because I thought, "If only I had clothing I could pull the threads and knot them or reweave them for something to do!" And, "If only I were sitting in a chair I could splinter it and try to make something of the splinters." And then the overwhelming realization that eternity was forever and ever, time without end! What to do in a vacuum forever? The thing that brought me around were the words "You have a girl," and for a while I thought the tormenting voices were again giving me another stage of torment, teasing me into thinking I didn't have to stay in that vacuum!

Two years later, I was again giving birth, and this time things went badly. I had a retained placenta and, in endeavoring to get the placenta I had an inverted uterus. During the delivery I was given ether and I had the same horrible "dream": the same stages of torment, the feeling of hurtling towards the vacuum. The thing that brought me around were the words, "You have a boy!" I reasoned that since they said "boy," not "girl," as they had during my first experience, it must be true and the nightmare I was experiencing was only a nightmare.

After all these years, the nightmare remains vivid in my mind. I assure you the worst form of Hell in my mind, at least, would be myself suspended, naked, in a vacuum.

The third example was reported by an artist, with no religious upbringing, to have occurred in an automobile accident at age eighteen. He had lost control of his car on a snowy winter evening and slid off the road and down an embankment. The car came to an abrupt stop as it slid into a brook, and he hit his head on the windshield and lost consciousness. He described leaving his physical body and watching as the icy water filled the car:

> I saw the ambulance coming, and I saw the people trying to help me, get me out of the car and into the hospital. And at that time I was no longer in my body. I had left my body. I was probably a hundred or two hundred feet up and to the south of the accident, and I felt the warmth and the kindness of the people trying to help me. I felt their compassion and all the good feeling that was emanating from these people. And I also felt the source of an that kind of kindness or whatever, and it was very, very powerful and I was afraid of it, and so I didn't accept it. I just said, "No." I was very uncertain about it and I didn't feel comfortable, and so I rejected it.
>
> And it was at that moment that I left the planet. I could feel myself and see myself going away, way up into the air, then beyond the solar system, beyond the galaxy, and out beyond anything physical. And at first I thought I'd just go with it, see where it went, and I stayed as calm as I could, just kind of went with the whole thing. And that part of it was all right for a while.
>
> But then as the hours went on with absolutely no sensation, there was no pain, but there was no hot, no cold, no light, no taste, no smell, no sensation whatsoever, none, other than the fact that I felt a slight sensation of travelling at an extremely fast speed. And I knew I was leaving the earth and everything else, all of the physical world. And at that point it became unbearable, it became horrific, as time goes on when you have no feeling, no sensation, no sense of light. I started to panic and struggle and pray and everything I could think of to struggle to get back, and I communicated with a sister of mine who passed away. And at that moment, I went back into my body, and my body at that point had been moved to the hospital.

Though our sample is still small, the majority of our cases of "eternal nothingness" experiences were reported to have occurred during childbirth under anesthesia. As already noted, this kind of distressing experience includes few features prototypically reported in peaceful near-death experiences. Instead, the common themes include eternal emptiness, an experience of being mocked, and a sense of all of life being an illusion. Individuals tend to react to these threats with logical arguments against them, a tactic not seen in response to the first type of distressing experience.

This kind of experience also tends to leave the individual with a pervasive sense of emptiness and fatalistic despair after the event, a further contrast to the first kind of distressing near-death experience. An office manager raised as a Protestant, who reported she had never heard of near-death experiences at that time in her life, described this type of experience during childbirth at age 24. She had been in labor with her second child for three days and was extremely exhausted and in severe pain. Her account of her experience includes a continuing sense of despair after her return to normal consciousness:

> I remember being in extreme pain and I remember thinking this is as far as pain can go, and then I lost consciousness. I then found myself floating in a narrow river toward a beautiful arched bridge. The bridge was made of large stones. I could see the shadow of the bridge getting closer and closer, and I was looking forward to getting in the shadow because I knew I would then be dead, and I wanted to die. I was floating with my body all down in the water, except my head was floating above it and bobbing up and down. I was very peaceful, but I wanted to get in the shadow.
>
> After I reached the shadow I was in the heavens, but it was no longer a peaceful feeling, it had become pure hell. I had become a light out in the heavens and I was screaming, but no sound was going forth. It was worse than my nightmare. I was spinning around and around and screaming. I realized that this was eternity for all mankind. I had become all mankind and this was what forever was going to be. You cannot put into words the emotions that I felt. I felt the quietness, except for the screaming within my own body, which was no longer a body but a small ball of light. I felt the aloneness except the awareness that I was all mankind. I felt the emptiness of space, the vastness of the universe except for me, a mere ball of light screaming.
>
> On returning home, I found myself not wanting to talk to anyone. I felt that no one existed except me. I continued my duties as wife and mother, but I would wonder why. I would watch TV and think that I created all that was shown on it. Then I would wonder why I didn't know the outcome of a movie, and then I would rationalize that I was creating as I

watched, so naturally I had not created an ending until the end.

It was very realistic to me and an experience I will never forget for the rest of my life. I wrote this poem a few weeks later:

I have been to Hell.
It is not as you say:
There is no fire nor brimstone,
People screaming for another day.
There is only darkness—everywhere.

3. Experiences with Hellish Imagery

A smaller number of individuals report a distressing near-death experience that includes more graphic hellish symbolism, such as threatening demons or falling into a dark pit. As with the second type of distressing experience, this kind generally contains fewer features of the prototypical peaceful near-death experience and appears not to convert to a peaceful one with time. Following are verbatim accounts of this type of experience.

The first example was reported by a woodworker with no background or interest in religion prior to this experience, though he was married to "a religious fanatic." At age 48, shortly before a vacation for which he had been saving for years, he was arrested for driving while intoxicated and heavily fined, losing both his license and vacation savings. He then tried to hang himself from a utility shed:

From the roof of the utility shed in my back yard I jumped to the ground. Luckily for me I had forgot the broken lawn chair that lay near the shed. My feet hit the chair and broke my fall, or my neck would have been broken. I hung in the rope and strangled. I was outside my physical body. I saw my body hanging in the rope; it looked awful. I was terrified, could see and hear, but it was different—hard to explain. Demons were all around me; I could hear them but could not see them. They chattered like blackbirds. It was as if they knew they had me, and had all eternity to drag me down into hell, to torment me. It would have been the worst kind of hell, trapped hopeless between two worlds, wandering lost and confused for an eternity.

I had to get back into my body. Oh my God, I needed help. I ran to the house, went in through the door without opening it, cried out to my wife but she could not hear me, so I went right into her body. I could see and hear with her eyes and ears. Then I made contact, heard her say, "Oh, my God!"

She grabbed a knife from the kitchen chair and ran out to where I was hanging and got up on an old chair and cut me down. She could find no pulse; she was a nurse. When the emergency squad got to me my heart had stopped: my breath too was gone.

The second example was reported by a Jewish woman to have occurred at age 27 following an automobile accident while traveling with her husband and two young sons:

> An oncoming vehicle slid over three lanes to hit us head on. The roof of our car collapsed and my head was stuck between windshield, dash, and roof. Supposedly—I was unconscious to all onlookers, yet something weird was happening to me.... I was in a circle of light. I looked down upon the accident scene.... I looked into my car and saw myself trapped and unconscious. I saw several cars stop and a lady taking my children to her car to sit and rest until the ambulance would arrive.... A hand touched mine and I turned to see where this peace and serenity and blissful feeling was coming from...and there was Jesus Christ—I mean the way he is made out to be in all the paintings—and I never wanted to leave this man and this place.
>
> I was led around a well, because I wanted to stay with him and hold his hand. He led me from a side of bliss to a side of misery. I did not want to look, but he made me look—and I was disgusted and horrified and scared...it was so ugly. The people were blackened and sweaty and moaning in pain and chained to their spots. And I had to walk through the area back to the well. One was even chained to the evil side of the well. The man was so skeletal and in such pain—the one chained by the side of well—I wanted them to help him, but no one would—and I knew that I would be one of these creatures if I stayed. I hated it there. I couldn't wait to get to the well and go around it. He led me to it, but he made me go through it alone as he watched. Someone else followed me through and then stepped in front of me to help me walk over the debris on the ground (snakes or something). I never looked at this thing, but I know it was dark. I knew that if I elected to stay because of the greatest, most serene feeling, that I would only have misery because he didn't want me to stay.
>
> I leaned over the well, and this young Jesus look-alike...put his hand on my back as I looked in. There were three children calling, "Mommie, Mommie, Mommie, we need you. Please come back to us." There were two boys and a girl. The two boys were much older than my two little ones, and I didn't have a little girl. The little girl looked up at me and begged me to go back to life—and then all at once I was in the circle again (his hand still on my shoulder) and I saw the accident scene again, and I cried that I did not ever want to leave him—and I knew I had to leave and get back. I moaned, awake in the car again, and I screamed for my children. I knew where they were, but I demanded that my husband tell me about the lady taking them to her car because I wanted to make sure that what I saw was real.

Well, several years later I had a baby. I knew it would be the little girl in the well.

The third example was reported by a woman to have occurred following an attempted suicide by overdose at age 26:

The doctor leaned over close to me and told me I was dying. The muscles in my body began to jerk upward, out of control. I could no longer speak, but I knew what was happening. Although my body slowed down, things around me and things happening to me went rather fast.

I then felt my body slipping down, not straight down, but on an angle, as if on a slide. It was cold, dark, and watery. When I reached the bottom, it resembled the entrance to a cave, with what looked like webs hanging. The inside of the cave was gray and brown in color.

I heard cries, wails, moans, and the gnashing of teeth. I saw these beings, that resembled humans, with the shape of a head and body. But they were ugly and grotesque. I remember colors like red, green, and purple, but can't positively remember if these were the colors of the beings. They were frightening and sounded like they were tormented, in agony. No one spoke to me.

I never went inside the cave, but stood at the entrance only. I remember saying to myself, "I don't want to stay here." I tried to lift myself up as though trying to pull myself (my spirit) up out of this pit. That's the last thing I remember.

DISCUSSION

Existing research findings in near-death studies tend to pose more questions than they answer. However, a brief perspective on some previous findings may help in interpreting the meaning of distressing experiences.

Because it is not yet possible to predict which individuals will have a near-death experience, we cannot yet assess either psychological or physiological status before and after the experience. The observations of researchers and the batteries of psychological instruments administered to near-death experiencers and control subjects over the past decade indicate that near-death experiencers are psychologically unremarkable (Ring, 1980; Locke and Shontz, 1983; Gabbard and Twemlow, 1984: Irwin, 1985; Greyson, 1991). In other words, there is no reason to question the mental health or psychological state of any group of individuals simply on the basis of their having reported near-death experiences, be it pleasant or distressing.

Experiences occurring in the course of an attempted suicide raise further questions about the mental state of the individual and its contribution to his or her experience. However, suicide attempters have reported radiant as well as distressing experiences, leading us to question the reliability of prior mental status as a determinant of experience type. Similarly, neither the general religious belief system of the individual nor specific prior knowledge of similar experiences appears to have any demonstrable bearing on the content of a near-death experience (Ring, 1980; Greyson and Stevenson, 1980; Sabom, 1982; Greyson, 1991), although beliefs are often *subsequently* influenced by the experience. Cross-cultural studies as well as Western case collections reveal a recognizable underlying pattern irrespective of background belief systems or specific content of a set of experiences.

Second, although many experiences occur in the course of medical procedures or to individuals taking medication, many others do not. Attributing the experience to anesthesia or other medications is therefore questionable. Indeed, several studies indicate that individuals who had received medication or anesthesia were *less* likely to recall a near-death experience than those who were drug-free (Osis and Haraldsson, 1977; Ring, 1980; Sabom, 1982; Greyson, 1982).

Further, although the role of neurotransmitters in near-death experiences remains of considerable interest, current notions remain quite speculative (Saavedra-Aguilar and Gómez-Jeria, 1989; Morse, Venecia, and Milstein, 1989; Jansen, 1990). Findings relevant to other physiological explanations put forward for the experience—such as anoxia, hypercapnia, and limbic or temporal lobe dysfunction—remain ambiguous. Schoonmaker (Audette, 1979) and Sabom (1982), who reported actual levels of blood gases in their samples of experiencers found no effect of anoxia, although Gliksman and Kellehear (1990) have questioned the relevance of blood gas measurements in estimating cerebral anoxia or hypercapnia. Likewise, empirical support for psychological explanations—such as depersonalization, regression in the service of the ego, cultural conditioning, and wishful thinking (Greyson, 1983b)—is still lacking. Although many of the existing theories might explain some aspects of the near-death experience, few do so with precision, and none adequately describes all aspects of this still idiopathic event.

The vivid recall and persistent aftermath of near-death experiences suggest comparison with posttraumatic stress disorder: Is the distressing experience in particular an extreme psychophysiological reaction to stress, and do the aftereffects reflect an atypical posttraumatic stress syndrome? While the changes in attitudes, beliefs, and behavior following pleasant near-death experiences rarely lead to psychiatric evaluation or treatment, less is known about the course of individuals who have had distressing experiences. The diagnostic validity of posttraumatic stress disorder as a discrete clinical entity is still debated (Ramsay, 1990); however, the past decade has produced a variety of psychological, neuroendocrine, and electrophysiological characterizations of individuals who have suffered severe trauma such as in rape or combat. A comparison of the psychobiological responses of individuals who have had distressing near-death experiences would help clarify whether these events lead to a similar persistent stress response syndrome.

Sampling Problems

As noted previously, there is at present no way to forecast which individuals are likely to have near-death experiences or when they might occur. Conventional prospective sampling techniques are therefore not feasible for most researchers. Sabom's (1982) hospital-based study of unselected consecutive resuscitation patients offers the most rigorous methodological approach; his findings mirror those of studies of less-controlled samples.

Hindering the collection of accounts immediately after a close brush with death is the near-death experiencers' reluctance or inability to talk about their experiences for weeks, months, or even years after the event. Commonly given reasons are that the near-death experience is "too personal" or that the individual fears (often justifiably) that it is so at variance from ordinary experience that it will be dismissed or considered a sign of mental illness (Garfield, 1979; Clark, 1984; Atwater, 1988).

Ameliorating this apparent weakness in data collection is the consistency of accounts over time. This temporal constancy may be accounted for by the frequent comment of experiencers that the experience was indescribably vivid, often "realer than real." Adults' accounts of their childhood near-death experiences are remarkably consistent with those told by children shortly after the event (Bush, 1983; Gabbard and Twemlow, 1984; Serdahely, 1991); they frequently include odd lapses into childlike locutions and observations that are out of character for the adult (Bush, 1983), suggesting that the story is presented now as it was experienced in childhood. As reported by Garfield (1979) and Greyson (1983a), individual accounts tend not to vary, even though considerable time may pass between retellings.

Unfortunately, the passage of time does affect the recollection of clinical details that might be of interest to those now studying the near-death experience. Memories of precipitating conditions and treatments are often vague—sometimes in startling contrast to the clarity of recall of the experience itself—and medical records may be sketchy when dealing with the often transitory and perhaps unnoticed events associated with these experiences. Stevenson, Cook, and McClean-Rice (1989), reviewing medical records of persons reporting near-death experiences, found documentation of close proximity to death in only 45 percent of those records. For the many near-death experiences that occur away from a medical environment, of course, no records exist.

Given the retrospective and phenomenological nature of near-death studies, any conclusions as to the circumstances that produce near-death experiences and the psychophysiological processes they may illuminate are at present largely conjectural. By contrast, the aftereffects of near-death experiences offer both more manageable research prospects and potentially greater significance.

CONCLUSION

Accounts of distressing near-death experiences, long withheld by experiencers and overlooked by investigators, are now being acknowledged openly by both groups. The typology described here, comprising three discrete categories of distressing experiences, may suggest further directions for research.

The first type, phenomenologically similar to peaceful near-death experiences but interpreted as terrifying, and sometimes resolving into a peaceful experience, may indeed be a variant of the prototypical type differing only in the individual's perception or response.

The second type, of eternal nothingness sometimes accompanied by a sense of cosmic trickery, has less in common with peaceful experiences phenomenologically and may be associated with different organic precipitating factors. In the midst of their distress, individuals with this kind of experience sometimes try to argue their way out through logic; although it may be an artifact of our small sample, this tactic does not seem to occur in other types of distressing experiences. Individuals in this group are often left not only with feelings of terror, as with other distressing experiences, but also with a persisting sense of emptiness and despair.

The third type is the "hellish" experience characterized by archetypal imagery, sounds of torment, and sometimes demonic beings. In some instances, a benevolent guide accompanies the individual through the experience. In keeping with "hellish" experiences reported by Rawlings (1978), Garfield (1979), and Grey (1985), we found these experiences quite variable in phenomenology. While this kind of distressing experience has been considered a delirious artifact of modern resuscitation (Rogo, 1989), it is reminiscent of medieval back-from-the-dead narratives (Zaleski, 1987). Furthermore, Irwin and Bramwell (1988) reported a near-death experience that began to unfold as a prototypical positive one but then evolved into a frightening one with demonic beings. Thus, it may be an over-simplification to conclude either that this type of distressing experience is unrelated to the pleasant type, or that it is a variant of the prototypical pleasant experience.

Further study of both peaceful and distressing near-death experiences is required to clarify their similarities and differences, and to elucidate the physical and psychological factors associated with these altered states at the threshold of death. The aftereffects of the distressing near-death experience have not yet been studied systematically. However, our preliminary observations indicate that ontological fear is a common result of the experience. Future investigations of the aftereffects of distressing experiences may clarify their relationship to more familiar posttraumatic stress syndromes, may yield important clinical insights for the individuals involved, and may help clarify the near-death experience's meaning and relevance to life.

REFERENCES

Atwater, P. M. H. (1988). *Coming Back to Life: The After-Effects of the Near-Death Experience.* Dodd, Mead.

Audette, J. (1979). Denver cardiologist discloses findings after 18 years of near-death research. *Anabiosis* [East Peoria] *1*(1), 1–2.

Bush, N. E. (1983). The near-death experience in children: Shades of the prison-house reopening. *Anabiosis: The Journal of Near-Death Studies,3*, 177–93.

Clark, K. (1984). Clinical interventions with near-death experiencers. In B. Greyson and C. P. Flynn. eds., *The Near-Death Experience: Problems, Prospects, Perspectives.* Charles C. Thomas.

Flynn, C. P. (1986). *After the Beyond: Human Transformation and the Near-Death Experience.* Prentice Hall.

Gabbard, C. O., and S. W. Twemlow. (1984).*With the Eyes of the Mind: An Empirical Analysis of Out-of-Body States.* Praeger.

Gallop, G., Jr., and W. Proctor. (1982). *Adventures in Immortality: A Look Beyond the Threshold of Death.* McGraw Hill.

Garfield, C. A. (1979). More grist for the mill: Additional near-death research findings and discussion. *Anabiosis* [East Peoria] *1*(1), 5–7.

Gliksman, M. D., and A. Kellehear. (1990). Near-death experiences and the measurement of blood gases. *Journal of Near-Death Studies, 9*, 41–43.

Grey, M. (1985). *Return from Death: An Exploration of the Near-Death Experience.* Arkana.

Greyson, B.(1982, May). "Organic brain dysfunction and near-death experiences." Presented to Annual Meeting, American Psychiatric Association. Toronto, Ontario.

Greyson, B. (1983a). The near-death experience scale: construction, reliability, and validity. *Journal of Nervous and Mental Disease,171*, 369–75.

Greyson, B. (1983b). The psychodynamics of near-death experiences. *Journal of Nervous and Mental Disease ,171,* 376–81.

Greyson, B. (1983c). Near-death experiences and personal values. *American Journal of Psychiatry,140,* 618–20.

Greyson, B.(1991). Near-death experiences precipitated by suicide attempts: Lack of influence of psychopathology, religion, and expectations. *Journal of Near-Death Studies, 9,* 183–88.

Greyson, B., and I. Stevenson. (1980). The phenomenology of near-death experiences. *American Journal of Psychiatry, 137,* 1193–96.

Grosso, M. (1981). Toward an explanation of near-death phenomena. *Journal of the American Society for Psychiatric Research, 75,* 37–60.

Irwin, H. J. (1985). *Flight of Mind: A Psychological Study of the Out-of-Body Experience.* Scarecrow Press.

Irwin, H. J., and B. A. Bramwell. (1988). The devil in heaven: near-death experience with both positive and negative facets. *Journal of Near-Death Studies, 7,* 38–43.

Jansen, K. L. R. (1990). Neuroscience and the near-death experience. Role for the NMDA-PCP receptor, the sigma receptor and the endopsychosins. *Medical Hypotheses, 31*, 25–29.

Lindley, J. H., S. Bryan, and B. Conley. (1981). Near-death experiences in a Pacific Northwest American population: The evergreen study. *Anabiosis: The Journal of Near-Death Studies, 1*, 104–24.

Locke, T. P., and F. C. Shontz. (1983). Personality correlates of the near-death experience: A preliminary study. *Journal of the American Society for Psychical Research, 77*, 311–18.

Moody, R. A., Jr. (1975). *Life After Life* . New York: Mockingbird/Bantam Books.

Moody R. A., Jr. (1977). *Reflections on Life After Life.* New York: Mockingbird/Bantam Books.

Morse, M. L., D. Venecia, and J. Milstein. (1989). Near-death experiences: A neurophysiological explanatory model. *Journal of Near-Death Studies, 8*, 45–53.

Noyes, R., Jr. (1980). Attitude change following near-death experiences. *Psychiatry, 43*, 234–42.

Noyes, R., Jr., and D. J. Slymen. (1978–1979). The subjective response to life-threatening danger. *Omega, 9*, 313–21.

Osis. K., and E. Haraldsson. (1977). *At the Hour of Death.* Avon.

Raft, D., and J. J. Andresen. (1986). Transformations in self-understanding after near-death experiences. *Contemporary Psychoanalysis, 22*, 319–56.

Ramsay, R.(1990). Invited review: Post-traumatic stress disorder: new clinical entity? *Journal of Psychosomatic Research, 34*, 355–65.

Rawlings, M. (1978). *Beyond Death's Door.* Thomas Nelson.

Ring, K. (1980). *Life at Death: A Scientific Investigation of the Near-Death Experience.* Coward, McCann and Geoghegan.

Ring, K. (1984). *Heading Toward Omega: In Search of the Meaning of the Near-Death Experience.* William Morrow.

Roberts, G., and J. Owen. (1988). The near-death experience. *British Journal of Psychiatry,153*, 607–17.

Rogo, D. S. (1989).*The Return from Silence: A Study of Near-Death Experiences.* Aquarian Press.

Saavedra-Aguilar, J. C., and J. S. Gómez-Jeria. (1989). A neurobiological model for near-death experiences. *Journal of Near-Death Studies, 7*, 205–22.

Sabom, M. (1982). *Recollections of Death: A Medical Investigation.* Harper and Row.

Serdahely, W. J. (1991). Childhood near-death experiences: A comparison of adult retrospective accounts with children's contemporaneous accounts. *Journal of Near-Death Studies, 9*, 219–224.

Stevenson, I., E. W. Cook, and N. McClean-Rice. (1989). Are persons reporting "near-death experiences" really near death? A report of medical records.*Omega, 20*, 45–54.

Zaleski. C. (1987).*Otherworld Journeys: Accounts of Near-Death Experience in Medieval and Modern Times.* Oxford University Press.

15

What Is Not Being Said About the Near-Death Experience

P. M. H. Atwater

Surviving does not make you enlightened or superhuman.

One cold morning in Idaho in 1977, P. M. H. Atwater died from a hemmorhage following a miscarriage. This was only the first of three deaths punctuating a very difficult time in her life, she says. During her NDEs she experienced out-of-body travel; an opportunity to learn about creation; a complete, joyous, and painful life review; the appearance of family members and Christ out of a shimmering Void. Then she witnessed a cyclone-like funnel full of souls and an explosive energy center in the cyclone that led to God. Her son's loving voice brought her back from her third NDE, and she has become a researcher and writer with a passionate, therapeutic mission.

Having interviewed numerous NDE survivors, Atwater emphasizes several important themes, especially the unpleasant elements of some NDEs, in contrast to the purely joyous, loving accounts so often publicized. NDEs do not automatically make survivors saints, she stresses. They are an awakening, a jolt into a spiritual mystery. They do not automatically solve problems. "Surviving does not make you enlightened or superhuman" (1988, 19). The constant challenge to survivors is to integrate their experience into life, she stresses, whether their NDE involved healing light and love or terrifying darkness.

P. M. H. Atwater, Lh.D., has published several books, including: *Coming Back to Life: The After-effects of the Near-Death Experience* (1988), *Beyond the Light: What Isn't Being said About the Near-Death Experience* (1994), and *Future Memory* (1995). Atwater lives in Virginia and speaks around the country.

⌐ What Is Not Being Said About the Near-Death Experience ⌐

The near-death experience represents an incredible unknown, resisting thus far many attempts to clinically define its scope or the "need" that drives it. We do know a lot about the phenomenon. After twenty years of study and the efforts of well over a hundred researchers, we have a better grasp today of the phenomenon's dynamics and aftereffects. Still, we have hardly scratched the surface of what can be learned about this incredible mystery. *We do not know as much as we think.*

I say this because I am not just a researcher. I have had three near-death experiences (Atwater 1988, 1994). My research is informed by powerful personal experiences of the subject in question. Although my initial motive for doing this work was to save my sanity, I have always been guided by revelations made to me while on "the other side" of death, revelations that gave me a purpose: clarifying and giving perspective to soul awakenings. The Russian proverb "Trust, but verify" has set my course as I have interviewed over 3,000 near-death experiencers of all ages, from many countries, 700 of them in depth, plus numerous "significant others."

My own near-death experience was precipitated by my 1977 miscarriage and extreme hemorrhaging. Months later I suffered three relapses, one of which was adrenal failure. As a result, I had to relearn how to crawl, stand, walk, climb stairs, run, tell the difference between left and right, see and hear properly, and rebuild my belief systems. I was never hospitalized, seeing doctors only after the fact, but it is both my opinion and that of the specialist who diagnosed my problems that I had indeed died. Each time I met death, I had a visionary experience, and each was different, although one seemed somehow to lead into the next.

Elisabeth Kübler-Ross first helped me understand that I am a near-death survivor when we met at O'Hare Airport in

1978. Although her description of the phenomenon's universal pattern was helpful, I was left with more questions than answers. I launched my own research project shortly afterward, employing the skills of investigative observation and analysis that were taught to me when a child by my police-officer father. I was rigorous in cross-checking my work and in forcing myself to be objective, even if that meant acknowledging what I did not want to face.

This effort convinced me that the near-death phenomenon is more complex and many-faceted than is commonly believed. Far from describing some heavenly travelogue or providing "proof" of an afterlife, the phenomenon actually challenges us to reconsider our very *aliveness* and the existence of *spirit*.

Because I kept the individual's near-death scenario in context with their previous and present life, I was able to find multiple connections, correlations, and parallels that led me to conclude that the experience could be "needed" by those who had it. It seems that a near-death experience quite probably is one of nature's more accelerated growth events, a powerful and complex dynamic that can foster major psychological and physiological changes in both adults and children. Viewing the near-death phenomenon in this manner, I have identified four distinctive types of experience with a general psychological profile for each category (Atwater, 1994).

THE FOUR TYPES OF NEAR-DEATH EXPERIENCES

1. Initial Experience (a minimal "seed" encounter)
Involves elements such as a loving nothingness, a living darkness, or friendly voice, or a brief out-of-body experience. Usually experienced by those who seem to need the least amount of evidence for proof of the soul's survival, or who need the least amount of shakeup in their lives at that point. Often this becomes a "seed" experience or an introduction to other ways of perceiving and recognizing reality.

2. Unpleasant or Hellish Experience (revolves around inner cleansing and self-confrontation)
Encounter with a threatening void, stark limbo, hellish purgatory, or scenes of a startling and unexpected indifference, even "hauntings" from one's own past. Usually experienced by those who seem to have deeply repressed guilts, fears, and angers, or those who expect some kind of punishment or discomfort after death.

3. Pleasant or Heavenly Experience (leads to reassurance and self-validation)
Heavenly scenarios of loving family reunions with those who have died

previously, reassuring religious figures or light beings, validation that life counts, affirmative and inspiring dialogue. Usually experienced by those who most need to know how loved they are, how important life is and how every effort has a purpose in the overall scheme of things.

4. Transcendent Experience (Expansive revelations, alternate realities)

Exposure to otherworldly dimensions and scenes beyond the individual's frame of reference; sometimes includes revelations of greater truths. Seldom personal in content. Usually experienced by those who are ready for a "mind-stretching" challenge, or individuals more apt to utilize, to some degree, these truths.

I have found that all four types can occur during the same near-death experience, can exist in varying combinations, or can spread out across a series of episodes. What may seem as negative or positive concerning any of these four types is very relative. *The value and meaning of an NDE depend on each individual involved and his or her response to what happened.*

1. *The Initial Experience.* One group of people had very brief experiences with one or two elements. Hardly more than "snatches" of anything otherworldly, these seemingly inconsequential events can have an impact on an individual every bit as powerful as a full-blown near-death scenario. Uncomplicated or simple out-of-body episodes account for about half of them.

What happened to the novelist Ernest Hemingway is an example of this type. During World War I, Hemingway was wounded by shrapnel while fighting in Italy. He made this cryptic statement in a letter he wrote from his hospital bed: "Dying is a very simple thing. I've looked at death and really I know." Years later, Hemingway confided to a friend the details that had occurred on that fateful night in 1918:

> A big Austrian trench mortar bomb, of the type that used to be called ash cans, exploded in the darkness. I died then. I felt my soul or something coming right out of my body, like you'd pull a silk handkerchief out of a pocket by one corner. It flew around and then came back and went in again and I wasn't dead anymore. (Josephs, Hoffman, 108)

Hemingway remained deeply affected by this out-of-body initial near-death experience throughout his life, and was never again as "hard-boiled" as he once had been. *A Farewell to Arms* contains a passage where the character Frederic Henry undergoes the same confrontation with death that Hemingway did:

> I ate the end of my piece of cheese and took a swallow of wine. Through the other noise I heard a cough, then came the chuh-chuh-chuh-chuh—then there was a flash, as when a blast-furnace door is swung open, and a roar that started white and went red and on and on in a rushing wind. I tried to breathe but my breath would not come and I felt myself rush bodily out of myself and out and out and out and all the time bodily in the wind. I went out swiftly, all of myself, and I knew I was dead and that it had all been a mistake to think you just died. Then I floated, and instead of going on I felt myself slide back. I breathed and I was back. (Hemingway, 54)

Those who have this type of near-death episode respond as if they had been suddenly "stimulated." They appear more alert, curious and open, exhibiting expanded sensory abilities. This is a "seed" event, an experience that grows over time, inspiring the survivor to think more creatively and abstractly. And, like most seed events, it can lead to lifestyle and personality changes. It seems that shorter lengths of exposure to otherworldly realities are quite enough for this stage in survivors' development. Young children often undergo this type of episode.

2. *Unpleasant or Hellish Experience.* This kind of fearful terror was experienced by Jeanne Eppley of Columbus, Ohio. She told me that, during the birth of her first child, she was frightened when:

> Everything was bright yellow. There was a tiny black dot in the center of all the yellow. Somehow I knew that the dot was me. The dot began to divide. First there was two, then four, then eight. After there had been enough division, the dots formed into a pinwheel and began to spin. As the pinwheel spun, the dots began to rejoin in the same manner as they had divided. I knew that when they were all one again, I would be dead, so I began to fight. The next thing I remember is the doctor trying to awaken me and keep me on the delivery table, because I was getting up.

Eppley expressed disappointment that her case did not match all the wonderful stories that other near-death survivors tell. A fellow experiencer suggested that maybe the reason for this was her refusal to "let go" and surrender to the experience. The battle she had waged so fiercely may have blocked any further development of an uplifting scenario. Other researchers have suggested that "surrender" may indeed be the factor that determines not only depth of experience, but who might possibly have an NDE to begin with.

Yet, if you explore Eppley's life before and after, a startling pattern emerges. This painful experience evoked some needed strength. It foreshadowed two disappointing marriages, the birth of three more children, verbal and physical abuse, an attempt on her life, plus the ordeal of raising her family without support. The battle fear generated in her near-death episode was *the first time* she had ever stood up for herself. By her own admission, the strength she gained from that fight enabled her to call upon deep reservoirs of power that she never knew she had. Thus, winning one battle gave her the courage to win many others. She has since remarried, and is now a radiantly happy woman. What was originally fearsome turned out to be a godsend.

Would Eppley have benefitted as much as she did had her scenario been sweetly angelic? In Eppley's case developing psychological muscle was more advantageous than becoming spiritually pious. She needed to get tougher and what happened helped her to do so. I have observed this curious characteristic with *all* the people I have interviewed: The phenomenon tends to provide experiencers with an opportunity to rectify behavior flaws or heal an emptiness; in some way the NDE inspires them to loosen up, open up, and grow.

With unpleasant cases, seldom has anyone I have met said anything about fiery hot or burning sensations where they went. Rather, most comment on how cold it was, or clammy or shivery or "hard" or empty. The light was dull, sometimes gray or "heavy" as if overcast or foggy. Invariably an attack of some kind or a shunning would occur, resulting in pain or surges of anxiety. The experiencer would have to defend him or herself or fight for survival. Common are themes of good and evil, devils and angels, great storms, sucking vortexes and a frightening void.

Also common with the frightening type are reports of hauntings after the individual revives and resumes life's routines. These hauntings are perceived as physically solid and real. I have heard numerous stories of "evil ones" who suddenly appear in broad daylight to chase the experiencer and do battle over his or her soul, then disappear. Manifestations such as these are depicted in the 1990 movie "Flatliners."

One out of seven in my research had unpleasant or hellish experiences, yet truly demonic scenarios were in the minority. Three puzzles emerged for me concerning this finding:

- *Elements* (Contrary Evaluations)—The same thing that one person would describe as "horrific," another would term "wondrous."
- *Scenarios* (Coping)—Whether or not an individual could cope with the experience stemmed more from their evaluation of "heavenly" or "hellish" than the actual content.
- *Experiencers* (Age)—Only older children and adults reported unpleasant or hellish episodes; little ones did not.

When I focused on these puzzles I noticed a glaring contrast in language among those I spoke with, even though many described *similar images in similar settings*. This chart compares these descriptive contrasts:

COMPARISON OF HEAVENLY AND HELLISH EXPERIENCES

Heavenly Cases	Hellish Cases
Friendly beings	Lifeless or threatening apparitions
Beautiful, lovely environments	Barren or ugly expanses
Conversations and dialogue	Threats, screams, silence
Total acceptance and an overwhelming sensation of love	Danger and possible violence or torture
A feeling of warmth and a sense of heaven	A feeling of temperature extremes, usually cold, and a sense of hell

These conundrums took on new meaning once I recognized a common denominator present in *every* episode of this type that I investigated: distressing near-death experiences seem to outpicture a process of inner purification, a fantastic housecleaning that operates on levels more powerful than personal or religious beliefs. Along this same line I noticed that those experiencers willing to confront "the shadow self," that aspect of their own nature either repressed or denied, were the ones who reported miraculous healings more often than did the others.

3. *Pleasant or Heavenly Experience.* Since these constitute the vast bulk of cases, it is no wonder that the basic storyline has become virtually mythologized as the classic NDE. But, just as there is more to the hellish version than meets the eye, more can also be found in tales of heaven.

For example, in 1932 Arthur Yensen, a university graduate and staunch materialist turned syndicated cartoonist, decided to take some time off to research his weekly cartoon strip, *Adventurous Willie Wispo*. Since his main character was a hobo, Yensen became one for a while, blending with the Depression's sixteen million unemployed. He bummed rides from Chicago into Minnesota, where he was picked up by a young man driving a convertible. Going too fast for road conditions, the car hit oiled gravel and flipped into a series of violent somersaults. Both men were catapulted through the cloth top before the car smashed into a ditch. The driver escaped unharmed, but Yensen was injured and nearly died:

> Gradually the earth scene faded away, and through it loomed a bright, new, beautiful world—beautiful beyond imagination! For half a minute I could see both worlds at once. Finally, when the earth was all gone, I stood in a glory that could only be heaven.
> In the background were two beautiful, round-topped mountains, sim-

ilar to Fujiyama in Japan. The tops were snow-capped, and the slopes were adorned with foliage of indescribable beauty. The mountains appeared to be about fifteen miles away, yet I could see individual flowers growing on their slopes. I estimated my vision to be about one hundred times better than on earth.

To the left was a shimmering lake containing a different kind of water—clear, golden, radiant, and alluring. It seemed to be alive. The whole landscape was carpeted with grass so vivid, clear and green that it defies description. To the right was a grove of large, luxuriant trees, composed of the same clear material that seemed to make up everything. (Yensen)

Yensen's rapturous visit was lengthy and involved many insights and teachings given to him by a heavenly being. His case rivals any of modern vintage. To say he was transformed and transfigured after his experience would be an understatement, yet his life is a study in contradiction. Force-fed religion as a youngster, he turned against church and challenged his parents at every turn, including the way they ate. His defiance of convention was compounded by his near-death event. Suddenly "knowing" more than before, he switched from atheism to mysticism and became a political activist, educator, organic gardener and nutrition expert. He married, helped raise three sons, and later was named one of Idaho's "Most Distinguished Citizens."

Even though he healed and helped thousands of people during his long life, Yensen died still questioning his worth and whether he had accomplished his mission in life. He suffered a deep loneliness and often claimed that it was his near-death experience that kept him going.

I have observed that once those who have a heavenly scenario experience what they recognize as *true* love, they feel tremendous pressure to pass it on. This may not be because they have become a fountain of that love—for many sense, as did Yensen, a gross inadequacy in themselves and are never quite able to accept the validity of "worthiness"—but because they now know they are connected to and in communion with a A Greater Reality. They have faced the awesome visage of RESPONSIBILITY and returned with a sense of mission.

Both pain and joy can be as instructive. Heavenly visions may leave some pain, and hellish experiences may stimulate some joy. I have consistently found this in my research. I no longer consider one type of near-death scenario to be more important than another. Rather, I now view all four categories as ways that evolving consciousness uses to stimulate progress.

4. *The Transcendent Experience.* Usually lengthy, complex and seldom personal, these cases are so otherworldly that they defy ordinary understanding. Scenarios can range from riding a light ray throughout the universe, or view-

ing creation as it happened, or witnessing the beginning and end of history, to attending classes in some "heavenly" university. Invariably the people who have them are inspired to take action when they return, to make a difference in the world. Although hearing remarkable claims by near-death survivors that they were privy to all knowledge during their experience is typical, coming back with that knowledge rarely occurs.

History gives us an example that shows how society can be affected by an individual who has had a transcendent episode. In 1837 a Chinese peasant farmer's son Hung Hsiu-ch'uan failed for the third time to pass the official state examination. He fell into a prolonged delirium, his body wasting away as he lay near death for forty days. He revived after having a miraculous vision that portrayed him and an "elder brother" searching out and slaying legions of evil demons in accordance with divine will. Six years later Hsiu-ch'uan came across a Christian missionary pamphlet. He used what he read in the pamphlet to "substantiate" his conviction that his vision was real and that he, as the younger brother of Jesus Christ and God's Divine Representative, was ready and willing to overthrow the forces of evil, which he saw as the Manchus and Confucianism. With the help of converts to his cause, he established the God Worshippers Society, a puritanical and absolutist group that quickly swelled to the ranks of a revolutionary army. Hsiu-ch'uan joined forces with the Taiping Rebellion of 1850 to help lead a massive, bloody civil uprising which lasted fourteen years and cost the lives of twenty million people (Chien 10, 36; Curwen, 11; Hamberg; Lee).

Near-death survivors such as Hsiu-ch'uan (who changed his name to T'ien Wang, the Heavenly King) may be transformed by their unusual near-death experiences and become zealous in their desire to "wake up" the so-called "deluded." They may be convinced that only REAL TRUTH has been revealed to them, and thus it is their sacred duty to "save" the populace. In the case of Hsiu-ch'uan, his near-death experience led to wholesale carnage and helped to forge a "Heavenly Dynasty" that ripped asunder the very fabric of China.

Transcendent cases are powerful in both content and consequences, yet they are a risky business because they can affect experiencers' lives *plus* the lives of countless others. This enigma repeats itself each time an individual is changed so utterly by the near-death phenomenon. Clearly, seeing "heaven" does not make one holy, nor does it make anyone "chosen" or "savior." *No single case* is more profound, complete, or better than any other. In truth, the real strength of near-death stories comes from *the combined message of the many,* a chorus that speaks with a voice of thunder about the reality of God, Soul and Oneness.

Only 21 percent of those I interviewed denied the existence of aftereffects. Of these, most reported having had only the initial type. The rest reported significant, life-changing differences afterward. 19 percent claimed radical psychological and spiritual turnarounds, almost as if they had become another person.

Any notion that, as a compensatory gift, some people are privileged to survive death, see heaven, and return dedicated to selfless service for all humankind, I call the "myth of Amazing Grace." That's because there are both positive *and* negative aspects to the aftereffects. Passing through death's door seems merely to be step one. Integrating the experience is the real adventure. Making what was learned real and workable in everyday life is difficult. No "set of instructions" covers how to do this. Thus lengthy bouts with depression are typical.

PSYCHOLOGICAL AFTEREFFECTS

I have observed that it seems to take a minimum of seven years for most experiencers to integrate the aftereffects. Although these cannot be faked, an individual can delay the onset of them or deny their existence. Seven major elements comprise the universal pattern.

1. *Unconditional love*—Experiencers perceive themselves as equally and fully loving of each and all, openly generous, excited about the potential and wonder of each person they see. Confused family members tend to regard this sudden switch in behavior as oddly threatening, as if their loved one had become aloof, unresponsive, even uncaring or unloving.

2. *Lack of boundaries*—Familiar codes of conduct can lose relevance or disappear altogether as unlimited avenues of interest and inquiry take priority. This new frame of reference can infuse experiencers with such an accepting nature that they can and do display childlike naïveté. With the fading of previous norms and standards, basic cautions and discernments can also fade.

3. *Timelessness*—Most experiencers begin to "flow" with the natural shift of time, rejecting clocks and schedules as they exhibit a heightened awareness of the present moment and the importance of "now." They are easily distracted and can appear "spacey" until they readjust to the demands of daily routines.

4. *Psychic insights*—Extrasensory perception and various types of psychic phenomena become normal and ordinary in the lives of experiencers. A person's religious beliefs do not prevent this expansion of faculties or enlargements of perceptual range. This can frighten the unprepared and be misconstrued as "the devil's work," whereas it is actually more akin to "gifts of the spirit."

5. *Reality switches*—Hard-driving achievers and materialists can transform into easy-going philosophers. But, by the same token, those previously

more relaxed or uncommited can become energetic "movers and shakers," determined to make a difference in the world. Such switches seem to depend more on what is "needed" to round out the individual's growth than on any uniform result.

6. *The soul as self*—Most come to recognize themselves as an immortal soul currently resident within material form so lessons can be learned while sojourning in the earthplane. They know they are not their body; it is a "jacket" they wear. The majority develop an interest in reincarnation, and some accept it as valid.

7. *Modes of communication*—what was once foreign becomes familiar, what was once familiar becomes foreign. Rationality of any kind tends to lose its logic as experiencers begin to think more abstractly and in grandiose terms. New ways of using language, even whole new vocabularies, emerge.

Within some households, relatives are so impressed by what they witness with their loved one that they too change, making the near-death experience a shared event. In other families, though, the response is so negative that alienation, separation, or divorce results. The situation with children, who undergo the same aftereffects as adults, can be doubly challenging, since they lack the ability to speak up for themselves, negotiate, or seek alternatives.

PHYSIOLOGICAL AFTEREFFECTS

More than the psyche is affected by the near-death phenomenon. A person's body and its patterns undergo change too. Mundane chores can take on surrealistic dimensions. I have found a number of typical physiological aftereffects, including: altered energy levels, hypersensitivity to light and sound, unusual sensitivity to chemicals (especially pharmaceuticals), reduced stress, lowered blood pressure, and even electrical sensitivity. This last effect makes a person's energy field affect electrical and electronic devices; many can no longer wear watches because they break, or microphones "fight" them.

EXTERNAL VERIFICATION

Every near-death incident I studied that had elements in it unknowable to the experiencer that could be checked, was checked, and every one of those details was verified. For example, in one of my cases, a four-year-old boy drowned in his parents' backyard swimming pool. Emergency crews were called. After fifteen minutes, the boy revived. Incredibly, but typical of most near-death incidents, there was no brain damage. Immediately, he spoke of meeting his little brother on "the other side," a little brother about two years old, yet able to converse. Since the youngster was an only child, his parents rightfully assumed that he was hallucinating—until the story spilled out.

Mommy made a "mistake" when she was 13 and had an abortion. Chalk-white and shocked, mommy confirmed the boy's revelation. No friends or family knew about the abortion, and the mother had long since forgotten it. But here was her "only" child quoting what her aborted child told him. Sadly, the schism that subsequently developed between the parents over this affair led to a divorce.

Again and again, detailed revelations such as this, absolutely impossible for the individual to know, are seen and later externally verified: descriptions of the accident scene, hospital room or family secrets. Obviously the dynamics of the human spirit defy what can be proven scientifically, or even what can be defined by our reason and sensory faculties.

The near-death phenomenon, both the experience and its aftereffects, reveals more about life than it does death. It reveals an aliveness and a power above and beyond anything we can presently fathom.

REFERENCES

Atwater, P. M. H. (1981–85). "Coming Back," a regular column in *Vital Signs*, published by IANDS, International Association for Near-Death Studies, P.O. Box 502, East Windsor Hill, CT 06028-0502; phone (860) 528-5144.

Atwater, P. M. H. (1988). *Coming Back to Life: The After-Effects of the Near-Death Experience.* New York: Dodd, Mead; New York: Ballantine Books, 1989.

Atwater, P. M. H. (1994). *Beyond the Light: What Isn't Being Said About the Near-Death Experience.* New York: Birch Lane Press; New York: Avon Books, 1995.

Atwater, P. M. H. (1995). *Future Memory.* New York: Birch Lane Press.

Chien, Yu'wen (1973). *The Taiping Revolutionary Movement.* New Haven, CT: Yale University Press.

Curwen, Charles A. (1977). *Taiping Rebel: The Disposition of Li Hiu-cheng.* Cambridge, England: Cambridge University Press.

Hamberg, Theodore. (1975). *The Visions of Hung-Siu-Tshuen and Origin of the Kwan-Si Insurrection.* San Francisco: Chinese Material Center. (First written in 1854 while Hamberg was in China, and during the Taiping Rebellion.)

Hemingway, Ernest. (1929). *A Farewell to Arms.* New York: Scribner's.

Hoffman, Frederick J. (1970). The Secret Wound, in Jay Gellens, ed. *Twentieth Century Interpretations of* A Farewell to Arms. Englewood Cliffs, NJ: Prentice Hall, 108–111.

Josephs, Allen. (1983). Hemingway's Out of Body Experience. *The Hemingway Review.* Spring, 11–17.

Lee, C. Y. (1990). *Second Son of Heaven.* New York: William Morrow. (A fictionalization of Hung's story.)

Yensen, Arthur. E. *I Saw Heaven.* P.O. Box 369, Parma, ID 83660: Eric Yensen.

16

Near-Death Reports
Evidence for Survival
of Death?

Robert Kastenbaum

Ten thousand reports are no better
than ten reports if they are offered
simply as further examples of the
fact that some people believed they
have died and come back to life.

Robert Kastenbaum, Ph.D., is a psychologist who has written and
edited numerous books and articles on aging and death, including
the *Encyclopedia of Death.* Kastenbaum agrees that NDEs are real
as experiences, and certainly significant and worthy of scientific
study. But he hastens to add, NDEs do *not* prove that the soul
survives death. Several difficulties with NDE research must be
taken into account. For example, there may be large gaps between
the direct experience of a paranormal death experience and the
report of it, which may include old memories, rumors, even
fabrications. Our definition of death is notoriously vague and

clouds interpretation. Furthermore, what are we to make of all the people who die and return who do *not* report visionary experiences?

Robert Kastenbaum, Ph.D., is a professor in the Department of Communication at Arizona State University. He is editor of several important works in the field of aging and death, such as *Omega, Journal of Death and Dying* and *The Encyclopedia of Death,* and author of numerous books and articles, including *The Psychology of Death,* and *Is There Life After Death?*

·‿ Near-Death Reports ‿·
Evidence for Survival of Death?

INTRODUCTION: WHAT IS THE CENTRAL QUESTION?
Do you believe there is a divine purpose at work in the cosmos, and that this plan includes survival or persistence of the soul? If so, let it be said immediately that nothing in this chapter will challenge your faith. On the other hand, nothing in this book adds a whit of support. The same must be said for other books that base their conclusions on near-death experience (NDE) reports. That many people have accepted NDE reports as proof of survival is an interesting social and cognitive phenomenon, but the popularity of a belief does not certify its accuracy.

Before focusing on the question of central issue here it will be useful to scan through several related questions:

- Are near-death experiences (NDEs) real?
- Are NDEs significant?
- Do NDEs constitute legitimate data for scientific and scholarly investigation?
- Have studies been carried out to investigate NDEs?
- Has it been found that NDEs sometimes are followed by powerful changes in thoughts, feelings, and attitudes?
- Have theories been offered to describe or explain NDEs from a scientific perspective?

Yes. There is no dispute here with the propositions that NDEs are "real" and "significant" in some meaningful sense of these terms, nor that they are proper subjects of scientific research and theory. The problem begins with the next question:

- Do NDEs prove survival of death?

No.

The emphasis here is on *prove*. Belief in survival of death per se is not the central issue. This is one of the most ancient, widespread, and persistent of human beliefs. Survival belief was deeply entrenched long before NDEs became a topic of general discussion. The sacred writings of the major religions do not depend on NDEs for validation. Survival belief was doing very well prior to the recent dissemination of NDE reports, and this belief does not depend on NDEs for its continuation.

The phenomenon that has become known popularly as the NDE is not the central issue here either. How could we not be interested in these reports? Our curiosity is natural and requires no defense or apology—it is a non-issue.

What is the issue, then? The issue is the connection between NDEs and the belief in survival. More specifically, it is the assumption that NDEs prove survival of death. This conclusion is usually drawn from the following basic schematic:

> I was dead
> While dead, I had a strange and beautiful experience
> I came back to life (stopped being dead)
> Therefore death is not the end

There is often the additional specification that:

> I returned with the knowledge that what is called "death" is nothing to
> fear, and since that time my life has been transformed.

Not all NDEs are reported as positive experiences, and not all experiencers conclude that they had returned to life after an episode of deadness. However, most of the NDEs that have been published or aired on talk shows do conform to this schematic. Once again: it is not the experience itself that is at issue here, but the assertion that such experiences provide evidence for survival of death.

We begin by looking at NDEs as a source of data for research.

PARANORMAL DEATH EXPERIENCES AS DATA

Raymond A. Moody, Jr., the person who first brought NDEs to general attention, has stated recently that he has never been completely satisfied with that term (Kastenbaum, 1995a). He now finds it more appropriate to speak of paranormal death experiences. This seems to be a useful term, particularly because it calls attention to a larger range of phenomena that have been reported around the time of death. For example, if we are interested in NDE reports, then we might also want to investigate reports of dying people who seem to be interacting with hallucinatory or spiritual entities such as angelic escorts. (We will not be pursuing this interesting topic here; sources include Barrett, 1926/1986; Burnham, 1990; Kastenbaum, 1995b; Osis & Haraldsson, 1977.)

Paranormal death experiences are not that rare. Talk to people who have had extensive interactions with dying persons and you will probably hear reports of experiences that were unexpected, memorable, and hard to explain. In my own clinical and research activities I have encountered a number of episodes that might well be called paranormal death experiences. Like many others who have worked with dying persons and their families, I am aware that there is much that we do not understand. Heard within this context, a near-death experience is not rejected and dismissed. Each listener, though, is likely to come to his or her own interpretation of what this experience might signify.

There is a problem, however, with the concept of paranormal death experiences. This term suggests that we have a full and secure knowledge of normal death experiences. We do not. Abysmal ignorance and morbid stereotypes about the dying process prevailed for many years. The introduction of hospice care and death education has improved this situation markedly, but it would be premature to say that we have a thorough understanding of "normal" experiences related to death. The boundary between the paranormal and the normal has not yet been well defined. This realization need not deter us from trying to make sense of the available observations, but might encourage a little more caution in drawing conclusions.

EXPERIENCES AND REPORTS

Here is what one might call either an NDE or a paranormal death experience:

> I floated over the scene of the accident, fairly high, maybe thirty feet, the height of a two story building. I could see myself on the pavement, lying on my side, almost a fetal position. My right side. There was a lot of commotion and noise. Cars stopping. People gathered around me including my boyfriend and two other kids from the front seat of our car. I think someone asked if I were dead. It was then that I noticed my skirt was hiked up and I was humiliated that everyone was staring at me. At the same time I was floating higher and could see or sense white light. Then I looked back down at my body and became angry. The next thing I remember is waking up in the hospital the next day to see my father's face.[1]

Here, then, is a fairly typical description, one that contains several but not all the elements that can be discerned in NDEs (Ring, 1993). Let us ask of this description a question that is not typical: is it an experience or a report? The failure to explore this question systematically has contributed to the indecisive nature of NDE studies although, as we will see, there are other problems that also have not been addressed adequately.

At the very least, this question reminds us that experience and report are not interchangeable ways of denoting the same thing. It is easier to begin with reports. A report is a communication. It is a message that has been constructed according to certain rules. This message may be constructed during or immediately after an experience, or it may not be framed until many years later. Furthermore, the message may be transmitted through one or more channels (e. g., speech, writing). It may be transmitted and received as a separate, self-contained communication, or it may be combined with other reports and perhaps modified in the process. The report may be received by one person, a great many people, or by no person. The report may be received almost immediately, or not for many years. When the message is received it may be understood, partially understood, or misunderstood, i.e., the recipient may have varying degrees of accuracy in decoding the meaning that was intended by the sender.

The relationship between report and experience is subject to marked variation. The report may be an attempt to report the sender's actual experience as accurately as possible. It is also possible, however, for a report to have a previous report as its source, or even a series of previous reports, as in sequences of gossip and rumor. A report can also be a fabrication, a work of fiction intended to be received as such, or an attempt to deceive the recipient. A recipient may or may not be able to determine whether a particular report conveys the gist of an actual experience.

Reports can be amassed. An interested person might succeed in collecting hundreds or thousands of reports, whether of NDEs or some other experiential state. There are only practical, not theoretical limits to the number of communications-about-experiences that might be obtained. By contrast, direct experiences cannot be gathered by the bushel. A person who is keenly interested in NDEs may never have had such an experience, and therefore be forced to rely on reports from other people. Even the researcher who has had a personal NDE must also rely primarily on reports. One can certainly use one's own NDE as a source of hypotheses, but the pursuit of these hypotheses will require a collection of reports about other people's experiences. The "scientificization" of NDEs usually comes down to studying reports and their correlates. In other words, we are somewhat at a remove from the direct experiential state.

But what is a direct experiential state? Philosophers and scientists continue to struggle with the concept of consciousness. There is hardly a statement one can make about conscious or experiential states without having it subject to criticism from one of the entrenched theoretical positions. There are three types of approach to the definition and understanding of conscious states.

The *biological* approach regards consciousness as a by-product of neural activity. This is the dominant approach at present because of the major advances being made by the neurosciences (Churchland, 1995; Damasio, 1994; Dennett, 1991). What we might call the *transcendental* approach regards the individual's consciousness as but one stream within a larger cosmic flow. In the past this approach has been associated almost entirely with religious ideation, but it also has been broached by some physicists and philosophers as they propose challenging new paradigms of the universe. The *phenomenological* approach focuses on direct experience itself. The guiding belief here is that we should attempt to describe and understand conscious activity on its own terms.

Which of these approaches we choose can be consequential for NDE research. To think "I am alive" is not different than to think "I am dead" from the biological perspective. The contents of consciousness have little place in most biological models, even in today's increasingly sophisticated models. I reject the biological-only model on several grounds, but for our purposes primarily because it would have the effect of dismissing the whole subject of NDEs as meaningless. (Theoretical models that accord reality both to conscious experience and neurophysiological processes are exempt from this criticism.) The transcendental approach considers conscious experience to be meaningful, but introduces additional propositions whose truth-value is asserted rather than established on the basis of consensual evidence. One thinks of the desperate student who answered an exam question: "God only knows!" The instructor's reply: "God passes. You flunk."

It appears most useful to pursue our questions about NDE in the sphere of direct experience. The definition of "consciousness" or "direct experience" is notoriously difficult. There is the temptation to define one by the other, e.g., "consciousness is direct experience." Strictly speaking, it may be impossible to wriggle out of the labyrinth of language and into a clear and independent definition of consciousness. As a practical alternative to a long and convoluted discussion, let us think of consciousness as *the awareness of circumstances, events, and symbols as we perceive them in the moment that we perceive them*. It is both a process (of perception or knowing) and a more or less structured field within which this process operates.

There are four important correlates of conscious experience. First, the "feel" of consciousness belongs only to the experiencing individual. A thousand people may be exposed to the "same" event, but no two people will feel the same relationship between themselves and the event (and, even if they did, we would have no way of establishing this fact). Second, consciousness is an activity that is not identical with its contents. If you are looking at a cat and I am looking at two cats, this does not mean that I am twice as conscious as you are. Third, conscious experience is always replacing itself, always moving on. I might think of myself as a continuous self with a history that spans many years, but this history consists of innumerable moments in which consciousness flickered before entering the next moment. Fourth, the "reality" of conscious experience does not depend on the relationship of its perceived content to external events and circumstances. Lovers, creative artists, and fortune seekers may have vivid presentations in their momentary phenomenological fields precisely because a desired state of affairs does not exist outside of their minds at present.

Conscious experience is real—as conscious experience. NDEs are a species of conscious experience and therefore also real—as experience: "I am floating." "I am floating." "I am floating." "I am floating." Assume the first statement is made by one's self to one's self during a dream. Assume the second statement is made by a person who is inventing a story. The third statement comes from a person who is under the influence of a chemical substance. Take for the last statement the opening words of the NDE excerpted above. Obviously, we cannot distinguish among these statements on the basis of their message structure. Can we distinguish among them with regard to conscious experience? Not likely. Each perception occurs within a unique consciousness. The special "tang" and meaning of each perception arises within the momentary context of that unique field of consciousness. The fact that "I am floating" has become a quality of awareness is sufficient demonstration of its reality. What, then, might be considered "not real?"—anything that does not win its way into conscious experience. For example, all of the above statements might have been made at 11:30 p.m., but this fact might not have gained admission into the momentary field of conscious activity.

Underlying the interpretation of NDEs is the question of what we should make of conscious experience in general. My suggestion is that we accept direct conscious experience as a given. The contents and characteristics of conscious experience are "real" within this frame of reference. To what extent these experiences correspond to external events is a separate question. NDEs therefore are no more nor less "real" than any other variety of conscious experience.

Perhaps this analogy will help. Suppose that a movie screen and audio system is substituted for the contents of your conscious experience. You observe a vivid dramatic sequence, say, a battle scene with a last-minute rescue. The wide-screen action is full of detail and incident. Close-ups reveal powerful emotions on the faces of the larger-than-life performers. Your own feelings are caught up—heart rate, respiration, and other physical functions respond to the drama. In short, you have a "real" response to a scene that appears "real." Later you might wonder: Is this the way that scene actually took place? How much of this drama—if any—is a faithful reconstruction of the historical events, and how much is the product of a screen-writer's and director's fantasy? This is certainly a legitimate line of inquiry. Nevertheless, the correspondence or lack of correspondence between the scene you have witnessed and external events and circumstances does not affect the reality of the experience itself. An accurate but poorly-crafted filmed presentation of a historic battle would provide a less persuasive experience than a brilliant presentation with little correspondence to the historical event. The "special effects" and intensity noted in many NDE reports can make this type of experience seem even "realer" than most everyday experiences. We cannot dismiss NDEs as "unreal experiences" without dismissing conscious experience in general.

Many of the challenges and obstacles that we face in trying to discover correlates of NDEs are encountered in any attempt to compare experiential states with events and circumstances in the external world. It has never been easy to define, study, and interpret conscious experience, so we should not be surprised to encounter difficulties with NDEs. Indeed, Moody's own abiding interest in paranormal death experiences is associated with his fascination for the mysteries of conscious experience (Kastenbaum, 1995b). Although it will be necessary below to criticize some aspects of NDE research, we should not forget that the study of conscious experience as conscious experience is a daunting challenge, with or without NDEs. Similar difficulties are encountered, of course, in examining other types of paranormal death experience.

From this very limited exploration of paranormal death experiences as data there are three major implications to be drawn:

1. *Reject the assumption that NDEs must either be fabrications ("unreal") or that they must provide valid information about death*. When I have had previous occasions to question the connection between NDE reports and death, the most common objection has been to insist that these reports are true—they are not lies or inventions. I agree with that proposition. For the most part, NDE reports are not lies or inventions. However, the fact that these are honest reports of "real experiences" does not establish these reports as proof that the people have been somewhat dead and that death has the characteristics of their experiences.
2. *A clear distinction should be made between experience and report*. The experience is private. The report is public. Few people have more than one NDE. Anybody can read a great number of reports. The "rules of

evidence" we use in examining personal experiences are not the same rules we use in examining information that is in the public domain. For example, if I have a NDE myself, I can hardly not believe it—and I am more inclined to attribute a variety of meanings to this episode.

If you tell me of your NDE, however, I have the perspective of the external observer, which does not include the feeling-state that you experienced during the episode. Most discussions of NDE phenomena in both the popular and the scholarly literature fail to respect the differences between experience and report. This continuing practice makes it very difficult to compare findings and theories from various sources. Are we talking about experiences as experiences—or reports? (We must pass by here the complex process by which an experience becomes a report.)

3. *It makes good sense to concentrate on reports and to apply methodologies that are best suited to analyzing texts.* The reports that are based on NDEs can be treated as texts, specifically, as self-narratives. The study of self-narratives and other texts has become a major new area of scholarly inquiry in recent years, drawing expertise from philosophy, linguistics, literature, psychology, communication, and other disciplines (Britton & Pellegrini, 1991; Bruner, 1990; Nelson, 1991). This suggestion does not mean that we should ignore direct experiential states. It does mean that we should take advantage of the increasing sophistication available in the study of texts and its less troubled philosophical/methodological status as a source of data. Whatever might be the "real reality" of paranormal death experiences, what we know about them is pretty much in the form of self-narrative texts and should be studied as such.

"I" AND "ME" IN NDE REPORTS
"I could see myself on the pavement."

This statement from our sample NDE report calls our attention to a key issue that has not received the attention it deserves. Who is observing whom? Who is telling the story, and who is the subject?

A very common—if not universal—characteristic of NDE texts is the split between the narrator-self ("I") and the subject-self ("Me"). We should be curious about this arrangement. Many general questions can be raised. These include:

- What are the rules that govern the splitting of self into narrator and subject, and what, if anything, is special about these rules in the NDE situation?
- Does the narrative perspective introduce systematic biases? And, if so, what are these biases?

- What circumstances alter the relationship between the "I" and the "Me?" and in what manner?
- How does the act of sharing one's experience affect the text that is produced?

We will touch briefly on the two last-mentioned questions as examples of the "I"/"Me" problems that have yet to be examined systematically in the realm of paranormal death experiences.

The person who reported the sample NDE was 17 years of age at the time that it occurred. She was 53 when she wrote the text (having just learned the name and address of a scientific investigator, Ian Stevenson, who was interested in such reports).

Is the "I" who wrote this report the same "I" who observed herself as the victim of an automobile accident 36 years ago? Or is she now a markedly different "I" who is reconstructing the "I" who observed a long-ago "Me?" The narrative voice that was operational when this woman prepared the text has incorporated both the observing and the observed self of the past. She wrote at this later time with a perspective gained from subsequent maturation and life experience. This perspective becomes obvious as she reflects upon the experience:

I don't believe I considered this to be a near-death experience at the time. This concept was not in my 17-year-old's comprehension. But I did consider it a "close call" at the time I woke up in the hospital.

When it was actually happening, there were no thoughts about what was occurring other than my anger at the public humiliation.

What I now think happened is that I was an angry person from the time I was a five-year-old child when my mother abandoned us. When the accident occurred, I wasn't ready to die as I still had that anger to reconcile.

It took a drinking problem at age 36 and subsequent contact with my mother to resolve my anger (as part of working through Alcoholics Anonymous' Twelve Steps).

I don't know when I started seeing that experience as a kind of matter of fact "near death." Perhaps as an inveterate reader I found enough accounts of similar experiences to eventually make that connection in my mid-thirties.

Then it was just a few years ago that my focus on the experience for a paper for a class on religion (I was earning a BS degree in organizational behavior and the class was a degree requirement) took on a slightly spiritual meaning. But I remained a kind of spiritual atheist, if that makes sense. I do think the experience changed my life in that I was aware of

having had a close call, that is, almost died, so life was to be savored, made
the most of and enjoyed fully. I was a bit of a hedonist; a reporter leading
a glamorous life in my twenties; then in my thirties, recovering from a
drinking problem and entering the alcohol treatment field to help others
recover—living my recovery to its fullest.

Also, I think it gave me the courage to be a lesbian when, in my early
twenties, it was very daring, even dangerous, as girls commonly got locked
up in institutions for it. I've flown a plane, back-packed in Alaska, and
generally lived an adventurous, unconventional life.

Today, I'm living on a Mendocino Coast headland with my long time
companion in a reduced-consumption life style, working part-time with a
drinking driver treatment program and writing novels, mysteries, and science fiction. My first one came out this spring and a second is to be
released this winter.

In her mid-50's, this woman reviews several past versions of herself to
provide a context for the NDE episode: the angry five-year-old, the still-angry
adolescent, the glamorous but danger-courting twenty-year-old, the alcoholic
thirty-year-old, and the more recent "I" who assigned a "slightly spiritual
meaning" to the event that had occurred many years before. Her narrative
voice at the time of preparing this text was different from all of the foregoing
(and might well change significantly in the future). Suppose that we had
reports of the NDE experiences from all of these voices, including future
versions of the self. Would these texts be identical? Probably not. How might
these different versions affect the value of these texts as data? Who knows?
The least likely possibility is that the texts would be identical or nearly so.

There are several other facets of this text that are worth considering. First,
it is clear that the meaning she attributes to the NDE episode is closely
associated with her overall life situation. This situation changed several times,
e.g., from the perspective of a rejected and angry child who focused on the
humiliation involved in the episode, to a mid-life adult with a "slightly
spiritual" orientation. Usually we have only one text per paranormal death
experiencer, so the meanings we discover (or invent) in these texts are
dependent on all the forces that affected that person at the time a current "I"
reconstructed a past "I" and "Me."

Secondly, we note that the rules governing social discourse had changed
between the episode and its report. At the time of the event she could not
have recognized this happening as a NDE: Moody's book was still two
decades away. Furthermore, in 1955 and for some years afterward, a woman
would have had to violate societal taboos to discuss one's lesbian orientation.
These differences in the rules of social discourse between the episode and its
report are easy to identify. It is probable that less obvious differences have

occurred as well—and not only in this particular instance. We should also include shifts in the context of interpretation—what scholars or other readers make of NDE texts. A text read two decades ago and the same text read today is likely to elicit different responses based on the intervening growth in knowledge base and theory.

Next, we recognize that the personal consequences of this episode are not described in the manner that one might expect from current writings on the NDE. Most of the attention in recent writings has focused on the supposed transforming effect of NDEs (e.g., Ring, 1984; Morse & Perry, 1992). Something about the experience itself is assumed to be the basis for the positive consequences. The present text does not conform to this assumption. Immediately after the episode, she had "no thoughts about what was occurring other than my anger at the public humiliation." The experience did not affect her thoughts about life and death: no sense of liberation, exaltation, enhanced appreciation of life, or transcendence of death anxiety. And yet she did consider that she had had a "close call." It is a reasonable proposition that a person who has been perhaps a hair's breadth from death might be affected by that experience in either a temporary or an enduring manner. Had this woman undergone a transformation, it might have been on the basis of the "close call" rather than the special quality of the experience itself.

As it happened, neither the brush with death nor the NDE as such led to an immediate and profound change. It was only many years later when she heard of NDEs and their reputed spirituality that this episode had a delayed (though not transfiguring) effect on her.

Why did she not respond to the NDE in the manner described by current writers? And how often have people rushed to the conclusion that the experiential state—rather than a close call with death—was responsible for transformation? It would not be that difficult to compare people who have had close calls with death (without NDEs) and people who have NDE-like experiences when not in a life-threatening situation. The texts they produce and the effect of these episodes on their thoughts and lives would be useful in evaluating the prevailing assumption that it is the NDE that leads to transformation, when transformation does occur.

Next, we might remind ourselves that all communications are acts of sharing. These acts occur within particular settings and everything about the messages—their construction, transmission, and reception—is subject to influence by contextual factors. This holds true for the self-narratives that are known as NDE reports. In the present example, the act of sharing was influenced by the sender's expectation that it would be read by a knowledgeable and sympathetic person; had she tried to communicate this experience at an earlier time she might well have been influenced by the negative attitude of prospective listeners or readers. NDE research must be careful about the conditions under which acts of sharing have taken place—but the literature reveals many examples of indifference to this issue. The reader should have no difficulty in finding "data" which the eager investigator shaped to suit his/her interests.

There is one further implication of the "I"/"Me" narrative relationship that completely undermines claims for NDE reports as proof of survival. No matter how vivid and fascinating the report, it always comes from the narrative self. These texts boil down to: "I saw me dead." Precisely who is dead? "Me." Who says so? "I do."

The report that death is pleasant and at times survivable comes invariably from an observer who was lively and alert through it all. The illogic here may be compared to what happens if we question a person who is resting with eyes closed. "Are you sleeping?" "Yes, thank you for asking." The very fact that there is a prompt and articulate response casts doubt on the substance of that response. So it is with NDE reports, only more so.

There are two possibilities: (1) "I" was there and alive to observe and classify "Me" as dead; (2) "I" was not functional and made no observations at the time; therefore, "I" was in no position to determine the condition of "I" and "Me." (This alternative is consistent with the theory that NDE reports should be regarded as memory fantasies that are created—not consciously—as one is recovering from the stress of a life-threatening episode (Kastenbaum, 1995c).

If "I" have survived to report the demise of "Me," then the report of Our death has been, in Mark Twain's words, "greatly exaggerated."

I raised this problem at scientific conferences and in print when NDEs were first attracting attention (e.g., Kastenbaum, 1978, 1979). One might think that those who believe that NDEs provide evidence for survival would respond to this criticism. Not so. Years later, this annoying little fact is still being neglected: reports presumably from the realm of death are offered only by people who were living observers of the experience.

NDE RESEARCH FINDINGS AND THE SURVIVAL QUESTION

Studies have not proven that people were dead at the time the experiences occurred which provided the basis for subsequent NDE reports. There are well studied cases in which it is clear that lives were in great jeopardy and in which the individuals did not seem capable of perception, thought, and response. Later (sometimes years later, as in our sample text) these people reported experiences that were then interpreted as having occurred while they were dead. Not established, however, was (a) convincing evidence that the person was dead; and (b) that the experience actually occurred precisely at the time when the person was out of this life.

There is a general problem that complicates the attempt to connect NDE communications with actual death. What is death? The development of life-support systems and organ transplant technology has ever-widening consequences in the medical, ethical, religious, legal, and economic domains (Brock, 1993; Madsen, 1993). The basic question seems to be: under what circumstances should we consider a person to be dead? To answer this question, one needs a firm definition of death. What we have at present, however, is a set of competing definitions and views. What is most relevant for us here is the possibility that death might be considered to be a matter of degree—or that death might even take more than one form (Kastenbaum, 1993; 1995b).

The challenging possibilities here go well beyond the scope of this chapter. However, we might well keep in mind the realization that alternative definitions of death could have major implications for the interpretation of NDEs. The interpretation that is best in accord with available knowledge at the moment might be expressed as follows:

- If death is to be defined as the total and irreversible cessation of functioning, then we must conclude that research has failed to support the claim that NDE reports constitute proof for survival.
- But if death is to be deconstructed into a variety of meaning-states (e.g., partial, temporary, situational), then it might be possible to show that some NDEs occurred during one of these states.

Today people usually take "survival of death" to mean recovery of function after a person was dead in the traditional, all-or-none sense of the term. It would be erroneous to claim that NDE research has proven survival within the traditional context of meaning, although the way is open for responsible exploration of the alternative approach.

NDE research has had its greatest success in the accumulation of texts. The relative ease in obtaining reports suggests that such experiences are not rare. There has also been some success in examining the correlates. The most useful findings here were well in hand more than a decade ago. For example, Gabbard and Twemlow (1984) found that NDE reports were not related to mental illness, previous interest in paranormal or mystical phenomena, or level of education. Other studies have found NDE reports among people of various ages, racial/ethnic backgrounds and historical periods (Zaleski, 1987). Although cultural factors do have an influence on content (Kellehear et al., 1994), it is reasonably clear that this general type of experience occurs across a broad spectrum of people. These findings support the position that NDEs tell us something significant about human experience in general.

As mentioned, research produced solid and useful results in the years immediately following Moody's (1975) introduction of NDE texts. This first wave of research activity, however, did not provide direct evidence for the survival-of-death assertion that has made NDEs of exceptional interest to many people. Perhaps the closest approach to viable evidence was a clinical study reported by cardiologist Michael B. Sabom and his colleagues (1982). Several patients reported having seen and/or heard events taking place around them while they in the operating room, under anesthesia, and presumably unresponsive. These details were confirmed by retrospective study of what had actually occurred during surgery.

Some people rushed to the unreflective conclusion that a spirit self had left the dead bodies of these persons and observed the goings-on. This conclusion was premature because Sabom's study did not establish that the patients were dead at the time, nor did it rule out alternative explanations of a less radical nature. Nevertheless, one might have expected these provocative findings to be followed up and extended by other studies. This did not happen. Why not? Perhaps a sufficient explanation is the fact that such studies are difficult to conduct, given the circumstances of operating rooms, intensive care units, and hospital systems in general. The one subsequent attempt known to have been made (Holden, 1988) encountered many practical problems, not the least of which was the absence of patients with NDEs to report.

The general scientific enterprise would not have progressed to its present state if researchers had retreated from the challenge of designing and conducting difficult studies. Up to now, few NDE researchers have taken on the challenge of examining their phenomena under rigorous conditions.

Indeed, research into the key issue of NDEs, death, and survival has come to a virtual halt in recent years. This is also Moody's current (Kastenbaum, 1995a) opinion. To test this conclusion, one need only read through the *Journal of Near-Death Studies* from its inception to the present day. One will notice a steady decline in articles that present data bearing directly on the question of whether or not people who report NDEs were dead, and death itself a state of exhilaration. The same time trend is evident in books. People are still adding more NDE texts to those already published, but there is nothing in the way these texts are obtained or analyzed that contributes to their evaluation as evidence. Ten thousand reports are no better than ten reports if they are offered simply as further examples of the fact that some people believed they have died and come back to life, rather improved for the experience.

Research attention has turned to other topics, such as the consequences of having had an NDE. Speculations and side issues have taken the place that we might expect to be occupied by quality data. There is no reason to believe that the *Journal of Near-Death Studies* and other publications have decided to reject competent data-based articles. The research is not being done, and the newcomer might well assume that the main questions have already been settled; not so!

What we do find in the available evidence are the following points (Kastenbaum, 1995c):

1. Many people who have returned from a close encounter with death do not have NDE reports to offer. Why are NDEs not a universal characteristic of brushes with death? We do not know.

2. Some of the reports are nightmarish rather than comforting. Why this variation? Again, we do not know (although, again, there is no shortage of speculation).

3. Reports with the features that have been found in NDE texts have also been made by people who were in situations in which their lives were not in danger. Why, then, should we associate such reports so strongly with death?

4. Some people who recovered from illness or injury over- or mis-interpreted what they had been told by health care providers (Stevenson et al., 1989–1990). They persuaded themselves or were persuaded by others into believing they had been dead.

5. People who were actually close to possible death have been found less likely to report an NDE than those who were less endangered (Greyson, 1981). This suggests that the production of NDE texts requires a central nervous system that is still in working order.

Taken together with the logical and methodological problems already noted, these findings do not provide the basis for concluding that NDE texts are reports from people who have made a round-trip journey to the realm of death. One can choose to believe that the complete and permanent cessation of life is followed by a blissful spiritual state, but NDE research has provided no evidence for this proposition. People who have died and stayed dead have not necessarily had the experiences reported by those who have shared their extraordinary episodes with us.

WHAT DO NDES MEAN AND HOW MIGHT WE LEARN MORE ABOUT THEM?

There is a reasonable alternative to the unconfirmed proposition that NDEs give us reliable information about death and survival. This alternative emphasizes the functional value of the episode as experienced and as reported. Psychiatrist Russell Noyes, Jr. provided the foundation for this approach with his analysis of the psychological states that manifest themselves in NDE reports, drawing upon the earlier observations of Roth and Harper (1962) who had examined other types of unusual experiences. Noyes concludes that most reports show both a state of *hyperalertness* and a state of *depersonalization:*

> On a psychological level depersonalization may be interpreted as a defense against the threat of death. Not only did people in the studies…find themselves calm in otherwise frightening situations but they also felt detached from what was happening…. The depersonalized state is one that mimics death. In it a person experiences himself as empty, lifeless, and unfamiliar. In a sense he creates psychologically the very situation that environmental circumstances threaten to impose. In so doing he escapes death, for what has already happened cannot happen again; he cannot die, because he is already dead. (Noyes, 1979, 79)

Noyes further suggests that these contrasting strategies—hyperalertness and depersonalization—might be mediated by the same neural mechanism whose function it is to help the organism deal with danger by intensifying alertness while at the same time inhibiting potentially disorganizing emotion. When this mechanism is working properly, a person is able to remain calm and effective in the midst of a crisis. In subsequent research I have found that the hyperalert/depersonalized state of mind described by Noyes also can occur when a dying person has the time and inclination to write a deathbed journal (Kastenbaum, 1995d).

This response-to-danger theory was expanded by my analysis of the role of the individual in the crisis situation (Kastenbaum, 1979). A driver faced with an impending collision is much more likely to execute an emergency maneuver than to split off into a detached, autoscopic experience. The experiential state that is known as an NDE tends to occur when the individual can do nothing directly to improve his or her chances of surviving the crisis. The sense of serenity associated with an NDE serves to quiet the nervous system and conserve energy. It is probable that the production of brain opiates (endorphins) is stimulated by these circumstances. In short: when we perceive a dangerous situation, we take practical action when we can—and when we cannot act, it is time to seek refuge in a pleasantly tinged state of withdrawal.

It is also a reasonable hypothesis that the report as well as the experience serves a useful function. The text is not created in the midst of the physical crisis, but on the way back as the individual is recovering. This is also characteristic of the way in which normal self-reports are generated. We construct a story to describe and account for what happened after it has happened. It is not unusual for these stories to be revised several times until they reach a more or less fixed form. Furthermore, the act of communicating itself contributes to the articulation of the text. Eventually, a profoundly unsettling and rather chaotic immediate experience becomes a text that explains the experience to one's self and can be shared with others. This is an adaptive process because it helps the individual to go ahead with his or her life as an integrated person after an episode of discontinuity and threatened disintegration.

It is not idle speculation to compare NDE reports with texts—NDE reports *are* texts. As previously noted, almost all of the data come to us in the form not of our own direct experiences, but in the form of texts whose precise relationship to experience is indeterminate. We are limited in the types of data available to us in NDE research, but texts are abundant. It would make sense to make more of what we do have; unfortunately, NDE texts have seldom if ever been subjected to sophisticated analyses. Perhaps these reports should be given over to specialists in linguistics, literature, philosophy, and communication who have more expertise in textual analysis than what has been demonstrated by most NDE researchers.

With more productive studies of NDE texts, we might also work ourselves into a better position for understanding their neural and contextual aspects. For example, Morse and his colleagues have proposed a fascinating (but untested) neural model for NDEs (Morse, Venecia, & Milstein, 1989). It is worth noting that the brain areas and functional networks he believes to be mostly responsible for such experiences are also involved in imagination, creativity, and fantasy. Texts can vary greatly with respect to their factual and imaginative content, a distinction that no amount of microneurological research can make on its own. Ironically, then, the most promising way to test neuroscience theories of NDE production may be to examine the voices of the "I" and the "Me" as they speak through these still-fascinating and still-elusive texts.

NOTE

1. This report is part of a set that was kindly made available to the author by Ian Stevenson, M.D., and Emily Williams Cooks, Ph.D. The comments made here reflect only the author's views.

REFERENCES

Barrett, W. (1926/1986). *Death-bed Visions*. Northampton, England: Aquarian Press.

Britton, B. K., and A. D. Pellegrini. (1990). *Narrative Thought and Narrative Language*. Hillsdale, NJ: Lawrence Erlbaum Associates.

Brock, D. W. (1993). *Life and Death*. Cambridge, England: Cambridge University Press.

Bruner, J. (1990). *Acts of Meaning*. Cambridge, MA: Harvard University Press.

Burnham, S. (1990). *A Book of Angels*. New York: Ballantine.

Churchland, P. M. (1995). *The Engine of Reason, the Seat of the Soul*. Cambridge, MA: MIT Press.

Damasio, A. (1994). *Descartes' Error: Emotion, Reason, and the Human Brain*. New York: G. P. Putnam's Sons.

Dennett, D. (1991). *Consciousness Explained*. Boston: Little, Brown.

Gabbard, G. O., and S. W. Twemlow. (1984). *With the Eyes of the Mind*. New York: Praeger.

Greyson, B. (1981). "Empirical evidence bearing on the interpretation of NDE among suicide attempters." Paper presented at the annual meeting of the American Psychological Association, Los Angeles.

Holden, J. M. (1988). Rationale and considerations for proposed near-death research in the hospital setting. *Journal of Near-Death Studies, 7*, 19–31.

Kastenbaum, R. (1978). "Recent studies of the NDE: A critical appraisal." Paper presented at the annual meeting of the American Psychological Association, Los Angeles.

Kastenbaum, R. (1979). Death through the retroscopic lens. In R. Kastenbaum (ed.), *Between Life and Death*. (pp. 156–184). New York: Springer Publishing Co., Inc.

Kastenbaum, R. (1993). Last words. *The Monist, An International Journal of General Philosophical Inquiry, 76*, 270–90.

Kastenbaum, R. (1995a). *Is There Life after Death?* Revised edition. London: Prion.

Kastenbaum, R. (1995b). Paranormal death experiences: An Omega interview with Raymond A. Moody, Jr. *Omega, Journal of Death and Dying, 31*, 87–97.

Kastenbaum, R. (1995c). *Death, Society, and Human Experience*. 5th edition. Boston: Allyn and Bacon.

Kastenbaum, R. (In press). "How far can an intellectual effort diminish pain?" William McDougall's journal as a model for facing death. *Omega, Journal of Death and Dying*.

Kellehear, A., I. Stevenson, S. Pasricha, and E. Cook. (1994). The absence of tunnel sensations in near-death experiences from India. *Journal of Near-Death Studies, 13*, 109–115.

Madson, S. K. (1993). Patient Self Determination Act: Implications for long term care. *Journal of Gerontological Nursing, 12*, 17–23.

Moody, R. A., Jr. (1975). *Life after Life*. New York: Mockingbird/Bantam Books.

Morse, M. L., D. Venecia, Jr., and J. Milstein. (1989). Near-death experiences: A neuro-physiological explanatory model. *Journal of Near-Death Studies, 8*, 45–53.

Morse, M. L., with P. Perry. (1992). *Transformed by the Light*. New York: Villard Books.

Nelson, K. (1991). Remembering and telling: A developmental story. *Journal of Narrative and Life History, 1*, 109–128.

Noyes, R., Jr. (1979). Near-death experiences: Their interpretation. In R. Kastenbaum (ed.), *Between Life and Death* (pp. 73–88). New York: Springer Publishing Co., Inc.

Osis, K., and E. Haraldsson. (1977). *At the Hour of Death*. New York: Avon.

Ring, K. (1984). *Heading toward Omega*. New York: William Morrow.

Ring, K. (1993). Near-death experiences. In R. Kastenbaum and B. Kastenbaum (eds.), *Encyclopedia of Death* (pp. 193–196). New York: Avon.

Roth, M., and M. Harper. (1962). Temporal lobe epilepsy and the phobic anxiety-depersonalization syndrome, Part II: Practical and theoretical considerations. *Comprehensive Psychiatry, 3*, 215–26.

Sabom, M. B. (1982). *Recollections of Death*. New York: Simon & Schuster.

Stevenson, L., C. W. Cook, and N. McClean-Rice. (1989–1990). Are persons reporting "near-death experiences" really near death? A study of medical records. *Omega, Journal of Death and Dying, 10*, 45–54.

Zaleski, C. (1987). *Otherworld Journeys*. New York: Oxford University Press.

17

Neuroscience, Ketamine, and the Near-Death Experience
The Role of Glutamate and the NMDA Receptor

Karl Jansen

In truth, the exploration of the mind-brain interface is one of the most exciting adventures which humans have ever undertaken, and the real reductionism lies in attempts to draw a mystical shroud over the NDE.

Karl Jansen, M.D., Ph.D., MRC Psych., is a psychiatrist whose research supports an extension of the neurophysiological argument that NDEs are side-effects of a flood of brain chemicals. He proposes that the amino acid glutamate, which is a key chemical messenger in the brain, floods the brain in crisis times, such as a death threat, and becomes toxic. Recent research strongly suggests, he says, that the drug ketamine can reproduce the characteristics of NDEs, because it prevents this toxicity. If the brain's natural chemicals, acting like ketamine, such as opiate-like endopsychosins, do block the toxic glutamate flood, they can provide the neurophysiological explanation for NDEs. Jansen is working to confirm his hypothesis.

Karl Jansen, M.D., Ph.D., MRC Psych., began his neurological research at the University of Auckland in New Zealand, then earned his D.Phil. at Oxford University. He has published several articles in neurophysiology. He is a member of the Royal College of Psychiatrists, practicing at the Maudsley Hospital, Denmark Hill in London, SE5 8AZ. Dr. Jansen would like to hear from persons who have had experiences with ketamine.

Neuroscience, Ketamine, and the Near-Death Experience
The Role of Glutamate and the NMDA Receptor

The near-death experience (NDE) is an altered state of consciousness with characteristic features. These can be reproduced by ketamine via blockade of a glutamate (N-methyl-D-aspartate, NMDA) receptor. Overactivation of these receptors by a glutamate 'flood' occurs under the same conditions which precipitate NDEs, resulting in neuro-toxicity. Ketamine prevents this neurotoxicity. Endogenous substances in the brain (e.g., endopsychosins) have similar actions to ketamine. Thus conditions which trigger an NDE may also trigger an endopsychosin flood, to protect cells. The NDE is a side-effect on consciousness with psychological functions.

The near-death experience is an important altered state of consciousness (Stevenson and Greyson, 1979; Greyson and Stevenson, 1980; Ring, 1980; Sabom, 1982; Jansen, 1989a,b, 1990). However, scientists have been deterred from research by claims that NDEs are evidence for life after death which impart the air of a pseudoscience to studies of the NDE (e.g., Osis and Haraldsson, 1977). Irrespective of religous beliefs, the NDE can never be evidence for life after death on logical grounds: death is defined as the final, irreversible end, and anyone who 'returned' did not, by definition, die.

There is overwhelming evidence that the mind is produced by the brain. The effects on the mind of adding drugs to the brain, and the religious experiences which sometimes result, provide further evidence (Grinspoon and Bakalar, 1981). Morse has noted the contradiction which 'after-lifers' must resolve, that "the spirit rises out of the body leaving the brain behind, but *somehow* still incorporating neuronal functions such as sight, hearing, and proprioception" (Morse, 1989).

The NDE can be reproduced by ketamine (Domino et al.,

1965; Rumpf, 1969; Collier, 1972; Siegel, 1978, 1980, 1981; Stafford, 1977; Lilly, 1978; Grinspoon and Bakalar, 1981; White, 1982; Ghoniem et al., 1985; Jansen, 1989a,b, 1990, 1993). With some exceptions, this has been seen as no more than a curiosity because the dying are not given drugs of this nature (Siegel, 1980, 1981; Jansen, 1990). Recent discoveries indicate that reproduction of the NDE by ketamine is more than a coincidence. These discoveries include the major binding site for ketamine, called the NMDA receptor (Thomson et al., 1985), the importance of NMDA receptors in the cerebral cortex, particularly in the temporal and frontal lobes, the key role of these sites in cognitive processing, memory, and perception, their role in epilepsy, psychoses, hypoxic ischaemic and epileptic cell damage (excitotoxicity), the prevention of this damage by ketamine, and the discovery of substances in the brain called 'endopsychosins' which bind to the same site as ketamine (Anis et al., 1983; Quirion et al., 1984; Simon et al., 1984; Benveniste et al., 1984; Ben-Ari, 1985; Coan and Collingridge, 1987; Collingridge, 1987; Contreras et al., 1987; Rothman et al., 1987; Mody et al., 1987, Quirion et al., 1987; Sonders et al., 1988; Barnes, 1988; Choi, 1988; Monaghan et al., 1989; Jansen et al., 1989a,b,c, 1990a,b,c, 1991a,b,c, 1993).

The above discoveries can be combined to extend and modify previous neurobiological hypotheses into a more contemporary model.

THE NEAR-DEATH EXPERIENCE
There is no agreed set of criteria which define the NDE. This lack allows those critical of neurobiological models to dismiss them because some particular criterion which they believe to be important may not have been fully accounted for by the model being proposed—although it may well be that a consensus, statistical definition of the key features of the NDE would not include those features—just as the American Psychiatric Association (APA) definition of schizophrenia (1980) represents an international consensus and avoids the sectarian views of a few, or inclusion of obscure cases which do not meet the general rule. For example, Gabbard and Twemlow (1989) state that Saavedra-Aguilar and Gomez-Jeria's neurobiological hypothesis (1989) does not have general validity because Gabbard and Twemlow had identified 5 cases in which hypoxia and stress did not appear to be a triggering factor (temporal lobe epilepsy can occur without any triggering factors).

Ketamine is capable of reproducing all of the features of the NDE which have been described in the most cited works in this field, and the following account is based upon these and also upon NDEs described to the author (Domino et al., 1965; Rumpf, 1969; Collier, 1972; Siegel,1978, 1980, 1981; Stafford, 1977; Lilly, 1978; Grinspoon and Bakalar, 1981; White, 1982; Ghoniem et al., 1985; Sputz, 1989; Jansen, 1989a, b,1990b, 1991c, 1993).

NDEs typically include a sense of ineffability, timelessness, a sense that what is experienced is 'real' and that one is actually dead, and feelings of calm and peace, although some cases have been frightening. There may be analgesia, apparent clarity of thought, a perception of separation from the body and hallucinations of landscapes, beings such as 'angels', people including partners, parents, teachers and friends (many of whom are alive at the time), and religious and mythical figures. Hearing noises during the initial part of the NDE has also been described (Noyes and Kletti, 1976a; Morse et al., 1985; Osis and Haraldsson, 1977; Greyson and Stevenson, 1980; Ring, 1980; Sabom, 1982).

A five-stage continuum has been described: 1. feelings of peace and contentment; 2. a sense of detachment from the body; 3. entering a transitional world of darkness (rapid movements through tunnels: 'the tunnel experience'); 4. emerging into bright light; and 5. 'entering the light' (Ring, 1980). Ring reported that 60% experienced stage 1, but only 10% attained stage 5. Transcendent mystical states are common while panoramic life reviews are rare (Greyson, 1983). As might be expected in a mental state with a neurobiological origin, more mundane accounts also occur, e.g. children who may 'see' their schoolfellows rather than God and angels (Morse, 1985).

KETAMINE

Ketamine is a short-acting, hallucinogenic, dissociative anaesthetic. Ketamine and phencyclidine (PCP) are arylcyclohexylamines. Unlike PCP, it is relatively safe, an uncontrolled drug in most countries, and remains in use as an anaesthetic (White et al., 1982). The effects are different from the psychedelic drugs such as LSD (Grinspoon and Bakalar, 1981). Ketamine can reproduce all features of the NDE, from rapid trips through dark tunnels into light and the conviction that one is dead, to 'seeing spirits', 'telepathic communion with God', auditory and visual hallucinations, out-of-body experiences, mystical states, peace and tranquillity, and occasional frightening experiences (see ketamine references above). If given parenterally, it has a short action with an abrupt end. Describing ketamine effects, Grinspoon and Bakalar (1981) wrote of:

> ...becoming a disembodied mind or soul, dying and going to another world. Childhood events may also be re-lived. The loss of contact with ordinary reality and the sense of participation in another reality are more pronounced and less easily resisted than is usually the case with LSD. The dissociative experiences often seem so genuine that users are not sure that they have not actually left their bodies.

Descriptions of the NDE have been closely matched with those produced by ketamine (e.g., Siegel, 1980, 1981). Explanations of NDEs as related to hallucinatory phenomena are sometimes rejected by spiritualists because so many persons insist that their experiences were 'real' (Osis and Haraldsson, 1977; Ring, 1980). It is significant that 30 percent of normal subjects given ketamine insisted that they had not been dreaming or hallucinating, but that the events had really happened (Rumpf et al., 1969; see also Siegel, 1978). The APA (1980) defines a hallucination thus: 'a hallucination has the immediate sense of reality of a true perception …transient hallucinatory experiences are common in individuals without mental disorder.' The clear sensorium of some dying patients has also been used to argue against hallucinations (Osis and Haraldsson, 1977; Ring, 1980). However, hallucinations in schizophrenia typically occur in clear consciousness and are believed to be real, sometimes for many years—despite incontrovertible evidence to the contrary (APA, 1980). Thus a personal conviction of the 'reality' of an NDE should not be used to argue against neurobiological hypotheses. It is worth noting that some users of LSD have claimed that their minds are clearer than usual (Grinspoon and Bakalar, 1981).

Much has been made of reports that some cardiac arrest survivors can describe the resuscitation in detail (Sabom, 1982). Ketamine sometimes permits sufficient sensory input to allow accounts of procedures during which the patient appeared wholly unconscious (Siegel, 1981).

GLUTAMATE AND THE NMDA RECEPTOR

The majority of large neurones in the cerebral cortex use the excitatory amino acid glutamate as their neurotransmitter. Glutamate is the key chemical messenger in the temporal and frontal lobes, and is central to the function of the hippocampus (Cotman et al., 1987; Fagg and Foster, 1983; Greenamyre et al., 1984; Monaghan, Bridges, and Cotman, 1989; Jansen et al., 1989c, 1990a). Glutamate plays a vital role in all cognitive processes involving the cerebral cortex, including thinking, and the formation of memories and recall, and it is vital in perception (Monaghan, Bridges, and Cotman, 1989; Oye et al., 1992).

Until recently, there was confusion about the meaning of the terms sigma, sigma-opioid, PCP, and NMDA receptors. There is a binding site for ketamine and PCP, called the PCP receptor, attached to the NMDA receptor which is like a harbour with several docks (Monaghan, Bridges, and Cotman, 1989). As they are part of the same entity, the two terms are sometimes used interchangeably. The sigma receptor is totally unrelated. It is not an opioid receptor and has a unique distribution in the CNS (Walker et al., 1990; Jansen et al., 1991b). The term 'sigma-opioid' is no longer in use. Ketamine is not an opioid.

When I first proposed the glutamate theory of the NDE (Jansen, 1990b), it was not clear whether the hallucinogenic properties of ketamine were due to NMDA or sigma receptors. It is now known that these effects are due to NMDA receptor blockade (Krystal et al., 1994), and that sigma receptors probably do not play an important role in the key cognitive aspects of the experience. Substances which bind to sigma receptors with a high degree of specificity (e.g. (+)pentazocine) do not produce the NDE at doses where most of the binding is to sigma rather than NMDA and kappa opioid receptors (substances which bind to sigma receptors frequently have some affinity for NMDA and kappa opioid receptors at higher doses) (Musacchio et al., 1990; Walker et al., 1990).

Glutamate is excitatory. When present in excess, neurons die via excitotoxicity. This is the mechanism of neuronal cell death in hypoxia/ischaemia and epilepsy, conditions which have been proven to lead to excessive release of glutamate (e.g. Rothman, 1984; Rothman and Olney, 1986, 1987). Blockade of the PCP receptor prevents cell death from excitotoxicity (e.g., Rothman et al., 1987). This suggests that the brain may have a protective mechanism against the detected glutamate flood: a counter-flood of a substance which binds to the PCP receptor, preventing cell death. The brain is a well-protected organ with many known defences. It is reasonable to propose protective mechanisms against excitotoxicity. This is the only speculation in the process outlined above: the other statements are strongly supported by data (Benveniste et al.,1984; Simon et al., 1984; Ben-Ari, 1985; King and Dingledine, 1986; Rothman et al., 1987; Westerberg et al., 1987; Hoyer and Nitsch, 1989).

Endogenous substances have been found in the brain which bind to the PCP receptor, one of which is a peptide called 'alpha-endopsychosin' (Quirion et al., 1984).

EXPLANATIONS FOR THE NDE

Some authors have declared that the NDE must have a single explanation and then presented anecdotes to counter each scientific theory (e.g. Ring, 1980), or required that any scientific theory put forward must explain all of the experiences ever given the name of NDE (e.g., Gabbard and Twemlow, 1989). It is more likely that the NDE is a final common expression of several different causes. Even then, the final 'common' expression contains sufficient variability to suggest different types of NDE with different explanations. A multi-levelled interpretation is the most useful. The 'glutamate hypothesis of the NDE' is not intended to apply to all NDE's, nor it is incompatible with many of the theories described below.

Psychological

1. *Depersonalisation*: this theory proposes that the NDE is an adaptive mechanism which alerts one to the threat of death while potentially overwhelming emotion is held at bay, allowing the reality to be integrated without panic (Greyson, 1983; Noyes and Kletti, 1976a,b). This model is most applicable when death is psychologically near, as when falling from a cliff. While protecting nerve cells from ischaemic damage is then largely irrelevant, glutamate and NMDA receptors would certainly be involved in producing the experience, as they play a key role in cognition and perception.

2. *Regression in the service of the ego*: confronting death cuts off the external world, resulting in regression to a pre-verbal level experienced as mystical ineffability (Greyson, 1983). A loss of contact with the external world is one of the most characteristic effects of ketamine, and this is probably due to blockade of NMDA receptors involved in sensory transmission. NMDA receptors play a central role in the transmission of incoming signals from all sensory modalities (Davies and Watkins, 1983; Greenamyre et al., 1984; Headley et al., 1985; Cotman et al., 1987; Cline et al.,1987; Monaghan, Bridges and Cotman, 1988; Kisvardy et al., 1989; Oye et al., 1992).

3. *A state-dependent reactivation of birth memories* (Grof and Halifax, 1977): this theory explains the movement through tunnels towards light as a memory of being born. The NDE is thus actually a 'near-birth experience'. NMDA receptor blockade could be the underlying mechanism for such a reactivation.

4. *Sensory deprivation*: memories may normally be suppressed by a mechanism which acts as a gate, admitting primarily external signals when we are fully conscious and concentrating upon an external task (Siegel,1980, 1981). If this input is dramatically reduced (e.g. by ketamine or a heart attack) in combination with central stimulation (e.g. by excessive glutamate release during hypoxia, epilepsy, or arising without external provocation), stored perceptions are released and become 'organised' by the mind. The 'white light' may result from CNS stimulation mimicking light on the retina, and a lowering of the phosphene perceptual threshold. Sensory deprivation itself produces a profound alteration in consciousness (Lilly, 1961,1978).

The hippocampus is the anatomical location of such a gate, and the NMDA receptor is the molecular substrate. NMDA receptors have their highest concentration in the hippocampus, a part of the medial temporal lobe where data from the external world is integrated with internal programs. The NMDA receptor plays an important role in learning, and in the formation and retrieval of memories. The PCP receptor is referred to as a 'gated channel'. Whether the gate is open or closed depends on the degree of excitation—specifically, the position of a magnesium ion in the channel. Ketamine blocks this channel and closes the gate to incoming data (Monaghan, Bridges, and Cotman, 1989; Morris et al., 1986; Collingridge, 1987; McNaughton and Morris, 1987; Cotman, Monaghan, and Ganong, 1988).

Drug-induced hallucinations

Administered drugs may explain some cases of NDE's, but in many no drugs were given with effects resembling the NDE (Sabom, 1982)

Temporal Lobe Epilepsy

Persinger and Makarec (1987) and Saavedra-Aguilar and Gomez-Jeria (1989) have reviewed evidence for the similarity between the phenomena experienced in temporal lobe epilepsy (TLE) and the NDE. Glutamate is the key neurotransmitter in the temporal lobe, particularly in the hippocampus, and plays an important role in epilepsy. The neuropathology of epilepsy is believed to result from excito-toxic cell death (Ben-Ari, 1985; King and Dingledine, 1986; Olney, Collins, and Sloviter, 1986; Mody and Heinemann, 1987; Cotman, Monaghan, and Ganong, 1988).

It is possible that the postulated endogenous neuroprotective system becomes active in any excitotoxic situation, including TLE. The degree of excito-toxic cell damage, and the mental state, resulting from an incident in which there is a glutamate flood, whatever the cause, may depend on the final balance in each neuronal pathway between excito-toxic forces and neuro-protective mechanisms. This theory is supported by reports of persons who were oxygen deprived for prolonged periods, had a profound NDE, and survived the episode unimpaired (Sabom, 1982). The lack of apparent brain damage in these cases is hard to be explain unless we postulate that these may be persons with a particularly effective mechanism for glutamatergic blockade.

It is also possible that there is no protective mechanism, and that ketamine has its effects by mimicing some of the processes seen in TLE. Even though ketamine blocks glutamatergic transmission, and prevents excitotoxic cell death, the effect of ketamine upon the human electroencephalograph (the EEG) suggests that the final result of ketamine acting in the brain is the result of a complex interplay of forces. There is a reduction in alpha wave activity, while beta, delta and theta wave activity are increased (Schwartz et al. 1974; Pichlmayr et al., 1984). Ketamine has been reported to act both as an anticonvulsant (e.g., McCarthy et al., 1965; Celesia and Chen, 1974; Taberner, 1976; Leccese et al., 1986; Mares et al., 1992) and as a pro-convulsant (Bennet et al., 1973; Gourie et al., 1983; Myslobodsky, 1981). Myslobodsky (1981) reported that ketamine could produce epileptiform

EEG patterns in human limbic and thalamic regions, but that there was no evidence that this affected other cortical regions or that clinical seizures were likely to occur. This is quite consistent with the NDE model presented by Saavedra-Aguilar and Gomez-Jeria (1989) which involved limited electrical abnormalites in the limbic system. Thus the production of the NDE by ketamine is not necessarily at odds with the proposal that the NDE may result from abnormal electrical activity in the brain. In a recent review, Reich and Silvay (1989) concluded: 'it is hard to draw objective conclusions regarding the anti-convulsant properties of ketamine...animal data are particularly difficult to interpret because of interspecies variations.' Nevertheless, the weight of the evidence favours the conclusion that ketamine is probably anticonvulsant at the doses required to produce the NDE (Myslobodsky, 1981) favoring the hypothesis that an NMDA receptor blocker is released to produce the NDE.

Endorphin Release

Carr (1981, 1989) proposed that the NDE might be the result of a flood release of endogenous opioids (endorphins) as survival time was increased by administering opiate antagonists such as naloxone, in fatal circumstances (Holoday and Faden, 1978). The concept of a flood release of endogenous compounds is valuable, and it has now been established that a glutamate flood results in excitotoxic cell death in hypoxia/ischaemia and epilepsy (see above). However, endorphins are not responsible for the NDE, as they are not potent hallucinogens (Oyama et al., 1980). Injection of beta-endorphin into the CSF has analgesic effects lasting well over 22 hours (Oyama et al.,1980). However, NDE's are typically brief. Ketamine produces brief, deep analgesia (White et al., 1982) due to NMDA receptor blockade (e.g., Schouenberg and Sjolund, 1986; Parsons et al., 1988). Such limited psychotomimetic properties as certain opioids (e.g., (-)pentazocine) do appear to result from binding to kappa opioid receptors, and to PCP receptors at higher doses (Pfieffer et al., 1986; Mussachio et al., 1990). However, the effects of (-)pentazocine binding to kappa receptors are described as 'feelings of cheerfulness and strength' (Belville and Forrest, 1968). The effects of selective and specific drug binding to kappa receptors do not match the profound alterations in consciousness produced by ketamine. When higher doses are employed, more marked effects may appear as a result of binding to PCP receptors. The claim that the (+)isomers of benzomorphan opiates, which are sigma preferring, have psychotomimetic effects is not supported by an extensive literature based on research in humans, carried out in the 1960's, which demonstrates that it is the (-)isomers which have psychotomimetic properties—and these may prefer PCP receptors (review: Mussachio,1990). The naloxone-reversible component is due to kappa opioid receptor binding, while the naloxone insensitive component is now known to be due to PCP (i.e., NMDA) receptor binding, not sigma binding (Walker et al., 1990). The role of opioid receptors in ketamine effects is contoversial, and has been reviewed by Reich and Silvay (1989). Amiot et al. (1985) found no evidence that naloxone could reverse the effects of ketamine in humans. Similar results were reported in a key study with dogs (Vaupel, 1983). It is important to note that ketamine is supplied as a mixture of (+)ketamine and (-)ketamine isomers. Some of the controversy may be resolved by an improved understanding of the separate effects of the isomers, and the dose levels at which these appear. As dose levels rise, the probability that drugs will bind to a wider range of receptors also rises. In this context, it is important to note that ketamine induces the NDE at doses much lower than those required for anaesthesia–sometimes stated as being about four times less : 35 mg by intravenous injection is quite sufficient to induce an NDE (Stafford, 1977; Lilly, 1979; Grinspoon and Bakalar, 1981; Sputz, 1989).

White et al. (1980) reported that it was (+)ketamine which has some opioid binding properties and which produced the most anaesthesia, while (-)ketamine produced more "psychic emergence reactions" (the NDE). White et al. (1985) went on to show that (+)ketamine is about four times more potent as a hypnotic and analgesic, and has different effects upon the EEG from (-)ketamine, which may explain some of the confusion concerning whether ketamine is an anticonvulsant or a proconvulsant (Myslobodsky et al.,1981).

Saavedra-Aguilar and Gomez-Jeria (1989) have presented evidence from some animal experiments that beta-endorphin may be epileptogenic to support their argument that beta-endorphins produce the NDE (e.g., McGinty et al., 1986; Henriksen et al., 1978). While beta-endorphin may have had these effects within the rat experimental paradigms used, it is common clinical experience that opioids produce calming, inhibitory effects in humans—not excitation or states resembling epilepsy (Meltzer, 1987). It seems more probable that released peptides would have protective functions rather than contributing further to excito-toxicity. Saavedra-Aguilar and Gomez-Jeria (1989) also cite the finding of Su, London, and Jaffe (1988) that some steroids have affinity for sigma receptors, suggesting that steroids could play a role in the NDE. In fact, the steroid in question was progesterone, which is certainly not a hallucinogen, and Schwartz et al. (1989) have suggested that the affinity is insufficient to result in significant receptor occupancy.

It is possible that the endogenous ligand for the PCP channel is not a peptide but an ion or some other class of compound. Magnesium and zinc are involved in inhibiting the action of the NMDA receptor (Thomson, 1986; Westbrook and Mayer, 1987; Cotman, Monaghan, and Ganong, 1988).

Abnormalities in Blood Gases

1. *Hypoxia*: the proposal that hypoxia might give rise to the NDE (Blacher, 1980) has been criticised by some authors (Sabom, 1982) because studies involving a slow fall in inspired oxygen show mental clouding rather than NDE phenomena (Henderson et al., 1927). However, these studies are not an accurate model of events in, for example, cardiac arrest. Hypoxia causes an excessive release of glutamate with resulting excitotoxicity, which can be prevented by ketamine (see previous references).

2. *Hypercarbia*: a CO_2-enriched breathing mixture can result in typical NDE phenomena such as bodily detachment, being drawn towards a bright light, etc., with diverse personality types producing similar results, suggesting that a shared neurological substrate is at work (Meduna, 1950).

Serotonin

Like endorphins, serotonergic effects may be contributory but do not play a central role in the NDE. Psychedelic drugs such as LSD are serotonergic in action and the psychedelic mental state is very different from the NDE. LSD frequently involves an overwhelming increase in sensory input from the environment (Grinspoon and Bakalar, 1981), in sharp contrast to the cataleptic dissociation produced by ketamine. Psychedelic visual phenomena bear little relationship to the dream-like images of ketamine and the NDE. The 'ego dissolution' experienced on LSD has a different quality from the conviction of having died which may arise with ketamine, and loss of contact with the environment leading rapidly to the 'tunnel experience' is not a typical psychedelic drug effect, although it may occur.

CONCLUSIONS

The NDE is an important phenomenon that can be safely reproduced by ketamine, and the 'glutamate theory of the NDE' can thus be investigated by experiment. Recent advances in neuroscience strongly suggest a common origin for ketamine experiences and the NDE in events occuring at glutamatergic synapses, mediated by the NMDA (PCP) receptor. This theory represents an extension of previous hypotheses, and incorporates most of the neurobiological and psychological theories which have been put forward. It links many of these ideas (hypoxia, peptide release, temporal lobe epilepsy, regression in the service of the ego, reactivation of birth memories, sensory deprivation etc.) rather than being an alternative to them. Most of the planks upon which the hypothesis is built are strongly supported by experimental evidence, published in leading journals, which implicate glutamate and the NMDA receptor as unifying entities in the processes leading to an NDE. The main exception to this is the postulate that anti-excitotoxic agents can flood the brain, which remains to be clearly established.

It is regrettable that 'after-lifers' have seen neuroscientific explanations as dull and reductionist. In truth, the exploration of the mind-brain interface is one of the most exciting adventures which humans have ever undertaken, and the real reductionism lies in attempts to draw a mystical shroud over the NDE.

REFERENCES

American Psychiatric Association. (1980). *Diagnostic and Statistical Manual of Mental Disorders.* Third Edition, APA, Washington, DC.

Amiot, J. F., Boujou, P. and Palacci, J. H. (1985). Effect of naloxone on loss of consciousness induced by iv ketamine (letter). *British Journal of Anaesthetics, 57,* 930.

Anis, N.A., Berry, S. C., Burton, N. R. and Lodge, D. (1983). The dissociative anaesthetics ketamine and phencyclidine, selectively reduce excitation of central mammalian neurons by N methyl-aspartate. *British Journal of Pharmacology, 79,* 565–75.

Barnes, D. M. (1988). NMDA receptors trigger excitement. *Science, 239,* 254–56.

Ben-Ari, Y. E. (1985). Limbic seizure and brain damage produced by kainic acid: mechanisms and relevance to human temporal lobe epilepsy. *Neuroscience, 14,* 375–403.

Bellville, J. and Forrest, W. (1968). Respiratory and subjective effects of d- and l- pentazocine. *Clinical Pharmacology and Therapeutics, 9,* 142–51.

Bennett, D. R., Madsen, J. A. and Jordan, W. S. (1973). Ketamine anesthesia in brain-damaged epileptics. *Neurology (Minneapolis), 23,* 449-50.

Benveniste, H., Drejer, J., Schouseboe, A. and Diemer, H. H. (1984). Elevation of the extracellular concentrations of glutamate and aspartate in rat hippocampus during cerebral ischaemia monitored by microdialysis. *Journal of Neurochemistry, 43,* 1369–74.

Blacher, R. S. (1980). The near-death experience. *Journal of the American Medical Association, 244,* 30.

Carr, D. B. (1981). Endorphins at the approach of death. *Lancet, 1,* 390.

Carr, D. B. (1989). On the evolving neurobiology of the near-death experience. *Journal of Near-Death Studies, 7,* 251–54.

Celesia, G. G. and Chen, R. (1974). Effects of ketamine on EEG activity in cats and monkeys. *Electroencephalography and Clinical Neurophysiology 37,* 345-53.

Choi, D. W. (1988). Glutamate neurotoxicity and diseases of the nervous system. *Neuron, 1,* 623–34.

Cline, H. T., Debski, E. and Constantine-Paton, M. (1987). NMDA receptor antagonist desegregates eye specific stripes. *Proceedings of the National Academy of Sciences, 84,* 4342–45.

Coan, E. J. and Collingridge, G. L. (1987). Effects of phencyclidine, SKF10,047 and related psychotomimetic agents on N-methyl-D-aspartate receptor mediated synaptic responses in rat hippocampal slices. *British Journal of Pharmacology, 91,* 547–56.

Collier, B. B. (1972). Ketamine and the conscious mind. *Anaesthesia, 27,* 120–34.

Collingridge, G. L. (1987). The role of NMDA receptors in learning and memory. *Nature, 330,* 604–05.

Cotman, C. W. and Monaghan, D. T. (1987). Chemistry and anatomy of excitatory amino acid systems. In: Meltzer, H. Y. (1987), pp.197–218.

Cotman, C. W., Monaghan, D. T., Ottersen, O. P. and Storm-Mathisen, J. (1987). Anatomical organisation of excitatory amino acid receptors and their pathways. *Trends in Neurosciences, 10,* 273–79.

Cotman, C. W., Monaghan, D. T. and Ganong, A. H. (1988). Excitatory amino acid neuro-transmission: NMDA receptors and Hebb-type synaptic plasticity. *Annual Review of Neuroscience, 11,* 61–80.

Davies, J. and Watkins, J. C. (1983). Role of excitatory amino acid receptors in mono and poly-synaptic excitation in the cat spinal cord. *Experimental Brain Research, 49,* 280–90.

Domino, E. F., Chodoff, P. and Corssen, G. (1965). Pharmacologic effects of CL-581, a new dissociative anaesthetic, in man. *Clin. Pharmacol. Therapeutics, 6,* 279-91.

Fagg, G. E. and Foster, A. C. (1983). Amino acid neurotransmitters and their pathways in the mammalian central nervous system. *Neuroscience, 9,* 701-71.

Foster, A. and Fagg, G.E.,(1987). Taking apart NMDA receptors. *Nature, 329,* 395.

Gabbard, G. O. and Twemlow, S. T. (1989). Comments on 'A neurobiological model for near-death experiences'. *Journal of Near-Death Studies, 7,* 261–64.

Ghoneim, M. M., Hinrichs, J. V., Mewaldt, S. P. and Peterson, R. C. (1985). Ketamine: behavioral effects of subanaesthetic doses. *Journal of Clinical Psychopharmacology, 5,* 70–77.

Gourie, D. M., Cherian, L. and Shankar, S. K. (1983). Seizures in cats induced by ketamine hydrochloride anaesthesia. *Indian Journal of Medical Research, 77,* 525–28.

Greenamyre, J. T., Young, A. B. and Penney, J. B. (1984). Quantitative autoradiographic distri-bution of l-[3H]glutamate binding sites in rat central nervous system. *Journal of Neuroscience, 4,* 2133–44.

Greyson, B. and Stevenson, I. (1980). The phenomenology of near-death experiences. *American Journal of Psychiatry, 137,* 1193–1200.

Greyson, B. (1983). The psychodynamics of near-death experiences. *Journal of Nervous and Mental Disease, 171,* 376–80.

Grinspoon, L. and Bakalar, S. B. (1981). *Psychedelic Drugs Reconsidered.* New York: Basic Books.

Grof, S. and Halifax, J. (1977). *The Human Encounter with Death.* New York: E. P. Dutton.

Headley, P. M., West, D. C., and Roe, C. (1985). Actions of ketamine and the role of N-methyl aspartate receptors in the spinal cord: studies on nociceptive and other neuronal responses. *Neurological Neurobiology, 14,* 325–35.

Henderson, Y. and Haggard, H. W. (1927). *Noxious gases and the Principles of Respiration Influencing their Action.* American Chemical Society. New York.

Henriksen, S. J., Bloom, F. E., McCoy, F., Ling, N. and Gullemin, R. (1978). B-endorphin induces non-convulsive limbic seizures. *Proceedings of the National Academy of Sciences, 75,* 5221–25.

Holaday, J. W. and Faden, A. L. (1980). Naloxone reversal of endotoxin hypotension suggests role of endorphins in shock. *Nature, 275,* 450–51.

Hoyer, S., and Nitsch, R. (1989). Cerebral excess release of neurotransmitter amino acids sub-sequent to reduced cerebral glucose metabolism in early-onset dementia of Alzheimer type. *Journal of Neural Transmission, 75,* 226–32.

Jansen, K. L. R. (1989a).The near-death experience. *British Journal of Psychiatry, 154,* 882–83.

Jansen, K. L. R. (1989b). Near-death experience and the NMDA receptor. *British Medical Journal, 298,* 1708–9.

Jansen, K. L. R., Faull, R. L. M., and Dragunow, M. (1989c). Excitatory amino acid receptors in the human cerebral cortex: a quantitative autoradiographic study comparing the distribu-tion of [3H]TCP, [3H]glycine, l-[3H]glutamate, [3H]AMPA and [3H]kainic acid binding sites. *Neuroscience, 32,* 587–607.

Jansen, K. L. R., Faull, R. L. M. and Dragunow, M. and Synek, B. (1990a). Alzheimer's disease: changes in hippocampal N-methyl-D-aspartate, quisqualate, neurotensin, adenosine, benzodiazepine, serotonin and opioid receptors–an autoradiographic study. *Neuroscience, 39,* 613–17.

Jansen, K. L. R. (1990b). Neuroscience and the near-death experience: roles for the NMDA-PCP receptor, the sigma receptor and the endopsychosins. *Medical Hypotheses, 31,* 25–29.

Jansen, K. L. R. (1990c). Ketamine: can chronic use impair memory? *International Journal of Addictions, 25,* 133–39.

Jansen, K. L. R. and Faull, R. L. M. (1991a). Excitatory amino acids, NMDA and sigma receptors: a role in schizophrenia? *Behavioral and Brain Sciences, 14,* 34–35.

Jansen, K. L. R., Faull, R. L. M., Dragunow, M. and Leslie, R. (1991b). Autoradiographic distribution of sigma receptors in human neocortex, hippocampus, basal ganglia, cerebellum, pineal and pituitary glands. *Brain Research, 559,* 172–77.

Jansen, K. L. R. (1991c). Transcendental explanations and the near-death experience. *Lancet, 337,* 207–43.

Jansen, K. L. R (1993). Non-medical use of ketamine. *British Medical Journal, 298,* 4708–9.

King, G. L., and Dingledine, R. (1986). Evidence for the activation of the N-methyl-D-aspartate receptor during epileptic discharge. In: *Excitatory Amino Acids and Epilepsy* (eds. R. Schwarz, Y. Ben-Ari) 520–70, New York: Plenum.

Kisvardy, Z. F., Cowey, A., Smith, A. D. and Somogyi, P. (1989). Interlaminar and lateral excitatory amino acid connections in the striate cortex of monkey. *Journal of Neuroscience, 9,* 667–82.

Krystal, J. H., Karoer, L. P., Seibyl, J. P., Freeman, G. K., Delaney, R., Bremner,. J. D., Heniger, G. R., Bowers, M. B. and Charney, D. S. (1994) Subanesthetic effects of the noncompetitive antagonist, ketamine, in humans. *Archives of General Psychiatry, 51,* 199–214.

Leceese, A. P., Marquis, K. L., Mattia, A. and Moreton, J. E. (1986). The anticonvulsant and behavioral effects of phencyclidine and ketamine following chronic treatment in rats. *Behavioral Brain Research, 22,* 257–33.

Lilly, J. C. (1961). Experiments in solitude, in maximum achievable physical isolation with water suspension, of intact healthy persons. In: *Physiological Aspects of Space Flight.* 238–47. New York: Columbia University Press.

Lilly, J. C. (1978). *The Scientist: A Novel Autobiography.* New York: Bantam Books/J. B. Lippincott.

Lobner, D. and Lipton, P. (1990). Sigma ligands and non-competitive NMDA antagonists inhibit glutamate release during cerebral ischaemia. *Neuroscience Letters, 117,* 169–74.

MacDonald, J. F., Miljkovic, Z. and Pennefather, P. (1987). Use dependant block of excitatory amino-acid currents in cultured neurons by ketamine. *Journal of Neurophysiology, 58,* 251–65.

Mares, P., Lansitiakova, M., Vankova, S., Kubova, H. and Velisek, L. (1992). Ketamine blocks cortical epileptic afterdischarges but not paired-pulse and frequency potentiation. *Neuroscience, 50,* 339-44.

Mayer, M. L. , Westbrook, G. L. and Guthrie, P. B. (1984). Voltage-dependent block by $Mg2+$ of NMDA receptors in spinal cord neurons. *Nature, 309,* 261–63.

McCarthy, D. A., Chen, G., Kaump, D. H. and Ensor, C. J. (1965). General anaesthetic and other pharmacological propperties of CL-581. *Journal of New Drugs, 5,* 21–33.

McGinty, J. F., Kanamatsu, T., Obie, J. and Hong, J. S. (1986). Modulation of opioid peptide metabolism by seizures: differentiation of opioid subclasses. *NIDA Research Monographs, 71,* 89–101.

McNaughton, B. C. and Morris, R. G. M. (1987). Hippocampal synaptic enhancement and information storage within a distributed system. *Trends in Neurosciences, 10,* 408–15.

Meduna, L. J. (1950). The effect of carbon dioxide upon the functions of the brain. In: *Carbon*

Dioxide Therapy (L. J. Meduna, ed.), Charles Thomas, Ill., 23–40.

Meldrum, B. S. (1987). Protection against hypoxic/ischaemic brain damage with excitatory amino acid antagonists. *Medical Biology, 65,* 153–57.

Meltzer, H. Y. (ed). (1987). *Psychopharmacology: The Third Generation of Progress.* New York: Raven Press.

Mody, I. and Heinemann, U. (1987). NMDA receptors of dentate gyrus cells participate in synpatic transmission following kindling. *Nature, 326,* 701–3.

Monoghan, D. T., Bridges, R. J. and Cotman, C. W. (1989). The excitatory amino acid receptors. Their classes, pharmacology and distinct properties in the function of the nervous system. *Annual Review of Pharmacology and Toxicology, 29,* 365–402.

Morris, R. G. M., Anderson, E., Lynch, G. S. and Baudry, M. (1986). Selective impairment of learning and blockade of EPT by NMDA antagonist AP5. *Nature, 319,* 744–76.

Morse, M., Conner, D. and Tyler, D. (1985). Near death experiences in a paediatric population. *American Journal of Diseases of Children, 139,* 595–63.

Morse, M. L. (1989). Comments on 'A neurobiological model for near-death experiences'. *Journal of Near-Death Studies, 7,* 223–28.

Mussacchio, J. M., Klein, M. and Canoll, P. D. (1990). Dextrometorphan sites, sigma receptors and the psychotomimetic effects of sigma opiates. Progress in *Clinical Biological Research, 328,* 13–16.

Myslobodsky, M. S., Golovchinsky, V. and Mintz, M. (1981). Ketamine: convulsant or anti-convulsant? *Pharmacology, Biochemistry and Behavior, 14,* 27–33.

Nowak, L., Bergestovski, P., Ascher, P., Herbet, A. and Prochiantz, A. (1984). Magnesium gates glutamate-activated channels in mouse central neurons. *Nature, 307,* 462–65.

Noyes, R. and Kletti, R. (1976a). Depersonalisation in the face of life threatening danger: a description. *Psychiatry, 39,* 19–30.

Noyes, R. and Kletti, R. (1976b). Depersonalisation in the face of life threatening danger: an interpretation. *Omega, 7,* 103–8.

Olney, J. W., Collins, R. C. and Sloviter, R. S. (1986). Excitotoxic mechanisms of epileptic brain damage. *Advances in Neurology, 44,* 857–77.

Osis, K. and Haraldsson, E. (1977). *At the Hour of Death.* New York: Avon.

Oyama, T.Y., Jin, T., Yamaga, R., Ling, N. and Guillemin, R. (1980). Profound analgesic effects of beta-endorphin in man. *Lancet, 1,* 122–24.

Oye, N., Paulsen, O. and Maurset, A. (1992). Effects of ketamine on sensory perception: evidence for a role of N-methyl-D-aspartate receptors. *Journal of Pharmacology and Experimental Therapeutics, 260,* 1209–13.

Parsons, C. G., Gibbens, H., Magnago, T. S. I and Headley, P. M. (1988). At which sigma site are the spinal actions of ketamine mediated ? *Neuroscience Letters, 85,* 322–28.

Persinger, M. A. and Makarec, K. (1987). Temporal lobe epileptic signs and correlative behaviors displayed by normal populations. *Journal of General Psychology, 114,* 179–95.

Pichlmayr, L., Lips, U. and Kunkel, H. (1984). *The Electro-encephalogram in Anaesthesia.* Berlin: Springer-Verlag, 102–5.

Peters, S., Koh, J. and Choi, D. W. (1987). Zinc selectively blocks the action of N-methyl-D-aspartate on cortical neurons. *Science, 236,* 589–92.

Pfieffer, A., Brantl, V., Herz, A. and Emrich, H. M. (1986). Psychotomimeis mediated by k opiate receptors. *Science (Washington, DC), 233,* 774–76.

Quirion, R., Chicheportiche, R., Contreras, P. C., Johnston, K. M., Lodge, D., Tam, S. W., Woods, J.H. and Zukin, S. R. (1987). Classification and nomenclature of phencyclidine and sigma receptor sites. *Trends in Neurosciences, 10,* 444–46.

Quirion, R., Dimaggio, D. A., French, E. D., Contreras, P. C., Shiloach, J., Pert, C. B., Evert, H.,

Pert, A. and O'Donohue (1984). Evidence for an endogenous peptide ligand for the phencyclidine receptor. *Peptides, 5,* 967–77.

Rauschecker, J. P. and Hahn, D. (1987). Ketamine-zylazine anaesthesia blocks consolidation of ocular dominance changes in kitten visual cortex. *Nature, 326,* 183–85.

Reich, D. L. and Silvay, G. S. (1989). Ketamine: an update on the first twenty-five years of clinical experience. *Canadian Journal of Anaesthetics, 36,* 186–97.

Ring, K. (1980). *Life at Death: A Scientific Investigation of the Near-Death Experience.* New York: Coward, McCann, Goeghegan.

Rothman, S. M. (1984). Synaptic release of excitatory amino acid neurotransmitter mediates anoxic neuronal death. *Journal of Neuroscience, 4,* 1884–91.

Rothman, S. M. and Olney, J. W. (1986). Glutamate and the pathophysiology of hypoxic/ischaemic brain damage. *Annals of Neurology, 19,* 105–19.

Rothman, S. M. and Olney, J. W. (1987). Excitotoxicity and the NMDA receptor. *Trends in Neurosciences, 10,* 299–302.

Rothman, S. M., Thurston, J. H., Hauhart, R. E., Clark, G. P. and Solomon., J. S. (1987). Ketamine protects hippocampal neurons from anoxia in vitro. *Neuroscience, 21,* 673–83.

Rumpf, K., Pedick, J., Teuteberg, H., Munchhoff, W. and Nolte, H. (1969). Dream-like experiences during brief anaesthesia with ketamine, thiopental and propiadid. In: *Ketamine* (ed. H. Dreuscher) 161–80, Berlin: Springer-Verlag.

Sabom, M. B. (1982). *Recollections of Death: A Medical Investigation.* New York: Harper and Row.

Saavedra-Aguilar, J. C. and Gomez-Jeria, J. S. (1989). A neurobiological model of near-death experiences. *Journal of Near-Death Studies, 7,* 205–22.

Schoenberg, J. and Sjolund, B. H. (1986). First order nociceptive synapses in rat dorsal horn are blocked by an amino acid antagonist. *Brain Research, 379,* 394–98.

Schwartz, M. S., Virden, S. and Scott, D. F. (1974). Effects of ketamine on the electroencephalograph. *Anaesthesia, 29,* 135–40.

Schwarz, S., Pohl, P. and Zhou, G.-Z. (1989). Steroid binding at sigma 'opioid' receptors. *Science (Washington, DC), 246,* 1635–37.

Siegel, R. K. (1978). Phencyclidine and ketamine intoxication: a study of recreational users. In: *Phencyclidine Abuse: An Appraisal.* (ed. R. C. Peterson and R. C. Stillman). 119–40, National Institute on Drug Abuse Research Monograph 21. NIDA, Rockville, Maryland.

Siegel, R. K. (1980). The Psychology of life after death. *American Psychologist, 35,* 911–50.

Siegel, R. K. (1981). Accounting for after-life experiences. *Psychology Today, 15,* 67.

Simon, R. P., Swan, S. H. , Griffiths, T. and Meldrum, B. S. (1984). Blockade of NMDA receptors may protect against ischaemic damage in the brain. *Science, 226,* 850–52.

Sloviter, R. S. (1983). "Epileptic" brain damage in rats induced by sustained electrical stimulation of t perforant path. *Brain Research Bulletin, 10,* 675–97.

Squire, L. R. and Zola-Morgan, S. (1988). Memory: brain systems and behavior. *Trends in Neurosciences, 11,* 170–75.

Stafford, P. (1977). *Psychedelics Encyclopaedia.* Berkely, CA: And/Or Press.

Sputz, R. (1989). I never met a reality I didn't like: A report on 'Vitamin K.' *High Times,* October 1989, 64–82.

Su, T. P., London, E. D. and Jaffe, J. H. (1988). Steroid binding at sigma receptors suggests a link between endocrine, nervous and immune systems. *Science, 240,* 219–23.

Taberner, P. V. (1976). The anticonvulsant activity of ketamine against seizures induced by pentylenetetrazol and mercaptopropionic acid. *European Journal of Pharmacology, 39,* 305–11.

Thomson, A. M., West, D. C. and Lodge, D. (1985). An N-methylaspartate receptor-mediated synapse in rat cerebral cortex: a site of action of ketamine? *Nature, 313,* 479–81.

Thomsom A. N. (1986). A magnesium-sensitive post-synaptic potential in rat cerebral cortex resembles neuronal responses to N-methyl-D-aspartate. *Journal of Physiology (London), 370,* 531–49.

Vaupel, D. B. (1983). Naltrexone fails to antagonise the effects of PCP and SKF 10,047 on the dog. *European Journal of Pharmacology, 92,* 269–74.

Walker, J. M., Bowen, W. D., Walker, F. O., Matsumoto, R. R., DeCosta, B. and Rice, K. D. (1990). Sigma receptros: biology and Function. *Pharmacology Reviews, 42,* 355–402.

Westbrook., G. L., Mayer, M. K. (1987). Micromolecular concentrations of Zn^{2+} antagonise NMDA and GABA responses of hippocampal neurons. *Nature, 328,* 640–43.

Westerberg, E., Monaghan, D. T., Cotman, C. W. and Weilock, T. (1987). Excitatory amino acid receptors and ischaemic brain damage in the rat. *Neuroscience Letters, 73,* 119–24.

White, P. F., Ham, J., Way, W. L. and Trever, A. J. (1982). Pharmacology of ketamine isomers in surgical patients. *Anaesthesiology, 52,* 231–39.

White, P. F., Way, W. L. and Treveor, A. J. (1982). Ketamine: its pharmacology and therapeutic uses. *Anaesthesiology, 56,* 119–36.

White, W. F., Nadler, J. V., Hamburger, A., Cotman, C. W., Cummins, J. T. (1977). Glutamte as a transmitter of the hippocampal perforant path. *Nature, 270,* 356–57.

·⌣ **18** ⌣·

Near-Death Experiences
In or Out of the Body?

Susan Blackmore

When you are almost asleep, very frightened, or nearly dying, the model from the senses will be confused and unstable.... Fantasies and imagery might become more stable than the sensory model, and so seem real.

Susan Blackmore, Ph.D., is a psychologist who interprets the NDE through a skeptical empiricism blended with with spiritual insights from Buddhism. She has brought together several stimulating theories into an original biological theory. She expands the view that NDEs are hallucinations with a new physiological explanation for the peculiar tunnel imagery, based on the structure of the brain's visual system. Out-of-body experiences are memory models, she proposes, which often come to us in bird's eye view, experienced as real. The brain's natural endorphins, she hypothesizes, account for the pleasant, blissful, emotional tone of NDEs.

From Blackmore's positivist perspective, other-world visions are pure imagination. From her cognitive psychology perspective, the world and the self are both the constructions of an information-processing system. From her Buddhist perspective, both self and world are impermanent illusions. NDE survivors return with a better understanding of these truths, she believes, and so they are less attached to this world and to themselves. Blackmore's theories offer several important ways to explain NDEs with concrete, testable hypotheses, as well as challenging philosophical and spiritual proposals.

Susan Blackmore, Ph.D., teaches Psychology at the University of the West of England, in Bristol. She has published numerous articles and three books, including *Beyond the Body: An Investigation of Out-of-the-Body Experiences* (1982) and *The Adventures of a Parapsychologist.* (1986). This article is a condensed version of her book *Dying to Live: Science and the Near-Death Experience* (1993).

·⌣ Near-Death Experiences ⌣·
In or Out of the Body?

What is it like to die? Although most of us fear death to a greater or lesser extent, there are now more and more people who have "come back" from states close to death and have told stories of usually very pleasant and even joyful experiences at death's door.

For many experiencers, their adventures seem unquestionably to provide evidence for life after death, and the profound effects the experience can have on them is just added confirmation. By contrast, for many scientists these experiences are just hallucinations produced by the dying brain and of no more interest than an especially vivid dream.

So which is right? Are near-death experiences (NDEs) the prelude to our life after death or the very last experience we have before oblivion? I shall argue that neither is quite right: NDEs provide no evidence for life after death, and we can best understand them by looking at neurochemistry, physiology, and psychology, but they are much more interesting than any dream. They seem completely real and can transform people's lives. Any satisfactory theory has to understand that too—and that leads us to questions about minds, selves, and the nature of consciousness.

DEATHBED EXPERIENCES
Toward the end of the last century the physical sciences and the new theory of evolution were making great progress. But many people felt that science was forcing out the traditional ideas of the spirit and soul. Spiritualism began to flourish, and people flocked to mediums to get in contact with their dead friends and relatives "on the other side." Spiritualists claimed, and indeed still claim, to have found proof of survival.

In 1882, the Society for Psychical Research was founded, and serious research on the phenomena began; but convincing evidence for survival is still lacking over one hundred years later (Blackmore, 1988). In 1926, a psychical researcher and Fellow of the Royal Society, Sir William Barrett (1926), published a little book on deathbed visions. The dying apparently saw other worlds before they died and even saw and spoke to the dead. There were cases of music heard at the time of death and reports of attendants actually seeing the spirit leave the body.

With modern medical techniques, deathbed visions like these have become far less common. In those days people died at home with little or no medication and surrounded by their family and friends. Today most people die in the hospital and all too often alone. Paradoxically it is also improved medicine that has led to an increase in quite a different kind of report—that of the near-death experience.

CLOSE BRUSHES WITH DEATH

Resuscitation from ever more serious heart failure has provided accounts of extraordinary experiences (although this is not the only cause of NDEs). These remained largely ignored until about fifteen years ago, when Raymond Moody (1975), an American physician, published his best-selling *Life After Life*. He had talked with many people who had "come back from death," and he put together an account of a typical NDE. In his idealized experience a person hears himself pronounced dead. Then comes a loud buzzing or ringing noise and a long, dark tunnel. He can see his own body from a distance and watch what is happening. Soon he meets others and a "being of light" who shows him a playback of events from his life and helps him to evaluate it. At some point he gets to a barrier and knows that he has to go back. Even though he feels joy, love, and peace there, he returns to his body and life. Later he tries to tell others; but they don't understand, and he soon gives up. Nevertheless the experience deeply affects him, especially his views about life and death.

Many scientists reacted with disbelief. They assumed Moody was at least exaggerating, but he claimed that no one had noticed the experiences before because the patients were too frightened to talk about them. The matter was soon settled by further research. One cardiologist had talked to more than 2,000 people over a period of nearly twenty years and claimed that more than half reported Moody-type experiences (Schoonmaker, 1979). In 1982, a Gallup poll found that about one in seven adult Americans had been close to death and about one in twenty had had an NDE. It appeared that Moody, at least in outline, was right. In my own research I have come across numerous reports like this one, sent to me by a woman from Cyprus:

> An emergency gastrectomy was performed. On the fourth day following
> that operation I went into shock and became unconscious for several

hours.... Although thought to be unconscious, I remembered, for years afterwards, the entire, detailed conversation that passed between the surgeon and anaesthetist present.... I was lying above my own body, totally free of pain, and looking down at my own self with compassion for the agony I could see on the face; I was floating peacefully. Then...I was going elsewhere, floating towards a dark but not frightening, curtain-like area.... Then I felt total peace.... Suddenly it all changed—I was slammed back into my body again, very much aware of the agony again.

Within a few years some of the basic questions were being answered. Kenneth Ring (1980), at the University of Connecticut, surveyed 102 people who had come close to death and found almost fifty percent had had what he called a "core experience." He broke this into five stages: peace, body separation, entering the darkness (which is like the tunnel), seeing the light, and entering the light. He found that the later stages were reached by fewer people, which seems to imply that there is an ordered set of experiences waiting to unfold.

One interesting question is whether NDEs are culture specific. What little research there is suggests that in other cultures NDEs have basically the same structure, although religious background seems to influence the way it is interpreted. A few NDEs have even been recorded in children. It is interesting to note that nowadays children are more likely to see living friends than those who have died, presumably because their playmates only rarely die of diseases like scarlet fever or smallpox (Morse et al., 1986).

Perhaps more important is whether you have to be nearly dead to have an NDE. The answer is clearly no (e.g., Morse et al., 1989). Many very similar experiences are recorded of people who have taken certain drugs, were extremely tired, or, occasionally, were just carrying on their ordinary activities.

I must emphasize that these experiences seem completely real—even more real (whatever that may mean) than everyday life. The tunnel experience is not like just imagining going along a tunnel. The view from out of the body seems completely realistic, not like a dream, but as though you really are up there and looking down. Few people experience such profound emotions and insight again during their lifetimes. They do not say, "I've been hallucinating," "I imagined I went to heaven," or "Can I tell you about my lovely dream?" They are more likely to say, "I have been out of my body" or "I saw Grandma in heaven."

Since not everyone who comes close to death has an NDE, it is interesting to ask what sort of people are more likely to have them. Certainly you don't need to be mentally unstable. NDEers do not differ from others in terms of their psychological health or background. Moreover, the NDE does seem to produce profound and positive personality changes (Ring, 1984). After this extraordinary experience people claim that they are no longer so motivated by greed and material achievement but are more concerned about other people and their needs. Any theory of the NDE needs to account for this effect.

EXPLANATIONS OF THE NDE

Astral Projection and the Next World

Could we have another body that is the vehicle of consciousness and leaves the physical body at death to go on to another world? This, essentially, is the doctrine of astral projection. In various forms it is very popular and appears in a great deal of New Age and occult literature.

One reason may be that out-of-body experiences (OBEs) are quite common, quite apart from their role in NDEs. Surveys have shown that anywhere from eight percent (in Iceland) to as much as fifty percent (in special groups, such as marijuana users) had OBEs at some time during their lives. In my own survey of residents of Bristol I found twelve percent. Typically these people had been resting or lying down and suddenly felt they had left their bodies, usually for no more than a minute or two (Blackmore, 1984).

A survey of more than fifty different cultures showed that almost all of them believe in a spirit or soul that could leave the body (Sheils, 1978). So both the OBE and the belief in body are common, but what does this mean? Is it just that we cannot bring ourselves to believe that we are nothing more than a mortal body and that death is the end? Or is there really another body?

You might think that such a theory has no place in science and ought to be ignored. I disagree. The only ideas that science can do nothing with are the purely metaphysical ones—ideas that have no measurable consequences and no testable predictions. But if a theory makes predictions, however bizarre, then it can be tested.

The theory of astral projection is, at least in some forms, testable. In the earliest experiments mediums claimed they were able to project their astral bodies to distant rooms and see what was happening. They claimed not to taste bitter aloes on their real tongues, but immediately screwed up their faces in disgust when the substance was placed on their (invisible) astral tongues. Unfortunately these experiments were not properly controlled (Blackmore, 1982).

In other experiments, dying people were weighed to try to detect the astral body as it left. Early this century a weight of about one ounce was claimed, but as the apparatus became more sensitive the weight dropped, implying that it was not a real effect. More recent experiments have used sophisticated detectors of ultraviolet and infrared, magnetic flux or field strength, temperature, or weight to try to capture the astral body of someone having an out-of-body experience. They have even used animals and human "detectors," but no one has yet succeeded in detecting anything reliably (Morris et al., 1978).

If something really leaves the body in OBEs, then you might expect it to be able to see at a distance, in other words to have extrasensory perception (ESP). There have been several experiments with concealed targets. One success was Tart's subject, who lay on a bed with a five-digit number on a shelf above it (Tart, 1968). During the night she had an OBE and correctly reported the number, but critics argued that she could have climbed out of the bed to look. Apart from this one, the experiments tend, like so many in parapsychology, to provide equivocal results and no clear signs of any ESP.

So, this theory has been tested but seems to have failed its tests. If there really were astral bodies, I would have expected us to have found something out about them by now—other than how hard it is to track them down!

In addition there are major theoretical objections to the idea of astral bodies. If you imagine that the person has gone to another world, perhaps along some "real" tunnel, then you have to ask what relationship there is between this world and the other one. If the other world is an extension of the physical, then it ought to be observable and measurable. The astral body, astral world, and tunnel ought to be detectable in some way, and we ought to be able to say where exactly the tunnel is going. The fact that we can't leads many people to say the astral world is "on another plane," at a "higher level of vibration," and the like. But unless you can specify just what these mean, the ideas are completely empty, even though they may sound appealing. Of course we can never prove that astral bodies don't exist, but my guess is that they probably don't and that this theory is not a useful way to understand OBEs.

Birth and the NDE

Another popular theory makes dying analogous with being born: that the out-of-body experience is literally just that—reliving the moment when you emerged from your mother's body. The tunnel is the birth canal and the white light is the light of the world into which you were born. Even the being of light can be "explained" as an attendant at the birth.

This theory was proposed by Stanislav Grof and Joan Halifax (1977) and popularized by the astronomer Carl Sagan (1979), but it is pitifully inadequate to explain the NDE. For a start the newborn infant would not see anything like a tunnel as it was being born. The birth canal is stretched and compressed and the baby usually forced through it with the top of its head, not with its eyes (which are closed anyway) pointing forward. Also it does not have the mental skills to recognize the people around, and these capacities change so much during growing up that adults cannot reconstruct what it was like to be an infant.

"Hypnotic regression to past lives" is another popular claim. In fact much research shows that people who have been hypnotically regressed give the appearance of acting like a baby or a child, but it is no more than acting. For example, they don't make drawings like a real five-year-old would do, but like an adult imagines children do. Their vocabulary is too large and in general they overestimate the abilities of children at any given age. There is no evidence (even if the idea made sense) of their "really" going back in time.

Of course the most important question is whether this theory could be tested, and to some extent it can. For example, it predicts that people born by Caesarean section should not have the same tunnel experiences and OBEs. I conducted a survey of people born normally and those born by Caesarean (190 and 36 people, respectively). Almost exactly equal percentages of both groups had had tunnel experiences (36 percent) and OBEs (29 percent). I have not compared the type of birth of people coming close to death, but this would provide further evidence (Blackmore, 1982b).

In response to these findings some people have argued that it is not one's own birth that is relived, but the idea of birth in general. However, this just reduces the theory to complete vacuousness.

Just Hallucinations

Perhaps we should give up and conclude that all the experiences are "just imagination" or "nothing but hallucinations." However, this is the weakest theory of all. The experiences must, in some sense, be hallucinations, but this is not, on its own, any explanation. We have to ask why are they these kinds of hallucinations? Why tunnels?

Some say the tunnel is a symbolic representation of the gateway to another world. But then why always a tunnel and not, say, a gate, doorway, or even the great River Styx? Why the light at the end of the tunnel? And why always above the body, not below it? I have no objection to the theory that the experiences are hallucinations. I only object to the idea you can explain them by saying, "They are just hallucinations." This explains nothing. A viable theory would answer these questions without dismissing the experiences. That, even if only in tentative form, is what I shall try to provide.

The Physiology of the Tunnel

Tunnels do not only occur near death. They are also experienced in epilepsy and migraine, when falling asleep, meditating, or just relaxing, with pressure on both eyeballs, and with certain drugs, such as LSD, psilocybin, and mescaline. I have experienced them many times myself. It is as though the whole world becomes a rushing, roaring tunnel and you are flying along it toward a bright light at the end. No doubt many readers have also been there, for surveys show that about a third of people have—like this terrified man of 28 who had just had the anesthetic for circumcision:

> I seemed to be hauled at "lightning speed" in a direct line tunnel into outer space; (not a floating sensation . . .) but like a rocket at a terrific speed. I appeared to have left my body.

In the 1930s, Heinrich Kluver, the University of Chicago, noted four form constants in hallucinations: the tunnel, the spiral, the lattice or grating, and the cobweb. Their origin probably lies in the structure of the visual cortex, the part of the brain that processes visual information. Imagine that the outside world is mapped onto the back of the eye (on the retina), and then again in the cortex. The mathematics of this mapping (at least to a reasonable approximation) is well known.

Jack Cowan, a neurobiologist at the University of Chicago, has used the mapping to account for the tunnel (Cowan, 1982). Brain activity is normally kept stable by some cells inhibiting others. Disinhibition (the reduction of this inhibitory activity) produces too much activity in the brain. This can occur near death (because of lack of oxygen) or with drugs like LSD, which interfere with inhibition. Cowan uses an analogy with fluid mechanics to argue that disinhibition will induce stripes of activity that move across the cortex. Using the mapping it can easily be shown that stripes in the cortex would appear like concentric rings or spirals in the visual world. In other words, if you have stripes in the cortex you will seem to see a tunnel-like pattern of spirals or rings.

This theory is important in showing how the structure of the brain could produce the same hallucination for everyone. However, I was dubious about the idea of these moving stripes, and also Cowan's theory doesn't readily explain the bright light at the center. So Tom Troscianko and I, at the University of Bristol, tried to develop a simpler theory (Blackmore and Troscianko, 1989). The most obvious thing about the representation in the cortex is that there are lots of cells representing the center of the visual field but very few for the edges. This means that you can see small things very clearly in the center, but if they are out at the edges you cannot. We took just this simple fact as a starting point and used a computer to simulate what would happen when you have gradually increasing electrical noise in the visual cortex.

The computer program starts with thinly spread dots of light, mapped in the same way as the cortex, with more toward the middle and very few at the edges. Gradually the number of dots increases, mimicking the increasing noise. Now the center begins to look like a white blob and the outer edges gradually get more and more dots. And so it expands until eventually the whole screen is filled with light. The appearance is just like a dark speckly tunnel with a white light at the end, and the light grows bigger and bigger (or nearer and nearer) until it fills the whole screen.

If it seems odd that such a simple picture can give the impression that you are moving, consider two points. First, it is known that random movements in the periphery of the visual field are more likely to be interpreted by the brain as outward than inward movements (Georgeson and Harris, 1978). Second, the brain infers our own movement to a great extent from what we see. Therefore, presented with an apparently growing patch of flickering white light your brain will easily interpret it as yourself moving forward into a tunnel.

The theory also makes a prediction about NDEs in the blind. If they are blind because of problems in the eye but have a normal cortex, then they too should see tunnels. But if their blindness stems from a faulty or damaged cortex, they should not. These predictions have yet to be tested.

According to this kind of theory there is, of course, no real tunnel. Nevertheless there is a real physical cause of the tunnel experience. It is noise in the visual cortex. This way we can explain the origin of the tunnel without just dismissing the experiences and without needing to invent other bodies or other worlds.

Out-of-Body Experiences

Like tunnels, OBEs are not confined to near death. They too can occur when just relaxing and falling asleep, with meditation, and in epilepsy and migraine. They can also, at least by a few people, be induced at will. I have been interested in OBEs since I had a long and dramatic experience myself (Blackmore, 1982a).

It is important to remember that these experiences seem quite real. People don't describe them as dreams or fantasies, but as events that actually happened. This is, I presume, why they seek explanations in terms of other bodies or other worlds.

However, we have seen how poorly the astral projection and birth theories cope with OBEs. What we need is a theory that involves no unmeasurable entities or untestable other worlds but explains why the experiences happen and why they seem so real.

I would start by asking why anything seems real. You might think this is obvious—after all, the things we see out there are real aren't they? Well no, in a sense they aren't. As perceiving creatures all we know is what our senses tell us. And our senses tell us what is "out there" by constructing models of the world with ourselves in it. The whole of the world "out there" and our own bodies are really constructions of our minds. Yet we are sure, all the time, that this construction—if you like, this "model of reality"—is "real" while the other fleeting thoughts we have are unreal. We call the rest of them daydreams, imagination, fantasies, and so on. Our brains have no trouble distinguishing "reality" from "imagination." But this distinction is not given. It is one the brain has to make for itself by deciding which of its own models represents the world "out there." I suggest it does this by comparing all the models it has at any time and choosing the stable one as "reality."

This will normally work very well. The model created by the senses is the best and most stable the system has. It is obviously "reality," while that image I have of the bar I'm going to go to later is unstable and brief. The choice is easy. By comparison, when you are almost asleep, very frightened, or nearly dying, the model from the senses will be confused and unstable. If you are under terrible stress or suffering oxygen deprivation, then the choice won't be so easy. All the models will be unstable.

So what will happen now? Possibly the tunnel being created by noise in the visual cortex will be the most stable model and so, according to my supposition, this will seem real. Fantasies and imagery might become more stable than the sensory model, and so seem real. The system will have lost input control.

What then should a sensible biological system do to get back to normal? I would suggest that it could try to ask itself—as it were— "Where am I? What is happening?" Even a person under severe stress will have some memory left. They might recall the accident, or know that they were in hospital for an operation, or remember the pain of the heart attack. So they will try to reconstruct, from what little they can remember, what is happening.

Now we know something very interesting about memory models. Often they are constructed in a bird's-eye view. That is, the events or scenes are seen as though from above. If you find this strange, try to remember the last time you went to a pub or the last time you walked along the seashore. Where are "you" looking from in this recalled scene? If you are looking from above you will see what I mean.

So my explanation of the OBE becomes clear. A memory model in bird's-eye view has taken over from the sensory model. It seems perfectly real because it is the best model the system has got at the time. Indeed, it seems real for just the same reason anything ever seems real.

This theory of the OBE leads to many testable predictions, for example, that people who habitually use bird's-eye views should be more likely to have OBEs. Both Harvey Irwin (1986), an Australian psychologist, and myself (Blackmore, 1987) have found that people who dream as though they were spectators have more OBEs, although there seems to be no difference for the waking use of different viewpoints. I have also found that people who can more easily switch viewpoints in their imagination are also more likely to report OBEs.

Of course this theory says that the OBE world is only a memory model. It should only match the real world when the person has already known about something or can deduce it from available information. This presents a big challenge for research on near death. Some researchers claim that people near death can actually see things that they couldn't possibly have known about. For example, the American cardiologist Michael Sabom (1982) claims that patients reported the exact behavior of needles on monitoring apparatus when they had their eyes closed and appeared to be unconscious. Further, he compared these descriptions with those of people *imagining* they were being resuscitated and found that the real patients gave far more accurate and detailed descriptions.

There are problems with this comparison. Most important, the people really being resuscitated could probably feel some of the manipulations being done on them and hear what was going on. Hearing is the last sense to be lost and, as you will realize if you ever listen to radio plays or news, you can imagine a very clear visual image when you can only hear something. So the dying person could build up a fairly accurate picture this way. Of course hearing doesn't allow you to see the behavior of needles, and so if Sabom is right, I am wrong. We can only await further research to find out.

The Life Review

The experience of seeing excerpts from your life flash before you is not really as mysterious as it first seems. It has long been known that stimulation of cells in the temporal lobe of the brain can produce instant experiences that seem like the reliving of memories. Also, temporal lobe epilepsy can produce similar experiences, and such seizures can involve other limbic structures in the brain, such as the amygdala and hippocampus, which are also associated with memory.

Imagine that the noise in the dying brain stimulates cells like this. The memories will be aroused and, according to my hypothesis, if they are the most stable model the system has at that time they will seem real. For the dying person they may well be more stable than the confused and noisy sensory model.

The link between temporal-lobe epilepsy and the NDE has formed the basis of a thorough neurobiological model of the NDE (Saavedra-Aguilar and Gomez-Jeria, 1989). They suggest that the brain stress consequent on the near-death episode leads to the release of neuropeptides and neuro-transmitters (in particular the endogenous endorphins). These then stimulate the limbic system and other connected areas. In addition, the effect of the endorphins could account for the blissful and other positive emotional states so often associated with the NDE.

Morse provided evidence that some children deprived of oxygen and treated with opiates did not have NDE-like hallucinations, and he and his colleagues (Morse et al., 1986) have developed a theory based on the role of the neurotransmitter serotonin, rather than the endorphins. Research on the neurochemistry of the NDE is just beginning and should provide us with much more detailed understanding of the life review.

Of course there is more to the life review than just memories. The person feels as though she or he is judging these life events, being shown their significance and meaning. But this too, I suggest, is not so very strange. When the normal world of the senses is gone and memories seem real, our perspective on our life changes. We can no longer be so attached to our plans, hopes, ambitions, and fears, which fade away and become unimportant, while the past comes to life again. We can only accept it as it is, and there is no one to judge it but ourselves. This is, I think, why so many NDEers say they faced their past life with acceptance and equanimity.

Other Worlds

Now we come to what might seem the most extraordinary parts of the NDE; the worlds beyond the tunnel and OBE. But I think you can now see that they are not so extraordinary at all. In this state the outside world is no longer real, and inner worlds are. Whatever we can imagine clearly enough will seem real. And what will we imagine when we know we are dying? I am sure for many people it is the world they expect or hope to see. Their minds may turn to people they have known who have died before them or to the world they hope to enter next. Like the other images we have been considering, these will seem perfectly real.

Finally, there are those aspects of the NDE that are ineffable—they cannot be put into words. I suspect that this is because some people take yet another step, a step into nonbeing. I shall try to explain this by asking another question. What is consciousness? If you say it is a thing, another body, a substance, you will only get into the kinds of difficulty we got into with OBEs. I prefer to say that consciousness is just what it is like being a mental model. In other words, all the mental models in any person's mind are all conscious, but only one is a model of "me." This is the one that I think of as myself and to which I relate everything else. It gives a core to my life. It allows me to think that I am a person, something that lives on all the time. It allows me to ignore the fact that "I" change from moment to moment and even disappear every night in sleep.

Now when the brain comes close to death, this model of self may simply fall apart. Now there is no self. It is a strange and dramatic experience. For there is no longer an experiencer—yet there is experience.

This state is obviously hard to describe, for the "you" who is trying to describe it cannot imagine not being. Yet this profound experience leaves its mark. The self never seems quite the same again.

The After Effects

I think we can now see why an essentially physiological event can change people's lives so profoundly. The experience has jolted their usual (and erroneous) view of the relationship between themselves and the world. We all too easily assume that we are some kind of persistent entity inhabiting a perishable body. But, as the Buddha taught, we have to see through that illusion. The world is only a construction of an information-processing system, and the self is too. I believe that the NDE gives people a glimpse into the nature of their own minds that is hard to get any other way. Drugs can produce it temporarily, mystical experiences can do it for rare people, and long years of practice in meditation or mindfulness can do it. But the NDE can out of the blue strike anyone and show them what they never knew before, that their body is only that—a lump of flesh—that they are not so very important after all. And that is a very freeing and enlightening experience.

And Afterwards?

If my analysis of the NDE is correct, we can extrapolate to the next stage. Lack of oxygen first produces increased activity through disinhibition, but eventually it all stops. Since it is this activity that produces the mental models that give rise to consciousness, then all this will cease. There will be no more experience, no more self, and so that, as far as my constructed self is concerned, is the end.

So, are NDEs in or out of the body?

I should say neither, for neither experiences nor selves have any location. It is finally death that dissolves the illusion that we are a solid self inside a body.

REFERENCES

Barrett, W. (1926). *Death-bed Visions.* London: Methuen.

Blackmore, S. J. (1982a). *Beyond the Body.* London: Heinemann.

Blackmore, S. J. (1982b). Birth and the OBE: An unhelpful analogy. *Journal of the American Society for Psychical Research,* 77, 229–238.

Blackmore, S. J. (1984). A postal survey of OBEs and other experiences. *Journal of the Society for Psychical Research,* 52, 225–44.

Blackmore, S. J. (1986). *The Adventures of a Parapsychologist.* Buffalo, NY: Prometheus.

Blackmore, S. J. (1987). Where am I? Perspectives in imagery and the out-of-body experience. *Journal of Mental Imagery,* 11, 53–66.

Blackmore, S. J. (1988). Do we need a new psychical research?*Journal of the Society for Psychical Research*, 55, 49–59.

Blackmore, S. J., and T. S. Troscianko. (1989). The physiology of the tunnel. *Journal of Near-Death Studies*, 8, 15–28.

Cowan, J. D. (1982). Spontaneous symmetry breaking in large-scale nervous activity. *International Journal of Quantum Chemistry*, 2, 1059–82.

Georgeson, M. A., and M. A. Harris. (1978). Apparent foveo-fugal drift of counterphase gratings. *Perception*, 7, 527–36.

Grof S., and J. Halifax. (1977). *The Human Encounter with Death*. London: Souvenir Press.

Irwin, H. J. (1986). Perceptual perspectives of visual imagery in OBEs, dreams and reminiscence. *Journal of the Society for Psychical Research*, 5, 210–17.

Moody R. (1975). *Life After Life*. New York: Mockingbird/Bantam Books.

Morris, R. L., S. B. Harary, J. Janis, J. Hartwell, and W. G. Roll. (1978). Studies of communication during out-of-body experiences. *Journal* of *the Society for Psychical Research*. 72, 1–22.

Morse, J. P., Castillo, D. Venecia, J. Milstein, and D. C. Tyler. (1986). Childhood near-death experiences. *American Journal of Diseases of Children*, 140, 1110–14.

Morse, J., D. Venecia, and J. Milstein. (1989). Near-death experiences: A neurophysiological explanatory model. *Journal of Near-Death Studies*, 8, 45–53.

Ring, K. (1980). *Life at Death*. New York: Coward, McCann & Geoghegan.

Ring, K. (1986). *Heading Toward Omega*. New York: Morrow.

Saavedra-Aguilar, J. C., and J. S. Gomez-Jeria. (1989). A neurobiological model for near-death experiences. *Journal of Near-Death Studies*, 7, 205–22.

Sabom, M. (1982). *Recollections of Death*. New York: Harper & Row.

Sagan, C. (1979). *Broca's Brain*. New York: Random House.

Schoonmaker, F. (1979). Denver cardiologist discloses findings after18 years of near-death research. *Anabiosis*, 1, 1–2.

Sheils, D. (1978). A cross-cultural study of beliefs in out-of-the-body experiences. *Journal of the Society for Psychical Research*, 49, 697–741.

Tart, C. T. (1978). A psychophysiological study of out-of-the-body experiences in a selected subject. *Journal of the Society for Psychical Research*, 62, 3–27.

Parting Visions
A New Scientific Paradigm

Melvin Morse

It is certainly scientifically responsible to state that the process of dying is not painful or scary and that people often think that they leave their body during the very times when the most painful and invasive things happen to dying patients.

Melvin Morse, M.D., is a pediatrician in Seattle who was the first to do extensive research into children's near-death experiences. He is now exploring creative ways to bridge the gulf among opposing NDE interpreters. He proposes theories to overcome the sometimes hostile gap between reductionistic materialism, which limits the NDE to internal brain activity, and pure mentalism, which sees the mind as separate from the brain. Morse is focusing on the role of the normal function of the temporal lobe of the brain as a possible mediator of many spiritual experiences, including the near-death experience. His interactionist approach acknowledges the essential role of neurology without denying the significance of spiritual experiences.

Morse also sketches the findings from his research into both Japanese and African NDEs, thereby expanding the needed database of international NDE research. He extends the framework of the NDE phenomena by placing it in the context of a number of death-related visions, such as premonitions of death, pre-death visions, and post-death visitations.

Melvin Morse, M.D., has published three books with author Paul Perry: *Closer to the Light: Learning from the Near-Death Experiences of Children* (1990), *Transformed by the Light: The Powerful Effect of Near-Death Experiences on People's Lives* (1992), and *Parting Visions: Uses and Meanings of Pre-Death, Psychic and Spiritual Experiences* (1994).

·- Parting Visions -·
A New Scientific Paradigm

In this chapter, I propose a new scientific paradigm to understand near-death experiences (NDEs). I propose that they are simply one of many associated spiritual experiences mediated by the right temporal lobe. A variety of clinical situations trigger psychological experiences which are similar to NDEs, including dying, childbirth, severe child abuse, severe emotional or physical stress, premonitions of death, after death visitations, religious prayer and spiritual meditation. The finding of a common neurobiological pathway for these experiences documents that they are as real as any other human experience. I will present a review of the existing mainstream peer reviewed scientific literature to support this new paradigm. Philosophical questions such as the absolute reality of spiritual perceptions are beyond the expertise of the author, a practicing Pediatrician, and will not be discussed. The knowledge that we will all most likely have such an experience when we die has profound implications for our society.

HISTORICAL PERSPECTIVE
The process of dying or surviving near death has been associated throughout history with spiritual visions which are strikingly similar to modern NDEs. *The Egyptian Book of the Dead* (1500 BCE) is a manual to provide magical means by which the dead soul can join the crew of a ship, pass through the dark valley of the Underworld and be united with the Sun God for eternity (1967). The Aztec God Hero Quetzalcoatl in his death poem describes "the darkness twist in him like a river," which led to his seeing his own face as if in a cracked mirror, seeing a shining city, meeting people and religious figures, and ends "with his body changed to light, a star that burns forever in that sky" (Rothenberg, 1969, 92–98). Primitive shamans often underwent initiatory experiences

which often involved either actual death or the perception of near-death, spirit helpers, a journey to another reality, which often was through a tunnel or a dark void, and a return to ordinary consciousness with new knowledge and understandings (Harner, 1990).

Anthropologist Chris Carl compared the contemporary NDEs of Americans of European descent with the death experiences as understood by Tibetan Buddhist lamas of the eighth through eleventh centuries AD. He found that the most clearly culturally shared events included hearing loud noises like a wind or a roar early in the death process, seeing religious figures, seeing a white or gold light that is separate from oneself defining a dualistic consciousness, merging with that light to create a sense of oneness, a life review or judgment, and more generally, events that reveal death to be a learning process (Carr, 1993).

Large anecdotal collections by mainstream scientists began in the 1800s. Emanuel Swedenborg, a mining engineer and inventor, collected hundreds of such cases (Swedenborg, 1928). Two meticulously documented collections of anecdotes surveyed the entire spectrum of parting visions, from premonitions of death to after-death visitations (Myers, 1903; Gurney,1956).

The modern concept of a near-death experience as triggered by death or after resuscitation was well established by the 1950s. Numerous prominent cases were reported, including those of Admiral Francis Beaufort, writer Ernest Hemingway, Catholic priest Louis Tucker, explorer Richard Byrd, flying ace Edward Rickenbacker, psychologist Carl Jung, and many others (Audette, 1982).

The first systematic study of critically ill patients was by Russian physician Vladimir Negovsky who routinely asked World War II soldiers who were "reanimated" from nearly dying of injuries and hypothermia what they remembered about the experience. He described "the great majority" as perceiving the experience as a deep sleep without dreams, although he acknowledges that some had memories of events around them and occasionally describes blissful scenes of an afterlife. He felt these were distortions of perception in a malfunctioning brain (Negovsky, 1962, 1982).

In a watershed article, Burch, Depasquale, and Philips report a series of survivors of cardiac arrest who simply reported "a pleasant feeling as though they were entering a peaceful sleep" (1968, 438–39). They were the first to recognize that interviewing survivors of cardiac arrest would perhaps give insights into the first three or four minutes of the dying process, which is the longest period recall of psychic processes might be expected. "As crude as the tool utilized in this study seems to be, there is no better model presently available to study the natural process of death."

By 1972, the term "Lazarus Complex" was coined for such experiences (Hackett). In 1975, the flood of modern reports of near-death experiences began with the publication of *Life After Life*, by psychiatrist and philosopher Raymond Moody. He examined "a large number of accounts," perhaps as many as 150, from which he selected fifty to interview in depth. He described fifteen distinct elements which are commonly associated with NDEs, as a sequence of events from hearing the news of death, to floating out of the body, feeling peaceful, meeting others, the being of Light, the life review, the border, coming back, telling others, and the transformation. This was intended to be a composed of the ideal case, but many patients only had fragments and pieces of the experience (Moody, 1975).

Numerous case reports and studies are reported. Oakes prospectively interviewed 21 survivors of cardiac arrest over a two-year period and reported sensory awareness yet an inability to communicate, out-of-body experiences of the autoscopic variety, a journey through a tunnel toward a light, and feelings of indescribable splendor (1978). I reported the first Pediatric NDE, a seven-year-old girl who was without spontaneous heartbeat for nineteen minutes and had fixed, dilated pupils. She recovered to give a detailed description of her own resuscitation, including hearing pieces of conversations in the emergency room, accurately describing her own resuscitation, with details such as nasal intubation, and being placed in a CAT scanner. This was followed by a spiritual journey with a spirit guide through a dark tunnel to a heavenly realm and a decision to return to consciousness (Morse, 1983).

There is little evidence or reason to believe that these experiences represent psychiatric pathology or dysfunction, according to German psychiatrist Michael Schroeter (1990). They can be easily distinguished from hallucinations of schizophrenia or organic brain dysfunction (Blackmore, 1986; Bates and Stanlely, 1985).

Although often described as reactive fantasies to the fear of death, NDEs are described as occurring to infants and young children who have a different concept of death than adults, and have not yet experienced ego differentiation. Pediatric nephrologists from Massachusetts General Hospital reported an NDE occurring to an eight-month-old (Hartzog and Herrin, 1985), and I reported a large series of NDEs in children as young as age four (Morse, Connor and Tyler, 1985; Morse, Castillo and Venecia, 1986).

Although a precise understanding of the developmental aspects of death anxiety does not exist, most authorities agree that the child under age two has no concept of death and that from two to five, there is a limited understanding that death is perhaps the temporary cessation of activity. The anxiety that children have at this age is comparable to separation anxiety and does not come from some deep-seated fear of death (Rothenberg, 1979).

EXPLANATORY MODELS

From the clinical perspective, it is important to understand when these experiences occur. Do they occur in the few minutes between the death of the body and the death of the brain, or are they artifacts of resuscitation, and secondary falsifications after the fact (Morse and Neppe)?

1. Secondary Falsifications:

I believe that most physicians and scientists interpret NDEs as secondary falsifications, distortions of man's perception of his environment while the brain is malfunctioning. As Negovsky speculates:

> auditory perception may be preserved when areas of the cerebral cortex serving vision has ceased functioning and after motor activity has ceased. Without any mystical explanations we can understand why the dying and then revived person can tell us they heard the voices of physicians. The fact that resuscitated people in different countries can recall similar images seen by them during dying or resuscitation, does not prove life after death. It can be explained by the dynamics of the disintegration of cerebral function due to different resistances to anoxia of the various areas of the central nervous system. (1982)

Blackmore has developed a sophisticated computer model of the images the brain receives from the retina at the point of death. The macula is doubly innervated and may cause a persistence of light images as the brain dies. As the brain dies, she speculates, an increase in cortical irritability could destabilize the uniform visual image that we perceive, and result in the perception of concentric rings, lines, and tunnels.

This model speculates that the out-of-body experience results from the dying brain attempting to reconstruct a model of the universe from limited sensory input. She points out that we are constantly constructing a model of reality from a wide variety of competing sensory input. When that input ceases, we rely on memories and fragments of perceptions to reconstruct a memory model of reality, from a bird's eye view. Such a model would seem perfectly real (Blackmore, 1988).

Any time that the brain is confronted with memory gaps and pieces of information that don't seem to fit, it will attempt to make its best effort at creating a memory, and will believe it to be true. We do not precisely remember dreams and memories, but are constantly recreating them (Taylor, 1979; Calvin, 1990). Memory expert Elizabeth Loftus has convincingly shown that false memories are fairly easy to create in experimental situations simply through gentle questioning (1991).

This respective falsification model depends on fragments of perceptions of a chaotic disorganized brain, which is either psychologically and/or physiologically stressed, coupled with a secondary reorganization into a coherent story.

2. Real Time Models

These models primarily depend on similarities between the known functions of the right temporal lobe and related structures and NDEs. They speculate that NDEs are either the dysfunction or normal function of the temporal lobe, depending on the philosophical outlook of the investigator. Since coma involves the cessation of cortical functioning and "wipes clean the slate of consciousness" (Plum and Posner, 1972), these models depend on aspects of consciousness and memory being mediated by deep subcortical structures.

Researchers have described NDEs as neurobiological events, either as temporal lobe dysfunction (Carr, 1982) or normal temporal lobe activity (Morse, 1990) occurring in dying patients. For nearly one hundred years, patients with temporal lobe tumors were noted to have vividly real hallucinations superimposed over ordinary reality. These included seeing people dressed in white and other spiritual visions (Horrax, 1928). Most, if not all, of the fifteen traits of the near-death experience as described by Moody have been replicated either by electrical stimulation studies, seizures, or other pathology of the right temporal lobe, based on my reading of the literature.

CASE REPORT

J. R. is a twelve-year-old right-handed girl who was presented to my office for evaluation of a funny dream which seemed to mean she was going to die. It frightened her. Her past medical history was remarkable for migraine headaches which occurred every one to two months. She stated that she had an intense headache and felt she had to lie down. While she was having pain, she felt herself "sucked out of my body, you know, and into the long tunnel." She floated to the ceiling of her room and looked down at herself "all miserable and in pain." She then traveled through the tunnel into a heavenly realm with bright colors that seemed to be flowers. She saw a shining castle. She did not encounter a spiritual being or see a spiritual light. She thought her mother would be sad and she knew she would die if she stayed in this realm. She made a decision to return to her body.

The neurological and physical exam were entirely benign. Her electroencephalogram was read by a neurologist blinded for clinical details as showing abnormal right temporal lobe activity.

This case report is an example of a "real time" near-death experience, except the patient was not near death or in an unusual amount of pain for her migraine headaches. Most of the fifteen elements of Moody's NDE have been described in the literature in case reports of temporal lobe seizures, electrical stimulation studies, or as otherwise arising from deep temporal lobe and related structures. Penfield performed electrical stimulation studies of the right Sylvian fissure and found that patients often heard heavenly music, saw vivid hallucinations of people, and recall memories so vividly that they seemed to be three dimensional and real. One patient is reported as saying: "Oh god, I'm leaving my body", and another saying "I'm half in and half out" (Penfield and Rasmussen, 1950; Penfield, 1955).

To understand the out-of-body perception, West uses the example of a man looking out the window, with a fire burning behind him in the room. As the night comes, and light ceases from outside the window, the man sees the fire reflected in the window glass, along with reflections of objects in the room. He might easily mistake these reflections as coming from outside (1975). This perceptual release explanation of NDEs is agnostic as to the "reality" of those other images; but only makes the point that the seemingly autoscopic out-of-body experience may simply be a reflection and reconstruction of an inner state. As one child who had an NDE said to me "it was kind of like floating out of my body, but it was also like walking into my mind" (Morse, 1990). Blackmore's model works just as well for the real time theorists in explaining the neurophysiological underpinings of the tunnels, geometric visions, and out-of-body perceptions. Her reminder that we do not directly perceive reality, but are always creating a model of what we surmise it to be, is just as pertinent for real-time models of NDEs.

A variety of different neurotransmitters and neuronal receptors are speculated to be involved with NDEs, including serotonin (Morse, et al., 1989), endorphins (Carr, 1992), or L-glutamate. As for the latter, Jansen speculates that NDEs are in fact a byproduct of the brain's attempt to heal itself at the point of death. The neurotransmitter at NMDA receptors is probably L-glutamate, which can kill neurons when in excess. The release during ischemia of an endopsychosin which may function as a protective blocking agent could serve the function of minimizing brain damage, and could have dissociative side effects on consciousness (Jansen, 1988).

Real-time models regard the NDE as occurring in the final moments of consciousness. There is philosophical dispute as how to interpret them, ranging from seeing them as an artifact of neuronal dysfunction, a real experience linked to normal temporal lobe function (Morse, 1994), possibly harmful experience wasting precious energy on generating hallucinations (Negovsky, 1982), or possibly helpful in blocking the harmful effects of ischemia while generating a pleasing dissociation fantasy (Jansen, 1988).

A RETROSPECTIVE/PROSPECTIVE CASE CONTROL STUDY OF
CHILDHOOD NEAR-DEATH EXPERIENCES

In 1994, our research group at Seattle's Children's Hospital published final results of a combined retrospective/prospective case controlled study of pediatric near-death experiences, designed to clarify these issues (Morse, 1994). Our experimental group consisted of 26 critically ill patients who had life threatening events with a 10% or greater mortality, given the care in our Pediatric Intensive Care Unit. This group was compared to 121 seriously ill control patients with life-threatening conditions with a low mortality rate. Both groups were age and sex controlled, had a similar range of abnormal blood gases, were treated with the same medications including benzodiazepenes, narcotics, anesthetic agents and seizure medications, were mechanically ventilated and intubated, and were subjected to the psychological stresses of the intensive care unity environment.

The authors had no preconceptions as to what constituted a near-death experience at the onset of this study, and any memories that a patient subjectively perceived as occurring during the time of unconsciousness qualified as a near-death experience. This was done to clarify whether NDEs are simply a subset of intensive-care unit psychosis. An interview formal was developed with sixteen open-ended questions, such as "what do you remember happened to you when you were in the hospital?" Once the open-ended questions were asked, then a second questionnaire requiring "yes" or "no" responses was administered, with questions such as "did you see a light?".

Twenty-two of twenty-six critically ill children described memories of being clinically dead, and furthermore virtually all of the memories were consistent with previous anecdotal collections of adult NDEs. All of this information was obtained in the open-ended question phase of the study and no new information was obtained from the "yes or no" direct questions. The children often subjectively perceived themselves as being awake and alert while seemingly in coma, and felt that the entire experience was real. In fact, one six-year-old boy emphatically stated "it was real, Dr. Morse, it was realler than real."

The content of the experiences was usually described as a fragment of a greater indescribable experience. One eight-year-old boy stated: "I have a wonderful secret to tell you. I was climbing a staircase to heaven. It was long and dark and I could see a light (that was heaven). I came back because my brother had already died and it wouldn't be fair (if I continued)." This is the entire description of his experience and all other questions were answered with "I don't know (or remember)." Another six-year-old boy stated, "it was weird. I thought I was floating out of my body. And I could see a light. There were a lot of good things in it." Again, he could not further define what this light was or what he meant by "good things" in it. A five-year-old girl described the light this way: "It told me who I was and where I was to go." A twelve-year-old girl stated: "I learned that life is for living and that light is for later." This was her complete statement about her experience, only further stating that she was somewhere besides her own body, but couldn't say where else she was or what else happened to her.

One case strongly suggests that near-death experiences occur at the point of dying. A fourteen-year-old boy with documented Long QT syndrome (Romano Ward Syndrome), Sick Sinus Syndrome, and juvenile onset diabetes, experienced a pacemaker failure resulting in reoccurrence of ventricular tachycardia and fibrillation. He described floating out of his physical body and watching his own resuscitation from a corner of the room, surrounded by a soft white light. He could "see my hair all messed up. They cut off my clothes and hooked me up to IVs and stuff. I saw the nurses put some grease on me and then Dr. Herndon put paddles on my chest and pressed a button. I was sucked back into my body."

Dr. Paul Herndon, Chief of Cardiology at Seattle Children's Hospital, and nurses present independently verified that within minutes of this patient's successful resuscitation, he regained consciousness and said: "You guys just sucked me (or pulled me) back into my body."

None of our control patients described any memories of the time they were seriously ill, in spite of the (erroneous) perception they were dying, severe lack of oxygen to the brain, and a wide range of medications and physiological and psychological stresses.

We identified a core near-death experience which consisted of the subjective sense of being dead yet conscious, autoscopic out of body perceptions, darkness followed by a spiritual light or perception of heaven, comforting images from one's past, spirit guides and religious figures, and the perception of a decision to return to life.

We have studied 400 Japanese near-death experiences, and fifty Native African experiences collected at the University of Zambia, and found the same core experience as seen in American children. For example, in a retrospective study of over 400 Japanese near-death experiences, Japanese adults described a wide range of experiences in keeping with their cultural traditions. However, Japanese children similarly describe simple experiences of seeing a bright light or seeing living teachers and playmates. A four-year-old boy who had fulminant pneumonia described floating out of his body and coming to the edge of a river. His playmates were on the other side, urging him to go back. There was a misty bright light on the other side (Morse, 1992).

Recent experimental evidence from the National Warfare Institute further confirms that near-death experiences are in fact the dying experience. Pilots subjected to tremendous centrifugal forces to the point of near-death have subjective experiences similar to near-death experiences. These "loss of consciousness experiences" typically do not begin until the pilot is profoundly unconscious and often is having seizures from poor cerebral circulation (Forster and Whinnery, 1988; Whinnery and Whinnery, 1990).

Persinger also presents experimental data that electrical stimulation studies of the right temporal lobe create what he terms "the god experience." This experience is similar to near-death experiences and is apparently as transformative (1987).

This evidence clearly suggests that near-death experiences in fact occur when they are subjectively perceived as occurring, at the point of death. Every scientific clinical study that I am aware of supports this conclusion (Levin and Curly, 1990; Merkawah-Research, 190; Owens, Cook, and Stevenson, 1990). As such, they must represent the best objective evidence of what it is like to die, regardless of which neurotransmitters or anatomical structures mediate the experience. They are as real as any other human experience, as real as math or language. They occur to subjects with isoelectric EEGs, suggesting that deep temporal lobe and associated limbic structures mediate the experience and that memory and perception of consciousness do not depend on functioning cortical structures (Schoonmaker, 1993).

The unmistakable conclusion of the scientific evidence on dying is that profoundly comatose dying patients do in fact have an expanded sense of awareness and consciousness. The processes of dying are often spiritual, involve out of body perceptions and paranormal abilities and perceptions (transformed). This represents circumstantial evidence of some sort of consciousness surviving physical death.

LONG-TERM EFFECTS

I studied one hundred adults who had NDEs as children, and tested them with a battery of psychological tests including the Ellsworth Profile of Adaptation to Life Survey, Greyson Value Survey, Greyson Near-Death Validity Scale, Tempter Death Anxiety Scale, Reker-Peacock Life Attitude Profile, Neppe Subjective Paranormal Events Questionnaire, Neppe Temporal Lobe Sensitivity Inventory, a complete medical and psychiatric history, family bonding and rating scales, Weinbeerger Anxiety Inventory, and open-ended essay questions. They were compared to control groups of 50 subjects each, including 1. parents of children in a private suburban pediatric practice, 2. adults who nearly died as children but did not have an NDE, 3. adults who describe themselves as being New Age Christians or Humanists, 4. adults who describe themselves as having psychic powers, and 5. adults who had spiritual experiences of a mystical light as children not in the context of illness.

We found that children who have mystical experiences of light, either in the context of illness or not, have a similar psychological profile as adults. This profile includes low death anxiety, few symptoms of repressed anxiety or depression, lower self-reported rates of drug and alcohol use, or use of over-the-counter health products, increased self-reported time spent meditating, eating fresh fruits and vegetables, and exercise, more time spent alone and with family members, and statistically significant increased scores on tests of general mental health and spiritual well being. These adults described themselves as giving more money to charity and spending more hours a week in volunteer activities. In contrast, adults who nearly died as children, but did not have an NDE, had increased death anxiety, increased repressive and defensive symptoms, and evidence of post-traumatic stress syndrome. The other control populations scored in the normal range of these various tests, as had been previously reported for control populations (Morse, 1992).

Our study replicates and confirms previous similar studies in adults (Noyes, 1980; Stack-O'Sullivan, 1981; Greyson,1983). It is, of course, unknown whether or not these observed differences represent predisposing factors or the consequence of the experience.

RELATIONSHIP TO OTHER DEATH-RELATED VISIONS

Research on near-death experiences validates a host of death-related visions, including premonitions of death, pre-death visions, and post-death visitations. NDEs cannot be understood as an isolated phenomenon, but should be interpreted as being a part of a spectrum of spiritual events which happen to the dying, their families, and caretakers. The salient feature of the NDE is that it is a mystical spiritual experience superimposed over ordinary reality, which is also the hallmark of the death-related vision.

Anecdotal collections of pre-death visions have been reported for nearly one hundred years, with comparable phenomenology to NDEs. Sir William Barrett, Professor of Physics at the Royal Academy of Science in Dublin, in 1926 meticulously collected anecdotes of pre-death visions in children and adults at the turn of the century (1926/1986 Reprint).

More recently, Yale Pediatric Oncologist Diane Komp reported children who had experiences similar to NDEs prior to their deaths, except that the experiences occurred in "dreams, visions, or prayer and the children were infrequently brain dysfunctional at the time." A seven-year-old girl, dying of leukemia, sat up and said "the angels, they are so beautiful, can't you hear them singing Mommy?" immediately prior to her death (1992).

A handful of case reports and studies exist in the medical literature, also documenting the similarities of NDEs and other death-related visions. A ten-year-old girl with leukemia had several experiences during bone marrow transplantation. After the third unsuccessful attempt, she told her nurses that she "had seen the light" and "spoke to Jesus." She told her best friend that she had been through a tunnel and had come back to say goodbye to the friend (Schoenbeck, 1993). Osis and Haroldsson surveyed 5000 doctors and nurses in the United States and 704 in India. They collected 471 cases of pre-death visions and comment on their similarity to near-death experience, which they also collected. Pre-death visions were typically of brief duration, within 24 hours of death, dead and living relatives were often seen, and the purpose of the experience was to take the dying person away and to provide comfort (1977).

Barrett, Doyle, Madrid et al. report in a prospective case controlled study that dying adults have a marked increase in hallucinations of apparitions in the final week of life (1990).

Shared spiritual experiences with dying patients are also reported, which again are strikingly similar to near-death experiences. An off-duty nurse described a vivid dream in which she accompanied one of her patients through a tunnel into a spiritual light, which occurred at the same time her patient died in the hospital. She stated that during the dream "we burst out into the open-bright light all around us. I felt incredibly peaceful and good. Then I thought, I can't stay, It isn't my time, I have things to do. I looked (at her patient). She had already become part of that glorious white light" (Houlberg, 1992) .

A teenage girl shared the dying experience of her brother who died when a car struck him while riding his bicycle. She was at home when he was fatally injured. His mother was called and immediately went to his bedside at Harborview Hospital in Seattle and then returned home to tell her daughter. She found her daughter sitting in the living room stating that she was floating out of her body and in a heavenly realm with her brother, who showed her his bicycle accident and subsequent death and told her it was all right. The teenager was able to simultaneously communicate with both her brother and her mother. She stated that this vision occurred before her mother told her of her brother's accident (Morse, 1992).

A retrospective case control study of premonitions of Sudden Infant Death Syndrome (SIDS) by the Southwest SIDS Research Group documented that 21 percent of parents had a premonition of their infant's subsequent death. Seven parents documented their premonitions in a journal prior to the death. A retrospective control group and two prospective control groups reported 3–5 percent of parents whose infants did not die of SIDS having pre-monitions and that the control premonitions were of a qualitatively different nature than the premonitions of SIDS. Some parents reported spiritual visions similar to near-death experiences, including spiritual voices telling parents that the child was to die, out-of-body visions, including angels who predicted the child's death, and a four-year-old sibling sharing the infant's dying experience. The control premonitions were primarily vague feelings of unease (Hardoin, Hensley, Morse, et al., 1993).

Post-death visitations, often described as grief-induced hallucinations, are also well described in both children and adults. Although these experiences are again strikingly similar to NDEs and pre-death visions, they are invariably described as a separate psychological entity. They are typically described in the context of a dream or a waking vision as involving a vividly real hallucination of a dead relative, patient or friend superimposed over ordinary reality. They often include spiritual intuitions and visions of a mystical light.

The anthropologist D. Lewis randomly interviewed 108 London nurses and found that 35 percent reported experiences with dead patients, ranging from vague feelings to visual and auditory hallucinations (1987). In 1769 Charles Bonnet described adults who had pleasant visions of deceased relatives and other presumed hallucinatory experiences in the context of sensory deprivation (1776). Now such experiences are reported as the Charles Bonnet syndrome (Alroe and McIntyre, 1983; Adair, 1988).

W. D. Rees found that 50 percent of widowers reported visions of departed spouses, which occurred to them while in the waking state (1971). E. Haroldsson, in a national survey in Iceland, reported that 31 percent of respondents reported visual encounters with the dead (1988–89). These experiences have also been reported in traditional Hopi Indians (Matchett, 1903). Early accounts in adults also contain elements which could not be explained by reactive grief reactions, such as living persons seeing apparitions of the dead prior to their knowledge of the death (Myers, 1903). The fact that these experiences are so common has led one investigator to advocate abandoning the word "hallucination" to describe them (Stevenson, 1983).

CLINICAL AND THEORETICAL IMPLICATIONS

It is my opinion that these experiences all represent a spiritual dimension to the dying process, a continuum from the pre-death vision, the shared dying experience, the near-death experience and the post-death visitation. It is my intent to present a new theoretical framework to understand these previously isolated clinical entities so as to stimulate research on the effects of these powerful spiritual events on dying patients and grief. I believe that all of these experiences represent the normal function of the right temporal lobe in response to various clinical situations, from grief, to dying, to true pre-cognition of future events. My review of the scientific literature shows a heretofore unappreciated understanding of a spectrum of normal and healthy spiritual dissociation in man, from spiritual visions and parting visions on one extreme, to the chaos of multiple personality disorder on the other (Schenk and Bear, 1981; Greaves, 1980).

RESTORING DIGNITY AND CONTROL TO THE DYING PROCESS

Dying can be a depersonalized, spiritually degrading, and dehumanizing process. Patients often die alone stripped of personal dignity. They feel useless and a burden to their families, often draining financial resources for terminal care of minimal benefit. But, if it is understood that dying and comatose patients are often conscious and capable of emotionally processing information, family members and friends may want to spend more time at the bedside. Anticipatory grieving, life reviews, dialogues, and education concerning the spiritual perceptions of dying patients may well reverse the isolation of the dying patient. Spiritual visions can empower the dying patient because they still have something important to share with others. I am aware of many cases in which children have used their spiritual visions to comfort their parents about their impending deaths. Such statements can be enormously comforting and allow the child to feel powerful and in control.

One important issue for children and adults is to know what will happen to them when they die. Parents and health care professionals can present what is known of near-death research in a straightforward manner and simply explain what others say they have experienced when they underwent the dying process. It is certainly scientifically responsible to state that the process of dying is not painful or scary and that people often think that they leave their body during the very times when the most painful and invasive things happen to dying patients.

DEATH-RELATED VISIONS MAY REQUIRE COUNSELING

These experiences can precipitate a state of spiritual emergency. Patients who have had near-death experiences may have difficulty understanding what has happened to them. Divorce is not uncommon in adults after such experiences, as patients reassess their life and goals. The experience may be frightening. In fact, studies of negative near-death experiences suggest that the experiences themselves are similar to positive ones, but that the patients misunderstand the experience. They may see it as a psychiatric pathology or interpret various elements of the experience (especially the dark void) to mean that they are in hell or having a negative experience (Greyson and Bush, 1992).

Some patients and family members wonder why they haven't had death-related visions. Others wonder whether every comatose patient is conscious and aware, or some have already "died." Why do some choose to return to life and others do not? Often death-related visions raise as many painful questions as they bring comfort.

DEATH-RELATED VISIONS CAN ASSIST IN THE GRIEVING PROCESS

A common model for mourning involves four tasks: accepting the reality of the loss, working through the pain of grief, adjusting to a new environment without the deceased, and emotionally relocating the deceased and moving on with life (Shackelton, 1984). The knowledge that it is scientifically respectable to understand death-related visions as representing a real event has enormous potential to facilitate normal grieving and theoretically impacts on each of these steps.

Death-related visions can affirm spiritual intuitions and faith. Death-related visions potentially can intervene at each of these steps if they are validated as meaningful experiences. Often these experiences involve only a faint smile at the point of death, or a brief comment such as "the light, the light," or "I'm on a rocket ship to the moon" but are not understood as being an important experience.

Premonitions of death often involve only vague perceptions or feelings which nonetheless can re-establish faith in the order of the universe and that death has meaning. Post-death visitations often involve dialogues with the dead which anecdotally have been reported to facilitate grieving by allowing the loss to be accepted, as well as allowing the survivors to reinvest emotional energy (Morse, et al., 1989). NDEs have the power to restore meaning to the process of death because of their mythical role within our society.

Death-related visions can restore a sense of order to the universe because they often imply that there is a purpose and meaning to death, even if that meaning is obscure. A parent who interprets their child's death-bed visions as hallucinatory ravings from drugs or physiological derangement is seemingly less likely to look for meaning in the experiences than one who views such experiences within a communal and spiritual context which accepts such visions as natural.

NOT SIMPLY A WARM FUZZY WAY TO DIE

Listening to and affirming death-related visions has the potential to dramatically reduce wasteful and irrational medical procedures and treatments. An enormous percentage of our health care dollar is spent on intensive care unit management of dying patients without clearcut benefit. Dr. William Knaus of George Washington University School of Medicine has said: "In many cases, intrusive and communicated machinery is wheeled in to keep vital signs going, to give treatment of no benefit and tremendous cost, depriving others of treatment while dignity disappears" (Knaus, Wagner, Lynn, 1991).

Studies in adults show that dying patients primarily die in hospitals and that we spend 30–60 percent of our health care dollar on the last three months of life (Oye and Bellamy, 1991; Gaumer and Stavins, 1992; McCuster, 1983). There is considerable debate in the adult medical literature over the cost effectiveness and ethics of intensive care unit medicine, especially the routine use of cardiopulmonary resuscitation and assisted ventilation for dying patients (Schapira et al., 1993; "Charges...," 1989).

On the surface, it may seem hard to perceive a connection between death-related visions and overuse of medical technology. Daniel Schuster, MD, of

Washington University in St. Louis, feels the problem is that "we must learn to distinguish between everything that can be done and everything that should be done." He feels the problem is that we do not openly and accurately discuss the cost and outcome of critical care medicine with patients, and feels the greatest cost is not in money, but in human suffering. He feels that families should not expect that mechanical life support should be initiated in dying patients and asks: "Why did we get to this point, as physicians, as a society, where we can let—no actually be—the cause of such suffering, and even do it in the name of patient autonomy?" He asks that physicians and patients enter into a tough, gut-wrenching, anxiety-provoking dialogue, and accept our responsibility to start to make decisions, instead of simply letting them occur by default (Schuster, 1992). A discussion of the parting visions of the dying and those who care for and love them may become a cultural icebreaker and assist us in a renewal of our society's approach to death.

REFERENCES

Adair, D. K., Keshavan, M. S. (1988, July). The Charles Bonnet Syndrome and Grief Reaction (letter). *American Journal of Psychiatry*, 145, 7, 895–96.

Alroe, C. J., Mcintyre, J. N. M. (1983). Visual Hallucinations: the Charles Bonnet Syndrome and Bereavement. *Medical Journal of Australia*, 2, 674–75.

Audette, J. R. (1982). Historical Perspectives on Near-Death Experiences and Episodes. In Lundahl C. R., ed. *A Collection of Near-Death Readings*. Chicago: Nelson Hall Publishers.

Barrett, E. A. M., Doyle, M. B., Malinski, V. M. et al. (1990). The Relationship among the Experience of Dying, the Experience of Paranormal Events, and Creativity in Adults. In Barrett, E. A. M., Ed. *Visions of Rogers' Science Based Nursing*. New York: National League for Nursing Publication No. 15–2285.

Barrett, Sir William. (1986). *Death Bed Visions: The Psychical Experiences of the Dying*. The Aquarian Press. Reprint of 1926 Edition.

Bates, B.C., Stanley, A. (1985). The Epidemiology and Differential Diagnosis of Near-Death Experience. *American Journal of Orthopsychiatry*, 55,4, 542–49.

Blackmore, S. (1986). Out-of-Body Experiences in Schizophrenia. *Journal of Nervous and Mental Disease*, 174,10, 615–19.

Blackmore, S. (1988, May 5). Visions from the Dying Brain. *New Scientist*, 43–46.

Bonnet, C. (1776). Essai Analytique sur les Facultes de l'Ame, 2nd Ed, Vol. II. Copenhengen/Geneva: Philbert, 176–77.

Budge, E. A. W. (1967). *The Egyptian Book of the Dead*. New York: Dover.

Burch, G. E., DePasquale N. P., and Phillips J. H. (1968, Sept.). What Death Is Like. *American Heart Journal*. 438–39.

Calvin, W. (1990). *The Cerebral Symphony: Seashore Reflections on the Structure of Consciousness*. New York: Bantam.

Carr, D. (1982). Pathophysiology of Stress Induced Limbic Lobe Dysfunction: A Hypothesis for NDEs. *Anabiosis: The Journal of Near-Death Studies*, 2, 75–90.

Carr, C. (1993). Death and Near Death: A Comparison of Tibetan and Euro-American Experiences. *Journal of Transpersonal Psychology*, 25, 1, 59–110.

Charges of CPR "Overuse" Debated by MEA Readers. (1989, April). *Medical Ethics Advisor*, 5,4, 45–56.

Forster, E. M., Whinnery, J. E. (1988). Recovery from +Gz-Induced Loss of Consciousness: Psychophysiologic Considerations. *Aviation, Space, and Environal Medicine*, 59, 517–22.

Gaumer, G. L., Stavins, J. (1992). Medicare Use in the Last 90 Days of Life. *Health Services Research*, 26, 725–42.

Greaves, G. B. (1980, Oct.). Multiple Personality 165 Years after Mary Reynolds. *Journal of Nervous and Mental Disease*, 168,10, 577–96

Greyson, B. (1983, May). Near-Death Experiences and Personal Values. *American Journal of Psychiatry*, 140, 5, 618–20.

Greyson, B., Bush, N. E. (1992, Feb.). Distressing Near-Death Experiences. *Psychiatry Vol. 55*, 95–110.

Gurney, E. (1956). *Phantasms of the Living*. London: Trubner, 1886.

Hackett, T. P. (1972). The Lazarus Complex Revisited. *Annals of Internal Medicine*, 76, 135–37.

Haraldsson, E. (1988–89). *Survey of Claimed Encounters with the Dead*. Omega, 19, 2, 103–13.

Hardoin, R., Hennsley, J., Morse, M. et al. (1993). "Premonitions of Sudden Infant Death Syndrome: A Retrospective Case Control Study." (In press). Presented at the National SIDS Research Meeting, Pittsburgh, October 1993.

Harner, M. (1990). *The Way of the Shaman*. New York: Harper.

Hertzog, D. B., and Herrin, J. T. (1985). Near-Death Experiences in the Very Young. *Critical Care Medicine*, 13,2, 1074–75.

Horrax, G. (1928). Visual Hallucinations As a Cerebral Localizing Phenomenon: with Special Reference to their Occurrence in Tumors of the Temporal Lobes. *Archives of Neurology and Psychiatry*, 533–47.

Houlberg, L. (1992, Feb.). Coming Out of the dark. *Nursing*, 43.

Jansen, K. R. (1988). The Near-Death Experience (letter). *Lancet*, 153, 883–84.

Knaus, W. A., Wagner, D. P., Lynn. (1991, October 18). Short-term Mortality Predictions for Critically Ill Hospitalized Adults: Science and Ethics. *Science*, 389–94.

Komp, D. M. (1992). *A Window to Heaven: When Children See Life in Death*. Grand Rapids MI: Zondervan Publishing.

Levin, C., Curley, M. (1990). "Near-Death Experiences in Children." Reported at the Conference for Perspective on Change: Forces Shaping Practice for the Clinical Nurse Specialist. Boston Children's Hospital, October 11, 1990.

Lewis, D. (1987). All in Good Faith. *Nursing Times*, 83, 40–43

Loftus, E. (1991). *Witness for the Defense*. New York: St. Martin's Press.

Matchett, W. F. (1992, May). Repeated Hallucinatory Experiences as a Part of the Mourning Process Among Hopi Indian Woman. *Psychiatry*, 35, 185–94.

McCuster, J. (1983). Where Cancer Patients Die: An Epidemiologic Study. *Public Health Rep*, 98, 170–76.

Merkawah-Research. (1990, Jan.). "Progress Report on the Research into Near-Death Experiences." (In October 1991, I met in the Netherlands with the Dutch research group Merkawah to review our data.)

Moody, R. (1975). *Life After Death*. New York: Bantam/Mockingbird.

Morse, M. L. (1983). A Near-Death Experience in a 7-Year-Old Child. *American Journal of Diseases of Children*, 137, 959–61.

Morse, M. L., Connor, D., Tyler, D. (1985). Near-Death Experiences in a Pediatric Population. *American Journal of Diseases of Children*, 139, 595–600.

Morse, M.L., Castillo, P., Venecia, D. (1986, Nov.). Childhood Near-Death Experiences. *American Journal of Diseases of Children*, 140, 110–14.

Morse, M. L., Venecia, D., Milstein, J. M. (1989, Fall). Near-Death Experiences: A Neurophysiological Explanatory Model. *Journal of Near-Death Studies*, 8,1.

Morse M. L., with Perry, P. (1990). *Closer to the Light: Learning from the Near-Death Experiences of Children*. New York:Villard Books.

Morse, M. L., Neppe, V. M. (1991, Apr. 6). Near-Death Experiences (Letter). *Lancet*, 386.

Morse, M. L., with Perry, P. (1992). *Transformed by the Light: The Powerful Effects of Near-Death Experiences on People's Lives*. New York: Villard Books.

Morse, M. L. (1994, Feb.). Death-Related Experiences in Children: Implications for the Clinician. *Current Problems in Pediatrics*, 3–84.

Morse, M. L., with Perry, P. (1994). *Parting Visions: Uses and Meanings of Pre-Death, Psychic and Spiritual Experiences*. New York: Villard Books.

Myers, F. W. H. (1903). *Human Personality and Its Survival of Bodily Death*. London: Longmans, Green and Co. Reprinted 1956. Society for Psychical Research.

Negovsky, V. A. (1962). *Resuscitation and Artificial Hypothermia*. New York: Consultants Bureau.

Negovsky, V. A. (1982). Reanimatology Today. *Critical Care Medicine*, 10, 2, 130–33.

Noyes, R. (1980, Aug.). Attitude Change Following Near-Death Experiences. *Psychiatry*, 43, 234–42.

Oakes, A. (1978). The Lazarus Syndrome: A Care Plan For The Unique Needs of Those Who've Died. *RN*, 41,6, 60–64.

Osis, K., Harroldsson, E. (1977). *At the Hour of Death*. New York: Avon Books.

Owens, J. E., Cook, E. W., Stevenson, I. (1990). Features of Near-Death Experience in Relation to Whether or Not Patients were Near Death. *Lancet*, 336, 11, 75–77.

Oye, R. K., Bellamy, P. E. (1991). Patterns of Resource Consumption in Medical Intensive Care. *Chest*, 99, 685–89.

Penfield, W., Rasmussen, T. (1950). *The Cerebral Cortex of Man: A Clinical Study of Localization of Function*. New York: MacMillan.

Penfield, W. (1955). The Role of Temporal Cortex in Certain Psychical Phenomena. *Journal of Mental Sciences*, 101, 451–65.

Persinger, M. A. (1987). *Neuropsychological Bases of God Beliefs*. New York: Praeger.

Plum, F. P., Posner, J. B. (1972). *Diagnosis of Stupor and Coma*. Edition 2. *Contemporary Neurology Series*. Philadelphia: F. A. Davis Co.

Rees, W. D. (1971). The Hallucinations of Widowhood. *British Medical Journal*, 4, 37–41.

Rothenberg, J. (1969). *Technicians of the Sacred*. New York: Anchor Books. 92–98.

Rothenberg, M. (1979). The Dying Child. In Call, J. D., Noshpitz, J. D., Cohen, R. L., et al., eds. *Basic Handbook of Child Psychiatry*. New York: Basic Books.

Schapira, D. V., Studnicki, J., Bradham, D. D. (1993, Feb. 10). Intensive Care, Survival and Expense of Treating Critically Ill Cancer Patients. *Journal of the American Medical Association*, 269, 783–86.

Schenk, L., Bear, D. (1981, Oct.). Multiple Personality and Related Dissociative Phenomena in Patients with Temporal Lobe Epilepsy. *American Journal of Psychiatry*, 138,10, 1311–16.

Schoenbeck, S. B. (1993, May). Exploring the Mystery of Near-Death Experiences. *American Journal of Nursing*, 93, 5, 43–46.

Schoonmaker, Fred. Personal Communication. (December 9, 1993). A Denver cardiologist, Schoonmaker has done electroencephalograms on his own patients resuscitated from cardiac arrest. He documented that 70–75 patients with isoelectric EEGs reported near-death experiences. He did not use temporal or deep cortical leads.

Schroter-Kunhardt, M. (1990). Erfahrungen Sterbender wahrend des klinischen todes. *Zeitschrift für Allgemein Medizin*, 66, 1014–21.

Schuster, D. P. (1992). Everything that Should Be Done—Not Everything that Can Be Done.

American Review of Respiratory Diseases, 145, 508–10.

Shackleton, C. H. (1984). The Psychology of Grief: A Review. *Advances in Behaviour, Research and Therapy*, 6, 153–205.

Stack-O'Sullivan, D. J. (1981, Dec.). Personality Correlates of Near-Death Experiences. *Dissertation Abstracts International 42*, 6, 2584–A.

Stevenson, I. (1983). Do We Need a New Word to Supplement "Hallucination"? *American Journal of Psychiatry*, 140, 1609–11.

Swedenborg, E. (1928). *Heaven and Hell*. New York: Swedenborg Foundation.

Taylor, G. R. (1979). *The Natural History of the Mind*. London: Penguin Book.

West. L. J. (1975). A Clinical and Theoretical Overview of Hallucinatory Phenomena. In Siegel, R. K., and West, L. J., eds. *Hallucinations: Behavior, Experience and Theory*. New York: Wiley.

Whinnery, J. E., Whinnery, A. M. (1990, July). Acceleration-Induced Loss of Consciousness. *Archives of Neurology*, 47, 764–76.

Who Might Survive the Death of the Body?

Charles Tart

It is clear to me that whatever mind is—mind, soul, essence, whatever you want to call it—it is not equivalent to the brain, or the body.

Charles Tart, Ph.D., a major voice in the field of consciousness studies and parapsychology, asks what evidence exists that the mind survives death. He concludes that consciousness may survive, but not the ordinary "I" who is conscious. Those materialists who reduce mind to brain, and see the death of the brain as the end of mind, he argues, have not accounted for phenomena he is studying. He sketches the current state of thinking in four major areas of parapsychology: telepathy, clairvoyance, precognition, and psychokinesis; then discusses out-of-body experiences and near-death experiences.

Tart is widely known for his careful scientific studies of altered states of consciousness and parapsychology, especially out-of-body experiences. Here he describes a controlled laboratory experiment with a woman who said that she habitually journeyed out of her body while asleep. He also reviews the recent case of Vicky, a blind woman who indicates that blind people are actually able to see during a near-death experience.

Charles Tart, Ph.D., has contributed to numerous articles and chapters on transpersonal and parapsychological states of consciousness. His books include *Altered States of Consciousness* (1969); *States of Consciousness* (1975); and *Psi: Scientific Studies of the Psychic Realm* (1977). After teaching for many years at the University of California in Davis, he recently joined the faculty at the Institute of Transpersonal Psychology in Palo Alto, California. This article is a version of his plenary lecture at the 1994 Institute of Noetic Sciences conference on "The Sacred Source: Life, Death and the Survival of Consciousness."

·⁓ Who Might Survive the Death of the Body? ⁓·

What is the scientific evidence for survival of the mind after death? After 25 years of studying this, I have come to two conclusions. One is that, as I die, after a period of confusion and fear, I won't really be too surprised if I regain consciousness. On the other hand, I will be very surprised if "I" regain consciousness. This is because so much of my ordinary self is dependent on a physical body and a physical environment. And without that sort of mold to shape the particulars of my consciousness, I suspect that things are going to be very different. And very interesting. I have discussed this as a detailed theory elsewhere (Tart, 1987), based on my systems theory approach to understanding states of consciousness (Tart, 1975).

I am trying to be objective about this topic, but on the other hand, I am a person, even though I attempt to be a scientist, and I have my biases. For one thing, I am sometimes afraid of death. Now it is not considered a very good thing to admit to being afraid of something, and yet when we don't admit to our fears, they control us, they become *implicit* prejudices that distort the way we live and die. So I want to be honest with you, that I may not be able to give a perfectly objective talk about death, because there are times when I am afraid of it. I suspect that I am not alone in my fear. I want to place my summary of the scientific evidence about survival into the context of two questions: "Who am I?" and "What does that mean for survival?"

MATERIALISM
The easiest position to cover that is supposed to be a scientific position, is the materialist position: life equals biology, mind equals biology, your thoughts, your feelings, your hopes, your fears are all electro-chemical reactions in the brain. The brain

obviously turns into mush after you die, leaving no more thoughts or feelings, so why worry about survival? We just have to tough it out and know that we are going to die. This is a very dominant position, and because we are Westerners, we believe it, whether we know it or not. That position is drummed into us all the time, as if it were scientific fact. But it is not actually scientific fact. It is a hypothesis, with some evidence for it, but hardly overwhelming evidence.

Also, I think we should recognize a certain psychological problem. Lurking in the background of many of our beliefs about survival is fear. If you believe that the soul survives death, and that you will be judged, then you may fear that you have an excellent chance of going to Hell, because you weren't good enough. The materialist position is marvelously psychologically appealing, because it rejects this belief. "Oh, materialists do not go to go to Hell; at least that fear is over." I don't think we recognize that psychological factor often enough, and how much it affects the way that we think about things.

Speaking as a working scientist, the main thing that I want to tell you about the materialist position is that it is not good science. The first rule of science is that you have to account for *all* the data, *all* the experience, *all* the information, all the facts that you can gather about something. And if your theory cannot account for all the facts, it is not very good. Well, the materialist equation of the mind with nothing but brain simply does not take into account all the facts. Of course, the brain has a lot to do with the mind, there is no doubt about it. We are working this personal bio-computer and it has its style. But that is not all that there is to mind. It is bad science simply to accept materialism without having looked at all the evidence.

PARAPSYCHOLOGY

The area of psychology that specifically looks at the things that don't fit is parapsychology. In this field basically you take all we know about the material world, the dominant understanding, and you set up a situation that is impossible, where nothing can happen. But, if something does happen, then there is something wrong with the completeness of your theories. So parapsychology has done things like set up telepathy experiments. Two people are put in different rooms, different buildings, sometimes partway around the world from each other, and there is no conceivable physical way that they can communicate with one another. And yet you can do very carefully and precisely controlled experiments to show that sometimes the receiver does pick up something that somebody else is trying to send. It almost never works 100 percent of the time—the results are usually at a low level—but too often for it to be coincidence, people pick up information from another living person's mind. And there are dozens and dozens of experiments, really well-controlled experiments.[1] In fact I would say that the experiments in parapsychology are generally far better quality experiments than in ordinary branches of science, because the criticism has been so intense that the methodology has gotten extremely good. Telepathy is one of what I call the big four psychic effects that we can't reasonably doubt, if we really look at the evidence. It suggests to me that mind is something more than brain.

A second major psychic phenomenon is clairvoyance, the direct perception of the physical world. Old classical experiments would do something like this: someone would thoroughly shuffle a deck of cards dozens of times without looking at it, then put it in a box, and lock it in a drawer. Nobody in the world knows what the order in that deck of cards is. A person then comes into the laboratory, and is asked to make a guess as to what the order of the deck of cards is. It works well enough above chance to know that sometimes the human mind can directly reach out and know the state of physical matter without any of the physical senses being involved.

Now already we can start to ask the question "Who am I?" Who am I if I have the potential (at least occasionally) to reach out into another mind, in spite of barriers of space, or reach directly into the material world, and know what the state of affairs is?

Precognition is the third of these four major phenomena, where you ask someone to predict the future, when the future is controlled by inherently random, unpredictable processes. If someone says that the sun will come up, we will not be terribly impressed. But for precognition tests someone says "Two hours from now, after you leave, I am going to very thoroughly shuffle this deck of cards. Would you write down *now* what the order of the cards will be?" Too often to account for by chance, people score significantly above chance. That is precognition. That means that our ordinary ideas about time are very useful for all sorts of ordinary things, but they are not ultimate. There are some things that the human mind can do that puts it out of ordinary time, in some sense.

Finally, the fourth of the big four is psychokinesis, the direct ability of the mind to affect matter. In the old days, they tried to make dice fall in a certain way with some Rube Goldberg-type machine throwing dice. Now it is all done with computers. You see a little black box with solid state circuits in it. Its internal workings are a total mystery to experimental subjects. It is making a red light and a green light blink at random. An experimenter says, "Make the green light blink more than the red light." And it works a good deal of the time. It is a small shift; instead of 50-50, you shift it up to 51%, 52%, but it keeps up. And of course nobody knows what they are doing. I mean, which chip do you push on? Which electron do you try to slow down or divert? It is incomprehensible. And yet sometimes, simply desiring has a direct effect on the physical world.

Now, again, "Who am I?" if, at times my mind can transcend time, if at times my mind can have a direct effect on the physical world? It does not happen that often, probably fortunately. People sometimes get kind of scared when psychic stuff works too well. That is a whole other topic. But it happens enough that I think, as educated Westerners, as people who have been taught to respect science, we have to know that we have very hard scientific data, well over a thousand experiments for all these parapsychological effects, effects which cannot, in theory, happen if the mind is nothing but the physical brain.

OUT-OF-BODY EXPERIENCES

There are other phenomena that begin to bear more directly on the survival question, even if they have not been investigated nearly as well. For example, out-of-the-body experiences (OBEs). Years ago, I was very fortunate to meet a young woman who, since childhood, had OBE experiences routinely, many nights of the week. In fact as a child, she thought that it was normal that you go to bed, you fall asleep, you have a dream, you float up near the ceiling for a few seconds, you have another dream, and you wake up and go to school. Isn't that what sleep is about? I was able to have her spend four nights in my sleep laboratory. She had electrodes attached to her head to measure her brain waves. That meant that she could not get out of bed without making the recording machine in the next room spray ink all over the walls! After she was ready to go to sleep, I would go off to another room and randomly select a five-digit sequence, and write it on a piece of paper. Then I would go in and put it up on a shelf near the ceiling by a clock, so that even a person walking around in the room could not read it. I told her "If you get out of your body, not only do I want you to wake up afterwards and tell me about it, but try to read the number and take a look at the time, so we get the timing down right." Well, she had a total of seven or eight OBEs. During these she was in a brain wave state that I had never seen before. I have looked at a lot of records of people sleeping and dreaming, and this was like the dreaming state Stage One EEG, except there was a lot of slowed down alpha rhythm. I even showed it to the world's foremost EEG expert on sleep and we had 100 percent agreement. He said "It looks weird to me, too." I wish we had actually known what it meant. But she certainly was not near death.

On all nights but one, though, she said, "I'm sorry. I floated out of my body, but I was on the other side of the room, and I could not look at the number before I got back into my body. On the one occasion when she said she saw the number, she correctly reported that it was 25132. Now that is odds of a hundred thousand to one to guess that on a single try (Tart, 1968). I would have thought that, in a rational world, people all over the country would say "Let's find the people who can do this, and let's study them extensively." But as you know, it did not happen.

THE NEAR-DEATH EXPERIENCE

The near-death experience that we all have now heard of may start with an OBE. But generally it changes into a profound altered state of consciousness, not just ordinary consciousness that happens to be off to the side of the room. People think differently, they know differently, and so forth.

There is a very interesting out-of-body case experienced by a woman named Vicky at age thirteen. She said:

> In that near-death experience I would describe it as going through a pipe or a tube, type of feeling. And I was shocked, I was just totally in awe. I mean I can't even describe it, because I thought, "so that's what it is like!" And I saw my body, and just before I got sucked into the tube, I was up on the ceiling and I saw my body being prepared for surgery, and I knew that it was me. (Editoral Staff, 1994)

Now this is a typical start for many near-death experiences, and she went on to have many of the elements of a classical near-death experience. She met other figures, she met a deity-like figure, she knew things she did not ordinarily know, and so forth, before coming back.

Near-death experiences change people's lives extraordinarily. Since a near-death experience that takes five minutes can produce more change in your life than everything else put together, obviously psychology must study near-death experience intensely. Right? Wrong. It is a very funny profession that I am in. Incidentally, if you are into changing your life, while the near-death experience is generally the most intense, I don't recommend it; the *near* part is tricky, as you all know! Most people who come that near don't give us interesting reports; they get buried!

Returning to Vicky's near-death experience, Vicky says:

> I was born premature and went down to one pound 14 ounces. They had this new airlock incubator to save babies such as myself, and they did not realize they were giving us too much oxygen. There were approximately 50,000 babies in this country who were blinded in that way, from 1947 through 1952. My optic nerve was destroyed. I can't see anything. No light, no shadows, no nothing. Ever. And so I have never been able to understand even the concept of light.

This blind girl had a near-death experience, and she could see. She was amazed at the near-death quality of sight. Now that says that there are frontiers of the human mind that we cannot begin to grasp in our ordinary state of consciousness.

It is clear to me that whatever mind is—mind, soul, essence, whatever you want to call it—it is not equivalent to the brain, or the body (Tart, 1981, 1993). That does not mean that we should neglect the body. We should treat it with great respect; it is the temple of our soul. But don't assume that whatever consciousness is, it is just like being in a body. It's like we have been sitting at the keyboard of this personal computer for so long that we don't know that there is another world out there. But there *is* another world out there.

There are two quite striking lessons for life that come out of the near-death experiences that touch me very deeply, and they are the typical reasons for coming back to life. One of those, quite common, is that you can still contribute to knowledge and human happiness in life. More important is that most people come back because they have not learned how to love yet. If you have not learned how to love, you have blown it. You might say, in an academic metaphor, that love is a required course. You will have to repeat it if you don't pass it. Most of us worry an awful lot about *being* loved. But I would emphasize that the lesson is rather learning how to *give* love.

There have been many other reasons that people have come back from the near-death experience. But there is one that has never been reported, as far as I know. No one has ever had their life review, talked with the Being of Light and come back concluding: "I really should spend more time at the office." If our interest in death teaches us nothing more than the importance of love, that is wonderful!

NOTE

1. For a general overview of modern parapsychology, both methods and findings, I recommend books by Broughton (1991), Edge, Morris, Palmer and Rush (1986), Jahn and Dunne (1987), Targ and Harary (1984), Targ and Puthoff (1977), and Tart (1977). For those who want to access the main scientific literature directly, the *Journal of the American Society for Psychical Research*, the *Journal of the Society for Psychical Research*, the *Journal of Parapsychology*, the *Journal of Scientific Exploration* and the *European Journal of Parapsychology* are the primary outlets where studies and theory are published. The journal *Exceptional Human Experience* also publishes cutting-edge work in this area and provides comprehensive guides to past and current litertature.

REFERENCES

Broughton, R. (1991). *Parapsychology: The Controversial Science.* New York: Ballantine.

Edge, H., Morris, R., Palmer, J. and Rush, J. (1986). *Foundations of Parapsychology: Exploring the Boundaries of Human Capability.* Boston: Routledge & Kegan Paul.

Editorial staff, (1994, Spring). Vicky: A blind woman's two near-death experiences. *Vital Signs,* 12, No. 2, 3–6,7.

Jahn, R.G. and Dunne, B. J. (1987). *Margins of Reality: The Role of Consciousness in the Physical World.* New York: Harcourt Brace Jovanovich.

Targ, R. and Harary, K. (1984). *The Mind Race: Understanding and Using Psychic Abilities.* New York: Villard.

Targ, R. and Puthoff, H. E. (1977). *Mind Reach: Scientists Look at Psychic Ability.* New York: Delacorte Press/Eleanor Friede.

Tart, C. (1968). A Psychophysiological study of out-of-body experiences in a selected subject. *Journal of the American Society for Psychical Research,* 62, 3–27.

Tart, C. (1975). *States of Consciousness.* New York: E. P. Dutton.

Tart, C. (1977). *Psi: Scientific Studies of the Psychic Realm.* New York: E. P. Dutton.

Tart, C. (1981). Transpersonal realities or neurophysiological illusions? Toward a dualistic theory of consciousness. In R. Valle and R. von Eckartsberg (eds.). *The Metaphors of Consciousness.* New York: Plenum, 199–222.

Tart, C. (1987). Altered states of consciousness and the possibility of survival of death. In J. Spong (ed.), *Consciousness and Survival: An Interdisciplinary Inquiry into the Possibility of Life Beyond Biological Death.* Sausalito, CA: Institute of Noetic Sciences, 27–56.

Tart, C. (1993). Mind embodied: Computer-generated virtual reality as a new, dualistic-interactive model for transpersonal psychology. In K. Rao (Ed.), *Cultivating Consciousness: Enhancing Human Potential, Wellness and Healing.* Westport, CT: Praeger, 123–37.

·⁓ 21 ⁓·

Evaluating Near-Death Testimony

Carol Zaleski

We can turn to the task of interpreting near-death visions with a renewed sense of the rightness of treating them as socially conditioned, imaginative, and yet nonetheless real and revelatory experiences.

Carol Zaleski, Ph.D., is a religious studies scholar. She made an important advance in near-death research by analyzing medieval cases of NDEs and showing the role of cultural imagination in shaping such spiritual visions. In her book *Otherworld Journeys: Accounts of Near-Death Experiences in Medieval and Modern Times* (1987), she explores the parallels between medieval and modern NDEs. Zaleski identifies four models of medieval Christian otherworld journey narration: 1. Apocalypse, as in a legendary elaboration on St. Paul's biblical vision, 2. Miracle Story, as in Pope Gregory the Great's *Dialogues,* 3. Conversion, as in the vision of the Anglo-Saxon Drythelm, and 4. Pilgrimage, as in the Irish St. Patrick's Purgatory. Some of these accounts of otherworld journeys offer wide-eyed stories of Hell's torments and Heaven's bliss; others, like Gregory's, take a more cautious approach, interviewing witnesses and exploring symbolic meanings.

Curiously, before Dante, many accounts of Hell placed it above this world, not below. Not so curiously, as texts circulated, they often served a morally and religiously didactic purpose. For example, after Drythelm was guided to witness Hell's horrors, then Heaven's clear Light, he returned to this world to join a Benedictine monastery. By the mid-thirteenth century the motif of journeying to the other world and back was well-known, because it was used widely in sermons and chronicles.

Zaleski also tackles the question of the interpretation of NDEs, and in this essay she provides a valuable outline of the main currents of current theological opinion on NDEs. At one extreme some believers see NDEs as a Satanic trick, or question them because they seem to offer otherworldly escape from social responsibilities. But other believers, including clergy, see NDEs as a great help to dying people which can certainly strengthen traditional faith.

Zaleski's interpretation is both imaginative and pragmatic. She emphasizes that the evidential character of NDEs is not possible to settle empirically. The role of cultural imaginative forms, she stresses, is a strong influence in shaping otherworldly visions, and this must be incorporated into the analyses. This does not negate their value for faith, however, because transcendent visions can bring about significant moral and spiritual transformations. Zaleski rejects both the reductive materialistic extreme and the naïve acceptance of NDEs at face value. She takes a middle path, acknowledging the reality of these transforming experiences, but holding them up for comparison to the full range of traditional religious experiences.

Carol Zaleski, Ph.D., teaches Religious Studies at Smith College in Massachusetts. Her book *Otherworld Journeys* is being translated into Japanese, German, and Slovene. She has published articles on near-death experiences, spiritual practices, and William James. Her 1996 book is *The Life of the World to Come: Near-Death Experience and Christian Hope.*

◡ Evaluating Near-Death Testimony ◡

EXPERIENTIAL CLAIMS

One conclusion to which the present study leads is that the West has seen no steady progress from literal to literary use of the otherworld journey motif. The line between fiction and confession is necessarily blurry, but contemporary near-death reports—like their medieval predecessors—at least claim to represent actual experience. In this final chapter we will consider whether it is possible to take this claim seriously without being naïve.

Some might feel inclined to disregard the question, as do the social and literary historians who concern themselves only with the cultural transmission of otherworld journey imagery. For if we take visionary accounts at face value, as a factual description of what happens after death, we run the risk of enclosing ourselves in a shrunken utopia, cut off from the scientific and historical awareness that is our culture's special gift. Theologians, as much as other intellectuals, might wish to ignore experiential claims in order to avoid having to weigh testimony that either conflicts with accepted religious and scientific principles or brings the mysteries of life, death, and the hereafter embarrassingly close. It is safer to treat the otherworld journey solely as a metaphor or literary motif that illustrates a psychological or moral truth. In this way, we render it harmless; we attenuate the visionary virus until it is so weak that it produces immunity instead of contagion.

This approach fails to account, however, for what makes the other world such a powerful symbol. We have seen that the otherworld journey motif remains potent only as long as it retains at least a hint of correspondence to a sensed, dreamed, or imagined reality. An image like the review of deeds continues to have some vitality because we imagine ourselves undergoing such an experience, we visualize this experience as taking place in another world, and we sense that the image has further possibilities as yet unexplored. By contrast, an expression like "The road to hell is paved with good intentions," which we recognize as exclusively metaphorical, seems trite. It has become a dead circuit, no longer connected to real or imagined experience. The experiential dimension must therefore be considered if we are to understand the whole range of otherworld journey imagery—from its vestiges in our ordinary discourse to the more overt forms found in near-death literature.

It is, moreover, unfair to the individuals who report near-death experience to discount their claims in advance. The current controversy surrounding the rights and needs of the dying—and the fact that many people are turning to books like *Life After Life* for guidance or consolation—puts us under an obligation to assess near-death literature in an informed and sympathetic way.

It is a good sign, then, that some religious thinkers have taken an interest in interpreting near-death literature. Before I make suggestions of my own, it will be useful to consider the main currents of theological opinion on the subject.

When *Life After Life* appeared, it provoked widely varying reactions (Moody, 1975). In *Reflections on Life After Life*, Moody remarks that there were some among the clergy who accused him of selling "cheap grace," while others thanked him for producing a book that was such an asset to their pastoral work with the dying and bereaved (Moody, 1977). This pattern of response continues as public awareness of near-death experience grows. The loudest reaction against *Life After Life* and its successors comes from conservative Christians who see these books as a Satanic trick, designed to lull us into a false sense of security about the future life, to lure us into occult practices such as astral projection, to beguile us into accepting the advances of demons disguised as departed spirits, and to sell us a secular (but fundamentally diabolic) bill of goods about salvation without Christ. At the same time, as we noted above, there has been a proliferation of "born again" versions of near-death experience—complete with recollections of hell which, according to Maurice Rawlings, are "repressed" by the Life After Lifers (Rawlings, 1978).

On the other side, Moody reports that Christian clergy often tell him that *Life After Life* has strengthened their faith in the traditional Church teachings which it is their office to represent. It gave one minister the confidence to affirm at a funeral that the woman he eulogized had gone to join her deceased husband with Christ: "I wasn't speaking figuratively or symbolically; I meant it. This gave them comfort...." (Moody, 1977, 54). Near-death testimonials play a similar role in the pages of *Guideposts*, *Soul Searcher*, *Spiritual Frontiers*, and other magazines of Christian or Christian/spiritualist inspiration.

Among professional Christian theologians, the idea that near-death testimony might make a case for life after death has received critical attention both favorable and dissenting. A few mavericks—notably John Hick and Paul Badham—suggest that clinical and parapsychological evidence might provide just the empirical elixir we need to invigorate our culture's withered eschatological imagination. Nonetheless, neither of these theologians relies on empirical arguments alone. In *Death and Eternal Life*, Hick combines the evidence from mediumship and parapsychology with scientific, philosophical, and moral grounds for conceiving the future life on an evolutionary model. Badham's view is that near-death experiences and other psychic phenomena, although they provide no guarantee of immortality, can at least disarm naturalistic objections and make room for a faith founded on the experience of relationship to God (Badham, 1980,1982).

In general, however, academic circles have not seen much theological debate over the implications of near-death research. The predominant trend has been to ignore or repudiate efforts to find evidence for existence after death. One reason for this is that many Christian thinkers believe that the idea of personal survival has been rendered obsolete by recent scientific, philosophical, and linguistic discoveries. Beyond this standard and widespread skepticism, however, several generations of liberal and neo-orthodox theologians have warned against preoccupation with the hereafter. It is a narcissistic distraction from the ethical and social mission of the church, they argue, and it is moreover both childish and arrogant to expect more from rational or empirical proofs than from biblical promises. A Lutheran pastor writes, "If life after death could be empirically verified 'beyond a shadow of a doubt,' then there would seem to be little need for faith."[1]

For some religious critics, the most serious flaw in near-death literature is its portrait of death as a pleasant, gentle transition. Converging streams of Freudian, existentialist, and neo-orthodox thought, along with modern biblical scholarship, have produced a strong sentiment among theologians that it is essential to the Christian message to affirm the reality and sting of death.[2] Ever since Oscar Cullmann drew (perhaps overdrew) the distinction between the resurrection faith of Christianity and the Greek philosophical idea of natural immortality, this contrast has been a recurrent theme, even a rallying cry, of theological writing.[3] Stephen Vicchio speaks for many when he complains that "the empty tomb for Kübler-Ross and Moody is superfluous if not redundant. There is no need for Easter if we are immortal."[4]

Those who pit Cullmann against Kübler-Ross and her ilk are heirs to a long tradition of Christian polemic against the opponent—pagan or straw man—who would ground our hopes in knowledge rather than faith, in nature rather than sacred history, in the soul's intrinsic purity rather than God's willingness to cleanse it. Pragmatically speaking, however, the real issue in these debates is whether the alternative views make a difference in religious life; do they breed complacency or catalyze conversion? The answer to this question cannot be decided solely on biblical, doctrinal, or philosophical grounds. A great deal depends on social climate and personal temperament; as I shall suggest below, the history of religion tells us that similar eschatological conceptions may serve, under different circumstances, either to awaken efforts to merit an afterlife or to make such efforts redundant by feeding people pie-in-the-sky consolations.

In the current atmosphere of skepticism and cultural fragmentation, fears and doubts about survival of death can be just as morally and spiritually paralyzing as a monolithic faith in its certainty. Those who testify to the transforming effect of near-death experience often say that their conviction that death is not the end gave them the freedom and energy to change their way of life. On the other hand, when the quest for immortality is isolated from other religious concerns, as in psychical research, it can become something tawdry, egoistic, and this-worldly. So, too, medieval Christian vision literature runs the gamut from profound to mechanical understanding of penance, purgatory, and conversion. Perhaps the doctrine itself is not at fault, but only its abuse; the present danger is not that people will become convinced of immortality, but that the whole subject will be trivialized by a narrow focus on the case for or against survival.

Clearly, a new approach is needed; to make near-death testimony an arena for restaging old philosophical or theological battles will not suffice. It appears to be impossible, in any case, to determine objectively whether near-death reports are accurate or inaccurate depictions of the future life. It might therefore be more fruitful for theologians to consider near-death visions as works of the religious imagination, whose function is to communicate meaning through symbolic forms rather than to copy external facts. This is the aspect of near-death literature that I have attempted to highlight.

DOUBLE VISION

The purpose of comparing medieval and modern vision narratives has been to benefit from the stereoscopic effect, the depth perception, which the juxtaposition of two separate perspectives can provide. It will be helpful, then, to review the results of this comparison before proceeding to generalize about the religious implications of otherworld journey narration.

In broad terms, the similarities we found were as follows: both medieval and modern narratives depict the death and revival of individuals whose experience is held up as an example of what we can expect in our own final moments. The manner of death—departure of the spirit from the body—is described in frankly dualistic terms, the separated spirit looking down upon its former dwelling place with indifference or contempt.

After leaving the body, the visionary finds himself in a liminal condition hovering just overhead and watching the scene of crisis in a mood of detachment. The beginning of the otherworld journey proper is signaled by the advent of a guide and by motifs of visionary topography and travel such as paths, valleys, and tunnels. The guide, who is the narrator's alter ego, escorts the visionary from place to place, pushing the story forward and interpreting the inner significance of otherworld scenes; he thus calls attention to the symbolic character of the other world, and to the need for spiritual instruction in this life and the next.

In the pivotal episode of both medieval and modern journeys, the visionary confronts himself by means of various graphic representations. He meets his thoughts, words, and deeds; learns the weight of his soul; or reviews his life in a book, play, or movie—and in such fashion brings judgment upon himself.

Although medieval hell and purgatory scenes find scarcely any counterparts in the near-death testimony collected by Moody and his colleagues, motifs of paradise topography are much the same in both periods: shining edifices, gardens, meadows, heavenly cities, and so forth. In addition, the ultimate experience of contemplative vision, though treated only rarely and briefly by medieval otherworld journey narratives, is consistently described as a comprehensive vision of the whole, in which cognitive and affective powers fuse. It is a moment when the dramatic action of the otherworld journey seems to be suspended and unmediated awareness floods in; but an instant later the play resumes, a message is formulated, and the visionary feels compelled, against his desires, to return to life.

Upon revival, the visionary is physically and spiritually changed. Reticent and overwhelmed at first, he is eventually persuaded to communicate his discoveries and share his mission with others. Once an ordinary *vir quidam*, average guy, or "just a housewife," the visionary takes on a prophetic role, teaching by word and by the example of a transformed life.

We also saw that in both periods the otherworld journey narrative evolves through the visionary's conversation with others, and that the narrator shapes the account to conform to the conventions of the genre in which it will appear, whether sermon, allegory, chronicle, Christian polemic, contemporary best-seller, tabloid testimonial, statistical study, or television talk show. In all these different formats, the vision story retains its didactic aim: the other world is described not to satisfy theoretical curiosity, but to serve as a goad toward transformation.

There is bound to be disagreement over whether these recurrent motifs—guides, paths, barriers, encounters with deeds, and so forth—constitute a universal lexicon or whether they provide only the syntactic structure of the otherworld vision. Many of the areas of similarity appear to be formal rather than material; for when we fill in the picture, supplying the emotional content and the culturally specific features that make up a concrete vision, we discover significant divergences.

Thus, despite the structural resemblance between descriptions of the soul's exit from the body, we find that medieval visions exemplify the two deaths theme, while modern visions portray only the comforting prospect of a good death. So, too, although the guide is essential in both periods as a narrative expedient, didactic instrument, guardian of the threshold, and psychopomp, his character and relation to the visionary are understood quite differently. In medieval visions, the guide stands for hierarchical and feudal authority; in modern visions, he represents benevolent parental acceptance. His role appears to be determined by presuppositions about social and family structure, judicial process, education, and pastoral or psychological cure of souls.

The most glaring difference is the prominence in medieval accounts of obstacles and tests, purificatory torments, and outright doom. Aside from continuing the hellfire traditions of early Christian apocalyptic, medieval narratives serve as vehicles for the consolidation of Catholic teachings on purgatory and penance. In modern accounts, on the other hand, a sense of inevitable progress softens the rigors of final reckoning; the review of deeds is transformed from an ordeal into an educational experience; and the only serious obstacle is the barrier marking the point of no return. These narratives are shaped throughout by optimistic, democratic, "healthy-minded" principles that transparently reflect a contemporary ideology and mood.

The contrast to medieval accounts is sharpened when we set near-death narratives against the background of nineteenth- and twentieth-century spiritualism and its intellectual offshoot, the psychical research movement. The spiritualist other world, like that of near-death literature, is a social utopia, mirroring the progressive causes with which many spiritualists and psychical researchers have been connected: prison, insane asylum, and school reform; abolition; feminism; socialism; Christian perfectionism; and other high-minded liberal concerns have been validated by mediumistic and clairvoyant descriptions of the ideal conditions of the spirit world.[5]

Although ours is a less fertile period for generating utopian schemes, near-death literature expresses and provides otherworld validation for similar progressivist ideas. It is no wonder, then, that it provokes the ire of conservative religious thinkers, whose objections to current near-death studies echo earlier reactions against spiritualism.[6]

In its otherworld cosmology, as well, near-death literature is as close to spiritualism as it is distant from medieval visions. Medieval vision narratives, as we saw, are the outcome of a long history of development and suppression of cosmological schemes for the soul's journey to God; they retain vestiges, sometimes sublimated or confused, of older conceptions of the planetary spheres as places of interrogation and punishment. Naturally, this idiom is completely foreign to modern accounts; near-death literature reflects instead a short history of attempts to reconcile the spirit world with the world of

Faraday, Maxwell, Darwin, and Einstein. Though less inclined than spiritualism to localize the other world in the outer atmosphere, modern narratives make similar use of scientific vocabulary—energy, magnetism, vibrations, dimensions, evolution—now supplemented by terms drawn from relativity theory, quantum mechanics, and holography to update the imaginative cosmology.

In focusing on the reports of those who return from death, however, modern accounts are closer to their medieval counterparts than to spiritualist literature. The return-from-death story, unlike mediumistic accounts of the afterlife, conforms to the pattern of a conversion narrative. Rather than mapping the spirit world in great detail, the return-from-death story emphasizes the visionary's special task, the message he is charged to bring back to humanity, and the transformation of his way of life.

On the other hand, medieval and modern narratives differ considerably in their understanding of the nature of the visionary's message, commission, and conversion. Moral rehabilitation is too vague a goal for medieval visions; they are concerned, as we have seen, to promote particular penitential and monastic institutions. Modern narratives, however, advocate the renunciation of worries and fears and conversion to a life of love, learning, and service; this is an individualistic, anti-institutional, humanistic ideal, of which churches, hospices, and other service organizations may be the incidental beneficiaries. Considered closely, then, the differences between medieval and modern accounts of return-from-death conversion are as impressive as the similarities.

These comparative observations force us to conclude that the visionaries of our own age are no more free of cultural influence than those of less pluralistic eras. We have seen that the otherworld journey story—which comprises every level of the experience to which we have access, as well as every layer of narrative reconstruction—is through and through a work of the socially conditioned religious imagination; it is formed in conversation with society, even if it takes place in the solitude of the deathbed and in the private chamber of inner experience.

Once we recognize this, we can no longer insist that *Life After Life,* Gregory's *Dialogues,* or any other work of visionary eschatology paints a true picture of what occurs at the extreme border of life. If we wish to avoid the self-defeating extremes of shallow relativism and naïve affirmation, then our only recourse is to focus on the imaginative and symbolic character of otherworld visions.

The remainder of this chapter will consider whether this approach can yield a fuller understanding of near-death literature and of visionary and religious testimony in general. I should explain at the outset, however, that I am not attempting to provide a systematic theory of near-death visions. Such a theory would require the collaborative efforts of many different interpreters. Perhaps the solution to the puzzle of near-death experience will always remain in the distance, drawing us along by receding as we approach it. What I offer here is not a conclusion designed to close the book on the subject, but a set of suggestions and thought experiments intended to point out promising directions for further inquiry.

Although this discussion is preliminary and open-ended, it is guided by certain assumptions about the symbolic character of religious discourse; in case these assumptions are not by now apparent, I will make them explicit.

In speaking of *symbolism*, I have in mind a definition that the reader may not share but may be willing to grant for the purpose of discussion. According to most dictionaries, a symbol is an image or object that represents something beyond itself. To this minimal definition I would add—following the view expressed in various ways by Samuel Taylor Coleridge, Paul Tillich, Ernst Cassirer, Suzanne Langer, and Paul Ricoeur, among others—that a symbol participates in the reality that it represents. It does not copy or fully contain that reality, but it does communicate some of its power. Unlike a metaphor, it cannot adequately be translated into conceptual terms.

By *religious imagination*, I understand the capacity to create or to appreciate religious symbols. In this book, we have caught a glimpse of some of the features of the religious imagination. We have seen that it works not only with universal patterns—such as death and birth—but also with culturally specific and idiosyncratic material, and that it can fuse the universal and the particular into a seamless narrative whole.

Connected to this understanding of symbol and religious imagination is an assumption about the nature of religious discourse and of theology. *Theology*, as I understand it, is a discipline of critical reflection on religious experience and religious language. As such, no matter how objective or systematic it becomes, it cannot escape the fundamental limitations that apply to religious discourse in general.

To put it bluntly, I do not believe that any of our notions of God, the soul, or the other world are likely to be true in the ordinary sense of the word. One reason for this is human weakness: we are too thick-headed, twisted, or frightened to see clearly. Another reason, which perhaps brings less discredit, is that we have no mode of expression that combines the virtues of analytic and symbolic thought: our concepts are too abstract and one-dimensional while our images and symbols are too concrete; we sense that both modes of understanding are necessary, yet they seem incompatible. For this and other reasons that have been adduced by countless philosophers and religious thinkers, there is no sensory, imaginative, or intellectual form capable of fully expressing the transcendent. We can intuit and be forever changed by a higher reality, but we cannot apprehend or describe it in the direct and unequivocal manner with which we seem to know the objects of ordinary experience. Such understanding as we do receive of the transcendent comes to us through symbols, and it is through symbols that we communicate this understanding to one another.

Thus, although theology involves analytic thought, its fundamental material is symbol. Its task is to assess the health of our symbols, for when one judges a symbol, one cannot say whether it is true or false, but only whether it is vital or weak. When a contemporary theologian announces, for example, that God is dead or that God is not only Father but also Mother, he or she is not describing the facts per se, but is evaluating the potency of our culture's images for God—their capacity to evoke a sense of relationship to the transcendent.

To say that theology is a diagnostic discipline is also to say that its method is pragmatic. In evaluating religious ideas and images, theology deals with ranges of experience that cannot be verified—which even overflow our normal categories of thought. One need not abandon the idea that there is an ultimate truth in order to recognize that for now, at least, pragmatic criteria must be used. If we have no direct sensory or conceptual access to the reality for which we aim, then we must judge those images and ideas valid that serve a remedial function, healing the intellect and the will. In this sense, all theology is pastoral theology, for its proper task is not to describe the truth but to promote and assist the quest for truth.

I suggest, therefore, that a pragmatic method and a sensitivity to symbol must go hand in hand if we wish to give a fair hearing to the claims of near-death literature. If we fully recognize the symbolic nature of near-death testimony (and accept the limits that imposes on us), then in the end we will be able to accord it a value and a validity that would not otherwise be possible; this in turn will yield further insight into the visionary, imaginative, and therapeutic aspects of religious thought in general.

CORPOREAL IMAGERY

The advantage of paying close attention to the way in which otherworld visions reflect imaginative modes of thought becomes evident when we look at visionary accounts of the soul's exit from the body. We have seen that near-death reports, like their medieval predecessors, presume an old-fashioned dualism that most contemporary philosophers and theologians find inadequate to deal with the complexities of mind-body interaction. For some, this makes it difficult to take near-death visions seriously. A philosophy professor told me that although he was fascinated by near-death studies, he would hate to have to give up his hard-won sophistication and go back to thinking of the soul as "housed in the body like an oyster in a shell."[7] He could not decide whether to heed his philosophical training or the empirical data of out-of-body experience; one or the other would have to go.

Fortunately, however, a third alternative becomes available if we enact what I have called the Copernican revolution of regarding the other world as the domain of imagination and interpret its features accordingly. Without requiring adherence to any particular school of philosophical or psychological idealism, this revolution or change in perspective allows us to reclaim a whole range of imagery and experiential testimony that we might otherwise have to reject on theoretical grounds. Not only dualism and somatomorphism but also personification imagery, theatrical and cosmological symbolism, and externalization of deeds can be understood and valued as imaginative forms rather than descriptive models. They provide coherent patterns for dramatizing inner experience, yet they entail no particular metaphysics. They have a logic of their own, but if we try to grasp them in theoretical terms, we lay hold of nothing but confusion; and, like other category errors, this can lead to unwarranted skepticism.

Several vexing issues are clarified, then, if we view otherworld visions as artifacts of the imagination; most important, it should silence those critics who invoke the "fallacy of misplaced concreteness" or similar vetoes against the claims of near-death literature. If the other world is the inner world projected on the stage of the imagined cosmos, then here, if anywhere, is the place where concrete and graphic, embodied and animated principles belong. When we think theoretically, we must guard against spatializing and hypostatizing our ideas; perhaps we could not think creatively at all, however, if we lacked the capacity to imagine, though only subliminally, a realm in which our ideas can act. For this reason, I have suggested that many symbolic and even metaphorical expressions contain latent reference to another world.

The concrete imagery of near-death visions is dictated not only by their imaginative character but also by their narrative quality. The otherworld journey, as we have seen, is at its very roots a story. In order to fulfill its narrative purpose of engaging interest and its didactic purpose of impelling the audience from ideology to action, it must portray the afterlife as an active realm, and the soul as a protagonist whose experiences epitomize and interpret those of earthly life. If the soul must take on the shape of the body for that purpose, then so be it; if near-death visions had to conform to the requirements of abstract philosophical theology they would make dull stories indeed.

In the context of religious storytelling, then, it is not necessarily progress when, in deference to subtler understandings of spiritual perfection, we pluck off the limbs, erase the features, and shave our image of the soul into a bald symmetrical bit of geometry, incapable of motion or life. The same is true of images of the divine; attempts to picture God as transcending time, space, and gender may end by making God appear unsubstantial, neuter, and inert. In either case, the religious imagination is at work; the question is whether it works vigorously, harnessed and disciplined by spiritual practice, or whether it works lamely, hindered by misplaced theoretical scruples.

Perhaps there is no need to forgo speaking of the divine or the self in ways that feed the imagination. This is the view William Blake endorses when he urges us to imagine God as a person rather than a metaphysical principle:

> God Appears & God is Light
> To those poor Souls who dwell in Night
> But does a Human Form Display
> To those who Dwell in Realms of day.[8]

Blake's attitude is a welcome antidote to the intellectualism that has poisoned academic theology; but his insistence on anthropomorphism is misguided. The point is to give up dull abstractions, not to espouse one form of imagery over another. Even the most vivid images for God and the soul can lose potency with time. Corporeal imagery can become tyrannical, as St. Augustine discovered during the long period in which he struggled to free himself from a childishly materialist understanding of God, good, and evil; sometimes what is most needed is a fresh gust of iconoclasm, a healthy disdain for imaginative forms. When an archetype degenerates to a stereotype, then the laws of religious imagination no longer bind us to it, but call on us to register the changes that a new situation demands. At its best, theology is the art of detecting and serving these changing needs of religious symbol systems; thus, it proceeds in a rhythm of creation and destruction rather than a progressive conquest of truth.

If we view theology in this way, as an essentially therapeutic rather than theoretic discipline, it is easier to come to terms with religious change while maintaining respect for tradition. Religious teaching is an art, an activity, and an interaction with others; doctrine is only its by-product. A gifted religious teacher is not only able to transmit a tradition, but also to read the historical and personal situation and respond appropriately, discerning spontaneously what is required. Similarly, the modes of speculative and systematic religious thought that we call theology succeed when they are attuned to the needs of their times. What is needed is not the pursuit of superficial "relevance" for its own sake, but a balance between preservation and innovation. Theology should maintain links to the authoritative sources and stored wisdom of the past, while remaining flexible enough to alter doctrinal formulas for the sake of progress or reformation in religious life. Such flexibility is only possible if we acknowledge that theology, like the primary acts of religious teaching and inquiry which are its material, has to do not with truth-telling but with truth-seeking.

This is especially true of eschatological doctrines; within every major tradition they vary greatly not only in ideological content but also in the extent to which they permit the imagination to visualize a concrete other world. If we recognize that religious teaching is a therapeutic art, then we can see the value of teachings which are evasive on the subject of an afterlife—from Jesus' parabolic sayings about the Kingdom of God to Thoreau's insistence on "one world at a time"—yet we can appreciate the elaborate depictions of heaven and hell that from a Christian legacy in sermon, scholastic sententia, and cathedral stone. We can acknowledge that the Buddha, as "Supreme Physician," correctly diagnosed the condition of his hearers when he refused to satisfy their curiosity about the destiny of saints after death, and when he maintained silence on the other leading metaphysical issues of his day, yet we can also see the *dharma* reflected in the Pure Land sects, which promise rebirth in a lush celestial paradise.

Gregory the Great, whose voice has been so prominent in the Christian literature of the other world, speaks directly to this point:

> The medicine that lessens one disease adds force to another; and the bread that enhances the life of the strong destroys that of little ones. Therefore the speech of teachers should be shaped according to the condition of the hearers.[9]

In short, when we sit in judgment on traditional or newly coined conceptions of God, the soul, or immortality, we should consider the context in which they appear, rather than measure them against a narrow intellectualist standard.

THE QUESTION OF INTERPRETATION

The present study has demonstrated the need to take into account the imaginative, narrative, didactic, and therapeutic character of eschatological visionary literature; at the same time it has yielded a guiding principle for the interpretation of religious discourse in general. This approach not only helps us to come to terms with the varied religious expressions of our own culture but also contributes to our effort to understand other traditions. Recognizing the imaginative character of religious utterances does not entail renouncing our faith in an ultimate and objective truth, but it does allow us to stop pitting one set of beliefs against another. It means that the hope for reconciliation does not depend on our ability to identify areas of conceptual agreement or to dissolve apparent differences among the world's religions into a vague consensus. Moreover, it enhances historical self-awareness to learn that, as the study of near-death narratives makes plain, we are not cut off from our myth-making past. Like our ancestors, and like people of other cultures today, we come into contact with reality in ways that are shaped by language, social structure, geography, and weather, along with the particular forces that differentiate us from our neighbors. If we can appreciate this in ourselves, we can appreciate it in others. We need not strip the temples and unclothe the gods in order to discover affinities between different religious world-views.

Yet the benefits of this outlook can be ours only if we are willing to renounce the notion that some original and essential religious experience can be discriminated from subsequent layers of cultural shaping. This is the error in method against which theologian Gordon Kaufman warns:

> Our "religious experience," whatever this turns out to be, is never a raw, preconceptual, pre-linguistic experience, the undialectical foundation on which theology can be built. It (like all the rest of experience) is always a construction or composite, heavily dependent for its form and qualities on the learned terms and concepts which give it particular shape. (Kaufman, 1975, 6)

In a sense, this observation can serve to protect the integrity of experiential testimony. If we heed Kaufman's rejection of the notion of raw experience, then we will not make the assumption that the visionary who sees Christ or Krishna is only "labeling" an underlying experience which can be described more accurately and directly as encounter with a "being of light" or the "higher self." As I have suggested, such modern expressions may seem more palatable, but they are no less culturally determined or mythically cultivated.

For Kaufman, the fact that we have no access to uncultivated religious experience means that theology should be seen as an act of deliberate imaginative construction, finding its materials in reflection on our language and social experience rather than private oracles. The advantage of this position is that it calls on religious thinkers to acknowledge and take responsibility for their own reflective and creative work in framing ideas of the universe and of God. Its disadvantage is primarily practical: if we follow Kaufman's suggestion that theology should be related to but not rooted in individual religious experience, then we run the risk of widening the gap between the amateur theologian who examines his own experience in the search for truths and the professional who knows better.

Indeed, it is already the case that academic theologians tend to avoid questions of inner experience rather than risk privatism, subjectivism, or the transgression of Kantian boundaries; yet this is happening at a time when—to judge by the success of *Life After Life* and other books about individual spiritual experience—the wider public is hungry for theoretical and practical guidance in precisely this area.[10] Just as scholars are becoming more sophisticated about the social character of religion, the social context for religion is growing increasingly individualistic. For many people, personal experience seems to be the only available arena for religious discovery and the only guide for choosing among the dizzying array of competing world-views and paths. Under the pressures of secularism and pluralism, religion has become more than ever a matter of "what the individual does with his own solitariness."[11] There has never been a period in which undue skepticism about religious experience could be more damaging.

All of this bears on the problem of interpreting otherworld visions. If we wish to maintain a middle path between reductionism and naïveté, then we must mediate between the impersonalism of social theories that stress the coerciveness of language and culture at the expense of individual experience and the exaggerated individualism of earlier interpreters like William James and Henri Bergson, who disregard the social side of religion in favor of its private dimension and its solitary "geniuses."[12] Since debates are often muddled by unacknowledged differences in usage, it will clarify our task to discriminate three ways in which the terms social and individual can apply to religious experience:

1. Religious experience is invariably social in that religious life and thought are shaped by linguistic and social forces; for this reason, Clifford Geertz describes religion as a "cultural system."

2. Religious traditions reflect and promote social order and, in many cultures, tend to value the group over the individual. In archaic societies, according to Mircea Eliade, religious experience is profoundly collective—the individual feels his identity securely only when merged with the community, reenacting the mythical acts of its foundation, purging himself of idiosyncrasy. Many of the historical religious traditions also have a communal focus; the Hebrew Bible is the story of a people's response to God's acts, not the diary of a solitary seeker. Yet the extent to which religious experience is communal depends on the degree and quality of social cohesion in a given group. The social character of religious experience, in this sense, is a variable rather than a constant. It can therefore, as Wilfred Cantwell Smith argues, be misleading to generalize about the fundamental significance of religious community on the basis of a particular situation (Smith, 1978, 177). To make archaic religion the standard is no more reasonable than to suppose, as James did, that the separation between personal and institutional religion which characterized his own intellectual milieu should stand for all time and apply to all forms of religious experience.

3. Religious experience is invariably individual in that, as Smith says, "to be religious is an ultimately personal act." No matter how communal their society may be, human beings are essentially alone in the

experience of life and death and in the encounter with transcendent values. This is as constant as the fact of social conditioning (number 1 above) and is not altered by changing conditions of social structure. Individual experience may not be the locus of authority, but it is the touchstone for authenticity; in this context the opposite of "individual" is not "social," but "insincere."

In interpreting contemporary near-death literature, therefore, we can say without contradiction that it records the genuine and irreducibly personal experiences of individuals (number 3), that it is nonetheless a product of the social religious imagination (number 1), and that one sign of its social character is its individualistic message (number 2). If we keep these three rudimentary distinctions in mind, then our awareness of the cultural shaping of near-death testimony need not lead to relativism or skepticism. The antireductionist principle of judging religious experience by its fruits rather than its origins applies as well to current sociological insights as it does to the "medical materialism" against which William James battled.

Having cleared the way by defending near-death testimony against the new reductionism of social science, we are free to apply pragmatic criteria toward interpreting the content of near-death visions. As I have suggested, a pragmatic method is ideally suited for dealing with testimony that cannot be verified in other ways. If there is validity to religious accounts of life or death it is not because they provide a direct transcript of the truth, but only because they act as a lure toward truth, by leading people out of anxious, mechanical or vicious patterns of thought and behavior. As long as our religious ideas and images perform this leading function, and do not falsify our experience along the way, then we can say, with James, that they are "true in so far forth" (James, 1975, 98–103).

We can use this pragmatic approach without necessarily embracing James's pragmatic theory of truth. We should not adopt James's pragmatic method, however, without stretching it to include attention to the workings of the religious imagination and the cultural forces that shape it. What James calls the "cash value" of a religious conception depends on the state of the economy in which it is circulated, and cannot be measured against any universal or timeless rate of exchange. With this in mind, I have criticized theological interpretations of near-death literature that do not take into account its particular implications for our culture.

We cannot return to James, then, but we can combine a Jamesian respect for the validity of individual religious experience with a greater sensitivity to the cultural shaping of that experience. We can expand his pragmatic method by incorporating into it an appreciation of the symbolic and therapeutic character of religious discourse. Having done so, we can turn to the task of interpreting near-death visions with a renewed sense of the rightness of treating them as socially conditioned, imaginative, and yet nonetheless real and revelatory experiences.

This is the approach that allows us to respect the visionary's claim that he experienced death, even if he did not meet medical criteria. As the previous chapter points out, it is enough to know that the shock of extreme danger or expected death opened him to a discovery of what death means to him at the core of his being. When he stepped onto the stage of the other world—which is the inner world, turned inside out—he confronted his own deeply held image and presentiment of death, perhaps just as he will at the time of his actual death. Thus we can say, in the fullest possible sense, that the visionary "met his death."

Indeed, it is no coincidence that the ordinary expression "he met his death" is compatible with the testimony of near-death visionaries. Here is one instance in which our language preserves a vestige of otherworld journey imagery in a saying that, though commonplace, nonetheless retains a vital charge. Dormant in our everyday speech, this expression has the potential to spring into a full-blown imaginative or visionary experience; its potency is a sign that the traditional and folkloric view of death as a symbolic encounter still has authority for us. If we recognize this, then the testimony of near-death visionaries will begin to seem less foreign. On the basis of this common ground of imaginative experience, we have reason to accord some validity to the visionary's claims. Certainly this is a more fruitful and more humane approach than the application of external medical tests.

The same logic applies to the conviction of having survived death. Though it proves nothing about our own prospects for life beyond the grave, we are entitled to accept an individual's report that he experienced something in himself that surpasses death. Given the immense practical significance of this claim, it would be foolish to deny it solely because of scientific opinions. Science can hardly have the last word on a subject about which it has so little to say; and the transforming effects of near-death experience speak for themselves.

So the benefits of reading visionary testimony as a work of the imagination keep accumulating; and if we move on to consider the near-death vision as a narrative whole, its immunity to reductionist criticism becomes even greater. We have seen that arguments against the validity of visionary experience depend on analyzing it into component parts. The critics of near-death research remind us that near-death experience is a composite and that its individual elements may be "explained" by distribution to various physical, psychological, and social facts.

Yet it is our prerogative as imaginative beings to form meaningful wholes out of the elements of sensation, perception, language, memory, and so forth, which we are given. Imagination, which Coleridge calls the power "to shape into one," fuses these bits of experience into a dramatic sequence, aimed toward a destination, and therefore not reducible to their origin or cause. In acts of telling and retelling, near-death experience takes shape as a unified and unifying whole. Once this narrative integrity is achieved, no amount of analytical dissection can destroy it.

This immunity is lost, however, the moment we begin to try to verify near-death experience by isolating veridical elements, ruling out pathological causes, or breaking it down into statistics. Paradoxically, the very method that permits us to respect visionary testimony prohibits us from using it to make a case for survival. To this extent, we must frustrate the truth claims of near-death literature.

In every respect, our defense of near-death reports depends on treating them as symbolic expressions that can never be translated into direct observations or exact concepts. This will disappoint those who wish to have their doubts about life after death resolved. It has positive religious implications as well, however, for it requires us to give up our insistence on objective verification (which has been the source of so much grief throughout history) and in its place to cultivate an appreciation of symbol. Instead of regretting the fact that religious experience is symbolic rather than descriptive, we might rejoice that the truth empties itself into our human language and cultural forms. To attempt to strip away those forms in the belief that they merely embellish, veil, or obstruct the truth is, in effect, a revival of the Docetist heresy.

Even if we grant that near-death visions convey something real, there is no reliable way to formulate what that something is. We cannot take a consensus of the visionaries; their visions are too culturally specific. We cannot crack their symbolic code; and we know before we start that every explanation or interpretation, however thoughtful, will leave the essential mystery untouched. As the remainder of this chapter will suggest, we can appropriate the messages of near-death literature only in an indirect fashion, and yet that may prove to be no insignificant thing.

ANOTHER WORLD TO LIVE IN

The narrative integrity of near-death visions derives not merely from the fact that a story is told but, more importantly, from the fact that the story has an aim. What seems at first glance to be a visionary travelogue describing for the curious the sights of an exotic supernatural realm turns out to be the story of a conversion experience; and, as we have seen, its main purpose is to communicate to others the new insights gained by the convert.

Otherworld vision stories resemble conversion narratives in two respects. Most obviously, they trace the protagonist's recovery from a condition of sin, melancholy, malaise—or from death itself, which is the fundamental reference point and emblem for all states of despair. Although modern near-death narratives give us deliverance without conviction of sin, they nonetheless follow the conversion pattern, often beginning with an allusion to the protagonist's long-standing enslavement to fear of death, and ending, as the medieval narratives do, with an account of his regenerated way of life. The death-first pattern of contemporary reports thus serves a function parallel to that of the hell-first pattern of medieval narratives.

The second, and more intriguing, similarity between conversion experience and near-death visions is the way in which inner transformation colors perceptions of the outer world. Not only do otherworld visions resemble conversion, but, in this respect, conversion narratives resemble otherworld visions. William James suggests as much in his discussion of conversion, when he points out that a sudden sense of inward illumination can spill over into the landscape, saturating it with beauty, light, newness, vitality, and harmony. James's prime example for this is Jonathan Edwards's account of his own conversion experience, in which the face of nature seemed to change, and the voice of thunder was transformed from a dreadful summons into a sweet invitation.[13] James also cites several anonymous witnesses who entered the "state of assurance" under the auspices of evangelical revival; the following narrative, taken from E. D. Starbuck, is representative:

> It was like entering another world, a new state of existence. Natural objects were glorified, my spiritual vision was so clarified that I saw beauty in every material object in the universe, the woods were vocal with heaven-ly music; my soul exulted in the love of God, and I wanted everybody to share in my joy.

For a secular variation on the same theme, we can turn to Gustav Fechner, a philosopher whom James admired, who attained to his "daylight view" of the panpsychic intelligence of plants and planets after emerging from a period of painful seclusion:

> I still remember well what an impression it made upon me when, after suffering for some years from an ailment which affected my sight, I stepped out for the first time from my darkened chamber and into the garden with no bandage upon my eyes. It seemed to me like a glimpse beyond the boundary of human experience. Every flower beamed upon me with a peculiar clarity, as though into the outer light it was casting a light of its own. To me the whole garden seemed transfigured, as though it were not I but nature that had just arisen. And I thought: So nothing is

needed but to open the eyes afresh, and with that old nature is made young again. (Fechner, 211)

In this passage there converges an entire spectrum of literal and metaphoric conversion and otherworld journey motifs. A comparable account by Alphonse Ratisbonne, also quoted by James, likens a sudden conversion experience to emerging "from a sepulchre, from an abyss of darkness," and finding that "in an instant the bandage had fallen from my eyes" (James, 1985, Lecture, 10). But the special charm of Fechner's account is that these age-old symbols of awakening and renewed sight—exit from a darkened chamber, having a covering drop from the eyes, entering a luminous garden—take on literal form. The same may be said of near-death narratives; here the literal sense comes to rest on the passage from death into life, from the darkened chamber of the body and its lidded vision to the lucid garden which, as Fechner puts it, "lies beyond the wall of this world."

William James holds that the principle by which a conversion experience transfigures the landscape can also operate in reverse, in a melancholic refiguring of the world which strips it of value, interest, and hence of visual allure; and we have seen that this is the chief feature of what psychologists now call depersonalization, the condition that resembles and yet is the very antithesis of visionary near-death experience. According to James, this is more than a psychological principle; he maintains that our exalted or depressed states, assisted by our ideals, beliefs, doubts, and philosophic opinions, positively shape the character of the world. Not conversion only, but all meaningful experience has the power to endow the environment with reality and value, just as pathological, disordered, or lethargic states of mind correspondingly denature it.[14]

Considered in this way, the otherworld vision seems less bizarre; though exceptional, it is part of the normal range of religious and, in the sense just mentioned, even of ordinary experience. As a special form of conversion experience, in which the landscape is transfigured as a corollary of subjective transformation, the visionary journey dramatizes the way imagination contributes to our perception of the world. To use a Blakean analogy, imagination plays the demiurge and—aided by the visionary's exalted mood—creates a new world to dwell in, or restores the natural world according to its Edenic exemplar.

If this is true, it still does not mean that we can decode the features of otherworld topography by tracing them to particular states or objects of mind. Such attempts usually betray dogmatic assumptions; thus Freudian Géza Róheim sees phallic imagery in the architecture of the other world, while neurologist Ronald Siegel relates it to optic and mnemonic structures, and Swedenborg proposes an elaborate system of correspondences in which houses and cities are thoughts, animals and birds are affections, gardens are ordered ideas, and so forth. If we are inclined to adopt a Jungian approach, or to apply the teachings of the *Tibetan Book of the Dead* (which counsels the deceased to recognize his afterlife visions as a projection of the mind's own radiance), we must realize that our impartiality is at risk. Nor does the "intentional" character of otherworld visions call for any particular brand of philosophical idealism or endorse any special school of phenomenology; to enter these intellectual frameworks requires a large added step.

Without committing ourselves to such a step, the main conclusion we can draw is that the other world—in its literal or metaphoric forms—plays a significant role in our imaginative appropriation of moral and religious ideals. George Santayana, though no friend of literal eschatologies, implies this in his famous definition of religion:

> Any attempt to speak without speaking any particular language is not more hopeless than the attempt to have a religion that shall be no religion in particular.... Thus every living and healthy religion has a marked idiosyncrasy; its power consists in its special and surprising message and in the bias which that revelation gives to life. The vistas it opens and the mysteries it propounds are another world to live in; and another world to live in—whether we expect ever to pass wholly over into it or not—is what we mean by having a religion.[15]

Like Fechner's story, this passage brings together metaphorical and literal senses. Santayana seems to suggest that myth, ritual, conversion, moral improvement, and other aspects of religious life are intimately related to a primitive—and perhaps consciously repudiated—understanding of the other world as an actual place. For those of us who have abandoned thinking about other worlds, this produces a shock of recognition, demonstrating that our metaphorical ways of having "another world to live in" exert their power on the imagination only because we continue, at least subliminally, to visualize a literal other world. It is better to acknowledge this, and look for its possible benefits, than to ignore it and be unconsciously determined by it. The chief virtue of our tendency to conceive of another world may be that it provides a sense of orientation in *this* world, through which we would otherwise wander without direction.

ORIENTATION

In the vision literature we have considered, conversion motifs merge with pilgrimage motifs because the journey to the next world is actually a guide for pilgrimage through life. The maps of death and afterlife that these accounts contain are meant to help us get our bearings, right now, in relation to the cosmos in which we dwell, or wish to dwell.

Biologists Peter and Jean Medawar have expressed this:

> Only human beings guide their behaviour by a knowledge of what hap-
> pened before they were born and a preconception of what may happen
> after they are dead: thus only human beings find their way by a light that
> illumines more than the patch of ground they stand on.[16]

Comparative study of religion shows that *homo religiosus* has never found it sufficient to orient himself solely in terms of his place in local history, in the rat race, in private concerns that devour his energy. The imaginative cosmologies and eschatologies of different cultures testify to our human need to find a place to occupy in a wider universe.

This has not always been formulated in terms of life after death. Even the contemplation of death, unadorned by images of the beyond, can have this orienting effect insofar as it makes us place ourselves, with greater urgency and purpose, in the midst of life, and a sense of the mystery of existence, of infinite presence or surrounding emptiness, can have the same value as a graphic depiction of the steps to paradise and hell. Buddhist evocations of the inexhaustibly productive void are as well suited as Dante's *Divine Comedy* to meet the need for orientation. The question they address is not necessarily "What was I before I was born, and what will I be when I die?" but rather "Where am I now in relation to the north, south, east, and west of the cosmos, the yesterday and tomorrow of history, the higher and lower ranks of being?" And the answer to this question can legitimately take many different forms, as long as it succeeds to some degree in correlating our position in the social order with our position in the cosmic order. Thus I have suggested that otherworld journey narration is most likely to become prominent at times when a culture develops, or encounters through contact with other cultures, new perspectives on the social and natural universe which—until assimilated by the religious imagination—give rise to "cognitive dissonance" and spiritual dislocation.

It is the religious imagination that turns map into cosmos and cosmos into home; in visionary literature this is accomplished by sending scouts to visit the farther reaches and return with eyewitness accounts that imaginatively appropriate the current world-picture. Without such reports of actual experience, we seem to live in an unevaluated and desacralized universe.

If the otherworld journey is a way for the religious imagination to digest a culturally fashioned cosmology, then it is not surprising that these narratives, today as in the past, raise questions of a scientific order. The narrators who attempt to provide verification, according to the investigative canons of their day, are only extending this original impulse to link cosmology with imaginative experience. Although they may never achieve a profound synthesis of scientific and religious worldviews, they are at least making an effort in that direction, unlike those religious thinkers who are so disenchanted by the failed alliances of the past that they look for religion only in those areas—such as ethics—that do not overlap with the domain of science.

Fortunately, these are not the only options. A third possibility, as Gordon Allport tells us, is the "ceaseless struggle to assimilate the scientific frame of thought within an expanded religious frame" (Allport,132). The intent of this essay has been to point the theological interpretation of near-death experience in this direction; acknowledging scientific and historical contributions without succumbing to positivism, taking experiential claims seriously, and yet posing the question of verification on a deeper level.

Otherworld journey narratives orient us in two ways: as works of visionary topography they provide an updated, culturally sanctioned picture of the cosmos, and as works of moral and spiritual instruction they call on us to inhabit this cosmos, by overcoming the fear or forgetfulness that makes us as insensible to life as to death. All this is the action of the religious imagination, that power that makes our ideas and ideals come to life and act on us. Although most of us do not seek visions (nor are we advised to do so by the visionary literature we have considered), we can at least respect the testimony of vision literature as an extreme instance of the legitimate imaginative means through which one can instill a religious sense of the cosmos.

It is one thing to acknowledge in general terms the orienting value of otherworld visions; it is quite another to decide whether their specific content might be relevant to our own view of life and death. In order to understand the conditions, both cultural and natural, that shape near-death experience, we have assumed the role of spectators and cannot easily divest ourselves of that role. In comparing medieval and modern visions, we seem to have stepped outside our own cultural context and may feel at a loss as to how to step back into it and make judgments. Such incapacity for wholehearted participation is the intellectual's occupational disease; among scholars engaged in the comparative study of religion it can produce a sense of nostalgia for days of innocence or for some idealized form of archaic or traditional religiosity.

When we try to evaluate near-death experience, we may feel stymied by our own sophistication. We have gotten beyond reductionism to the extent that we can say of near-death visions, as William James says of mysticism, that they "usually are, and have the right to be, absolutely authoritative over the individuals to whom they come"; but we find ourselves effectively collared by the corollary that these revelations cannot legislate to—perhaps cannot even be shared with—the general public. As a result, those individuals whose understanding has been shaped by an overwhelming visionary experience seem to be isolated from the rest of us who are trying to make sense of things without the aid of direct revelation.

To some extent, this quarantine is necessary. At this stage I see no justification for treating contemporary near-death testimony as the foundation for a new eschatology or religious movement. Near-death literature is at its best when it is modest and anecdotal; pressed into service as philosophy or prophecy, it sounds insipid. There is no match here for the revelatory literature of the great religious traditions; and it seems unlikely that a Gregory the Great or a Dante will emerge to shape near-death testimony into a religiously sophisticated or artistically ordered statement. Neither could the medieval visions we considered stand on their own; they thrived insofar as they exemplified a wider tradition.

In the end, a revelation is binding only if it binds. On a personal scale, it must organize life into a meaningful whole, without excluding other experiences. On a social scale, it must create or serve a community; and on this score near-death testimony breaks down into private testaments which, despite their common features, have not mustered the collective energy to produce a coherent worldview. Those who experience near-death visions, as well as those who are affected by hearing them, still face the problem of finding a community and a context in which to search again for and apply the insights they have received.

In our fragmented religious situation, the otherworld journey narrative has lost some of its orienting power. It can remind us of the need for orientation, the need to have a consecrated cosmos as the setting for a spiritual journey, but it cannot provide the means or material to accomplish this. We are thrown back on our own devices, our own partial and provisional solutions.

Under these circumstances, the most significant contribution made by near-death literature today may be that it puts in experiential terms questions about life and death which are so urgent as to call not for answers but for vital response. The moment of death—whether it is an imminent prospect or just an idea—still has a salutary shock value; it can make what James would call "live options" out of metaphysical notions that might otherwise seem remote, abstract, or obsolete.

If near-death literature is to have any prophetic value or evidential weight, it will be because it communicates insights capable of being verified—not in medical charts, but in our own experience. We may find no difficulty in respecting the testimony of those whose lives have been transformed by a near-death vision, but we can verify their discoveries only if, in some sense, we experience them for ourselves. The same can be said of other forms of religious testimony; for, unlike the generalizable truths of science, religious truths are true only insofar as religious people make them their own.

In this respect, there is no great distance between those who have experienced near-death visions and those who have only read of them. The visionary—who must continually struggle to understand and not to betray his or her original vision—is in the same boat with the rest of us. All of us need to work at verifying our beliefs, whether they derive from personal experience or from venerated hearsay. A conviction that life surpasses death, however intensely felt, will eventually lose its vitality and become a mere fossil record, as alien as any borrowed doctrine, unless it is tested and rediscovered in daily life.

This study has demonstrated a fundamental kinship between otherworld visions and the more common forms of imaginative experience. Whether we fall into the "experiencer" or the "nonexperiencer" category on a near-death survey, we are all, in a sense, otherworld travelers. Otherworld visions are products of the same imaginative power that is active in our ordinary ways of visualizing death; our tendency to portray ideas in concrete, embodied, and dramatic forms; the capacity of our inner states to transfigure our perception of outer landscapes; our need to internalize the cultural map of the physical universe; and our drive to experience that universe as a moral and spiritual cosmos in which we belong and have a purpose.

Whatever the study of near-death visions might reveal about the experience of death, it teaches us just as much about ourselves as image-making and image-bound beings. To admit this is no concession to the debunkers; on the contrary, by recognizing the imaginative character of otherworld visions, we move beyond the merely defensive posture of arguing against reductionism. Within the limits here discussed we are able to grant the validity of near-death testimony as one way in which the religious imagination mediates the search for ultimate truth.

NOTES

1. Robert Herhold, "Kübler-Ross and Life after Death," p. 363. See also J. D. Ousley, Letter to the Editor on "Death-bed Visions and Christian Hope," by Paul Badham, *Theology*, 84 (January 1981: 44). In response to Herhold's argument, however, James W. Woelfel points out that it represents the fideistic stance of "vigorously biblical Protestant theologians"; Catholics, he maintains, still consider immortality demonstrable by reason, even if it is won only by faith. "Life After Death: Faith or Knowledge?" (Readers' Response), *The Christian Century*, 93 (July 7–14, 1976): 632–34.

2. See, for example, Paul Tillich in *The Meaning of Death*, ed. Herman Feifel (New York, 1959), p. 30.

3. "Immortality of the Soul or Resurrection of the Dead?" in *Immortality and Resurrection*, ed. Krister Stendahl (New York, 1965), pp. 9–53.

4. "Against Raising Hope of Raising the Dead: Contra Moody and Kübler-Ross," p. 65. Herhold makes the same remark in "Kübler-Ross and Life after Death."

5. Discussed by R. Laurence Moore, George Lawton, Geoffrey K. Nelson, and Frank Miller Turner.

6. See R. Laurence Moore, "Spiritualism and the Complaint of Christian Orthodoxy," *In Search of White Crows*, pp. 40–69.

7. He probably had in mind Plato's remark in Phaedrus 250c.

8. From "Auguries of Innocence." William Blake, *Complete Writings*, ed. Geoffrey Keynes (London, 1971), p. 434. Here, with characteristic poetic polemics, Blake anticipates the Romantic tradition in literature and theology that sought to elevate the prestige of imagination, making it almost an organ for the perception of higher truths. Elsewhere he chides the Greek philosophers for conceiving of God "as abstracted or distinct from the Imaginative World," and contrasts this to the way Jesus, Abraham, and David "consider'd God as a Man in the Spiritual or Imaginative Vision" (Annotation to Berkeley's "Siris," *Complete Writings*, p. 774). Coleridge, whose distinction between Imagination and Fancy resembles Blake's distinction between Imagination and Memory, provides a more balanced and philosophically astute defense of the imagination, in such writings as *The Statesman's Manual* and the *Biographia literaria*.

9. *Regula pastoralis liber*, ed. H. R. Bramley (Oxford and London, 1874), part 3, prologue, p. 128.

10. Theological discomfort with experiential claims has a long history, but in its current forms it reflects the influence of such diverse thinkers as Hume, Kant, Feuerbach, Marx, Freud, and Barth. In setting boundaries on the theoretical and practical use of reason, Kant established that God—as Absolute—cannot be an object of possible experience. Many theologians have since felt compelled to characterize religious experience as categorically different from all other kinds of experience and hence not recognizably empirical, or even to condemn interest in religious experience as a self-centered, idolatrous fixation that substitutes for pure faith. A pragmatic view of religious experience has the potential to release us from some of these vetoes; as William James points out, the God of religious experience is a More rather than a categorically transcendent All. Perhaps God is willing to descend from the status of "wholly other" in order to become available to human experience.

11. Alfred North Whitehead, *Religion in the Making* (New York, 1926; reprint ed., New York, 1960), p. 16. On the other hand, the fast-growing conservative and evangelical Christian communities constitute a significant exception to, and reaction against, this trend.

12. See James, *The Varieties of Religious Experience*; and Bergson, *The Two Sources of Morality and Religion*, (New York 1935). The sociological approach to cognitive religious claims reflects the influence of Marx, Weber, and especially Durkheim, who insists that the reality expressed by religious symbols is primarily a social one and, as such, cannot be understood by introspection.

13. *A Personal Narrative*, quoted by James in Lecture 10, "Conversion," *The Varieties of Religious Experience*.

14. In putting forward this view, James occupies a theoretical position somewhere between the practical idealism of the optimistic Mind-Cure philosophies he describes and criticizes in the *Varieties* and the more complex doctrines of intentionality that have become the specialty of modern schools of phenomenological inquiry. The details of his position cannot be covered here. I have only extracted the general insights that are relevant to interpretation of near-death testimony and are compatible with many different philosophical systems.

15. From *Reason in Religion*, quoted by Clifford Geertz as an introductory maxim to "Religion as a Cultural System"; in *The Interpretation of Cultures* (New York, 1973), p. 87.

16. *The Life Science* (London, 1977), quoted by Karl R. Popper and John C. Eccles in the frontispiece to *The Self and Its Brain* (New York, 1977).

REFERENCES

Allport, Gordon. (1950). *The Individual and His Religion*. New York.

Badham, Paul. (July, 1980). Death-bed visions and christian hope.*Theology 83*, 269–75.

Badham, Paul and Linda. (1982). *Immortality or Extinction?* Totowa, NJ.

Bergson, Henri. (1935). *The Two Sources of Morality and Religion*. (R.A. Audra and C.Brereton, Trans.). New York.

Blake, William. (1971). *Complete Writings*. (Geoffrey Keynes, Ed.). London.

Fechner, Gustav. (1946). *The Soul Life of Plants*, Conclusion. (Walter Lowrie, Trans.). *In Religion of a Scientist*. New York.

Feifel, Herman. (1959). *The Meaning of Death*. New York.

Gregory the Great. (1874). *Regula pastoralis liber.* (H. R. Bramley, ed.). Oxford.

Gregory the Great. (1924). *Dialogi*. (Umberto Moricca, ed.). Rome.

Gregory the Great. (1959). *Dialogues*. (Trans. Odo John Zimmerman). New York.

Herhold, Robert M. (April 14, 1976). Kübler-Ross and life after death. *The Christian Century 93*, 363–64.

Hick, John. (1976). *Death and Eternal Life*. London.

James, William. (1975). *Pragmatism*. Cambridge, MA.

James, William. (1985). *The Varieties of Religious Experience*. Cambridge, MA.

Kaufmann, Gordon. (1975). *An Essay on Theological Method*. Missoula, MT.

Lawton, George. (1932). *The Drama of Life After Death: A Study of the Spiritualist Religion*. New York.

Moody, Raymond. (1975). *Life After Life*. NY: Mockingbird/Bantam Books.

Moody, Raymond. (1977). *Reflections on Life After Life*. NY: Bantam Books.

Moore, R. Laurence. (1977). *In Search of White Crows: Spiritualism, Parapsychology and American Culture*. New York.

Nelson, Geoffrey. (1969). *Spiritualism and Society*. London and NY.

Rawlings, Maurice. (1978). *Beyond Death's Door*. Nashville: Nelson.

Rawlings, Maurice. (1980). *Before Death Comes*. Nashville: Nelson.

Roheim, Geza. (1930). *Animism, Magic and the Divine King*. London.

Smith, Wilfred Cantwell. (1978). *The Meaning and End of Religion*. San Francisco.

Stendahl, Krister. (1965). *Immortality and Resurrection*. New York.

Vicchio, Stephen J. (1979). Against hope of raising the dead: contra Moody and Kübler-Ross. *Essence 3*, 51–67.

Whitehead, Alfred North. (1926). *Religion in the Making*. New York.

22

The Near-Death Experience and the Perennial Wisdom

David Lorimer

The deeper aspects of the [NDE] experience are a kind of *gnosis* that give an insight into the nature of a reality which transcends the physical.

David Lorimer is a leading voice speaking for the transcendental, mystical interpretation of near-death experiences. He argues that the NDE has the same elements as the common core of world religions and that NDEs transcend physical reality. The "Perennial Philosophy" indicates the underlying beliefs that unite all genuine religious traditions: 1. the phenomenal world is the manifestation of a Divine Ground, 2. humans are capable of realizing the Divine Ground by direct intuition, 3. the soul is composed of both a mortal ego and an eternal Self, and 4. the purpose of life is to identify with the eternal Self and so absorb and practice the love and wisdom of the Divine Ground. The NDE, Lorimer says, exhibits the same elements, especially the love and wisdom. Initiation, conversion, the meanings given for life and death; these are characteristic phenomena deeply rooted in the transcendent soul's vision of its true Ground.

Lorimer develops his theory of "empathetic resonance" to explain NDEs in his 1990 book *Whole in One*. Empathetic resonance for him is the state of consciousness available when the alienating boundaries between in/out, self/other are softened. For example, many cases of people sharing dreams, illnesses, or premonitions, are recorded, such as the woman who suddenly felt water rushing into her ears and knew with horror that her brother or son had just drowned. Sadly, her empathetic resonance was confirmed when someone rushed in to tell her that her son had just drowned (Lorimer, 1990, 74–75). Such phenomena point to an underlying unity behind ordinary existence that links all individuals and helps explain some of the dilemmas of NDEs. When we experience empathic resonance, Lorimer says,

> the boundaries dissolve and there dawns the realization that one's ground is the unitive consciousness field out of which other individual self-consciousnesses also arise: the many arise out of the One and are linked to each other through participation in that One. (Lorimer, 1990, 90)

David Lorimer, M.A., is Director of the Scientific and Medical Network, an international organization of physicians and scientists that seeks to extend the framework of assumptions of contemporary scientific and medical thinking beyond materialist reductionism. He is also Chairman of the International Association for Near-Death Studies (UK) and author of *Survival: Body, Mind and Death in the Light of Psychic Experiences* (London: Routledge, 1984) and *Whole in One: The Near-Death Experience and the Ethic of Interconnectedness* (London: Arkana-Penguin, 1990). He studied at Eton, St. Andrews, and Cambridge, and lives in Buckinghamshire, England.

The Near-Death Experience and the Perennial Wisdom

The eye with which I see God is the same eye with which God sees in me: my eye and God's eye, that is one eye and one vision, one knowledge and one love.

– Meister Eckhart

It is not we who know God, it is God who knows himself in us.

– Frithjof Schuon

The human intellect can reach 'theosis'—knowledge of God—through the rediscovery of its own essence...to know God is to recall what we are.

– Seyyed Hossein Nasr

It is now some twenty years since the appearance of the first books explicitly devoted to the near-death experience (NDE) (Moody, 1975). Public interest in the phenomenon has been sustained over that period by a spate of new books ranging from the academic to the popular. Journalists and broadcasters still regularly make contact, wanting to produce programmes and speak to experiencers. The field has branched out in a number of directions and disciplines: neurobiology, medicine, psychiatry, various psychologies—ranging from cognitive to transpersonal—anthropology, sociology, philosophy (including the nature of perception), metaphysics and religion. The NDE lends itself to an interdisciplinary approach, and indeed cannot be fully understood without considering a variety of aspects and levels. This essay will focus on the relationship between the NDE and what I call the perennial wisdom, arguing that the deeper aspects of the experience are a kind of *gnosis* that give an insight into the nature of a reality which transcends the physical.

The term "Perennial Philosophy" was popularised by Aldous Huxley's 1945 book of the same name, but the ancestry of the term goes back a good deal further (Nasr,

1989). I am using it here in the sense advanced by Frithjof Schuon and others, that there exists an underlying thread which unites all expressions of religious traditions. Two of the cardinal principles of this are love and wisdom, principles which can be used as a benchmark or criterion of religion and spirituality: if love and wisdom are not central within a tradition, then, in my view, such a tradition is not a genuine expression.

By no means would all researchers agree that reality can transcend the physical dimension. The dominant philosophy in modern neuroscience, medicine and psychology is mechanistic, materialistic and reductionist, whether this is formulated as physicalism, functionalism or even 'biological naturalism' (Searle, 1992). It amounts to stating that conscious experience is produced by brain activity and that perception is only possible by means of the five senses. It follows from this that the NDE must be a purely physical phenomenon and that brain death spells the extinction of personal identity and memory. Without an active physical brain, no consciousness is possible.

An alternative view postulates that consciousness is not so much produced by as transmitted through the brain (James, 1899; Schiller, 1891; Lorimer, 1984). Thus conscious states would be correlated with rather than caused by brain activity. The distinction is a crucial one, since it allows the possibility that the mind or soul might operate independently of the physical brain and have access to non-physical aspects or dimensions of reality. Furthermore, the death of the brain need not necessarily spell the extinction of the individual, but possibly a transformation or shift to a different state of consciousness. In this view, the brain could be regarded as the space-time limitation or localisation of consciousness, which itself is not intrinsically limited or localised. This theory is capable of accounting for the kind of out-of-the-body perception reported in NDEs, while the brain-based approaches are obliged to ignore or dismiss such evidence. The fundamental issue here is this: is the physical world a closed self-sufficient system so that everything can be causally explained in physical terms? Or does it open into inner dimensions which transcend the physical realm? The modern scientific worldview assumes the former position, while all types of spiritual worldviews insist that there is something more.

The quotations at the top of this essay make very little sense to those who do not believe that there is a God to discover or know. Yet throughout history there have been reports of 'otherworld journeys' from those who have come back from the borderland of death (Zaleski, 1986). One of the earliest analogies to the traveller's tale is Plato's simile of the cave in the Republic (Lee, 1974). The prisoners in the cave take the shadows thrown by the fire on the wall opposite as reality, and are reluctant to believe in the existence of anything else. Yet, as Plato argues, there are many other degrees of reality which are more real than what can be perceived inside the cave. There is a gradual ascent from illusion through belief, reason *(dianoia)* and intelligence *(nous)* to a 'vision of the form of the good' represented by looking at the sun.

It is here that Plato's symbolism begins to meet the phenomenology of the NDE. The stages described seem to indicate a gradual withdrawal from the physical realm and entry into another, spiritual realm which is always sensed as more real than the physical on the traveller's return. An interesting reflection on this point is provided by 'Bertrand Russell', ostensibly communicating after his death through the medium Rosemary Brown:

> Now here I was, still the same I, with capacities to think and observe sharpened to an incredible degree. I felt earth-life suddenly seemed very unreal almost as if it had never happened. It took me quite a long time to understand this feeling until I realised at last that matter is certainly illusory although it does exist in actuality; the material world seemed now nothing more than a seething, changing, restless sea of indeterminable density and volume. How could I have thought that that was reality, the last word of Creation to Mankind? Yet it is completely understandable that the state in which a man exists, however temporary, constitutes the passing reality which is no longer reality when it has passed. (Brown, 1974)

Russell's remark that his capacities to think and observe were sharpened to an incredible degree is typical of the NDE and flies in the face of the materialistic assumption that a dying brain could only result in confused perceptual processes. The evidence for this comes from reports of veridical OBEs during the NDE, where subjects are able to give an accurate report of events going on around them when they were apparently completely unconscious. In one Dutch case, a man was brought into hospital following a heart failure and subsequently transferred to intensive care without recovering consciousness. Ten days later he was brought back to the ward. Not only did he recognise the nurse (whom he had never seen before) as having been present at his resuscitation, which he described in detail, but he even asked her where she had put his false teeth! The subject had seen her place them in a glass of water. The nurse was flabbergasted, as there was no normal way in which the subject could have known this.

Sceptics argue that such reports could have been reconstructed from residual hearing, but such an interpretation does scant justice to the detailed visual nature of the experience and the fact that many actions or phenomena reported were not actually verbalised by the medical staff. This stage of the NDE is the first point of contact with the perennial wisdom, which speaks of subtle bodies or vehicles of consciousness beyond the physical form or envelope. The subjects realise that they are more than their physical body, and sometimes even hear themselves pronounced dead in spite of the fact that they are still conscious and often looking down on the scene from above.

The next stage of 'going through the tunnel' almost sounds like emerging from the Platonic cave into the light. The 'light' is described as very bright, but harmless to the eyes. It is clearly not physical light, but rather spiritual light, a distinction which has its counterpart in Latin *(lumen/lux)* and Bulgarian *(videlina/svetlina)*. Light has from time immemorial been the symbol of the Divine, but, as Eckhart indicates in the quotation above, this light is also knowledge and love. One near-death experiencer writes:

> I found myself travelling towards this tremendous light, so bright that it would have blinded me if I'd looked at it here, but there it was different. I reached the light which was all around me…and I felt this wonderful love enfolding me and understanding me. No matter what my faults, what I'd done or hadn't done, the light loved me unconditionally.

Another near-death experiencer says:

> A light was glowing invitingly—I was encouraged by a strong feeling to enter the light. I approached without haste as I felt that the light was part of the jigsaw to which I rightfully belonged. As I entered, I felt the light glow. I was peaceful, totally content and I understood why I was born on earth and knew the answer to every mystery. (Lorimer, 1990)

These two accounts show that the light has both cognitive or intellectual and affective or emotional aspects. In the Perennial Philosophy this can be translated into wisdom and love respectively. It is significant that the root of the Latin word for wisdom—*sapientia*—comes from *sapere*, which means to taste. Wisdom, therefore, is derived from experience, and the NDE, in this sense, could be regarded as a taste of love and wisdom. This experience in turn influences the documented after-effects of the experience. Melvin Morse (Morse, 1992) even goes on to argue that the transformative effects of the NDE are due to the light, a hypothesis consistent with other research in religious experience (Hardy, 1979) indicating transformation following spiritual encounters.

A central feature of the experience of the light is that it is unitive: there is a sense of complete oneness—at-onement—in which the sense of self is nevertheless retained and expanded at the same time. Plotinus writes that the infinite can only be grasped 'by entering into a state in which you are your finite self no longer…when you cease to be finite and become one with the infinite'. The poet Tennyson similarly records: 'All at once, out of the intensity of the consciousness of individuality, individuality itself seems to fade away into boundless being'. The Zen scholar Suzuki suggests that satori is an expansion of the individual into the infinite. It is as if the normal boundaries of the limited and contracted and seemingly separate self are suddenly dissolved. It is perhaps this transcendence of the ego which produces a loss of the fear of death.

Modern NDE accounts are typical of what is known in the West as absorptive mysticism, where the self is absorbed into a higher or deeper order of reality in which light, life, intensity and certainty all meet. Consider this classic account from Ruysbroeck:

> And all those men who are raised up above their created being into a God-seeing life are one with this Divine brightness. And they are that brightness itself, and they see, feel and find, even by means of this Divine Light, that, as regards their uncreated essence, they are that same onefold ground from which the brightness without limits shines forth in the Divine way, and which, according to the simplicity of the Essence, abides eternally onefold and wayless within. And this is why inward and God-seeing men will go out in the way of contemplation, above reason and above distinction and above their created being, through an eternal, intuitive gazing. By means of this inborn light they are transfigured, and made one with that same light through which they see and which they see. (Lorimer, 1990)

This last sentence recalls the circular paradox in the Eckhart quotation, only here Ruysbroeck refers to light rather than the eye. This change of perspective and perception is a form of *gnosis* whereby, as Schuon puts it, we 'participate in the perspective of the Divine Subject'. And, in the words of Parmenides 'to be and to know are one and the same thing'. This kind of knowledge itself represents a change of being which overcomes the division between subject and object.

In the Indian tradition this state is the union of being, consciousness, bliss *(Sat, Chit, Ananda)*. There is no separation between knower and known, only the knowing; none between the lover and the beloved, just the love. Such a union between love and knowledge is beautifully expressed by St. Maximus: 'If the life of the spirit is the illumination of knowledge and if it is love of God which produces this illumination, then it is right to say: there is nothing higher than the love of God'. Seyyed Hossein Nasr makes the same point (Nasr, 1989): 'This illumination in turn enables man to realise that the very essence of things is God's knowledge of them and that there is a reciprocity and, finally, an identity between being and knowing. The intellect becomes transformed into what it knows, the highest object of that knowledge being God'. Such *gnosis*, according to both Nasr and Schuon, is through the eye of the heart, which is the eye of the intellect *(nous)* not reason (the two are often wrongly conflated—the intellect is what enables us to grasp unity, while reason is dialectical and dualistic). The essence of the intellect, according to Schuon, is 'light as well as vision, nor is it reason which is a reflection of intellect on the human plane, but it is the root and centre of consciousness and what has traditionally been called the soul'.

There is one further crucial feature of this *gnosis:* it is the truth which makes you free, the *moksha* or deliverance of Hinduism which is beyond form, beyond limitation and beyond ego. It is not just a concept, but a profound experience and, as Schuon says, 'if we want truth to live in us, we must live in it'. The return from the light can be painful and disappointing as the subject wakes up again in limitations of the physical body. The NDE, though, leaves an indelible impression in most of the experiencers. It is as if they try to live out the values of love, wisdom, truth, joy, beauty and peace which have transfused their beings. Such a shift of attitude and perspective can create difficulties for close relationships where the partner remains unchanged. There tends to be a change from 'having' to 'being', that is away from purely material concerns and priorities. Subjects embark on a pursuit of wisdom and make love the central value of their lives.

It is illuminating to compare the NDE and its accompanying transformation of values with the effects of conversion and initiation. William James (James, 1903) characterises conversion as a change in what he calls 'the habitual centre of personal energy', which precipitates 'a mental rearrangement' or reordering of priorities and values. The parallels with initiation are even more apparent, since one of its essential features is a ritual death and rebirth, a separation from the old and an embracing of the new (Eliade, 1958; Grosso, 1986). Grosso quotes an early Greek writer, Themistios, as stating that the soul has the same experience at the point of death as those who are being initiated: 'First one is struck by a marvellous light, one is received into pure regions and meadows'. In this sense, expe-riencers of NDEs are unwitting initiates who have usually had no preparation whatsoever, in contrast with the careful instruction which preceded ancient initiation rituals. In this vein the poet Rumi writes:

> O man go die before thou diest,
> So that thou shalt not have to suffer death when thou shalt die,
> Such a death that thou wilst enter into light,
> Not a death through which thou wilst enter into the grave.

In other words, die a death leading to a new or second, spiritual birth. In speaking of patterns of initiation, Mircea Eliade (Eliade, 1958) remarks on the initiatory character of the ordeals and spiritual crises of life: 'it remains true nonetheless that man becomes himself only after having solved a series of desperately difficult and even dangerous situations; that is after having undergone "tortures" and "death", followed by an awakening to another life, qualitatively different because regenerated. If we look closely, we see that every human life is made up of a series of "deaths" and "resurrections"'. Eliade observes that such initiations are usually effective only at a psychological rather than ontological level, which I think is by and large true for NDEs, although transformations can be so profound as to be clearly ontological when there is literally a change (or revelation) of being.

Some people refer to the NDE as a 'telephone call from God', which acts as a reminder of their true nature. Plato's myth of Lethe illustrates human forgetfulness of the nature of being and the purpose of human life. It is a spiritual awakening which makes people conscious of their journey and responsibilities. Typically, the spirituality of experiencers is deepened and they experience a spiritual feeling of closeness to the Divine. The emphasis is therefore on the inner life more than on outer ritual and church attendance. Church goers find themselves taking a more mystical approach and become more concerned with an underlying universal core of religions—what Schuon calls 'the transcendent unity of religions'. They also enjoy spending more time alone and in Nature.

In their search for the meaning of life and death, a significant number of NDE experiencers become interested, as I said, in more esoteric aspects of religion and spirituality. The lifework of Frithjof Schuon has been to formulate the transcendent unity of religions, showing that esoterism is the true form of ecumenism, not a watered down and compromised liberalism. The problems arise from the fact that Revelation is intrinsically absolute and extrinsically relative. In other words, the essence is absolute and the form relative: 'Religious revelation is both a veil of light and a light veiled'. Restrictive dogma arises when the form is taken to be equivalent to the essence. The esoteric aspects of a religion are its hidden inner essence only accessible through gnosis to those who have developed the appropriate organs of perception; while the exoteric aspects are the doctrines, dogmas and rituals in which the churchgoer is expected to believe implicitly and often unquestioningly.

Schuon characterises the relationship between esoterism and exoterism as follows (Nasr, 1986):

> Esoterism on the one hand prolongs exoterism—by harmoniously plumb-
> ing its depth—because the form expresses the essence and because in this
> respect the two enjoy solidarity, while on the other hand esoterism oppos-
> es exoterism—by transcending it abruptly—because essence by virtue of
> its unlimitedness is of necessity not reducible to form, or in other words,

because form, inasmuch as it constitutes a limit, is opposed to whatever is totality and liberty. (Nasr, 90)

He continues further on:

> We could say, simplifying a little, that exoterism puts the form—the credo —above the essence—Universal Truth—and accepts the latter only as a function of the former; the form, through its divine origin, is here the criterion of the essence. Esoterism, on the contrary, puts the essence above the form...the essence is the criterion of the form; the one and universal Truth is the criterion of the various religious forms of the Truth...the particular or the limited is recognised as the manifestation of the principal and the transcendent, and this in its turn reveals itself as immanent. (Nasr, 96)

In contemporary terms, we have here the tension and conflict between the esoteric, universal and mystical approach and the exoteric, literalist, fundamentalist view. The fundamentalist pronounces his own revelation as absolute, exclusive and unique, so that anyone not accepting it on those terms is cast into outer darkness and forfeits salvation. The near-death experiencer will tend to express a more inclusive philosophy corresponding to the ineffability of the experience. Indeed one fundamentalist who had an NDE came back with the (to them) surprising thought that 'God isn't interested in theology'! Another experiencer tells of a presence which asked 'What is in your heart?' and added that what mattered most was the love expressed in one's life; also that there is no such thing as sin, as humans commonly understand the term. The emphasis throughout is on being rather than belief, and actions infused with spiritual qualities.

A modern initiate and spiritual Master who was also an exponent of the perennial wisdom is the Bulgarian Beinsa Douno (Peter Deunov, 1864–1944). He taught in Bulgaria from 1900, and began giving systematic lectures in 1914. Between that time and his passing, he gave some 7,000 lectures and talks on every aspect of human existence. The cardinal principles of his Teaching, though, are simple: Love, Wisdom and Truth (Lorimer, 1991a):

> The first principle on which the whole of existence is based is Love; it brings the impulse to life; it is the compass, the stimulus within the human soul.
>
> The second principle is Wisdom, which brings knowledge and light to the mind, thus enabling human beings to use the forces of Nature in a noetic way.
>
> The third principle is Truth; it frees the human soul from bondage and encourages her to learn, work well and make efforts towards self-sacrifice.

> There is nothing greater than these three principles; there is no straighter or surer path. In these three principles lies the salvation of the world.

These are the principles which we have already encountered in connection with the perennial philosophy and the NDE. They are expressed in practical form through the sacred dance movements of paneurythmy (Lorimer, 1991b). Douno echoes Schuon's remarks about essence and form, but with a distinct emphasis:

> Love does not recognise any religion. It is Love itself which creates religions. In the Divine World there are no religions.
> There, only Love exists. Love is the very atmosphere of the Divine World. And everything in it breathes Love.
> Since Love cannot manifest on earth, there arose the need for religions. However, if you wish to fulfil the will of God, it is essential to substitute Love for religion (Douno, 21).

Religions are therefore the various forms and expressions of the Divine, and all have love or compassion at their core. The statement that Love is the very atmosphere of the Divine World expresses the experience in the NDE of being immersed in love and light (wisdom); and the centrality of the principle of Love in the NDE and its aftereffects unites it with the mystical and wisdom traditions in world religions. The success of two recent books on the NDE (Eadie, 1992; Brinkley, 1994) suggests to me that the spiritual content contains a message which resonates with many contemporary seekers. It comes directly out of an individual's experience and yet contains universal elements which speak to our condition and yet point beyond it to the more profound and systematic teachings expressed in the perennial wisdom and outlined above.

Some aspects of the NDE, then, can be seen as an opening into the transcendent realms beyond and within the apparently self-sufficient and closed physical system. It reveals to the experiencer hitherto unknown and little explored dimensions of the self, indicating that human beings are more than a physical body-mind. The experience can be regarded as a seed for spiritual growth in the perennial principles of Love, Wisdom and Truth. Although these principles are universal, they are lived and experienced by individuals. Future forms of spirituality will, I believe, draw both on individual experience and timeless tradition, which remains a yardstick of its authenticity and sets it in a broader and deeper context.

REFERENCES

Brinkley, D. (1994). *Saved by the Light*. New York: Villard.

Brown, Rosemary (1974). *Immortals at My Elbow*. London: Bachman and Turner.

Douno, B. (Deunov, P.). *Le Maître Parle*. Paris: Le Courrier du Livre.

Eadie, B. (1992). *Embraced by the Light*. Placerville, CA: Goldleaf Press.

Eliade, M. (1958). *Rites and Symbols of Initiation*. New York: Harper and Row.

Grosso, M. (1986). *The Final Choice*. Walpole, NH: Stillpoint.

Hardy, Sir A. (1979). *The Spiritual Nature of Man*. Oxford: Oxford University Press.

Huxley, Aldous. (1954). *The Perennial Philosophy*. New York: Harper & Row.

James, W. (1899). *Human Immortality*. London: Constable.

James, W. (1903). *The Varieties of Religious Experience*. London: Longman.

Lee, Sir H. D. P. (1974) *Plato's Republic*. London: Penguin.

Lorimer, D. (1984). *Survival?* London: Routledge & Kegan Paul.

Lorimer, D. (1990). *Whole in One*. London: Arkana.

Lorimer, D. (1991a). *Prophet for Our Times*. Shaftesbury: Element.

Lorimer, D. (1991b). *The Circle of Sacred Dance*. Shaftesbury: Element.

Moody, R. A. (1975). *Life after Life*. New York: Mockingbird/Bantam Books.

Morse, M. (1992). *Transformed by the Light*. New York: Villard.

Nasr, S. H. (ed) (1986). *The Essential Writings of Fritjhof Schuon*. Warwick, NY: Amity House.

Nasr, S. H. (1989). *Knowledge and the Sacred*. New York: State University of New York Press.

Schiller, F. C. S. (1891). *Riddles of the Sphinx*. London: Swan Sonnenschein.

Schuon, Frithjof. (1975). *The Transcendent Unity of Religions*. New York: Harper & Row. Trans. Peter Townsend from *L'Unité Transcendante des Religions*. (1948). Paris: Gallimand.

Searle, J.R. (1992). *The Rediscovery of the Mind*. Cambridge, MA: MIT Press.

Zaleski, C. (1986). *Otherworld Journeys*. New York: Oxford University Press.

23

Mysticism and the Near-Death Experience

Judith Cressy

In general, one can say that the phases of the NDE develop in a way which resembles the stages of the mystic way.

Judith Cressy, a Protestant Doctor of Ministry, had a near-death-like experience herself, and is now convinced that the NDE is a mystical experience, not a case of madness. Here she compares the typical elements of NDEs to the life of the medieval Catholic mystic St. Theresa of Avila. Each shared experiences of ecstatic out-of-body travel, visions of God, clairvoyance, loss of fear of death, and healing transformations. They differ, however, in intention, preparation, understanding, techniques, and communities for reintegration.

NDE survivors are usually thrust unsuspecting into a totally unexpected realm and come back confused and alienated. Mystics usually undertake gradual and regular practices guided by a long tradition. NDE survivors could benefit from finding a spiritual practice to develop their newfound, shocking awareness, Cressy suggests, because in most cases, "one mystical experience does not make a mystic."

In Cressy's experience, some NDErs have achieved the summit of mystical experience, described in the Christian tradition as illumination, God-union, or in the East as no-self and enlightenment. Some NDEs are a mystical awakening, just the beginning of a long transforming path toward illumination and union with the light. Cressy is saying that there is no reason that NDE survivors should undertake such a journey alone, confused and alienated from conventional society. Spiritual communities exist, both within and without conventional religious institutions, that can guide and support the NDErs struggling to integrate their incredible experiences into daily life.

Judith Cressey, M.Div., D.Min., who lives in upstate New York, has been a college chaplain, a minister, a pastoral counselor, a spiritual center director, and is author of the book *Near-Death Experiences: Mysticism or Madness* (1994).

ᔑ Mysticism and the Near-Death Experience ᔐ

> I thought I was being carried up to Heaven: the first persons I saw there were my mother and father, and such great things happened in so short a time.... I wish I could give a description of at least the smallest part of what I learned, but when I try to discover a way of doing so, I find it impossible, for while the light we see here and that other light are both light, there is no comparison between the two and the brightness of the sun seems quite dull if compared with the other. (Afterwards) I was...left with very little fear of death of which previously I had been very much afraid. (Theresa 1960, 361–63)

That is not a survivor of a near-death experience speaking, but the great Christian mystic St. Theresa of Avila, describing what happened to her during the raptures which accompany contemplative prayer or meditation. The resemblance between Theresa's experience and the NDErs I have met is remarkable. Are they the same? In what ways is the NDEr like the mystic? What distinguishes the two? Near-death researchers have called the NDE an experience of mystical illumination and a spontaneous spiritual experience, but what do they mean?

Here I intend to extend the near-death discussion into the realm of the spiritual and mystical in a basic way. I compare the life-long mystical experiences of two Christian mystics, St. Theresa of Avila and St. John of the Cross, to the NDE and its aftereffects. In doing so, I discover the relationship between these mystics and most NDErs to be more remarkable than I supposed. Many NDErs have had a profound mystical experience. The details of the picture begin to emerge, however, when the NDE is compared to models of mystical and spiritual growth. On closer inspection, not all NDEs are spiritually similar, and most NDErs have not attained the heights of spiritual consciousness. Consequently, while many have had profound mystical experiences, none is a perfected saint.

Thus the NDEr may desire to begin or continue a spiritual practice, preferably on one of the spiritual paths attached to the world's religions, to convert the spiritual treasure discovered during the NDE into a permanent asset. One should seek a suitable Yogi, Zen Buddhist Roshi, Sufi Murshid, Native American Medicine Man, or similar teacher from other legitimate traditions. These teachers are available for the NDEr to continue spiritual growth and learn techniques for reentry, and also for those who hope to have a near-death-like mystical experience.

In these spiritual traditions, through thousands of years, the understanding of the dimension of spirit has been developed, and teachers have been trained and legitimized to lead the disciple into the other world and back to earth again. Within the spiritual paths exist the techniques to accomplish transcendence, the intellectual comprehension that accompanies that experience, and the tools for effective reentry.

These spiritual paths of the world's religions should also be the authority on what constitutes spiritual/mystical experience. Many NDErs have had their experiences recognized by legitimate spiritual teachers. The spiritual teacher knows that many NDErs have transcended the realm of this world and ordinary consciousness. They have become, if only for a moment, citizens of heaven. They have had a taste of the afterlife. However, they need more training. One mystical experience does not make a mystic. A mystic intentionally practices a spiritual discipline toward achievement of the goals established by his or her tradition.

On the other hand, the NDE has achieved public visibility, credibility and clarity for those mystical experiences achieved through experiencing one's own death, the death of another, childbirth, or personal crisis. Eight to twelve million *known* NDErs represent a larger *unknown*, and for the most part, silent minority: the masses who have had transcendent experiences. If one has had an experience similar to an NDE, with attendant light, love, information, and especially transformation, then one has had a mystical experience.

To those who believe death and mysticism to be two different categories, I say that death has always been a factor on the spiritual path, the mystic way. A great Sufi teacher has called mysticism "learning to die before you die." For the Christian mystics Theresa and John, mysticism was both the reason for life and a preparation for death. On the spiritual path, the soul becomes pure enough to blend into the light, and during ecstasy the soul glimpses the afterlife, as with Theresa:

I think that this experience has been of great help to me in teaching me where our true home is and in showing me that on earth we are but pilgrims; it is a great thing to see what is waiting for us there and to know where we are going to live. For if a person has to go and settle in another country, it is a great help to him in bearing the trials of the journey if he has found out that it is a country where he will be able to live in complete comfort. (St. Theresa, 1960, 363–64)

Both death and the NDE have been intimately connected with Christian mysticism. Many of the great mystics began their path with one. Elizabeth Petroff tells us that:

A surprising number of biographies and autobiographies tell of an apparent dying, often when a teenager, of being taken for dead and perhaps even put in a coffin but then miraculously coming back to life, often with an explicit visionary message for the world. This happened to Christina Mirabilis, Catherine of Siena, Madalena Beuthler, St. Theresa of Avila, and Julian of Norwich. (1986, 40)

Carol Zaleski has pointed to the historic development of mysticism from the NDE:

The near-death medieval narratives…correspond to what historian Peter Dinzelbacher calls the first phase of medieval Christian vision literature (lasting until the mid-thirteenth century) in which the visionary travels out of his or her body to visit heaven, hell and purgatory, and returns to life transformed. (1987, 6)

Though united in a common intimacy with death, NDErs and mystics differ, however, in intention, preparation, understanding, techniques, and communities for reintegration. On the spiritual path, growth is slow. Each experience is accompanied by an integration of the emotional intellectual, physical components of the individual. Unlike the mystic, the NDEr is suddenly jettisoned unprepared into another world and the higher reaches of spiritual consciousness. Often the NDEr must make up emotional and intellectual deficiencies by entering school, counseling, a new career, or a spiritual path. Unlike the mystic, NDErs return to an alien community rather than to a monastery. They return to a culture dominated by secular materialism, with little understanding of and less interest in mysticism. They may misunderstand their own experience. The difficult task of reentering life and recovery from death is compounded by the often negative feed-back provided the NDEr by his/her own community. The conflicts and tensions that result may create pathology where previously only a penchant for mysticism existed.

THE NDE AND THE MYSTICISM OF ST. THERESA OF AVILA AND ST. JOHN OF THE CROSS

The sixteenth-century Spanish world of St. Theresa of Avila and St. John of the Cross was equally dangerous to mystics. Fear of the Inquisition silenced many. St. John of the Cross did not speak openly about his mystical experiences, but disguised them in the metaphoric nuances of poetry. Theresa, however, did write of her mystical experience in *The Autobiography of Theresa of Jesus*. Because of her courage we have a legacy of personal mystical experiences to compare to modern near-death accounts.

Any NDEr unfamiliar with Theresa's writings will be surprised, I believe, to discover that, from beginning to end of her mystical career, Theresa appeared to experience the same events as an NDE. Theresa's may have been a different style of mysticism from the Christian norm, but she has been accorded a high status by the Church. She was the spiritual companion and friend of the mystical doctor of the Church, St. John of the Cross. They understood and aided one another in their earthly careers, as well as spiritual journeys. Theresa tells us about her ecstatic out-of-body spiritual experiences:

> Turning now to this sudden transport of the spirit it may be said…that the soul really seems to have left the body; on the other hand it is clear that the person is not dead…. He feels as if he had been in another world, very different from this in which we live, and has been shown a fresh light there, so much unlike any to be found in this life long, it would have been impossible for him to obtain any idea of them. In a single instant he is taught so many things all at once, that, if he were to labor for years on end in trying to fit them all into his imagination and thought, he could not succeed with a thousandth part of them. This…is seen with the eyes of the soul very much more clearly than we can see things with the eyes of the body; and some of the revelations are communicated to it (the soul) without words. (1961, 160)

During rapture Theresa obtains all knowledge instantaneously and tele-pathically, has a life review, sees the light, and like the NDEr below, loses all fear of death.

> If this is what death is like, then I'm not afraid to go…. If that's anyway like the hereafter is, then I'm not afraid to go at all. I have absolutely no fear at all…I'm not afraid of dying, I'm not really afraid and I used to be scared to death. (Ring, 1982, 177)

The similarity of Theresa's mystical experience to that of the NDE survivor does not end with a heavenly journey. Having tasted death, both are capable of seeing the souls of the dying. Among many such instances, Theresa recounts:

> Another friar of our Order—a very good friar—was extremely ill; and while I was at Mass I became recollected and saw that he was dead and was ascending into Heaven without passing through purgatory. He had died, as I afterward heard, at the very hour at which I saw him. (1960, 374)

Kenneth Ring discovered that NDE survivors have reported similar sightings:

> Seeing apparitions of dead persons is by no means as rare as many people think...and there are several such cases from my own files. Often these forms seem to coincide with the time of their death. A suggestive example of this was furnished by one of my correspondents who had her near-death experience in 1953. She writes: "Five years ago, my brother, age fifty-two, passed away. At 4:00 AM. that day, I was awakened by a soft, luminous light at the foot of my bed. It slowly ascended upward and disappeared. Half an hour later, I was notified of his passing, exactly at 4:00 AM. While the light was present, I felt extremely tranquil and didn't move." (1984, 176)

Theresa, like some NDErs, often returned from ecstasy healed of any illness and stronger and more energetic than before. Others were not so fortunate. "There are people of so frail a constitution that one experience of the Prayer of Quiet has killed them" (St. Theresa 1961, 49). This "Prayer of Quiet" (a high degree of contemplative prayer) is marred for Theresa by the mistaken madness of poetic but confused utterance. "I used often to commit follies because of this love," she says, like the NDEr who hugged everyone when he returned (1960, 164–66). Theresa also composed poetry at this stage and was unable to reason: "Many words are spoken during this state, in praise of God, but unless the Lord Himself puts order into them, they have no orderly form" (1960, 164).

At this stage, Theresa used the boldly metaphoric speech of the mystic, which is often mistaken as psychotic babble. She too was called mad, even telling her superior: "I beseech your Reverence, let us all be mad for the Love of Him who was called mad for our sakes" (1960, 277).

A MYSTICAL ATTITUDE AND NEAR-DEATH AFTER-EFFECTS

During the beginning or purgatorial stage of the mystic way, effort is required to practice the virtues of detachment from wealth, status, and personal relationship. Rapture brings achievement when, according to Theresa:

> The Lord helps and transforms a soul, so that it seems no longer to be
> itself, or even its own likeness…. It is no longer bound by ties of relation-
> ship, friendship, or property. Previously all its acts of will and resolutions
> and desires were powerless to loosen these and seemed only to bind them
> the more. (St. Theresa, 1961, 107)

The NDEr also no longer cares for wealth or status:

> Before I was living for material things…. Before I was conscious of only
> me, what I had, what I wanted…. I have gradually sloughed off the desires
> to have and to hold earthly possessions, material possessions to any great
> degree. (Ring, 1984, 132)

Competitive status seeking, so prevalent in our culture, is perceived by
another NDEr as false.

> Now…I'm starting to see that God didn't want me as a professional psy-
> chologist, dragging in the big bucks, getting all involved with the big words
> and labels for other people's conditions, and me getting all puffed up with
> my importance. He has made me a candle, lighting the place where I am.
> (Ring, 1984, 130)

The frantic search for wealth and material status which characterizes our
culture has nothing to do with what the NDEr learns is the meaning of life,
which is simply "…love. Fulfilling yourself with that love—by giving" (Ring,
1980, 57).

The NDE expands the capacity to feel and express other emotions, as well
as love. When remembering the light, NDErs often weep copious tears.
Theresa, too, shed tears of joy during her raptures. They were for her a
validation that the experience was real. Theresa was not alone. Petroff tells
us that:

> In the middle ages, women mystics often wept uncontrollably: among
> them Marie d'Oignies, Angela of Foligno and Margery Kempe…[their]
> tears were accompanied by loud sobbing resulting in embarrassment for
> them and their supporters. (1986, 38–39)

The weeping of the mystics was called "the gift of tears." The supernatural
visions and voices which accompany the mystic life were also considered
gifts.

VISIONS AND VOICES

Theresa heard the Voice of her Lord throughout her entire life. At times He was her only companion and counsel. Theresa believed these supernatural experiences to be divine favors, and offers advice for distinguishing between the Voice of God and the works of the devil. If the experience is powerful, memorable and has a good effect upon the soul, it can be said to come from God. The NDE is the most memorable and wonderful event in the life of the experiencer. It leaves them more compassionate, energetic, and eager to serve God and humanity in some helping capacity.

St. John of the Cross both affirms that supernatural events do occur in the life of the spiritual aspirant, and utters warnings of the dangers inherent in these supernatural gifts. In the *Ascent of Mt. Carmel*, John provides instructions to those who pass through the stage of supernatural visions in their ascent to the God who is beyond all form. He also discusses the supernatural visions and voices that the aspirant is likely to encounter, including revelations which are "the intellectual understanding of truths about God, or...a vision of present, past or future events which bear resemblance to the spirit of prophecy" (St. John, 194). Similarly, NDErs such as Tom Sawyer have this clairvoyant and prophetic ability. Tom has told me that he views all events now in three dimensions. He says he can see all the causes that have led to an event, perceive eventual outcomes, and intuitively read a person's heart.

John of the Cross affirms that "those who have reached perfection or are already close to it usually possess light and knowledge about events happening in their presence or absence...and can perceive the talents of men and what lies in their hearts" (1979, 198). These supernatural talents are signs, then, of spiritual growth, but are to be avoided because they detain the spiritual aspirant on his or her journey to the God who is beyond all images, or serve as occasions for spiritual inflation.

INEFFABILITY

The task of communicating mystical experience to those who have not had one is difficult. Theresa complains of the same essential "ineffability" which plagues NDErs' attempts to explain a spiritual experience in earthly language. "However clearly I may wish to describe these matters which concern prayer," she says, "they will be very obscure to anyone who has no experience of it.... Anyone who has attained to raptures will, I know, understand it well. If he has not experienced it, it will seem ridiculous" (1960, 124, 176).

Similarly, "anticipation of ridicule or doubts about their sanity," Zaleski says, "prevent the NDEr from speaking about their experience" (147–48). Silence, however, presents as great a risk as speaking. NDErs who remain silent never heal. Talking about the experience may be part of their personal healing and the healing of the culture, but to speak requires courage. Women mystics suffered from the same conflict between speech and silence, according to Elizabeth Petroff:

> Many women mystics speak of a period of illness that precedes their decisions to write down their experiences. They are fearful about what they expect to be a negative response to their writing, yet inwardly compelled to speak publicly of what they have experienced. The resolution to their dilemma comes only when a divine voice tells them they must write. Once they begin, they find that it is a healing process and that they gain strength from articulating what they know about the spiritual life. (1986, 42)

PAIN AND PERSECUTION

NDErs who do gather the courage to speak of their experiences have met with envy, fear, ridicule, and skepticism, as did St. Theresa when people learned of her raptures and supernatural favors:

> When this (her raptures) became known, people began to have a good opinion of one whose wickedness all were not fully aware.... Then suddenly began evil-speaking and persecution.... They said that I wanted to become a saint and that I was inventing new-fangled practices. (1960,186)

Apparently Theresa, like the NDEr, suffered from "the pedestal effect", first undeservedly elevated and then persecuted. A number of NDErs I know complain that their families alternatively view them as saints or insane. Neither is true. NDErs, like Theresa in the early stages of her mystical career, are not yet perfected saints. Nor are they mad, as society called St. Theresa of Avila, St. Francis of Assisi and now the NDEr.

Theresa's most serious persecutions came from those who believed she was possessed by the devil, a charge that some fundamentalist Christians bring against NDErs. Theresa was forbidden to pray or to be alone or go to communion. This went on for two years, until she found someone who had shared her experience and knew it was of value. "But just then," she complained, "I needed someone who had gone through it all for such a person alone could understand me and interpret my experience" (1960, 277).

Elaine Winner also complains of the loneliness that followed her NDE.

> I felt totally alone. I began wondering about my sanity.... I didn't know what to do, who to turn to.... I was frustrated and I begged God to let me die again—I wanted the pleasantness. There are so many experiencers out there who need to be reached, she said. They need to be told they are not

crazy, that they are not alone and that they should not be afraid of being made fun of. (Steinbuch, 62)

Elaine had entered the "dark night of the soul," like Theresa, who, alienated from the world and abandoned by God, felt "Crucified between heaven and earth" (1960, 194).

By virtue of these shared experiences and changes, the NDEr has often unwittingly entered the ancient community of mystics. However, they have not yet become perfected mystics or saints. To retain the spiritual treasure and continue growth toward higher mystical states, NDErs might find it helpful to seek out a competent spiritual guide. The availability of both learned and experienced spiritual guides is as poor today, however, as it was in Theresa's time. She considered poor spiritual direction part of her dark night of the soul.

CHRISTIAN MYSTICISM

Three typical stages of the Christian mystical way are: (1) Purgation as a Beginner, (2) Illumination as a Proficient, and (3) Union in Perfection. At the stage of the beginner, the spiritual pupil does all the work, and God does very little. Discipline is required to remain in prayer or meditation, and to detach from the things of this world. In the later stages, according to Theresa, God begins to do the work through the gift of ecstatic raptures. The act of purgation, or cleansing the soul of negativity, however, continues throughout the spiritual journey of both the mystic and the NDEr.

The second stage of the mystic way, Illumination, is achieved through a vision of a real, unearthly light, according to Evelyn Underhill:

> What is the nature of this mysterious illumination? Apart from the message it transmits, what is the form which it most usually assumes in the consciousness of self? The illuminative, one and all, seem to assure us that its apparently symbolic name is a realistic one; that it appears to them as a kind of radiance, a flooding of the personality with new light…. "Light rare, untellable!" said Whitman. "The flowing light of the Godhead," said Mechtild of Magdeburg, trying to describe what it was that made the difference between her universe and that of normal men. "*Lux vivens dicit*," said Hildegard of her revelations, which she described as appearing in a special light, more brilliant than the brightness around the sun. It is an "infused brightness," says St. Theresa, "a light which knows no night; but rather as it is always light, nothing ever disturbs it." (298–99)

The NDEr who has seen this light knows its reality. I believe they have had an experience of mystical illumination. They have ceased to be beginners, and entered the next phase of spiritual growth.

The final goal of Christian mysticism is, however, Union with God. St. John of the Cross describes this as a union of the soul with the Trinity of Love, Power, and Wisdom. The NDEr who encounters the Light also experiences this totality of Love, Power, and Wisdom. One woman who nearly died from childbirth and saw the Light said:

> It was a dynamic light, not like a spotlight. It was an incredible energy—a light you wouldn't believe. I almost floated in it. It was feeding my consciousness feelings of unconditional love, complete safety, and complete, total perfection.... It just dived into you. My consciousness was going out and getting larger and taking in more; I expanded and more and more came in. It was such rapture, such bliss. And then, and then, a piece of knowledge came in, it was that I was immortal.... Later when I was saying the Lord's Prayer, and I got to that part that says, "thine is the kingdom, and the power and the glory," I thought that nothing could describe this experience any better. It was pure power and glory." (Zaleski, 125)

Another woman, during open-heart surgery, was bathed in the Light: "It was in, around and through everything. It is what halos are made of. It is God made visible." (Zaleski,125).

As NDErs are transformed when united with the Light, so are mystics. According to John, union with the Light transforms or "divinizes" the soul, for "He created her in his image and likeness that she might attain such resemblance." In divinization:

> God makes the soul die to all that He is not, so that...He may clothe it anew.... This renovation is an illumination of the human intellect with supernatural light so that it becomes divine, united with the divine; an informing of the will with love of God so that it is no longer less than divine and loves in no other way than divinely.... And this soul will be a soul of heaven, heavenly and more divine than human. (St. John, 1979, 569, 36)

Entering or merging with the Light during an NDE results in a spiritual transformation of the soul which, however, may be only temporary and therefore imperfect. Even those NDErs who have momentarily achieved the heights of mystical consciousness need to continue their spiritual work upon return, to turn that glimpse into permanent attainment.

Christian mysticism may emphasize the Light, but a number of respected mystics speak of the Darkness of God beyond the light, or a paradoxical union of light and darkness at the highest levels of mystical awareness.

Dionysius the Areopagite speaks of a self-loss "wherein we pass beyond the topmost altitudes of the ascent, and leave behind all divine illuminations and voices and heavenly utterances; and plunge into the darkness where truly dwells as scripture saith, that one which is beyond all things" (Underhill, 39). The contemporary Christian mystic Bernadette Roberts underwent an experience of loss of self into a condition which she describes as "no-self." Prior to that final loss of self, she experienced some of the same paranormal phenomena as the NDEr or the mystic Theresa:

> Matters stood this way for twenty years (the interior flame of union was stable) when suddenly, in this phase, there was a movement in the center, deep inexplicable rumblings which gave me the idea of an impending explosion. When the thermostat was turned up, there came with it an energy never encountered before, a problematic energy in that it gave rise to a rash of extra-ordinary experiences, fore knowledge, knowledge of others, and even the possibility of healing. Whatever the true nature of these energies, it was obvious they wanted to reach outside and find expression.
>
>   I felt about to be used as a medium for these powers, and what that meant, I had no idea. (Roberts, 168–69)

Roberts chose to ignore these as alien to her experience and says that "from the start, I can compare this difficult regime to sitting on a volcano or riding a bronco" (169–72). The sudden explosion of alien energy and extraordinary experiences served as a prelude, for Roberts, to a higher state of mystical consciousness, the Void or Formlessness.

The phase model for the NDE, as developed by Kenneth Ring (1. OBE, 2. Heaven, 3. the Light), is helpful in our endeavor to compare mystical experiences to the NDE, discovering thereby both differences and similarities. In general, one can say that the phases of the NDE develop in a way which resembles the stages of the mystic way. At each phase of the NDE a higher stage of mystical consciousness is achieved. The relationship between near-death phases and mystical stages is further strengthened by examining a universal model of mystical consciousness developed by transpersonal psychologist Ken Wilber, as discussed in *Spiritual Choices*.

In my observations, those who abort at the OBE phase may return as psychics, but not mystics. Those who enter heaven may encounter specific spiritual beings, usually from their own tradition, and return as converts to a specific religious tradition. Entrance into the Light or Darkness of God usually results in a more universal spirituality, in which the new mystic feels at home in all the spiritual traditions of the world. The difference in depth of NDE, as measured by the phase at which the experience ends, may therefore account for the differences in religious and spiritual responses that occur together with a more universal spirituality.

MYSTICS AND METAPHYSICS

Emotional response to the NDE is hardly apathetic. People are usually either attracted or repelled. Negative reactions are often fear, anger, or envy. Indeed, intellectual skepticism may be a rationalization for a more instantaneous and primal emotional reaction to the challenge presented by the NDE to one's norms or world-view. The NDE presents the potential for shattering the structure of reality upon which one's life rests, however precariously. Fear and anger to such a threat is understandable. The imminent destruction of a worldview is a kind of death, and the worldview threatened is our society's materialism.

But there are other viable philosophical options that make better sense of the both the NDE and mysticism. In Hinduism and Buddhism, for instance, the metaphysical substructure is Idealism, in which mind or consciousness assumes ultimate reality. During my mystical experience, I made a similar discovery: mind, not matter, is the ultimate building block of the universe. By mind, I do not mean the brain's rational, dualistic consciousness, but the existence of another dimension: higher consciousness, Christ-consciousness, or Spirit—the source of Truth and inspiration.

Much of Hindu philosophy is based on information received during the meditative state. This information is accorded a higher place in the scale of human intelligence than the technical or rational reason that we so admire in the West. In industrial society the development of science and technology appeared to justify the conclusion that materialism was correct. The function of philosophy to discover Truth became obsolete, as science became the sole authority, and God became a figment of human imagination.

In the midst of this materialistic gloom, one philosophical light is Alfred North Whitehead. In his *Process and Reality*, he constructs a philosophy that can explain both mystical experience and the ordinary reality of the average man or woman living in a scientific age. Reality, for Whitehead, is not static nor mechanical, but organismic, a process of the evolution of interrelated systems. Howard Storm tells me that Whitehead's view of reality corresponds to what he learned during his NDE.

Though Whitehead's philosophy has the obvious advantage of providing a metaphysical system which could unite theology and science, his most important contribution to a metaphysical understanding of the NDE is to be found in his epistemology. Whitehead calls his philosophy a modified idealism. Mind or subject once more becomes the basis for reality. Though Whitehead agrees that there is something out there which we can call objective reality, he doubts that we will every be able to know what it is. The "symbol," an inextricable and unavoidable union of concept and percept, is all we shall every know. We are confined by the limits of our perceptual capacities and by the concepts, or ideas, or beliefs about reality that we hold in our minds. Hence, according to Whitehead, Zaleski is essentially correct in calling the NDE a set of symbols. Symbols, however, form the basis of our ordinary human, earthly, experience, also. We are no more likely to observe objective reality directly in this world than we are in the next. Whitehead's epistemology, therefore, reduces real distinctions between this world and the next, and potentially subjects them both to intellectual scrutiny.

From the sociological perspective, Peter Berger has described the process by which all cultures create and define their reality: through common language, experience and consensus. In *The Sacred Canopy* and *Rumor of Angels*, Berger contends that theology has reneged on its function to represent the transcendent in culture and joined the mainstream majority. Theology should, he feels, remain a minority culture committed to discovering "rumors of angels" such as these near-death stories.

In *The Social Construction of Reality*, Berger and Luckmann describe how each culture defines its safe circle, or "nomos," its norms for reality and behavior. He describes what happens to the deviate, the one who stands on the edge of the safe circle. Since the deviate reminds the inhabitants of the "nomos" of their own mortality and capacity for insanity, deviates are scapegoated. Berger has here described the situation of the NDEr who, having returned from death and the experience of a new reality, threatens the comfort, safety, and security of others.

Furthermore, Berger goes on to suggest that minority cultures shape themselves in the same fashion as the majority: through common experience, language, and consensus. Thus the NDErs and the mystic together shape a minority community based on a world-view that differs radically in many respects from the majority culture. The majority consider matter the ultimate reality, and unquestioningly accept the conclusions of their five senses. To the average American, the rational intellect or ego is the epitome of intellectual development, science is the accepted arbiter of truth, and God either doesn't exist or is a figment of imagination or creation of the human mind. Language is linear and limited to signs or words that have a single meaning. To them, objects have an ultimate reality "out there." Anything in the mind is merely subjective and less real.

On the other hand, the mystic and NDEr have learned by experience that spiritual realities do exist. For the NDEr, the Divine, Spirit, is the Ultimate Reality, and this world merely a poor reflection. NDErs trust their supersenses. Mystics believe that Truth resides in the Mind of God, and that true information and inspiration flow from there, however distorted they may be by the human channel. Mystics and NDErs understand the nature of both language and reality to be multidimensional, and they often speak in metaphors, symbols, and images. Communication is often telepathic, and community is shaped on the common bond with God as well as each other. Through mutual experience and insight, they validate each other's world-view. A minority mystical community created by consensus and validating its own norms is not mad; it is merely different. The power of the near-death movement is, therefore, that it is providing an opportunity to create an alternative minority community, which in turn can effectively challenge and change our models and perhaps our world.

REFERENCES

Berger, Peter. (1967). *Sacred Canopy: Elements of a Sociological Theory of Religion*. Garden City: Doubleday.

Berger, Peter A. (1969). *A Rumor of Angels: Modern Society and the Rediscovery of the Supernatural*. Garden City: Doubleday.

Berger, Peter, and Thomas Luckmann.(1966). *A Social Construction of Reality: A Treatise in the Sociology of Knowledge*. Garden City: Doubleday.

Petroff, Elizabeth A. (1986). *Medieval Women's Visionary Literature*. Oxford: Oxford University Press.

Ring, Kenneth. (1980). *Life at Death*. New York: William Morrow.

Ring, Kenneth. (1984). *Heading Toward Omega*. New York: William Morrow.

Roberts, Bernadette. (1985). *The Path to No-Self*. Boston and London: Shambhala.

St. John of the Cross. (1979). *The Collected Works of St. John of the Cross*. Kiernan Kavanaugh and Otilio Rodriquez, translators. Washington, D.C.: ICS Publication.

St. Theresa of Avila. (1960). *The Life of Theresa of Jesus*. Allison E. Peers, translator and editor. Garden City, New York: Image Books, Doubleday.

St. Theresa of Avila. (1961). *Interior Castle of St. Theresa of Avila.*. Allison E. Peers, translator. Garden City: Doubleday.

Steinbuch, Yaron A. (1986). "The Near-Death Experiences: The After Effects." Unpublished manuscript.

Underhill, Evelyn. (1923). *Mysticism*. London: Methuen.

Whitehead, Alfred North. (1929). *Process and Reality*. London: Collier Macmillan.

Wilber, Ken, Dick Anthony,and Bruce Ecker. (1987). *Spiritual Choices: The Problems of Recognizing Authentic Paths to Inner Transformation*. New York: Paragon House.

Zaleski, Carol. (1987). *Otherworld Journeys: Accounts of Near-Death Experience in Medieval and Modern Times*. New York: Oxford University Press.

⁓ 24 ⁓

The No-Thing-ness of Near-Death Experiences

Lee W. Bailey

Look for no-thing in the release of experience, the joy of paradox, and the transparent glass-ness of story.

Lee W. Bailey, Ph.D., is a religious studies scholar who detects plenty of no-thing in near-death experiences. Our culture has mastered many techniques of thing-ness, he says, but no-thing-ness tends to slip away. NDEs offer many glimpses of no-thing-ness in a fresh light, such as the no-thing-ness of language, the no-thing-ness of meaning, the no-thing-ness of ego-consciousness, the no-thing-ness of finitude, and the no-thing-ness of God. Looking over the edge of thing-ness at death, what does thing-ness consciousness see? Nothing it can think of. From that view death seems an empty, dark, terrifying void to be denied as far as possible.

But the no-thing-ness sensed in NDEs opens another realm, and it welcomes thinkers on a new/old path to its fullness. Near-death survivors stammer from the ineffability of their experiences, because ordinary language is inadequate to its majesty. They tell of unbelievable journeys into the energetic void of no-thing behind existence. Parallels in philosophy, psychology, and religion, especially in Taoism, welcome the ineffable element of NDEs, pointing to three varieties of consciousness that convey a little no-thing-ness: the release of experience, the joy of paradox, and the transparent glass-ness of story.

Lee W. Bailey, Ph.D., teaches Religion and Culture at Ithaca College in upstate New York. His publications include *Rudely Stamp'd: Imaginal Disability and Prejudice*, and articles on mythology, projection in psychology and religion, and the philosophy of technology. He is listed in *Who's Who in the East*.

∿ The No-Thing-ness of
Near-Death Experiences ∿

There is a neglected paradox in the accounts of near-death experiences (NDEs). Survivors keep saying that NDEs are ineffable: nothing can adequately express such a powerful mystery as the possible return from death in merely human mutterings. Of course this problem has not stopped us from endless scribbling and debate. But if we are to honor this report from the edge of life, we might ask how to be warmed by the ineffable no-thing never quite said. For as T. S. Eliot noted: "the communication of the Dead is tongued with fire beyond the language of the living" (Eliot, 50). One near-death survivor says he was pulled by Light far into the cosmos, where he drifted amidst the infinite "NO THING from which all things emerge" (Atwater, 70).

Before questioning no-thing, we must ask "What is a thing?" (Heidegger, 1967). Our industrial society defines a thing not as a substance made by a God, but as an object that can be known by a subject. The procedures for knowing things object-ively have been developed in the scientific method, which has effectively ruled out individual subjective bias by collective verification. The utility of this procedure has led to the belief that science gains a "value-free" knowledge of things. However, this belief neglects the collective "values" underlying this understanding of thing-ness. This system is placed at the altar of serving humans. Thing-ness is based on the collective "value" of anthropocentric power and pleasure.

The mystique of modernism that made thing-ness seem self-evidently valid is dissolving in late twentieth-century post-modern doubt. Many presuppositions underlying industrial society's faith in thing-ness have been deconstructed (Norris). A massive repression of other-ness was required to strengthen thing-ness. This repression denied, for example, the role of imaginative images at the level of basic definitions. But the very image of the differentiation between subject and object now evokes a radical uncertainty because, as the psychoanalytic revolution has shown, there is an indeterminate amount of unconscious-ness in any conscious formulation. Dualisms such as this can claim no privileged authority or absolute truth. Inner and outer, facts and interpretations, history and imagination, are constantly intertwined. Soul and world are relatively useful distinctions within a never-ending communion, an unconscious prior participation.

Thing-ness is a powerful cultural construct, so its de-construction sends around shivers of nihilism and despair. Outside thing-ness, the other seems fearfully insane, childish, or primitive. But the relativization of thing-ness need not be nihilistic. When the bright dominance of thing-ness dims, then no-thing-ness gently rises over the horizon. Or thing-ness may stimulate an angry reversal. "Men are mad," charges the comparative mythologist David Miller, "It is now the time of the return of the repressed. Nothing is coming again" (Miller, 74). Miller evokes the silent voice of no-thing and no-self in the many gods of polytheism and in the archetypal depths of Christianity. The decline of thing-ness brings a revolutionary change in consciousness. Mark C. Taylor exposes the death of a theistic God and his correlative human ego, the end of history as a sequence of facts, closure of the book as final revelation, and a wandering, amazing opening into communion with otherness (Taylor, 1984).

Near-death experiences are one way that no-thing-ness has wandered into the post-modern soul. The modern thing-ness of skillful medical resuscitation has uncovered one face of no-thing-ness, and we call it "near-death experiences." It evades much of the mastery, control and certain knowledge sought by thing-ness. It thrives in experience, paradox and story. No-thing can be thought, but only if there is no-thing to it.

We can differentiate five openings where no-thing comes to light in near-death experiences: 1. the no-thing-ness of language, 2. the no-thing-ness of meaning, 3. the no-thing-ness of ego-consciousness, 4. the no-thing-ness of finitude, and 5. the no-thing-ness of God.

FIVE PATHS OF NO-THING

1. The no-thing-ness of language

When near-death survivors emphasize, with a rush of feeling or a sigh, that the intensity and power of their experience is just beyond words, beyond the narrow capability of ordinary language, they are echoing the ancient theme of ineffability. One survivor said:

Now, there is a real problem for me as I'm trying to tell you this, because all the words I know are three-dimensional.... And of course, our world—the one we're living now—*is* three-dimensional, but the next one definitely isn't. And that's why it's so hard to tell you this. (Moody 1975, 26)

Such a brush with the wings of mystery flows more freely through poetic metaphor than literal prose, but even poetry only glimpses the vast silent awe.

A bold text about the impossibility of adequately communicating no-thing comes out of the Taoist tradition of China: the *Tao Te Ching*, by Lao Tsu, a legendary sixth-century BCE mystic who, according to legend, almost refused to write it down. Those who insist that we should not speak of things mystical at all would agree with Lao Tsu's strictest view of ineffability:

Those who know do not talk.
Those who talk do not know. (Lao Tsu, 56)

Of course Lao Tsu broke his own rule by writing this down, striving to capture in language the ineffable something that is no-thing. In some theories the no-thing glimmering on the edge is judged to be meaningless because it cannot be worded according to conventional rules of discourse. Then it is repressed, but only until some powerful burst of no-thing, such as a near-death experience, breaks into the field of consciousness again. Then, if those who *glimpse* no-thing do not talk, even tongued with fire, poetically and paradoxically, those who do *not* glimpse no-thing will do all the talking. "Get the nothingness back in to words," urges Norman O. Brown:

The aim is words with nothing to them; words that point beyond themselves rather than to themselves; transparencies, empty words. Empty words, corresponding to the void in things. (Brown, 259)

Both speakers and listeners need an ear for the vast rumbling clouds of no-thing trailing behind each word spoken about a near-death experience.

2. The no-thing-ness of meaning

A major theme of Western cultural criticism is that industrial society suffers from the anxiety of meaninglessness. Critics charge that the industrial revolution has traded off the world of deeper spirit and meaning for the power to manipulate things and satisfy pleasures. In our modern consciousness we have lost our sense of "ultimate concern," and we have become estranged from the whole of reality (Tillich). So we shop till we drop, numb the anxiety with various drugs, and vainly seek meaning in the passing fantasies of commercialized popular culture. Full of modern culture, we feel a knawing emptiness, a painful void, a confused shallowness, in the midst of an excess of thing-ness. In this mode, we look over the edge of thing-ness and have to ask "What is meaning?"

This attack is not quite fair, though, because the scientific and technological revolution is full of meaning, the meaning of thing-ness. Visions of utopian technical progress and heroic conquest of evil are inspiring, but the most dynamic meanings of thing-ness are the quest for unlimited power and pleasure, epitomized in modern war and consumerism.

This opens to a yearning for no-thing-ness.

If we leap past modernity and listen to the repressed void bursting out through extraordinary encounters such as near-death experiences, strange new springs of meaning are released from no-thing, and lives are transformed. The repressed and denied no-thing is paradoxically full of transforming surprises, full of healing energy, full of loving Light. Serious drug addicts and alcoholics have NDEs and are turned into caring people. Dannion Brinkely, once a covert assassin, has a NDE and comes back saying "You are a co-creator with God!" Betty Eadie comments that the Light shoved her into a new sense of meaning:

> Until then, I had felt no purpose in life; I had simply ambled along look-ing for love and goodness but never really knowing if my actions were right. Now, within his words, I felt a mission, a purpose; I didn't know what it was, but I knew that my life on earth had not been meaningless. (Eadie, 42)

No-thing-ness, shining through near-death experiences, sparkles with new meanings. Well, not really new meanings. Actually, very old.

3. The no-thing-ness of ego-consciousness

Modern industrial culture has whole-heartedly constructed the world of thing-ness, understood as objects outside and subjects inside. But thing-ness is not an independent world. It is a cultural creation of industrial society's scientifically and technologically cultivated collective ego-consciousness. The ego of industrial consciousness, making a world literal, causal, naturalistic, humanistic, ordinary, strives for control and identity. Exercising the will to power and pleasure, this ego lives in what it imagines to be a dead realm of matter to be exploited and polluted at will for its own desires.

For modern Western consciousness, experience has been forced through the strict censorship of a strong but narrow ego-consciousness. We have accepted this in order to gain the power to control nature. But the price has been the severe repression of a great depth, soul and mystery. For example, people from other cultures are often struck by the extreme individualism of our ego-consciousness. The Japanese philosopher Keiji Nishitani, in his book *Religion and Nothingness*, comments that "Inevitably each individual becomes like a lonely but well-fortified island floating on a dead sea of matter" (Nishitani, 11).

Whatever the thing-ness style of consciousness cannot know is denegrated as entertainment to be commercialized, illusion to be denied or no-thing to be ignored. And indeed it is no-thing, not fitting the industrial ego's mold of thing-ness. In this Western world-picture, no-thing-ness was turned into the lack of thing-ness and judged unreal. But no-thing-ness is not simply a fearful lack or shadow of thingness. No-thing-ness is reversed when ego is softened. And ego is softened when no-thing reverses it.

But, when experienced outside the walls of the well-fortified subjective ego of industrial culture, no-thing-ness donates its transforming energy to the weary ego itself. No-thing-ness flows gently into the soul when the strong grip of the controlling ego is relaxed, in wonder, in play, in therapy, in meditation, in near-death experiences. Only a broader field of consciousness beyond the industrial ego can sense no-thing-ness, awash in paradox and story. The near-death experience has plenty of no-thing, like the silence between the crashing of the waves. One near-death survior named Bob Helm says:

> I had a natural aptitude for the sciences and mathematics, disciplines based on logic. A childhood faith in some sort of Divine Father had been erod-ed by alcohol and materialism very early in life, and my logical mind would not accept what it could not rationalize. Yet here I was in a hospital, reliv-ing the most important experience of my life, something that had occurred during unconsciousness; and I had never experienced anything more real to me than this.... Death holds little fear for me now, and I know myself and all humankind to be spirit, clad temporarily in body, here on earth to learn and grow. (Ring, 1991, 28, 33)

To glimpse the no-thing-ness in NDEs, researchers must be what we call "objective," but not "objective." On the "objective" side, detached, fair consideration of various positions is important to avoid prejudgment, bias and merely personal opinion. We should acknowledge the many voices in the community of thinkers and the collective nature of good judgment by offering views for discussion, refutation and refinement. We should honor the rules of logic and avoid fallacies as far as possible. We should collect as much data as possible to compare to our theories. These are the guidelines for the quest for truths of all kinds, not just "objective" truth of ego-consciousness about thing-ness. But even in the most strenuous scientific efforts to be "objective," there are non- "objective" factors rich in no-thing-ness, such as honesty and serving humanity. Indeed, these scientific research guidelines themselves are not "objective" principles carved in stone external to human consciousness, but are valuable collective rules for inquiry.

At the same time we are compelled be *not* "objective." The study of NDEs, pro or con, inevitably has a fascination factor, an unconscious motivating element that grabs us and compels us to study this mystery. Otherwise, who cares? Caring may be seen as a large dose of no-thing-ness coming to presence in being (Heidegger, 1962). Occasionally I read an analysis of NDEs that curiously lacks this quality of the experience of care-ful face-to-face listening to survivors of NDEs.

We must also be honest with ourselves about our motives for caring about and therefore researching NDEs, for or against. Am I afraid of something such as death and anxious to overcome that with a compelling story? Am I angry about something such as an authoritarian religious background, and determined to resist all spirituality? Accepting such hidden feelings as possible motives for my arguments requires both honesty and detachment, because they go beneath ordinary ego-consciousness.

Western religions have supported this strong ego development by stressing the importance of the will, although this should be softened by each faith's teachings on humility and transcendence. Sigmund Freud, even while clinging to thing-ness and ego, opened the basement door to no-thing and saw the unconscious lurking in the dark. The subsequent development of Western psychotherapy and all its spin-offs has brought an important new stream of healing no-thing-ness into the soul of industrial society's ego-consiousness. The archetypal psychologist James Hillman beckons the old heroic ego into the imaginal underworld, the basement and cave below. He re-introduced the word "soul" into public discourse and its spreading use is a sign of the ego's softening into imaginal depth. The fantasy of the ego in charge, Hillman stresses, ignores the larger soul's embrace of our little consciousness, the archetypal depths that quietly, unconsciously guide ego's ideas, visions and passions (Hillman, 1975). No-thing-ness passes through soul on its way to consciousness.

Eastern religions, of course, long ago heard the echo of no-thing-ness, and this led straight to their teachings on the no-thing-ness of ego. Buddhists listen for the Unborn, Unoriginated, Uncreated and Unformed Emptiness, Void, No-thing, your face before you were born, the universe before creation. Consequently, Nishitani says that the "Nothingness in Buddhism is non-ego" (33). "When the 'nothing at all' opens up on the near side of the personal self, however, and is seen as the sheer self itself, then nothingness really becomes actualized in the self as the true self" (Nishitani, 71).

No-thing-ness is not contained in dualisms such as our supposedly self-evident subject/object dichotomy. No-thing-ness preceeds and underlies such useful tools for thing-ness thinking. As Nishitani says:

> When the field of nihility opens up simultaneously at the ground of both subject and object, when it appears behind the relationship of subject and object, it always presents itself as a field that has been there from the first at the ground of that relationship. (Nishitani, 109)

At times very subtle, at other times like a blow to the head, no-thing is awakening in the West a resistance to the controls of the in-charge modern ego. Vast like the ocean, no-thing-ness is flowing below our industrial ego's quest for certain knowledge of thing-ness. The near-death experience offers an opportunity to soften the hard edge of ego-consciousness with the gentle stream of its no-thing-ness.

4. The no-thing-ness of finitude

The strong this-worldly will to power and pleasure of industrial culture has denied immortal soul and life after death so forcefully that even religious believers rarely speak of Heaven (until someone dies). What comes after the finitude of life? Nothing I can think of. No-thing. Just live for now in this world of thing-ness, and forget the rest. But why is the power of this anxious denial fading in our time? Perhaps it is the spectre of mass annihilation, made possible by the very success of the industrial ego's powerful military weapons, that has taken our culture over the edge of this denial of death.

Was it the accumulated successes of World War I's massive trench slaughters, World War II's fire-bombing of civilians, the Holocaust, Hiroshima, and the Cold War's mutually assured nuclear destruction that softened the industrial ego's defenses against the no-thing-ness appearing in NDEs? Elisabeth Kübler-Ross, who opened many eyes to the reality of repressed grief, was transformed by her work as a young woman helping to clean up Europe's devastation after World War II. Now NDEs are presenting industrial culture with the possiblity of immortal soul, giving a larger picture for death, a broader context for the finitude of thing-ness. Perhaps the industrial ego's intensified anxiety about finitude will not be satisfied until it releases the repressed no-thing-ness of infinity.

5. The no-thing-ness of God

No-thing-ness is a minor but important theme in Western religions. First, theologians long ago concluded that God created the universe and its light *ex nihilo*. This was an important statement against some cosmologies that envisioned the cosmos to be created out of a pre-existing matter. The creation *ex nihilo* ontologically reaches far behind matter. Second, Western icono-clasm, enshrined in the second commandment against graven images of Gods, is a recognition that no *thing* can adequately picture the divine mystery. So Jews, Christians and Muslims alike are instructed to resist the yearning to paint and carve portraits of the Creator. How can mere stardust picture the invisible no-thing that made all the stars possible? (We won't mention that Michelangelo was allowed to break the second commandment—gloriously— in the Sistine Chapel by portraying God as a wise old man touching Adam's finger to give him life at creation.) Narrowing God down in images may be an unavoidable communication tool, but the tendency to literalize such metaphors in thing-ness thinking promotes forgetfulness. Western religions remember but forget the no-thing-ness of God.

In the midst of these problems arrives the near-death experience, surprising, even annoying some theologians with the dazzling light rather than the expected biblical father figure. But what is light but electromagnetic energy, and ultimately, what is energy, cosmic gravitational energy, tiny subatomic energy? Since mass is energy in formation, according to Einstein, energy is the mysterious underlying structure of thing-ness. What lies behind the many masks of God? Visible energy, called Light, says the near-death experience, not merely an objective, neutral thing, but full of healing power and love. The NDE's Light challenges both theologians and scientists. Can theologians explore the impersonal Light behind the image of a personal God? Can scientists explore the compassion unexpectedly flowing out of supposedly neutral energy? Who can listen for the sparkling silence within that mystery, the no-thing-ness of energy, the *nihilo* out of which the Light flows?

So in the midst of this tangle of the no-thing-ness of language, meaning, ego-consciousness, finitude and God, how can we best hear the far-away echo of no-thing-ness in near-death experiences, sounding just barely in the distance? Look for no-thing in the release of experience, the joy of paradox and the glass-ness of story. Through these flow the no-thing-ness of NDEs.

THE RELEASE OF EXPERIENCE

All knowledge requires experience, of course, but no-thing-ness eludes the structured, controlled lab experiment and appears at its own leisure, when the industrial ego's guard is down, for example, in meditation, dreaming, loving or dying. The mark of no-thing experience is both strong participation and strong observation. The closer the thinker can get to such experience, the more no-thing-ness emerges. No theory about NDEs should be published without plenty of face-to-face listening to the very people who have experienced it. Of course such experience is not far away, for death puts us all in its shadow, making it personal.

My sister died recently, after only eight months of knowing she had cancer. One night during her first hospitalization she lay awake, depressed and discouraged, staring in the darkness at the table full of flowers from family and friends at the foot of her bed. Suddenly she felt a rush of Light and love flow from the flowers into her body, filling her with total acceptance and caring compassion. Her depression lifted and she felt transformed by the peace and joy of the loving Light. She left the hospital saying "I'm just going to forgive everybody." This glimpse of no-thing in the Light gave her a great deal of comfort in the coming months. Often when she was in pain I would whisper to her "Remember the Light?" and she would nod "yes" and smile. So I cannot be a completely detached observer, because I am one who has participated. I have felt death brush by, I have caught a glimpse of no-thing in the effects of the Light.

Near-death survivors know the depth, the pain, the joy, the ineffable no-thing-ness that throws you out of the saddle of familiar definitions of experience into the far broader experience of no-thing. But no one needs to endure a painful brush with death to feel the breeze of no-thing. It is easily available, in smaller doses. Just do no-thing. Think no-thing. Just be. Let the grip of modern ego-centric consciousness relax. Release the control, play without goals, meditate without purpose, love without conditions. As Lao Tsu says:

> A truly good person does nothing,
> Yet leaves nothing undone.
> A foolish person is always doing,
> Yet much remains to be done. (38)

THE JOY OF PARADOX

You may have noticed that no-thing-ness seems to revel in paradox. Dannion Brinkley was struck by lightning and pronounced dead, awoke near the morgue, and now he goes around telling everyone about it! Like other NDE survivors, Dannion is *paradoxically* defying the iron law of death, puzzling physicians who so rarely see anyone return from the dead. Another survivor, a heart attack victim, told me about floating above his damaged body in the ambulance, vainly striving to communicate with the emergency medical technician. He was suddenly overtaken by a flood of dazzling light, comforted and loved. Floating above his body, he was *paradoxically* in this world and out of it. When expected opposites collide like this, ordinary logic stops cold. The paradox smiles like the Cheshire cat in Alice's Wonderland, silently asking who can transcend and see.

When Aristotle systematized many of the logical rules for inquiry that are accepted today, he ruled out paradox. But no-thing-ness does not find Aristotelian logic to be sufficient. While very useful for knowing thing-ness, logic closes too many doors on no-thing-ness. An older Greek philosopher, Heraclitus, kept the doors open, saying: "If one does not expect the un-expected one will not find it, since it is not to be searched out, and difficult to compass" (Kirk and Raven, 195). What is unexpected? Simply whatever a worldview and its logic delare to be impossible, out of bounds, no count, no-thing. The difficulty is not the availablity of paradoxical experiences, but the tendency of worldviews to want to be comprehensive and explain everything. Conventional logical boundaries are challenged by the no-thing-ness of NDEs. This may seem frightening or annoying, but it need not be, if we simply welcome the occasional joy of paradox.

The ineffability of NDEs is an obvious paradox. Like the sound of one hand clapping, these unbelieveable journeys just cannot adequately be expressed in the clumsy language of ordinary thing-ness. The feelings, moods and otherworldly sights are just too intense and incredible because they propel one into a world beyond thing-ness, a world of spiritual, silent communication, of instant out-of-body travel anywhere, of spectacular visions of dazzling otherworldly scenery, of overwhelming love and acceptance, of unbelievably rapid life reviews, and anguished returns to painfully wounded bodies. How can these outrageous experiences be reduced to mere words? Keep paradoxical no-thing-ness in your language, says the *Tao Te Ching*, and come upon something greater than you imagined:

> Something mysteriously formed,
> Born before heaven and earth.
> In the silence and the void,
> Standing alone and unchanging,
> Ever present and in motion.
> Perhaps it is the mother of ten thousand things.
> I do not know its name.
> Call it Tao.
> For lack of a better word, I call it great. (Lao Tsu, 25)

The Tao, or "the Way," is just a pointer to the unnameable greatness, silent and void, the unchanging mystery un-born before heaven and earth. This pointer is like a finger pointing to the moon, as the Zen saying goes: "When I point my finger to the moon, do not look at my finger. Look at the moon." Thing-ness points to no-thing-ness. Follow the pointer all the way. Obviously the language describing NDEs is not merely the language of thing-ness; it is not just literal, not just factual. While NDE language may describe things, such as the furniture and instruments in a hospital room, it also points to the presence of no-thing-ness in the love, the Light, the transformation. While I should know what a *bed* is, or a *scalpel*, how definite and final is knowledge of the realm beneath them, called *atoms* or *energy*? How much no-thing-ness is in such thing-ness? Lao Tsu kept pointing in this direction when he said:

> Look, it cannot be seen—it is beyond form.
> Listen, it cannot be heard—it is beyond sound.
> Grasp, it cannot be held—it is intangible
> These three are indefinable;
> Therefore they are joined in one....
> It returns to nothingness.
> The form of the formless,
> the image of the imageless,
> It is called indefinable and beyond imagination. (Lao Tsu,14)

This echoes another paradoxical element of the NDE, the way the Light appears as an impersonal yet personal energy, a God-like power that may be in human form or merely Light, but survivors just "know" that it is God, or Jesus, or Vishnu. Some theologians distinguish between God and the Godhead, or the ineffable mystery, the impersonal power behind the personified image of God the Father. The humanized earthly father is an image, a thing-ness picture of the creative, life-giving and loving parent quality of the great mystery. But it cannot be a literally masculine picture, because that force itself made humans through evolution and the male gender as half of the reproductive team of our species. How could the creator of all the reproductive systems of the universe literally be a human with only male reproductive plumbing? Follow the person metaphor past itself. Behind the personal phenomena glows the Light, behind the Light pulses the great no-thing from which the Light of Being flows and becomes phenomena.

In contemporary NDEs, the personal-impersonal conflict in religious thought is clearly resolved in favor of the impersonal-yet-personal, Light-filled mystery behind the personal deity of patriarchal tradition. If the NDE shows us anything about the great mystery beyond death, it is that the great loving, knowing Light behind the gods is most often formless, yet full of of love and caring. Perhaps this is because it is so close to the no-thing. As Lao Tsu says, the eternal no-thing is the nameless beginning:

> The Tao that can be told is not the eternal Tao.
> The name that can be named is not the eternal name.
> The nameless is the beginning of heaven and earth. (Lao Tsu, 1)

The personhood of the Biblical God may be seen as an archetypal image of the Light's creative power, and loving care, much like a parent. But, as a part of creation, the personal qualities of God are simply earthly manifestations of the no-thing behind all creation. Yet that no-thing-ness is too remote and intangible for daily use. Each person, each culture, needs a particular face of God, a local thing-like appearance of the vast universal force of no-thing. For example, the Gospel of John sees Christ as the Light between things and no-thing: "While you have the Light, believe in the Light, that you may become sons of Light" (John 12:36). The NDE reflects the paradox of God's impersonal Light, yet personal qualities of love and wisdom.

Another important implication of the impersonal Light behind the many faces of the divine mystery is the unity of world religions. While the many specific ethnic, cultural variations tend to separate religions for historical reasons, the Light of the NDE clearly points to the unifying source of them all. One NDE survivor born in India told me that she died and was lifted up by a tall figure of light. It seemed to be Vishnu, one of the three great Hindu deities. For Betty Eadie, the Light is Christ. Heraclitus put a paradoxical slant on this problem, saying: "One thing, the only truly wise, does not and does consent to be called by the name of Zeus" (Kirk and Raven, 204). A Buddhist adds the other twist: "There is one Lord revealed in many scriptures, who becomes clearly manifest at your wish" (Conze, 176). The joy of this paradox is affirmed by near-death experiences.

THE GLASS-NESS OF STORY

Where there is experience and paradox, then story, image and symbol cannot be far behind. Overflowing with imagery, NDEs present the glass-ness of story, the transparency of symbol, the Light shining through, like the heavenly cities and plants that seem to glow from within. The challenge is to see all the way through the glass-ness of familiar earthly forms and sense the ineffable glow of no-thing.

NDEs cannot simply be taken at face value, because they are loaded with images, often influenced by one's local culture. In the Light some Christians see Jesus and some Hindus see Vishnu. Some Americans see cities and some Africans see elephants. Some medieval visionaries go to Hell before Heaven, some contemporary near-death travelers discover a kindly psychotherapist, spiritual evolution or subatomic physics. Carol Zaleski rightly emphasizes the role of imagination in shaping NDEs when she says: "otherworld visions reflect imaginative modes of thought" (Zaleski, 192).

Let us examine some prevalent theories of imagination as they might apply to NDEs. Is the imagination a private picture show, a wholly subjective fantasy stimulated by brain chemicals, unrelated to "objective" thing-ness? Are NDE visions like dreams were to Freud, imaginative portrayals of real unconscious, internal, personal psychological states? Are NDEs symbolic pictures of real worldwide, collective, archetypal themes, much as dreams, visions and myths were to Jung? Is imagination in NDEs simply a local cultural filter, like stained glass, for the endless dazzling wonders of all the no-thing-ness generating existence?

The strongly reductive neurological interpretation tends to argue that

NDE stories are just a subjective picture show of the brain's meaningless illusions—merely tranquilizing hallucinations. Obviously neurological activity contributes in some form to NDEs, and the most comprehensive theories will incorporate both neurological and spiritual explanations. Neither side should reductively deny the other.

Three types of evidence argue against the reduction of NDEs to "nothing but" the play of meaningless imagination. First, as Raymond Moody emphasizes, are the verified psychic experiences, such as Jung's confirmed foreknowledge of his own physician's immanent death. Jung was under medication during his vision, but his psychic insight was too accurate to be merely a subjective illusion rooted in nothing but drugs (Jung, 1961, 293). Now this view must be tempered by the psychic insights that are not verified or are flat-out wrong, but nevertheless the verified ones cannot easily be dismissed.

Secondly, the powerful transformations that NDE survivors undergo are also strong arguments against the hallucination position. As Kenneth Ring has documented, people on a downward spiral of addiction and despair have been suddenly flipped over by an NDE and transformed into healing, loving, even inspiring persons (Ring, 1991). Now this data must also be tempered by the few negative, distressing NDEs and the many survivors who still struggle. As P. M. H. Atwater stresses, being awakened to the Light in an NDE is just the start of a long journey of taking responsibility and integrating it into one's life. And this is a constant challenge.

Third, if, as the extreme thing-ness position argues, we are nothing but mechanistic animals whose consciousness is a random by-product of the brain, why would a jumble of meaningless hallucinations stimulate verifiable psychic insights and powerfully transformed lives, instead of more mechanistic, brutish reactions? Why doesn't the brain produce blueprints and flow charts, x-rays and evolutionary ancestors? Where are the visions of ego-satisfying bodily pleasures? boundless fame? victory over opponents? Why would nothing but brain chemistry come up with so much moral concern, transcendent beauty, forgiveness and love? There is a large gap between the narrowly reductive, mechanistic, thing-ness of brain chemistry and the soulful no-thing-ness of people's lives transformed from shallow despair and violence to meaningful compassion and generosity. The reductive neurological arguments need to fill in this gap convincingly.

What about the view that NDE images are like dreams to Freud, portraying subjective but real, unconscious, personal dramas? Exploring the role of the unconscious in NDEs is fruitful. For example, Freud could point to Dannion Brinkley, who implies that his being forced in his NDE to endure the pain of all the people he harmed in his violent days expresses the burden of his unconscious guilt. He is admirably taking responsibility for this level of personal meaning.

Taking a next step, Jung would say that the unconscious is not merely personal; it is collective and expressed in myth as well as dream, as Freud's own use of Oedipus and Narcissus shows. So NDE visions, while dream-like, symbolize archetypal patterns of the collective human drama, not just personal stories. Furthermore, these images are not just the result of repressed feelings and mechanistic instincts. For Jung the archetypal soul undergoes serious spiritual quests and is presented with numerous images of divinity such as the circular mandala, the wise old man/woman, the spiritual guide, and cosmic Light. These express various images of God within and without each dreamer, seen in cultures around the world. No one image of the divine Light is final or absolute, because symbolic language is not literal. So the NDE could easily be analyzed for its archetypal content. The Light may be seen as Jesus, Buddha, Vishnu or a mandala, depending upon the person's archetypal orientation.

Each archetypal image is like an earthly stained-glass filter for the light flowing out of the ineffable, powerfully transforming no-thing. The NDE is told in story because the language of thing-ness cannot adequately convey no-thing. But no-thing flows readily through the glass-ness of images and stories.

In 1982 a young man in North Carolina named Mellen-Thomas Benedict died of cancer. His soul moved out of his body, through the darkness toward the Light. The Light kept changing into various symbols: Jesus, Buddha, Krishna, and other archetypal images. "If you were a Buddhist or Catholic or Fundamentalist, what you get is a feedback loop of your own stuff," he realized. The Light gives us a chance to examine our own versions of no-thing. Each image is a picture of our higher Self, he understood, in our personal and collective unconscious world. The Light, he saw, gladly wears these earthly faces for us, but each is only an earthly appearance of the infinite energy behind creation, swirling inside each atom: no-thing-ness.

Incredibly, unlike most NDE survivors, Mellen-Thomas' consciousness was thrust through the light, he says, past the big bang of creation, into the Void of no-thing. This Void, he discovered, is paradoxically full of energy, "the energy that has created everything that we are." The impersonal Godhead behind the person of God is in the Void, he saw, "which is not really a time, not a place. It is so hard to describe. It is a point where there is not vibratory action as we know it. It is beyond vibration. It is zero point." Of course no-thing has no is-ness, no it-ness; here language must grope for images.

Mellen-Thomas returned after being dead at least an hour and a half, as documented by his trained hospice caretaker. He was free of cancer and a transformed man. Before his NDE he was depressed and discouraged, but he returned loving everyone and full of creative insights about nature, science and spirituality. "We are stardust," he says, created many times over, free to help the creator evolve new forms, for the world and our souls are "God expanding itself through us." We have soul lessons to learn in each incarnation, but we all have immediate access to the Light through spiritual practices such as meditation.

Mellen-Thomas tells an incredible story full of transforming experience, baffling paradox and intense image. This story, like all NDE survival stories, is full of no-thing-ness. While the thing-ness elements can be checked by the medical tests confirming the disappearance of his cancer, the no-thing-ness slips through that net. The no-thing-ness of NDEs is not verifiable in the same way as thing-ness can be. The experiences, the paradoxes and the stories cannot be seen simply as true or false, illusion or reality. As Mellen-Thomas says, he had his questions answered, but others have different questions to be answered. He entered no-thing-ness full of despair and emerged full of faith.

NDEs are not simply experiences of fact and information, to be confirmed or rejected by empirical testing. Near-death experiences are about the meaning of each person's own death. So each investigator is involved; none can be "objective," none "subjective." No theory about NDEs can linger in the shopworn assumptions of modern industrial ego-consciousness. Mellen-Thomas says:

> The mystery of life has very little to do with intelligence. The universe is not an intellectual process at all. The intellectual is helpful; it is brilliant, but right now that is all we process with, instead of our hearts and the wiser part of ourselves. (Benedict)

Or, as Mark C. Taylor says:

> Thought needs what it cannot bear. This is the passion of thinking...the crucifixion of understanding.... The paradox of thinking is to learn how to think not without not thinking or ceasing to think.... Thinking is forever interrupted by the not it can never think. (Taylor, 1993)

"Near-death experiences" as we call them, have plenty of no-thing between each breath, between each death. The unbearable joy of this paradox has no-thing to offer suffering industrial ego-consciousness but a few tattered stories of uncertain, unsystematic experiences of no-thing-ness.

REFERENCES

Atwater, P. M. H. (1994). *Beyond the Light*. New York: Birch Lane Press.

Benedict, Mellen-Thomas. *Journey Through the Light and Back*. Audiotape. Golden Tree Productions, PO Box 1898, Soquel, CA 95073.

Brinkley, Dannion. (1994). *Saved by the Light*. New York: Villard Books.

Brown, Norman O. (1966). *Love's Body*. New York: Random House.

Chan, Wing-Tsit. (1963).*The Way of Lao-Tzu*. Englewood Cliffs, NJ: Macmillan.

Eadie, Betty. (1992). *Embraced by the Light*. Placerville, CA: Gold Leaf Press.

Eliot, T. S. (1971). "Little Gidding." *Four Quartets*. New York: Harcourt, Brace, Jovanovitch.

Freud, Sigmund. (1974). *The Standard Edition of the Complete Psychological Works of Sigmund Freud*. 24 Vols. Ed. J. Strachey. London: Hogarth.

Greyson. Bruce. (1989,Winter). Editorial: can science explain the near-death experiences? *Journal of Near-Death Studies,8, 2*, 77–92.

Heidegger, Martin. (1962). *Being and Time*. (Trans. J. Macquarrie and E. Robinson.) New York: Harper and Row. (German *Sein und Zeit* , Tübingen.)

Heidegger, Martin. (1967). *What Is a Thing?* (Trans. W. B. Barton and Vera Deutsch.) Chicago: Regnery. (Originally lectures 1935–36, first published in German as *Die Frage nach dem Ding*, Tübingen.)

Hillman, James. (1975). *Revisioning Psychology*. New York: Harper and Row.

Jung, Carl G. (1953-78). *The Collected Works of C.G. Jung*. 20 Vols. Ed. W. McGuire. Princeton: Princeton University Press.

Kirk, G. S. and Raven, J. E. (1976). *The Presocratic Philosophers*. Cambridge: Cambridge University Press.

Kübler-Ross, Elisabeth. (1969). *On Death and Dying*. New York: Macmillan.

Lao Tsu. (1972). *Tao Te Ching*. (Trans. Gia-Fu Feng and Jane English.) New York: Vintage.

Miller, David L. (1974). *The New Polytheism*. NewYork: Harper and Row.

Miller, David L. (1981). *Christs: Meditations on Archetypal Images in Christian Theology*. New York: Seabury Press.

Miller, David L. (1991). Why men are mad; nothing-envy and the fascration complex. *Spring, 51*, 71–79.

Miller, David L. (1995). Nothing almost sees miracles: self and no-self in psychology and religion. *Journal of Psychology and Religion*, 1–26.

Moody, Raymond. (1975). *Life After Life*. New York: Mockingbird/Bantam Books.

Moody, Raymond. (1988). *The Light Beyond*. New York: Bantam Books.

Norris, Christopher. (1987). *Jacques Derrida*. Cambridge, MA: Harvard University Press.

Ring, Kenneth. (1980). *Life at Death*. New York: William Morrow Co.

Ring, Kenneth. (1984). *Heading Toward Omega*. New York: William Morrow Co.

Ring, Kenneth. (1991, Fall). Amazing grace. *Journal of Near-Death Studies*, 10,1, 11–39.

Taylor, Mark C. (1984). *Erring: A Postmodern A/theology*. Chicago: University of Chicago Press.

Taylor, Mark C. (1993). *Nots*. Chicago: University of Chicago Press.

Tillich, Paul. (1952). *The Courage to Be*. New Haven, CT: Yale University Press.

Tillich, Paul. (1963). *Systematic Theology*. Chicago: University of Chicago Press.

Zaleski, Carol. (1987). *Otherworld Journeys*. New York: Oxford University Press.

·⌣ Bibliography ⌣·

Adams, Jay E. (1979). Counseling, Death and Dying: The Doctrine of the Future. In *More Than Redemption: A Theology of Christian Counseling.* 297–300. Grand Rapids, MI: Baker Book House.

Atwater, P. M. H. (1988). *Coming Back to Life.* New York: Dodd, Mead.

———. (1994). *Beyond the Light.* New York: Birch Lane Press.

Ayer, A. J. (1988a, Oct. 14). What I Saw When I Was Dead. *National Review 40, 20,* 8–40.

———. (1988b, Oct. 15). Postscript to a Postmortem. *The Spectator 261, 8362,* 12–14.

Basford, Terry K. (1990). *Near-Death Experiences: An Annotated Bibliography.* New York: Garland Publishing.

Becker, Carl B. (1981, Dec.). The Centrality of Near-Death Experiences in Chinese Pure Land Buddhism. *Anabiosis 1,2,* 154–71.

———. (1982). Why Birth Models Cannot Explain Near-Death Phenomena. *Anabiosis 2,* 102–9.

———. (1984a). On the Objectivity of Near-Death Experiences. *Journal of Religion and Psychical Research 7,* 66–74.

———. (1984b). The Pure Land Revisited: Sino-Japanese Meditation and Near-Death Experiences of the Next World. *Anabiosis 4, 1,* 3–20.

———. (1984c, Spring). Religious Visions: Experiential Grounds for the Pure Land Tradition. *Eastern Buddhist 17,* 138–53.

———. (1985, Spr.). Views from Tibet: NDEs and the Book of the Dead. *Anabiosis 5,1,* 3–20.

Blackmore, Susan. (1983, July). Birth and the OBE: An Unhelpful Analogy. *The Journal of the American Society for Psychical Research 77,* 229–38.

———. (1986). *The Adventures of a Parapsychologist.* Buffalo, NY: Prometheus Books.

———. (1993). *Dying to Live.* Buffalo, NY: Prometheus Books.

Brinkley, Dannion. (1994). *Saved by the Light.* New York: Villard Books.

———. (1995). *At Peace in the Light.* New York: HarperCollins.

Brooke, Tal. (1979). *The Other Side of Death.* Wheaton, IL: Tyndale House.

Brown, J. A. C. (1961). *Freud and the Post-Freudians.* Baltimore, MD: Penguin.

Carr, Daniel. (1981, Feb.14). "Endorphins at the Approach of Death." *Lancet 8261,* 390.

———. (1982, June). Pathophysiology of Stress-Induced Limbic Lobe Dysfunction: A Hypothesis Relevant to Near-Death Experiences. *Anabiosis 2, 1,* 75–89. Reprinted in Greyson and Flynn, eds. (1984). *The Near-Death Experience: Problems, Prospects, Perspectives.* Springfield, IL: Charles Thomas. 125–39.

Clapp, Rodney. (1988, Oct. 7). Rumors of Heaven. Review of Zaleski's *Otherworld Journeys. Christianity Today 32, 14*, 16–21.

Cox-Chapman, Mally. (1995). *The Case for Heaven*. New York: G. P. Putnam's Sons.

Cressy, Judith. (1994). *The Near-Death Experience: Mysticism or Madness?* Hanover, MA: Christopher Publishing.

Crookall, Robert. (1960). *The Study and Practice of Astral Projection*. Secaucus, NJ: University Books.

Davenport, Arlice W. (1984, Jan.). Science and the Near-Death Experience: Toward a New Paradigm. *Journal of Religion and Psychical Research 7, 1*, 26–37 [Part I] and 7, 2 (1984, April) 98–108. [Part II].

Dippong, Joseph F. (1982, Jun/July). Dawn of Perception: A True Rebirth. *CHIMO: The New Age Magazine 8*, 31–37.

Eadie, Betty. (1992). *Embraced by the Light*. Placerville, CA:Gold Leaf Press.

Ehrenwald, Jan. (1978). Survival After Death? Chap. XXII in *The ESP Experience: A PsychiatricValidation*, 231–36. New York: Basic Books.

Eliot, T. S. (1943). *Four Quartets*. New York: Harcourt Brace Jovanovich.

Evans-Wentz, W. Y., Complier and Translator. (1927/1960). *The Tibetan Book of the Dead*. New York: Oxford.

Flynn, Charles P. (1986). *After the Beyond: Human Transformation and the Near-Death Experience*. Englewood Cliffs, NJ: Prentice-Hall.

Fremantle, Francesca, and Chogyam Trungpa, Translators. (1975). *The Tibetan Book of the Dead*. Berkeley: Shambhala.

Gabbard,Glen, and Twemlow, Stuart. (1984).*With the Eyes of the Mind: An Empirical Analysis of Out-of-Body States*. New York: Praeger.

Gallup, George Jr. (with William Proctor). (1982). *Adventures in Immortality*. New York: McGraw Hill.

Gibbs, John C. (1981). The Near-Death Experience: Balancing Siegel's View. *American Psychologist 36, 11*, 1457–58. Reprinted in Greyson and Flynn. (1984). *The Near-Death Experience: Problems, Prospects, Perspectives*. Springfield, IL: Charles Thomas. 63–72.

Gibson, Arvin. (1992). *Glimpses of Eternity*. Bountiful, UT: Horizon Publishers.

Giovetti, Paola. (1982). Near-Death and Deathbed Experiences: An Italian Survey. *Theta 10,1*, 10–13.

Grey, Margot. (1985). *Return from Death*. London:Arkana/Routledge and Kegan Paul.

Greyson, Bruce. (1983a). The Near-Death Experience Scale: Construction, Reliability and Validity. *Journal of Nervous and Mental Disease 17*, 369–75.

———. (1983b). Increase in Psychic Phenomena Following Near-Death Experiences. *Theta 11,2*, 26–29.

———. (June 1983c). The Psychodynamics of Near-Death Experiences. *Journal of Nervous and Mental Disease 171,6*, 376–81.

———. (1985, Aug.). A Typology of Near-Death Experiences. *American Journal of Psychiatry 142, 8*, 967–69.

———. (1990). Appendix: Clinical Approaches to the NDEr. In Harris, Barbara, and Bascom, Lionel. (1990). *Full Circle: The Near-Death Experience and Beyond.* New York: Simon and Schuster/Pocket Books, 271–85.

———. (1993, Nov.). Varieties of Near-Death Experience. *Psychiatry 56*, 390–99.

———, and Bush, Nancy E. (1992, Feb.). Distressing Near-Death Experiences. *Psychiatry*, 95–110.

———, and Flynn, Charles, eds. (1984). *The Near-Death Experience: Problems, Prospects, Perspectives.* Springfield, IL: Charles Thomas.

Grof, Stanislav, and Halifax, Joan. (1977). *The Human Encounter with Death.* New York: E.P. Dutton.

Grootius, Douglas. (1995). To Heaven and Back? *Christianity Today*, April 3; reprint in *Vital Signs*, xiv: 4, 1995, Fall, 4–7.

Grosso, Michael. (1985). *Final Choice.* Walpole, NH: Stillpoint Publishing.

———. (1992). *Frontiers of the Soul.* Wheaton, IL: Quest Books.

———. (1992). *Soulmaker.* Norfolk, VA: Hampton Roads Publishing.

———. (1995). *Millenium Myth: Love and Death at the End of Time.* Wheaton, IL: Quest Books.

Harris, Barbara, and Bascom, Lionel. (1990). *Full Circle: The Near-Death Experience and Beyond.* New York: Simon and Schuster/Pocket Books.

Heaney, John J. (1983, Summer). Recent Studies of Near-Death Experiences. *Journal of Religion and Health 22, 2*, 116–30.

Heim, Albert von st. Gallen. (1892). Notizen über den Tod durch absturz [Remarks on Fatal Falls]. *Jahrbuch des Schweizer Alpenclub 27*, 327–37. Trans and Intro. by Roy Kletti and Russell Noyes, Jr. (1972). The Experiences of Dying from Falls. *Omega 3*, 45–52.

Hill, Brennan. (1981). *The Near-Death Experience: A Christian Approach.* Dubuque, IA: William Brown Co.

Hobson, Douglas Paul. (1983). *A Comparative Study of Near-Death Experiences and Christian Eschatology.* M.A. Thesis, Baylor University.

James, William. (1902). *The Varieties of Religious Experience.* New York: Macmillan.

Jansen, Karl L. R. (1991). Transcendental Explanations and the Near-Death Experience. *Lancet 337*, 207–43.

Jung, Carl. (1961). *Memories, Dreams, Reflections.* New York: Random House.

Kastenbaum, Robert. (1995). *Death, Society and the Human Experience.* 5th Ed. Boston: Allyn and Bacon.

Kastenbaum, R. and B. (1993). *The Encyclopedia of Death*. New York: Avon.

Kellehear, Allan. (1996). *Experiences Near Death: Beyond Medicine and Religion*. New York: Oxford University Press.

Kohr, Richard. (1983). Near-Death Experiences, Altered States, and PSI Sensitivity. *Anabiosis 3, 2*, 157–76.

Kübler-Ross, Elisabeth. (1969). *On Death and Dying*. New York: Macmillan.

———. (1991). *On Life After Death*. Berkeley: Celestial Arts.

Kuhn, Harold B. (1981, Mar. 13). Out-of-Body Experiences: Misplaced Euphoria. *Christianity Today 25, 5*, 78, 82.

Küng, Hans. (1984). *Eternal Life*. Garden City, NY: Doubleday Co. Trans. Edward Quinn, from *Ewiges Leben?* Munich: Piper Verlag, 1982.

Lorimar, David. (1990). *Whole in One: The Near-Death Experience and the Ethic of Interconnectedness*. London: Penguin Arkana.

Lowental, Uri. (1981, Fall). Dying, Regression and the Death Instinct. *Psychoanalytic Review 68, 3*, 363–70.

Lundhal, Craig R. (1979, Nov.). Mormon Near-Death Experiences. *Free Inquiry in Creative Sociology 7, 2*, 101–4. Reprinted in *A Collection of Near-Death Research Readings*, (1982). 165–79. Chicago: Nelson-Hall.

———, Ed. (1982). *A Collection of Near-Death Research Readings*. Chicago: Nelson-Hall.

———. (1982, April). The Perceived Other World in Mormon Near-Death Experiences. *Omega 12, 4*, 319–27.

——— and Harold Widdison. (1983, June). The Mormon Explanation of Near-Death Experiences. *Anabiosis 3, 1*, 97–106.

MacDonald, Jeffery. (1986, Jul./Aug.). The Anthropology of Consciousness: Anthropology and Parapsychology Reconsidered. *Parapsychology Review 17, 4*, 13–15.

McDonagh, John. (1982). *Christian Psychology: Toward a New Synthesis*. New York: Crossroad.

Menz, Robert. (1984, Winter). The Denial of Death and the Out-of-body Experience. *Journal of Religion and Health 23, 4*, 317–29.

Moody, Raymond. (1975). *Life After Life*. New York: Bantam/Mockingbird.

———. (1977). *Reflections on Life After Life*. New York: Bantam/Mockingbird.

———. (1988). *The Light Beyond*. New York: Bantam Books.

——— and Perry, Paul. (1993). *Reunions: Visionary Encounters with Departed Loved Ones*. New York: Villard.

Morse, Melvin. (1989, Fall). Near-Death Experiences: A Neurophysiologic Explanatory Model. *Journal of Near-Death Experiences 8, 1*, 45–53.

——— (with Paul Perry) (1990). *Closer to the Light: Learning from the Near-Death Experiences of Children*. New York: Ivy Books.

——— (with Paul Perry). (1992). *Parting Visions: Uses and Meanings of Pre-Death, Psychic and Spiritual Experiences*. New York: Villard.

Neumann, Jonathan. (1990, Winter). Near-Death Experiences in Judaic Literature. *Journal of Psychology and Judaism 14, 4,* 225–53.

Newsom, Rosalie. (1988, Winter). Ego, Moral and Faith Development in Near-Death Experiencers: Three Case Studies. *Journal of Near-Death Studies 7, 2,* 73–105.

Nietzke, Ann. (1977, Sept.). The Miracle of Kübler-Ross. *Human Behavior,* 18–27.

Noyes, R., Jr. (1972). The Experience of Dying. *Psychiatry, 35,* 174–84.

——— and Kletti, R. (1976). Depersonalization in the Face of Life-Threatening Danger: A Description. *Psychiatry, 39,* 19–27.

——— and Kletti, R. (1976). Depersonalization in the Face of Life-Threatening Danger: An Interpretation. *Omega 7,* 103–14.

Osis, Karlis, and Haraldsson, Erlendur. (1977/1986). *At the Hour of Death.* New York: Hastings House.

Pennachio, John. (1986, Spring). Near-Death Experience as Mystical Experience. *Journal of Religion and Health 25, 1,* 64–71.

Persinger, M. A. (1983). Religious and Mystical Experiences as Artifacts of Temporal Lobe Function: A General Hypothesis. *Perceptual and Motor Skills 57,* 1255–62.

Quimby, Scott L. (1989, Winter). The Near-Death Experience as an Event in Consciousness. *Journal of Humanistic Psychology 29, 1* 87–108.

Rawlings, Maurice. (1978). *Beyond Death's Door.* Nashville: Nelson Publishers.

———. (1980). *Before Death Comes.* Nashville: Nelson Publishers.

Rhodes, Leon S. (1982, June). The NDE Enlarged by Swedenborg's Vision. *Anabiosis 2, 1,* 15–35.

Ring, Kenneth. (1980). *Life at Death.* New York: William Morrow Co.

———. (1984). *Heading Toward Omega.* New York: William Morrow Co.

———. (1991, Fall). Amazing Grace: The Near-Death Experience as a Compensatory Gift. *Journal of Near-Death Experiences 10,1,* 11–39.

———. (1992). *The Omega Project.* New York: William Morrow Co.

———. (1995, Aug.). Near-Death Experiences in the Blind—Can They Actually See? IANDS Annual Conference. Audiotape. Boulder, CO: Perpetual Motion.

Ritchie, George. (1978). *Return from Tomorrow.* Waco, TX: Chosen Books.

———. (1991). *My Life After Dying.* Norfolk, VA: Hampton Roads Publishing.

Rodin, Ernst A. (1980, May). The Reality of Death Experiences: A Personal Perspective. *Journal of Nervous and Mental Disease 168, 5,* 259–63. Reprinted in Greyson and Flynn. (1984). *The Near-Death Experience: Problems, Prospects, Perspectives.* Springfield, IL: Charles Thomas, 63–72.

Royce, David. (1985, March). The Near-Death Experience: A Survey of

Clergy's Attitudes and Knowledge. *Journal of Pastoral Care 39, 1,* 31–42.

Sagan, Carl. (1974). The Amniotic Universe. Chapter XXV in *Broca's Brain.* New York: Ballantine Books.

Sabom, Michael. (1982). *Recollections of Death: A Medical Investigation.* New York: Harper & Row.

Schnarr, Grant R. (1984). *Swedenborg and the Near Death Experience.* Glenview, IL: Swedenborg Center.

Sharma, Arvind. (1979, July–Sept.). Near-Death Experiences and the Doctrine of Subtle Body. *Journal of Dharma* 4, 278–85.

Sharp, Kimberly Clark. (1995). *After the Light.* New York: William Morrow Co.

Siegel, Ronald K. (1975). *Hallucinations: Behavior, Experience and Theory.* New York: John Wiley & Sons.

———. (1980, Oct.). The Psychology of Life After Death. *American Psychologist 35,* 911–31. Reprinted in Greyson and Flynn. (1984).*The Near-Death Experience: Problems, Prospects, Perspectives.* Springfield, IL: Charles Thomas. 77–120.

———. (1981, Jan.) Accounting for the "Afterlife" Experiences. *Psychology Today 15,1,* 64–75. Reprinted under the title "Life After Death" in *Science and the Paranormal.* New York: Scribner's, 159–84.

——— and Ada E. Hirshman. (1984, Spring). Hashish Near-Death Experiences. *Anabiosis 4, 1,* 69–86.

Sogyal Rinpoche. (1993). *The Tibetan Book of Living and Dying.* New York: HarperCollins Publishers.

Steiger, Brad. (1994). *One with the Light.* New York: Penguin Signet.

——— and Stieger, Sherry Hansen. (1995). *Children of the Light.* New York: Penguin Signet.

Stevenson, Ian, and Bruce Greyson. (1980, Oct.). The Phenomenology of Near-Death Experiences. *American Journal of Psychiatry 137,* 10, 1193–96.

——— and Satwant Pasricha. (1986). Near-Death Experiences in India: A Preliminary Report. *The Journal of Nervous and Mental Disease 174, 3,* 165–70.

———, et. al. (1989–90). Are Persons Reporting "Near-Death Experiences" Really Near-Death? A Study of the Medical Records. *Omega 21, 1,* 45–54.

Sutherland, Cherie. (1992). *Reborn in the Light.* New York: Bantam Books.

Swihart, Phillip. (1978). *The Edge of Death.* Downers Grove, IL: Inter-Varsity Press.

Tart, Charles, Ed. (1969). *Altered States of Consciousness.* Garden City, New York: Doubleday Anchor.

Tart, Charles. (1975). *States of Consciousness.* New York: E. P. Dutton.

Thurman, Robert A. F., Translator. (1994). *The Tibetan Book of the Dead.* New York: Bantam.

Vicky: A Blind Woman's Two Near-Death Experiences. (1994, Spring). *Vital Signs 13*, 2, 1–8.

Von Franz, Marie-Louise. (1987). *On Dreams and Death*. Boston: Shambhala.

Wilkerson, Ralph. (1977). *Beyond and Back: Those Who Died and Lived to Tell It*. New York: Bantam Books.

Woodhouse, Mark B. (1981, July). Near-Death Experiences and the Mind-Body Problem. *Anabiosis 1*, 1, 57–65.

Yogananda, Paramahansa. (1946). *Autobiography of a Yogi*. Los Angeles: Self-Realization Fellowship.

Zaleski, Carol. (1987). *Otherworld Journeys: Accounts of Near-Death Experiences in Medieval and Modern Times*. New York: Oxford University Press.

———. (1996). *The Life of the World to Come: Near-Death Experience and Christian Hope*. New York: Oxford University Press.

VIDEOGRAPHY

Conversations with God. (1995). [Videotape.] (Goldhil Home Media International, Thousand Oaks, CA).

Darrah, Marlin. (Director). (1995). *The Death and Times of Dannion Brinkley*. [Videotape.] (Saved by the Light Productions, P.O. Box 13255, Scottsdale, AZ 85260.)

An Evening with Betty J. Eadie. (1995). [Videotape.] (Onjinjinkta Productions P.O. Box 66119, Seattle, WA 98166. 1-800-433-8978.)

The Near-Death Experience: Transcending the Limits. [Videotape.] (Seattle: Pacific Northwest IANDS 1991 Conference—Seattle IANDS Productions. 2841 Northwest 74th Street, Seattle, WA 98117. (206) 789-2278.)

O'Reilly, Tim. (Producer and Director). (1991). *Round Trip: The Near Death Experience*. [Videotape.] (Tim O'Reilly Productions, P.O. Box 1701, Cranford, NJ 07016-1701.)

Schokey, Peter (Producer and Director). (1992). *Life After Life*. [Videotape.] (Cascom International, Inc. 1-800-397-3397.)

Van Rooy, Norman. (Producer). (1994). *Shadows: Perceptions of Near Death Experiences*. [Videotape.] (Norman Van Rooy, 23632 Highway 99 #343, Edmonds, WA 98026.)